Advances in Cognitive–Behavioral Research and Therapy

Volume 1

Contributors

Frank Andrasik

Diane B. Arnkoff

Thomas J. D'Zurilla

Carol R. Glass

Steven C. Hayes

Kenneth A. Holroyd

Daniel S. Kirschenbaum

Arthur Nezu

Andrew J. Tomarken

Robert D. Zettle

Advances in Cognitive–Behavioral Research and Therapy

Volume 1

Edited by

PHILIP C. KENDALL

Department of Psychology
University of Minnesota
Minneapolis, Minnesota

1982

ACADEMIC PRESS

A Subsidiary of Harcourt Brace Jovanovich, Publishers

New York   London

Paris   San Diego   San Francisco   São Paulo   Sydney   Tokyo   Toronto

ACADEMIC PRESS, INC.
111 Fifth Avenue, New York, New York 10003

United Kingdom Edition published by
ACADEMIC PRESS, INC. (LONDON) LTD.
24/28 Oval Road, London NW1 7DX

ISBN 0-12-010601-9

ISSN 0730-5389
This publication is not a periodical and is not
subject to copying under CONTU guidelines.

PRINTED IN THE UNITED STATES OF AMERICA

82 83 84 85   9 8 7 6 5 4 3 2 1

Contents

Rule-Governed Behavior: A Potential Theoretical Framework for Cognitive–Behavioral Therapy

Robert D. Zettle and Steven C. Hayes

On Facing the Generalization Problem: The Study of Self-Regulatory Failure

Daniel S. Kirschenbaum and Andrew J. Tomarken

Social Problem Solving in Adults

Thomas J. D'Zurilla and Arthur Nezu

A Cognitive–Behavioral Approach to Recurrent Tension and Migraine Headache

Kenneth A. Holroyd and Frank Andrasik

Contributors

Numbers in parentheses indicate the pages on which the authors' contributions begin.

Frank Andrasik (275), Department of Psychology, State University of New York, Albany, New York 12222

Diane B. Arnkoff (1, 35), Department of Psychology, Catholic University of America, Washington, D.C. 20064

Thomas J. D'Zurilla (201), Department of Psychology, State University of New York, Stony Brook, New York 11794

Carol R. Glass (1, 35), Department of Psychology, Catholic University of America, Washington, D.C. 20064

Steven C. Hayes (73), Department of Psychology, University of North Carolina, Greensboro, North Carolina 27412

Kenneth A. Holroyd[1] (275), Stress and Coping Project, University of California, Berkeley, California 94720

Daniel S. Kirschenbaum (119), Department of Psychology, University of Wisconsin, Madison, Wisconsin 53706

Arthur Nezu[2] (201), Division of Psychological Services, Fairleigh Dickinson University, Teaneck, New Jersey 07666

Andrew J. Tomarken (119), Department of Psychology, University of Wisconsin, Madison, Wisconsin 53706

Robert D. Zettle (73), Department of Psychology, University of North Carolina, Greensboro, North Carolina 27412

[1]Present address: Department of Psychology, Ohio University, Athens, Ohio 45701.
[2]Present address: 139 Temple Avenue, Hackensack, New Jersey 07601.

Preface

Recent years have witnessed a dramatic increase in the quality and quantity of research and applications pertinent to the integration of cognition and behavior. Indeed, the sheer bulk of relevant material (both current and historical) is so vast that researchers, clinicians, and students are confronted with not only a formidable reading list but also the onerous task of tracking down diverse sources. Moreover, the growing field itself requires an outlet for authoritative reviews, critical commentaries, and theoretical treatises, as well as more speculative analyses.

Advances in Cognitive–Behavioral Research and Therapy is broadly conceived to include a diversity of topics relating cognition and behavior. For example, systematic exploration of assessment issues, theoretical analyses, treatment strategies for distinct clinical disorders, basic studies in pathology, and advanced research methodologies are a few of the topics appropriate for inclusion. Drawing on the developments in the study of cognition, behavior modification, development, learning, personality, and social interaction, and occasionally including dialogues on pertinent issues, this serial publication draws together the advances in diverse areas related to cognitive–behavioral research and application. All contributions are prepared with the academic researcher and practicing clinician in mind.

These books are not intended to be only a collection of literature reviews, nor are they designed to serve solely as a display of treatment successes. Rather, each volume will contain a collection of articles that deal with a sample of the numerous content areas that are of interest to researchers and clinicians struggling with the interplay of cognition and behavior. There will not be a single theme or mold to each volume. Rather, each contribution will stand by itself. Most important, perhaps, contributors are encouraged to develop their thinking and present these advances in the written product.

Volume 1 brings together the work of innovative scholars dealing with contemporary concerns in cognitive–behavioral research and therapy. Specifically, there have been recent calls for theoretical developments, and several of the present contributions provide stimulating theoretical insights, commentaries, and proposals. The two lead articles provide a cognitive-side perspective on theory, assessment, and treatment. In the first article, Diane B. Arnkoff and Carol R. Glass examine the prevalent cognitive clinical constructs, evaluating their present course and elaborating on promising directions. In a related article, Carol R. Glass and Diane B. Arnkoff address some of the assumptions of cognitive assessment and therapy and provide consideration of the organizational models needed to guide future cognitive assessment and treatment efforts. These collaborative and coordinated articles represent a masterful retaliation to my challenge (invitation) to prepare the lead articles. A behavioral-side analysis is evident in the second pair of articles. Robert D. Zettle and Steven C. Hayes present a carefully reasoned analysis of rule-governed behavior as a radical behavioral framework for cognitive–behavioral therapy. Daniel S. Kirschenbaum and Andrew J. Tomarken provide an integrative review and scholarly appraisal of self-regulatory failure and treatment generalization.

The two closing articles consider the basic and applied advances in specific content areas. Social problem solving is discussed by Thomas J. D'Zurilla and Arthur Nezu. Their comprehensive coverage includes an analysis of the process of social problem solving, the relationship between social problem solving and psychological dysfunctions, and the issues involved in assessing and training social problem-solving skills. Recurrent headaches are examined by Kenneth A. Holroyd and Frank Andrasik. Information from multiple approaches (e.g., demographics, epidemiology, physiology, vulnerability factors) is presented and the procedures for and the effects of cognitive–behavioral treatments are described. I am encouraged by the truly significant contributions made by each of the authors.

Portions of the present book were completed while I was a Fellow at the Center for Advanced Study in the Behavioral Sciences, Stanford, California. It is with a great deal of pleasure that I express my gratitude to the Center staff, and its director, Gardner Lindzey, who (somehow) maintains the ideal academic and social environment. I am especially grateful for financial support provided by the National Institute of Mental Health (#5-T32-MH14581-05) and the John D. and Catherine T. MacArthur Foundation. I also wish to recognize the support of my home institution, the University of Minnesota, and to acknowledge the assistance of the staff of Academic Press, who played an important part in the production of this volume. Finally, I would like to thank each of the authors for being a part of this venture.

Philip C. Kendall

Clinical Cognitive Constructs: Examination, Evaluation, and Elaboration

DIANE B. ARNKOFF AND CAROL R. GLASS[1]

Department of Psychology,
Catholic University of America,
Washington, D.C.

The cognitive movement in clinical psychology is no longer in its infancy. Therapeutic strategies and assessment devices in particular have grown to awesome proportions. Conceptualization of clinical procedures, however, has until recently lagged behind (Mahoney & Arnkoff, 1978).

[1] This article was the joint effort of both authors. Order of authorship was determined randomly.

1

ADVANCES IN COGNITIVE-BEHAVIORAL RESEARCH
AND THERAPY, VOLUME 1

In the cognitive movement, it seems obvious to turn to cognitive psychology for sources of conceptualizations of clinical phenomena. Cognitive psychology itself is very young, often dated to Neisser's publication of *Cognitive Psychology* in 1967. Nevertheless, a great number of competing views have emerged in recent years. As clinical psychologists have turned to their cognitive colleagues for theoretical constructs, it is not surprising that concepts in cognitive psychology and developmental–cognitive psychology are now appearing in the writings of clinical psychologists. For example, in a short span of years, diverse clinical frameworks based on different cognitive paradigms have appeared by Mahoney (1974), Meichenbaum (1977), Goldfried (1979), Arnkoff (1980b), Landau and Goldfried (1981), and Merluzzi, Rudy, and Glass (1981); a framework based on a developmental–cognitive framework was proposed by Sollod and Wachtel (1980); and Mischel (1981) has developed a framework based on cognitive social learning theory.

Readers of these various works will encounter a vast array of terms for cognitive phenomena, including self-statements, beliefs, expectancies, attributions, egocentrism, metacognition, schemata, distortions, current concerns, thinking styles, plans, and strategies. While some may infer terminal confusion in the field, we choose to interpret the ferment as indicating progress. Many cooks in the kitchen are better than none!

The purposes of this article, as the title suggests, are to examine the constructs that have been most prevalent in the cognitive–clinical literature to date, to evaluate the course in which the work seems to be headed, and, primarily, to elaborate what we see as the most promising directions to take for the future. Initially we will discuss criteria that an adequate cognitive–clinical theory will be obliged to meet, followed by a discussion of relationships among cognitive constructs. We will then turn to a more detailed evaluation and elaboration of the three sets of constructs that have been most studied to date: self-statements, beliefs, and distortions and thinking styles. (See Glass and Arnkoff, this volume, for a presentation of the implications of the directions suggested here for both assessment and psychotherapy.)

I. THEORETICAL CRITERIA

The systems and models for conceptualizing cognitive–clinical phenomena that have appeared have numerous similarities. For example, all reject (some explicitly, some implicitly) the associationistic, mechanistic processes hypothesized by behavioral models. In their place, these models posit cognitive structures and processes that "mediate the impact of social experience and guide information processing" (Mischel, 1981, p. 488). Cognitive processes are seen in these models as heuristics (Tversky & Kahneman, 1974), in other words, as more or less successful methods of categorizing and simplifying events so that they may be dealt with by an organism with finite capabilities. In all of the models, individuals are seen as active creators of their experience.

Although the models differ considerably in terminology and content, the extent of overlap and basic agreement is interesting, especially in light of the fierce competition among the parent systems in cognitive and developmental psychology. However, we would like to repeat Meichenbaum and Butler's (1980b) caution that it would be a mistake to think that we have now explained cognitive–clinical structures and processes just because we have borrowed words to describe the phenomena. No final word on theory is possible or even desirable, but we can offer several criteria that an adequate conceptual scheme for cognition in clinical psychology must meet:

1. An adequate theory must attend more to the function of cognitive phenomena than to their content. As will be discussed in detail later in this article, much of our current work deals with the content of cognitive processes such as beliefs, self-statements, and expectancies. While this work has been fruitful, the content is really secondary to the function or meaning of such cognitive processes and events (Goldfried, 1979; Meichenbaum & Butler, 1980c). Adaptive living is not necessarily incompatible with holding a belief that diverges somewhat from reality or with saying negative things to oneself; the determinant of adaptation is the meaning or function of the belief or self-statement. An adequate theory must therefore predict the circumstances under which cognitive processes become maladaptive.

2. An important task for theory is to explain the relationship between cognition and other aspects of functioning. Although the pie is usually divided into the familiar slices of behavior, affect, and cognition, Schwartz (1978) points out that this division is based on methods of assessment rather than on a theory of the relationships among components of behavior. A more useful attitude, he says, would be to view the different approaches as "reflecting different levels of analysis of the same organism" (p. 68).

Schwartz' (1978) emphasis on integrated functioning is important to take into account in any theory. As Landfield (1980) reminds us,

Kelly's (1955) Personal Construct Theory is not about disembodied behavior, but about *persons* and *processes*. However, sufficient evidence does exist of differentiated functioning of different components of the organism so that any theory which does not consider components would be incomplete. An adequate theory, therefore, must account for differentiated functioning in the context of the integrated functioning of the organism (Wallett, 1979). A theory of cognitive–clinical structures and processes, then, must address the relationships among and integration of observable behavior, self-reported thoughts, self-reported affect, inferred cognitive processes, and inferred affect.

It is clear from a scholarly viewpoint that a theory would be incomplete if it could not delineate such relationships. It is also a matter of practical import that clinicians have a framework for relating these aspects of functioning. Projective methods of assessment, for example, are gaining interest in the cognitive literature (Sobel, 1981). Their use, however, requires a theory relating the verbal production to inferred constructs and behavior. In fact, theory is no less important in any form of assessment, since one measured behavior is always inferred to stand for others.

3. In accounting for the relationships among cognition, behavior, and affect, cognitive conceptualizations have encountered most difficulty in explaining the relationship between cognition and affect. An adequate theory must especially address the ties between these aspects of the organism. The hallmark of many clinical problems is a disorder of affect; any theory that deals only with ideas and not with that affect would be bound to fail.

In the cognitive–clinical movement, the most common position on the relationship between cognition and affect has been that the cognition precedes and causes the inappropriate affect. This idea is the cornerstone of the theories of Ellis (1962) and Beck (1976). Velten's (1968) method of inducing affect through reading self-referent statements is often cited as support for this idea.

Recent conceptualization and empirical evidence suggests, however, that a one-way relationship between cognition and affect is too simplistic (Coyne, 1982; Meichenbaum & Butler, 1980a; Zajonc, 1980). Mancuso and Ceely (1980) argue, in fact, that a mechanistic attempt to explain the cause of any one event, such as an expression of affect, ignores the essential flow of processes over time. A contextualist paradigm, in contrast to a mechanistic paradigm, describes change "in *terms of the shifting interconnections of fused strands within the context*" (Mancuso & Ceely, 1980, p. 8). A contextualist theory of cognition and affect, then, will concern itself not with the cause of each as determined by static temporal priority, but with their "shifting interconnections."

4. An adequate theory of cognitive–clinical phenomena must explain *change* in these phenomena. Such a statement may seem obvious, but our examination of the literature suggests that to date clinicians have paid more attention to seemingly static cognitive structures such as maladaptive beliefs than to cognitive processes such as change. Clearly, any theory in psychology, particularly a clinical theory, must explain change.

Cognitive–clinical psychologists have begun to recognize the value of examining normal development in its implications for the process of change.[2] The relationship between change in psychotherapy and change in development is well worth exploring. As Sollod and Wachtel (1980) argue, Piaget's theory is especially applicable to clinicians because of its conceptualization of the *process* of cognitive development.

In the cognitive–clinical literature to date, we have generally studied the end product of a cognitive process, such as the rate of positive and negative self-statements of a subject in an evaluative situation. The Piagetian strategy, however, is not to focus on the end product, but rather on the cognitive process. It is on the basis of the process of reasoning, for example, that a child is said to have attained the concept of conservation. Similarly, it may be valuable in clinical endeavors for us to study the cognitive *process* of the subject in one situation as well as across time, rather than simply the rate of positive and negative self-statements at one point in time. As Mischel (1981) points out, cognitive assessment is in fact better suited to the task of studying process than a traditional assessment strategy, which determines the individual's place on a static trait dimension.

Although change may be of greatest interest in a clinical theory, failure to change requires equal explanation. In addition, we must not overlook fluctuations in change within one individual. The high return rate to therapy of successfully treated individuals indicates that change does not mean irreversible transformation, but rather a (sometimes temporary) shift in the prepotency of various cognitive processes (Mahoney, 1980).

5. Following from the need for an explanation of the process of change, an adequate clinical theory must address the procedures to produce change. More specifically, we need a theory of which activities

---

[2] The authors are grateful to Michael Furlong for his suggestions in this section.

in therapy will produce which kind of change. Questions such as the utility of behavioral or verbal change procedures demonstrate the importance of this criterion (Bandura, 1977). While some research suggests the specificity of our interventions (Jesness, 1975), other studies find striking generalization (Arnkoff, 1980a; Zeiss, Lewinsohn, & Muñoz, 1979). Both specificity and generalization require explanation. A theoretical framework must be capable of guiding research on the therapeutic activities that will facilitate various types of change, as well as the conditions that result in resistance to change.

To date, the relationship between cognitive psychology and clinical psychology has been one-way, with cognitive psychology providing the constructs that clinicians use in formulating clinical theories. Clinicians have had to modify or elaborate their cognitive sources, however, in order to address the complexity of clinical phenomena. An example is the role of affect, discussed by Merluzzi et al. (1981). If we are successful in making these theories our own, or in devising our own theories, the tutelage should begin to go in the other direction as well, since the clinic is an outstanding, if complex, natural cognitive laboratory.

II. INTERRELATIONSHIPS AMONG COGNITIVE CONSTRUCTS

An examination of the numerous constructs posed in cognitive conceptualizations reveals several dimensions along which the constructs may be placed. These dimensions will be discussed with the goal of revealing researchers' conceptualizations of the cognitive–clinical domain. (See Glass and Arnkoff, this volume, for a discussion of the practical implications for assessment of some of these findings.)

One dimension along which cognitive constructs may be placed is the *awareness* indicated by the construct. While self-statements by definition involve self-report of conscious thought, automatic thoughts (Beck, 1976) may be presently out of awareness. Scripts, or specific actions that must be performed to reach a goal (Landau & Goldfried, 1981), may influence behavior even if outside of awareness, and dynamics are usually thought of as unconscious.

Related to the variable of awareness is that of *level of inference* of a cognitive construct. Arnkoff (1980b) borrows Chomsky's surface and deep structure terms to propose a relationship between observable behavior and inferred meaning. In linguistics, the surface structure of a sentence is the words composing the sentence. The meaning of the sentence is not in the words, but rather is in the deep structure of the sentence; deep structure is an inference from surface structure. Meaning is ambiguous when surface structure alone is considered. The sentence, "Flying planes can be dangerous" is an example of one surface structure that has at least three deep structural meanings. Extrapolating to other behavior, the surface structure may be said to be observable behavior, including self-reports such as self-statements. The meaning or deep structure of the behavior is not immediately apparent, but is an inference from the observed behavior. The surface-to-deep inference is complex because there is no one-to-one correspondence between them. One behavior could have several different meanings, and, conversely, one meaning can be expressed by any number of behaviors. The meaning or deep structure of an event is the essential element for both client and therapist, but it is not automatically identifiable from the content. Meaning, beliefs, schemata, and other constructs implying depth must be inferred from observable events.

In clinical work and clinical research, one type of cognitive event is elicited as material for inference to deep structure and process. Self-statements, for example, are elicited in assessment and therapy as evidence of beliefs (Sutton-Simon, 1981). However, two aspects of this process must be stressed. First, any inference can be questioned. Just as the early behavioral assessment literature criticized traditional assessment for its reliance on unsubstantiated inferences (Goldfried & Kent, 1972), so cognitive assessment must not fall prey to the menace of careless inference. It is dangerous to assume, for example, that the thought, "I'm going to fail" has the same meaning for everyone. One person may be discouraged and give up after such a thought, while another may counter the thought, become encouraged, and try harder (Kendall & Hollon, 1981). We are most likely to err in our inferences about meaning if we extrapolate from the content of a cognitive "snapshot" taken at one point in time. We must consider the shifting interconnections of the threads of experience (Mancuso & Ceely, 1980) and the *function* that a thought process plays.

The second aspect of the inference from surface to deep structure that must be emphasized is that the cognitive processes that are in an individual's awareness at any time are only the tip of the iceberg (Arnkoff, 1980b). However, we are suggesting neither a defensive blocking, nor a vast ignorance by individuals of their own processing. As Mischel (1981) says, psychologists can gain a great deal of information by asking the right questions. Nevertheless, we must be willing to make inferences from what the person tells us. Furthermore, we must also supplement self-report by other types of assessment, such as behavioral observation and responses to projective material, each of which requires its own type of inference to cognitive constructs.

Some types of structures and processes in particular may be less amenable to direct self-report than others because of their inaccessibility to language. One important structure of this type is a belief that was formed prior to the development of language (Mahoney, 1980). A client's belief in her worthlessness, for example, may predate self-talk. Current self-statements would deal not with the core belief of worthlessness, but with consequences of it, such as "I'd better not be demanding." Some of Beck's automatic thoughts, then, may never have been conscious.

Other structures and processes may be accessible to self-report, but only if we learn to ask the right questions. For example, some processes may have originated following the development of language, but were present so frequently that they faded into the background (Kendall, 1981; Mahoney, 1980). Vygotsky (1934/1962) hypothesized that private speech with the goal of self-regulation changes from overt self-directed speech modeled from adults to covert inner speech with its own structure and content. Frequently given examples with relevance to adults are learning to drive a car and learning to ski: initially the instructor's directions are meticulously repeated, but eventually the instructions fade as the activity is learned. Such speech which was once overt should be capable of being recovered or reconstructed. According to Vygotsky, the right questions to ask would involve reintroducing the information desired into the subject's consciousness (Wertsch, 1979). Because the subject's covert inner speech differs from overt communicative speech (Vygotsky, 1934/1962), even when the self-directions are reconstructed, the subject must translate the speech into grammatical sentences.

One final point that must be made with regard to the inference from overt behavior, or surface structure, to meaning, or deep structure, is that such inferences must be justified in the same manner as any other generalization. We can do no better than to quote Mischel on this point: "Such justification requires empirically demonstrating reliability, validity, stability, cross-situational consistency, and utility, and it is the assessor's burden regardless of theoretical orientation. The deeper the inference, the wider the generalizations and the greater the responsibility to justify them with evidence" (1981, p. 498).

In addition to level of awareness presumed and inference required, another dimension on which cognitive constructs may be placed is their *relationship in time* to an event of interest. Kendall and Braswell

(1982) present a temporal model of constructs. The model allows for feedback from the outcomes of previous behavioral events, and consequent changes in cognitions preceding later events. The model has as its starting point a state of motivation to reach a specific goal, where cognitions indicate one's current concerns (Klinger, 1971). These cognitions persist concurrently with a particular action taken or "behavioral event." At the termination of the behavioral event, the attributional process comes into play as attempts are made to explain the cause or outcome of one's behavior. The repetition of multiple behavioral and cognitive events increases the likelihood of cognitions which are more stable and consistent, such as cognitive or attributional styles and belief systems. A history of behavioral events and their outcomes also leads to the presence of anticipatory cognition in the form of outcome and self-efficacy expectancies (which may be situationally specific) as well as more generalized and transsituational factors such as intentions, plans, and commitments. In the most generalized state, expectancies can in turn influence both situational outcome predictions and postperformance attributions. Self-statements, imagery, and cognitive problem-solving skills can occur at any point in the temporal flow, where self-statements can function as instances of beliefs, attributions, or expectancies.

Kendall and Braswell's (1982) temporal model is a valuable addition to the cognitive literature. It may be coupled with Landau and Goldfried's (1981) schemata model, which delineates targets of assessment for both structure and process of cognition, and Mischel's (1981) framework of cognitive social learning variables. These models set the stage for a more careful consideration of the appropriate targets for assessment than we have seen to date. As Mischel (1981) has stated, "a coherent view of cognitive assessment . . . requires that we consider not only what alternative methods are available for the enterprise but also what aspects of the person need assessment within the cognitive perspective" (p. 483). Yet, surprisingly, little work in this area has been done. The difficulty of the task and the overwhelming narrow focus in the literature on assessing self-statements and beliefs (perhaps because they are key constructs in cognitive therapy efforts?) most certainly have contributed to this state of affairs.

The final dimension along which cognitive constructs may be placed is their *situation specificity*. Expectancies are usually thought of as situation specific (Kendall & Braswell, 1982); for example, an individual's self-efficacy expectations for touching a snake may differ considerably from the same person's expectations for climbing to the top of a tall building. On the other hand, beliefs may be thought of as state or as trait variables (Sutton-Simon, 1981). For example, the debate over the usefulness of the Irrational Beliefs Test (Jones, 1969) may stem in part from its goal of assessing a trait of irrationality, when irrational beliefs may be best thought of as situation-specific (Craighead, 1979; Glass & Merluzzi, 1981; Lohr & Bonge, 1982). Conversely, the beliefs implicated in evaluation anxiety may cross different types of situations (Glass & Arnkoff, 1980; Wine, 1980). Related to situational specificity is the variable of *breadth*, with themes representing a broader construct than, for example, situational scripts (Landau & Goldfried, 1981).

According to Mischel (1981), the assessment of cognitive constructs may be especially well suited to the determination of situation specificity or generality, provided that we "focus more specifically on what the person *constructs* in particular conditions instead of attempting to infer the global traits that he or she generally *has*" (p. 484). The assessment of cognitive and behavioral skills, or *competencies*, rather than dispositions, may afford not only "much better temporal and cross-situational stability," but also "more pervasive consequences for coping and adaptation" (Mischel, 1981, p. 485).

We have considered dimensions that characterize interrelationships among the vast range of cognitive–clinical constructs that have been proposed. To date, however, only three constructs have been extensively studied: self-statements, irrational beliefs, and cognitive distortions. We will now turn our attention to a more detailed consideration of these constructs.

III. SELF-STATEMENTS

Although there have been several proposed organizations for the variety of *methods* for assessing self-statements (Genest & Turk, 1981; Glass & Merluzzi, 1981; Kendall & Hollon, 1981; Meichenbaum & Butler, 1980a), less attention has been focused on conceptualizing the *content* and *nature* of internal dialogue. The cognitive therapy literature has tended to use dichotomous classifications when referring to self-statements: negative vs positive, inhibitive vs facilitative, negative vs coping, irrational vs rational, unrealistic vs realistic, dysfunctional vs functional, and task-irrelevant vs task-relevant. These bipolar distinctions appear to be used almost interchangeably in the literature. Notice that underlying these classifications is the inherent assumption that it is better to be rational, realistic, task-relevant, and positive than it is to be irrational, unrealistic, etc. In self-statement therapy, clinicians often help clients to identify the "bad" thoughts and replace them with "good" ones.

The question we would like to pose concerns whether the use of these interchangeable dichotomies to categorize self-statements is conceptually accurate or useful. Clinical experience suggests that using the terms "negative" and "positive" self-talk is beneficial to clients, in the sense that such a distinction may aid the client in viewing his or her problems from a cognitive perspective. But theoretically, the manner in which we have used this distinction may hinder our efforts to understand the role of cognition in the process of self-regulation and coping.

A. Differential Influence

Dichotomous classification of self-statements tends to imply that each pole of the dichotomy has equal influence or is of similar importance. Positive and negative self-statements may, in fact, play different roles in influencing behavioral outcome. Recent research suggests that positive, facilitative thoughts may be less important than the presence of negative self-statements. In one study, negative (but not positive) scores on the Social Interaction Self-Statement Test (SISST) correlated significantly with confederates' and judges' ratings of subject skill and anxiety following a heterosocial interaction (Glass, Merluzzi, Biever, & Larsen, 1982). Negative self-statements listed in anticipation of a social interaction were found to be inversely related to self-evaluations, although the number of positive and neutral/irrelevant thoughts were not (Cacioppo, Glass, & Merluzzi, 1979). In addition, Kendall, Williams, Pechacek, Graham, Shisslak, and Herzof (1979) report that an absence of negative self-statements was related to positive adjustment during cardiac catheterization, while the presence of positive thoughts did not necessarily aid in the coping process. In a study by Klass (1981), negative self-statements showed a stronger relationship to feelings of guilt about assertion than did positive self-statements.

These findings have important implications not only for treatment but also for our conceptualization of the role of cognitive processes in adjustment and maladaptive behavior. To the clinician, they suggest that helping the client to become aware of and change negative patterns of thinking may be more important than merely increasing the number of positive thoughts. Kendall and Hollon (1981) offer an interesting analysis of the power of nonnegative thinking. Meichenbaum (1977) also points out that just saying the "right" things to yourself may not be sufficient to induce change. Component analyses of cognitive restructuring allow for the direct examination of the relative importance of examining and challenging negative self-statements as opposed to learning and practicing new positive self-talk. Studies of this sort by Carmody (1978), Glogower, Fremouw, and McCroskey (1978), and Thorpe, Amatu, Blakey, and Burns (1976) have yielded inconsistent results, however, and do not offer evidence to support conclusions about negative cognitions being more important than positive thoughts.

It may be the case that the differential influence of negative versus positive self-statements is a result of *when* such thoughts occur in relation to behavior in a particular situation. For example, negative self-talk emitted during behavioral performance may be crucial in contributing to failure, yet thoughts reflective of high self-efficacy expectations prior to behavior may be equally predictive of successful performance. The importance of other variables that may interact with self-statement valence must not be ignored.

B. Misleading Assumptions in Scoring Systems

Many paper-and-pencil self-statement assessment measures have relied on a negative–positive scoring system. Structured self-statement inventories typically ask subjects to indicate which of a predetermined list of thoughts they experienced in a previous situation or task. The Assertion Self-Statement Test (Schwartz & Gottman, 1976), Social Interaction Self-Statement Test (Glass et al., 1982), Checklist of Positive and Negative Thoughts (Galassi, Frierson, & Sharer, 1981), and Self-Statements Inventory (Kendall et al., 1979) all yield total scores for positive and negative items. Thoughts generated on thought listings (Cacioppo et al., 1979), in which subjects are asked to list what they were thinking during the period immediately preceding assessment, have also tended to be scored on the valence dimension (positive, negative, and neutral/irrelevant).

These cognitive assessment inventories, by virtue of the assumptions involved in their construction and scoring systems, perhaps are steering us toward a "uniformity myth" about our subjects' cognitive experiences. A negative–positive dichotomy, while helpful to the researcher concerned with reliable scoring and quantification, may also serve to oversimplify a considerably more complex picture.

It is misleading to assume that all thoughts which are rated by judges as "negative" always function to inhibit responding and/or elicit negative emotions. The seemingly negative self-statement, "I'll never get my work done" is not negative, in that it may serve as a cue to certain individuals to get back to work (Kendall & Hollon, 1981). In a similar vein, Glass and Merluzzi (1981) suggest that assessing the frequency of positive and negative statements may not be as important as when a thought occurs or what it *means* to the person. Two men may both report thinking, "She's probably not interested in me" when contemplating asking an attractive woman out for a date. However, this may mean "I'm a real loser" to one man, yet "I'll really have to turn on the charm, then" to the other. Thus, a "negative" thought is seen as a challenge and serves a motivating function, while the identical thought to another person may reflect a belief of inferiority and serve to heighten anxiety and avoidance. It may be a mistake to infer the valence of a thought by examining its verbal expression in isolation.

C. Functional Classifications

Alternative classification systems for internal dialogue thus need to be considered. We would propose that a useful way to conceptualize self-statements is in terms of the *function* they play, as opposed to looking at content alone. In this section, we would like to discuss several possibilities that represent more functional classifications.

One of the earliest examples of a more functional analysis can be found in Meichenbaum and Cameron's (1972) initial stress-inoculation training study. Clients learned to monitor negative, self-defeating thoughts and use these as cues to employ four types of coping self-statements which were believed appropriate to different stages of fear reactions. These self-statements fell into the general categories of preparing for the stressor, confronting and handling the stressor, coping with the fear of being overwhelmed, and providing self-reinforcement. Thus, these statements served the function of encouraging clients to assess the reality of the situation, control negative thoughts and images, recognize, use, and relabel arousal, prepare to confront the situation, cope with intense fear, and reflect on performance and reinforce coping attempts (Meichenbaum, 1977). Not all of these self-statements, however, were of equal utility to all clients. Meichenbaum (1977) notes that, over the course of training, different clients chose to use specific combinations of self-statements.

Meichenbaum's self-statements were derived according to a *model* of fear reactions. We would encourage other investigators to allow theoretical considerations to guide functional conceptualizations of self-statements. For example, Wine's cognitive–attentional theory of test anxiety (Wine, 1980) postulates that task-irrelevant self-preoccupation, characterized by self-depreciation and ruminative self-critical worry, contributes to an attentional focus away from the task to be solved. She suggests that test-anxious individuals have negative, self-focused thoughts, but that low test-anxious persons do not thus have positive, self-focused thoughts—rather, it is task-focused thoughts that characterize their cognitive process.

Thus, being able to assess or manipulate the attentional focus of thoughts should be important for further understanding of their function in social-evaluative situations. Thought-listing measures and videotape thought reconstructions can be easily scored to determine the locus of attention of each particular thought. For example, Merluzzi, Cacioppo, and Glass (1979) found that high socially anxious men tended to focus more on themselves and less on the other person or the interaction than low-anxious subjects. A similar system was employed by Hollandsworth, Glazeski, Kirkland, Jones, and Van Norman (1979), who asked subjects to view a videotape of their test behavior and relate what they were thinking and feeling. Judges categorized thoughts into facilitative (on-task, positive self-referent) and debilitative (off-task, negative self-referent) categories.

The use of subcategories imbedded within several dimensions of content, focus, or function can yield increasingly sophisticated cognitive analysis. Structured self-statement questionnaires, which typically have yielded scores on a single positive–negative dichotomy, can also be adapted for multidimensional assessment. Merluzzi and Glass (1981) are currently exploring the possibility of devising a self-statement inventory relevant to social interaction which could be scored for locus of attention and also whether the thought manifested a belief, a current concern, an attribution, or an expectation.

It is important, however, to look broadly for models to guide self-statement conceptualizations. It is possible for defense mechanisms, from traditional psychodynamic theory, to be incorporated into cognitive assessment to examine the function of self-statements. Houston (1977), for example, in an examination of the cognitive coping behavior of high and low trait-anxious individuals in stressful situations, devised a postexperimental questionnaire to measure thoughts conceptualized as indicative of intellectualization, isolation, denial, rationalization, reversal of affect, projection, avoidant thinking, search for and lack of strategies, and preoccupation. Higher trait anxiety scores were associated with lack of strategy, preoccupation, and not using intellectualization during a shock avoidance task. These cognitive responses were also associated with greater pulse rate and reported anxiety (stress response) than other cognitive coping behaviors.

Finally, Lazarus' (1981) work on stress and coping offers yet another model with implications for a functional analysis of self-statements. He views coping as a flexible (but not necessarily rational or realistic) set of strategies to comprehend and deal with stressful events. Coping, according to Lazarus, has two functions: to change the situation (problem solving) and to manage the somatic and subjective components of stress-related emotions (palliation). He also offers a delineation of four modes of coping that could be used as the basis for an additional categorization system for self-statements. These coping modes include (1) information seeking, (2) direct action, (3) inhibition of action, and (4) intrapsychic processes—what a person says to himself or herself to regulate emotion, including defenses (denial, projection) and avoidance. Specific self-statements thus could be classified on the basis of their role in guiding information seeking, directing or inhibiting action, or dealing with affect.

Although content is important, it may result in oversimplification and lead away from even more important issues such as meaning, differential influences, and individual differences. The reader has seen that there are several exciting ways in which assessment can encompass functional issues. To conclude our discussion of self-statement conceptualization, we would like to go one step further and suggest an alternative to categorization itself.

D. Continuous Dimensions

We propose to view self-statements along a continuous dimension from *maladaptive* to *adaptive*. Our earlier discussion of the importance of the meaning of self-statements becomes especially crucial now, because where a thought falls on this continuum is probably related to the *meaning* or *impact* the cognition has for the individual. Goldfried (1979) and Meichenbaum and Butler (1980a) stress this issue when they refer to connotative, affective, or personal meanings. It may not be the content of the self-statements but their subjective meaning that contributes to one's cognitive appraisal of a stressful situation as threatening as opposed to challenging.

Since the meaning of a particular thought may differ from individual to individual, a maladaptive thought for one person may actually function in a more adaptive way for another. Kendall and Hollon (1981) make the point that behavioral procedures may change the subjective meaning of self-statements and thus the behavior, so that clients say the same things to themselves but employ the self-statements differently. Therefore a self-statement that is maladaptive for one individual at time X may serve a more adaptive function for that same person at time Y! Our challenge, therefore, is to devise ways of assessing subjective meaning so that we may truly assess where a thought falls on this continuum (see Glass & Arnkoff, this volume).

IV. BELIEF SYSTEMS

A well-known cognitive intervention is Albert Ellis' (1962) Rational–Emotive Therapy (RET), which focuses on challenging and disputing clients' irrational beliefs. These rigid, absolutistic demands, commands, and musts are seen as the basic cause of disturbed emotions (Ellis, 1979). Ellis' earlier work on RET identified a group of 10 to 12 irrational beliefs (Ellis, 1962, 1970) that form the basis for several measures of irrationality, including the Irrational Beliefs Test (IBT; Jones, 1969) and the Irrational Beliefs Inventory (Alden & Safran, 1978). (For an excellent review of irrationality scales, see Sutton-Simon, 1981.) Recently, Ellis has reduced his original number of basic irrational beliefs to three major "musts," which include from 3 to 13 subcategories (Ellis, 1977). He also maintains that there are probably hundreds or thousands of irrational ideas and that he has already compiled a list of 259 major self-defeating ones.

A. Classification of Beliefs

Ellis' conception of irrational beliefs is based on an analysis of their content, and relies on a specific hierarchical organization scheme. There appears to be no theoretical or empirical basis for adopting this particular system, however. More specifically, we would argue that there is no "correct" list of irrational beliefs that can be decided on for all people on an a priori basis. The conceptual distinctions between each of 3, 12, or 259 beliefs are not clear-cut, and the existence of subcategories falling under each belief is also problematic. For example, Ellis says that the three major beliefs "merely seem basic in the sense that virtually all the others you can think of . . . fall into subcategories under these major headings" (Ellis, 1977, p. 14). Any number of different hierarchical belief systems would fulfill this same criterion, and there is no theoretical basis for favoring one over another.

Evidence that beliefs may not be easily classified into a limited number of conceptually distinct categories is provided in Lohr and

Bonge's (1982) cross-validation of the IBT. Factor loadings of some items necessitated their reassignment to more appropriate subscales on a modified IBT devised by these authors, and 24 of the initial 100 items which had been presumed to reflect particular irrational beliefs were discarded due to weak component loadings. In fact, the analysis of the IBT, conducted for the sake of comparability with Jones' analysis (1969) to yield 10 factors, found these factors to account for only 32% of the total variance. Eight of these belief components accounted for less than 5% apiece, and no evidence was found for the existence of Jones' Frustration Reactive subscale.

Ellis' conception of irrational beliefs, however, is only one of several definitional models of belief systems (Sutton-Simon, 1981). Assessment strategies can be developed not only from a definition of irrational beliefs as a set of life rules, but also from a view of such beliefs as a set of qualities (such as rigidity) underlying thought, or as dysfunctional thinking styles. We will address conceptual issues involved in this third alternative, Beck's (1976) notion of cognitive distortion and faulty thinking styles, in the next section of this article.

At the present time, we would like to expand on Sutton-Simon's distinction by suggesting a fourth definitional model of irrational beliefs, one based on the function or role they play. Many criticisms of both self-statement and belief assessment presented earlier in this article have centered on the problematic nature of adopting a content perspective on clinically relevant cognitions. In order to consider a totally different conception, it is perhaps important to begin by asking the questions: "What do we mean by rationality and irrationality?" or "What is the irrational component in an irrational belief?"

B. Rationality and Irrationality

Simon (1979) makes the distinction between *substantive* rationality, in which behavior is appropriate to the achievement of given goals, and *procedural* rationality, in which behavior is the outcome of appropriate deliberation, reasoning, and decision making. Clinical psychologists such as Ellis appear to combine both aspects, defining criteria of rationality as "using efficient, flexible, scientific, and logico-empirical ways" of attempting to achieve the basic values, purposes, or goals one has chosen and to avoid self-defeating results (Ellis, 1979, p. 400). Similarly, Tosi (1979) describes rationality as "implying logical thinking and acting as a way of achieving some personal goal or set of goals" (p. 182). Irrationality, then, involves thinking, emoting, and behaving in illogical ways that interfere with the achievement of these goals and lead to self-defeating or self-destructive consequences (Ellis, 1977, 1979).

It is the substantive approach that is consistent with our emphasis on the function, and not the content, of irrational beliefs. Rationality and irrationality are closely tied to the concepts of maladaptive and adaptive thought highlighted earlier in the article. Irrational beliefs should be seen as maladaptive for an individual relative to his or her own goals. While discussing goals, however, Ellis also attempts to categorize and list which beliefs are irrational on the basis of *content*. For example, the belief "I must become the best in my field" could be considered an irrational "must." By logical deduction, then, the conclusion follows that this belief should interfere with the achievement of individual goals. Yet we all know persons who hold this belief and do *not* experience consequent maladaptive affect or goal-blocking behavior: in fact, they report that this belief is *adaptive* for them in having some success in reaching the lofty goals they have set for themselves in extremely competitive fields. Continuing with our logical analysis, since this is a valid argument, and since the conclusion is not always true, we must conclude that one of the premises is in error.

We would like to suggest that the second premise, which states that there are particular beliefs that are, by definition, irrational, is where the difficulty lies. Such "irrational" ideas can sometimes be adaptive, just as rationality can sometimes be maladaptive. A functional view of irrationality would take this into consideration, and allow a given belief to be adaptive or "rational" for one individual, yet be "irrational" or maladaptive for another. We agree with Lazarus (1980) that it is not the case "that only accurate perceptions of reality (or assumptions about life) can be adaptationally effective and desirable" (p. 123). Perhaps the term "maladaptive belief," instead of irrational belief, could be used in the literature to avoid the inconsistency. We will discuss the sometimes positive role of illusion and distortion further in the final section of this article.

In summary, Ellis sometimes focuses on the *content* of specifically delineated irrational beliefs, yet at other times highlights the *function* more rational beliefs play in attaining personal goals. We have argued that this is problematic and that we would stress a focus on the function a belief has for a given individual. Specific lists of irrational beliefs, which do not also assess function, may be helpful when working with specific clients but counterproductive in terms of conceptual and theoretical understanding. As Kelly (1955) stated, the therapist must not impose preexisting personal constructs or preferred hypotheses upon the behavior and symbolism of the client.

C. Beliefs and Situation Specificity

Another important issue concerns the organization and situation specificity of irrational beliefs. Sutton-Simon (1981) raises the fascinating question of whether irrational beliefs represent trait or state variables. The most widely known concept of such beliefs (Ellis, 1962) appears to view them as a reflection of a generalized disposition or personality trait, and measures such as the IBT yield overall scores reflecting an individual's cross-situational cognitive style. Mischel (1981) cautions that a comprehensive cognitive assessment must focus not only on cognitive person variables, but also pay attention to situations and person–situation interactions.

The A-B-C theory of irrational thinking and disturbance (Ellis, 1979), in fact, does take situational variability into account by maintaining that it is the person's beliefs about what is occurring at or during an activating experience or event that cause the emotional or behavioral consequence. The situation–belief interaction would play an important role in our functional approach to irrational beliefs, since it may be that a particular belief is maladaptive for a given person in some situations but not in others. For example, a belief that one must be thoroughly competent in everything one does might be a great motivator on the job but lead an individual to be insufferable in his or her interpersonal relationships. Whether the specification of situational context may thus increase the predictability of behavior compared to more global, trait-like measures is an empirical question.

One approach to a situational assessment of maladaptive beliefs is to create a measure of beliefs relevant to a particular type of problematic situation. In the context of a cognitive therapy outcome study, Craighead (1979) employed a measure of Irrational Beliefs about Assertion, consisting of 24 general belief statements about the value and consequences of assertive responding. Ginsburg, Glass, and Heinssen (1981) have recently devised a similar measure of adaptive and maladaptive beliefs which may influence affect and responding in heterosocial situations.

A program of research by Lohr (Lohr, Brandt, & Bonge, 1977; Lohr & Bonge, 1979) has taken a slightly different approach to situational belief assessment. The Situational Irrational Cognitions Inventory (SICI) requires subjects to examine irrational syllogistic interpretations that follow social vignettes (objective statement or description of the event—unreasonable or illogical judgment or inference—negative emotional consequence or reaction) and to rate the degree to which each interpretation is personally applicable and how anxious or upset they would feel in the situation. Subscales correspond to the same preestablished 10 irrational belief categories used by Jones (1969).

These assessment instruments represent initial attempts to address the role of situational variables in belief systems. In addition to normative, between-subjects comparisons on global measures of irrational beliefs, research must be initiated on intraindividual (ipsative) performance across time and situations (Lazarus, 1981). Before concluding this section on irrational beliefs, we would like to share a few additional conceptual questions.

D. Additional Questions

Although the content of irrational beliefs is typically assessed through interviews and questionnaires, we have argued that a more functional analysis is in order. If one truly wishes to study belief systems, there must be a greater emphasis on the analysis not only of belief content but also the investigation of the organization or structural interrelationships between beliefs. Neimeyer and Neimeyer (1981) provide a cogent description and analysis of personal construct assessment, based on Kelly's (1955) Personal Construct Theory. Such assessment can yield structural measures of the independence of construct clusters, flexibility of construing, and extremity of ratings ("meaningfulness" of constructs). We wonder if it also might be possible to study the interrelationships and hierarchical structure of subordinate and superordinate beliefs.

A related issue concerns the role and interrelationship of general versus personally relevant beliefs. The IBT (Jones, 1969) contains a large number of irrational beliefs, some of which are stated in a general form, such as "People need a source of strength outside themselves." Other items on the same subscales are worded with specific reference to the subject, such as "I try to consult an authority on important decisions." Are these two forms functionally equivalent, or do they have a differential impact upon affect and behavior? For example, an individual might answer "true" to the first statement, because he or she believes that, in general, most people do need to rely on others. However, this need not mean this same person believes that he or she personally needs such an external source of strength. Indicating an "irrational" belief in the general sense may be quite different from acknowledging it is true for you.

And what of the role of faulty logic in contributing to maladaptive beliefs? If these beliefs are based on "illogical thinking" about the reasons for our own and others' behavior, what can we say about the logical abilities or competencies of persons who hold a large number of these beliefs or hold them to an extreme extent? Our position (which you can probably guess by this time) is that an individual can be a very logical person—be good at completing analogies, critical thinking, detecting invalid arguments, etc.—and yet seemingly be blind to the presence of certain "illogical" deductions or inferences on his or her part in particular life areas. This issue may also be addressing Sutton-Simon's (1981) distinction between irrational belief systems based on life rules and irrational belief systems based on faulty thinking. We can envision a fascinating dialogue between philosophers and psychologists relating to this question.

Finally, if our goal as psychologists is to seek a cognitive–functional analysis (Meichenbaum, 1977) of cognition, we need to further our knowledge of how cognitive factors, such as irrational beliefs, relate to the other cognitive events and processes discussed at the beginning of this article. In the final section of the article, we now turn to some critical issues and conceptual distinctions relating to a third cognitive construct: faulty thinking styles and cognitive distortions.

V. DISTORTIONS, MALADAPTIVE IDEAS, AND ILLUSIONS

In discussing distortions, maladaptive ideas, and illusions, our theme will again be that the content of an idea or thinking process alone is misleading. To assess the adaptive or maladaptive nature of a cognitive process, we must attend to the *function* or *meaning* for the individual.

A. Cognitive Distortions

Beck has identified a number of maladaptive cognitive distortions, which are misperceptions of reality or disorders of thinking. These distortions have been found in depression (Beck, 1963) and anxiety (Beck, Laude, & Bohnert, 1974), and Beck (1976) proposes that similar processes underlie other emotional disorders. Bedrosian and Beck (1980) list 10 common types of distortions. When we examine the distortions, it seems that they can be divided into two major types: misuse of information (selective abstraction, arbitrary inference, overgeneralization, personalization, incorrect assessments regarding danger versus safety), and extreme types of thinking (polarized thinking, magnification and exaggeration, assuming excessive responsibility, dysfunctional attitudes about pleasure versus pain, tyranny of the shoulds).

Some readers may disagree with our categorization of the distortions; for example, it is not entirely clear that overgeneralization should be defined only as a misuse of information, and magnification as a type of extreme thinking. Each may fit both categories, and, in fact, the boundaries between overgeneralization and magnification are fuzzy. This confusion illustrates a problem with a listing of distortions which implies that they are separate and distinct. Just as the content of Ellis' irrational beliefs may not be distinct, so each of Beck's cognitive distortions may not be conceptually separate from the others.

There is some empirical evidence of the difficulty in uniquely identifying the distortions. Krantz and Hammen (1979) have developed a cognitive distortion questionnaire for assessing depressed, distorted thinking. In devising the questionnaire, they presented each item to graduate student raters and asked them to rate whether the item showed depressed mood, and whether it showed distorted thinking. For each item that was rated as distorted, Krantz and Hammen asked the judges to rate the type of distortion it represented, such as overgeneralization, selective abstraction, etc. Although there was agreement as to which items were distorted, the raters were unable to identify the different types of distortions reliably.

In discussing Ellis' irrational beliefs, we made the point that even though the types of beliefs may not be conceptually distinct, it may be clinically useful to retain the individual terms. The same conclusion can be drawn with regard to Beck's 10 types of cognitive distortions. A client may more easily learn to identify maladaptive patterns by labeling some as arbitrary inference and others as overgeneralization. A general term such as "cognitive distortion" or "misuse of information" may not convey sufficient information for the client to identify problematic patterns.

For conceptual clarity, however, it may be useful to keep in mind the reason that Beck considers these thinking processes to be distortions. In discussing irrational beliefs, we suggested an examination of the function of beliefs in order to determine which ones are maladaptive. Similarly, we suggest that the *function* of a thinking style be examined to determine if it is maladaptive. Only certain types of outcomes lead us to label a thinking style as distorted. For example, selective attention to the environment may be seen as adaptive when the environment is extreme. A better future adjustment might be predicted for a rock star who is skeptical of his or her popularity, who attends selectively to it, than for the star who correctly perceives the worship of adoring fans. Similarly, caution is called for in labeling all extreme thinking as distorted until more information is available on good copers as well as those whom we see in our clinics. How many chairpersons of the boards of major corporations will be found to have a "tyranny of the shoulds"? In fact, in a study of "super insurance producers," whose annual production equals or exceeds six million dollars, Abrahms (1979) found ample evidence of maladaptive cognitions. She reports, for example, the prevalent idea among her very successful subjects that their self-worth was determined solely by the volume of their sales.

Clinicians appear to label a thinking process as distorted only if it serves the function of leading to unnecessarily unpleasant, maladaptive conclusions, emotions, or behavior. Examples of maladaptive outcomes are unnecessarily critical self-evaluations, disorganizing anxiety, and failure to take action because of feelings of hopelessness. Thinking processes that covary with such outcomes are likely to be labeled as distorted. It may be the case that extreme thinking usually leads to maladaptive outcomes. But it may be fruitful to determine the circumstances under which extreme thinking may be adaptive as well as maladaptive.

Our point may be clarified by considering one type of distortion in detail. Polarized thinking is identified as a distortion by Beck (1976; Bedrosian & Beck, 1980). Another term for the same process is dichotomous thinking (Neuringer, 1961). In polarized or dichotomous thinking, the person is able to see only the extremes of black and white; gray does not appear in his or her spectrum. For example, some people with evaluation anxiety appear to believe that they either get a perfect score on a test, or they have failed. (Clearly, distortions other than polarized thinking, such as overgeneralization, may also be said to operate here.)

Beck (1976) describes polarized thinking in neurotics as being likely in "sensitive areas" (p. 92), and not necessarily as a general trait. Yet it is our impression that clinicians often think of dichotomous thinking as a trait; it is as if people could be divided into dichotomous or continuum thinkers. But such a bipolar division of people is itself an example of dichotomous thinking. We would like to raise two questions about the dichotomous thinking issue. First, we wonder to what extent thinking in bipolar opposites is cross-situational, or trait-like, and to what extent it is situation-specific. Beck (1976) clearly hypothesizes that the tendency will be seen primarily in the areas that are most problematic for the individual. In depression, he predicts polarized thinking in self-evaluations, while in anxiety neurosis, he

predicts it in the expectations of personal danger. An empirical evaluation of the extent and specificity of dichotomous thinking in various
disorders would be most interesting.

Our second question about dichotomous thinking refers again to our
emphasis on the *function* of a cognitive process. Beck (1976) seems
to consider that polarized thinking is always maladaptive. Yet, as
Landfield (1980) points out, an a priori characterization of dichotomous thinking as maladaptive is paradoxical—another example of
dichotomous thinking. Perhaps there are certain conditions under
which polarized thinking is maladaptive, but other conditions under
which it is adaptive.

Our question arises, in part, because of the apparent similarity between polarized thinking and Kelly's (1955) theory of bipolar personal
constructs. Kelly, of course, theorizes that people organize their construction of events around bipolar constructs such as success–failure,
integrity–dishonesty, etc. For Kelly, bipolar thinking is the norm; yet
for Beck, it is a distortion. Since we are attracted to both Beck's and
Kelly's theories, we were faced with the dilemma of how to reconcile
them!

Kelly himself addresses the question of the relationship between
dichotomous constructs and continuous constructs (1955, pp. 141–145).
He proposes a number of different means of creating graduated scales
from dichotomous constructs. For example, the hierarchical nature of
constructs allows us to create a scale by arranging the constructs in
hierarchical order and assigning the poles of each construct the binary
values of 0 and 1. To explain this procedure more specifically, let us
use Kelly's example of a scale called "integrity vs dishonesty," which
is made up of the four constructs of honesty vs dishonesty, candor vs
deviousness, courage vs defeatism, and objectivity vs subjectivity, arranged hierarchically in that order. If the digit 1 represents the first
pole of each construct, and the digit 0 represents the second pole, any
individual may be described by an arrangement of 0s and 1s. A dis-
honest, devious, courageous, and objective person would therefore be
represented by the digits 0011. The reader can see that the four constructs may be arranged in 16 different permutations. Since the constructs are hierarchically arranged, the 16 possible permutations create
an ordinal scale. Using a larger number of such constructs would result
in an approximately continuous scale.

Kelly's theory does not imply the kind of rigid, polarized construction that a casual reading might imply. In fact, the ultimate reconciliation of the apparent contradiction of Beck and Kelly, we believe,
comes in the emphasis of both on *flexibility* in construing events.

Though Kelly's theory is about dichotomous constructs, an important aspect of the theory is his term *permeability*. A construct is permeable to the extent that it allows the inclusion of new elements of experience. If a person has the construct "intelligent vs unintelligent," the construct is permeable if new acquaintances can be included as intelligent or unintelligent. "A construct which 'takes life in its stride' is a permeable one" (1955, p. 81). Flexibility characterizes permeable constructs: "when new elements are added to the context of a construct there is a tendency for the construct itself to change somewhat" (1955, p. 80). The permeability of constructs sounds similar to the Piagetian notion of accommodation of the schema in light of new experience. Kelly adds that permeable constructs are "less shaken by the impact of unexpected minor events" (1955, p. 80).

We suggest that Beck's intent in focusing on polarized thinking is also to highlight the notion of flexibility. Polarized thinking is problematic insofar as it is rigid and inflexible. As we have said, the outcome of a thinking process seems to determine whether it should be called distorted. Dichotomous thinking may often be characteristic of rigidity, as Beck theorizes. But an investigation of competent functioning may also reveal instances of adaptive polarized thinking. Landfield (1977) specifically points to the *motivating* effect of thinking in dichotomies. "Strong positions and commitments are necessary to initiate important undertakings, and ... final decisions often involve dichotomies" (p. 137). Interestingly, one illustration of the need to adopt a dichotomy comes in the advance of scientific knowledge (Mahoney, 1976). When we adopt a theory such as Beck's or Kelly's, we know that, like all theories, it is imperfect. We must nevertheless dichotomously adopt it as if it were true to provide the impetus to test it.

B. Illusion—Maladaptive or Adaptive?

The emphasis in cognitive–clinical writings might lead an observer to expect that functioning is adaptive to the extent that it is consistent with reality. Indeed, Arnkoff (1980b) discusses adaptation as symmetry with reality. Empirical evidence and recent arguments, however, necessitate a rethinking of that position (J. C. Coyne, personal communication).

Lazarus (1980) argues that "positively toned emotions" play a large role in coping. It is a mistake, he says, to rule out as useless "all the things people do and think that simply make them feel good or produce positively toned emotions, even when one has to bend reality a bit to maintain certain illusions" (p. 123). Denial, for example, is a viable way to cope when direct action is not possible. Kendall, Finch, and Montgomery (1978) found that subjects who characteristically employed reversal defenses (denial, negation, and reaction formation) and projection tended to respond to a vicarious threat to self-esteem with a *decrease* in state anxiety. In general, being able to put a "good light on things" (Lazarus, 1980, p. 123) is associated with adaptive functioning (Lazarus, Cohen, Folkman, Kanner, & Schaefer, 1980; Lazarus, Kanner, & Folkman, 1980).

Lazarus, Kanner, and Folkman (1980) suggest that positively toned emotions may arise from false assumptions as well as from accurate appraisals. There is evidence in particular of false self-enhancing appraisals in perceived control over the environment. Control may be divided into the perception of contingency between actions and outcome, and the perception of personal competence. Small children are hypothesized to overestimate the contingency between their actions and outcomes (Weisz & Stipek, 1982). Development in the contingency aspect of control involves a decrease in the perception of contingency. Yet even adults make the "fundamental attribution error" of attributing outcomes to personal dispositions when environmental forces are actually more responsible (Ross, 1977). The depression literature contains empirical evidence of the adaptive role of illusion or self-enhancing appraisals of contingency. For example, Alloy and Abramson (1979) conducted four experiments in which subjects estimated the degree of contingency between their behaviors (pressing or not pressing a button) and an environmental outcome (the onset of a green light). While depressed subjects were generally accurate in their estimates of contingency in all experimental conditions, nondepressed subjects overestimated the degree of contingency when the green light was presented frequently and when the appearance of the light was associated with monetary reward for the subject, and nondepressed subjects underestimated the degree of contingency when the green light was associated with monetary loss for the subject. The authors interpret the results for the nondepressives as reflecting a motivation to enhance self-esteem. Results consistent with this "rosy glow" formulation have also been found by Golin, Terrell, and Johnson (1977).

The perception of contingency is one form of perceived control. A second form is the perception of personal competence (Weisz & Stipek, 1982). Lewinsohn, Mischel, Chaplin, and Barton (1980) and Nelson and Craighead (1977) have found that nondepressives overestimate their competence at various tasks. For example, in the study by Lewinsohn *et al.*, a comparison was made between self- and observer ratings of social skill in both depressives and nondepressives. Depressed individuals were accurate in their self-evaluations with respect to the observer ratings at the outset of therapy. During the course of treatment, however, they began to enhance their evaluations relative to the observers'. Nondepressed subjects consistently showed this "illusory glow."

How shall we understand this departure from reality? As the Alcoholics Anonymous Prayer says, adaptive functioning involves accepting what we need to accept and changing what we can change (Lazarus, 1980). It appears that whatever processes allow us to be adaptive are functional, even if such processes involve distortion. Positive emotions and belief in our abilities are adaptive in situations in which action can have a self-enhancing outcome. If mild illusions are required to keep us motivated and active, then mild illusions are adaptive. Here again we focus on the *function* of the appraisal process as more indicative of adaptation than the content.

An illustration of illusion as potentially adaptive is provided in a charming fashion by the children's story of Dumbo and the Magic Feather, immortalized in the Disney animated film (M. Cunningham, personal communication). Dumbo, for those readers who are no longer children, is an elephant, an outcast all his life because of his oversized ears. Dumbo lives in a circus, his only friend a clever mouse who sits in Dumbo's hat. One night Dumbo and his friend watch the circus clowns have a party, and Dumbo and the mouse themselves drink huge quantities of pink champagne. The pink champagne leads to visions of pink elephants flying all around, and in the morning, Dumbo and his friend wake up in the highest limb of a very tall tree. The mouse tells Dumbo that Dumbo flew them both up there, but Dumbo does not believe his friend and in his fright, falls from the tree to the ground.

In the meantime, five black crows on a nearby telephone pole have observed all these events with great amusement. The leader offers to help the mouse persuade Dumbo of his ability to fly. The crow pulls a big black feather out of his tail and tells Dumbo that maybe he can't fly by himself, but with the help of the feather, he will indeed be able to fly. Dumbo grasps the feather, flaps his ears, and takes off in flight.

Dumbo and the mouse plan to show off to the clowns by demonstrating that he can fly. At the big moment, however, as Dumbo jumps off his high perch, he loses his feather. Without faith in his ability to fly alone, he begins to fall. The mouse yells to Dumbo that he could really fly all along. Just as he is about to plunge to the ground, Dumbo begins to believe in himself and starts to fly!

The story of Dumbo is an especially colorful illustration of the power of both illusion and self-efficacy expectations. The attribution illusion was essential to convince Dumbo that there were some circumstances under which he could fly. It seems important that in the end, Dumbo was able to give up the illusion and believe in himself. Margaret Cunningham, who reacquainted us with Dumbo, makes a parallel between Dumbo's experience of relying on a feather to find his own wings, and the experience of a client relying on the therapist to find strength that was always available within.

We would like to make three further points with regard to illusion. The first deals with the cognitive processes involved. In the studies showing inaccurate perception of competence, the subjects either had no information on their performance, or ambiguous information. In the study by Lewinsohn et al. (1980), no feedback was provided to the subjects. In the study by Nelson and Craighead (1977), the "feedback" was experimenter controlled and not actually contingent on the subject's performance. Subjects may have been surprised at times by the feedback they received. It seems that in both studies, judgments were made under conditions of uncertainty. In such situations, individuals tend to rely on past experience with similar tasks. Tversky and Kahneman (1974) describe several "heuristics" which aid judgment in uncertain situations. One such heuristic is *representativeness*, the tendency to judge the present situation by its similarity to past situations. Even if the probabilities of outcomes in the current situation make one outcome far more likely than another, an individual is likely to ignore such base rate information and make a judgment by representativeness alone. In the studies of the illusion of personal competence, nondepressed subjects apparently make their self-ratings by referring to their experience in past situations. Nondepressed individuals would tend to have a positive self-evaluation, even a self-enhancing evaluation. Under conditions of random or nonexistent feedback, there is every reason to expect a carry-over of the positive evaluation.

Our second point with regard to the illusion findings is that the methodologies used to date are probably the optimal conditions under which to observe illusion. Though we apparently benefit from self-confidence, it would hardly be functional to be entirely unresponsive to reality. Mischel (1981) proposes that, in the absence of new information, individuals will act in accord with behavior-outcome expectancies they have obtained in similar situations. New information, however, can override the previous expectancies so that the new expectancies, tailored to the situation, come to direct behavior (Mischel & Staub, 1965). We propose that if individuals are provided with unambiguous, nonrandom feedback discrepant with their previous expectancies, the "illusory glow" will decrease. The discrepancy between "reality" and subject judgments will decrease either through an increase in effective behavior with no change in self-evaluations, or through a lowering of self-evaluations, depending on whether an alternative response is available (Lazarus, 1980). Such a procedure has not yet been employed in studies finding inaccurate judgments on the part of nondepressed individuals. We suggest that the "glow" will decrease, but we predict that it will not disappear. According to the "anchoring and adjustment" heuristic (Tversky & Kahneman, 1974), feedback will result in adjustment of mistaken judgments, but always relative to the starting point. The judgment will move *toward* a more realistic level, but is not likely to reach it. Illusory judgments, once made, are quite stubborn (Ross, 1977).

Finally, the serendipitous findings of an illusory glow in nondepressives underscore the need for normative data before models of abnormality can be confidently created (Meichenbaum & Butler, 1980c). Clinicians tend to construct models only from knowledge of pathology (Lazarus, 1980), and the example of illusion shows the danger of such a restricted view. A knowledge of functioning will greatly inform our understanding of malfunctioning.

VI. CONCLUSIONS

In this article, we have examined, evaluated, and elaborated on a number of conceptual issues relevant to the cognitive therapy literature. We suggested that cognitive constructs differ on a number of important aspects, including the amount of awareness indicated, their level of inference, temporal relationships to behavior or events, and situational specificity. A model of clinical cognitive phenomena must not lose sight of theoretical criteria necessary for an adequate conceptual scheme.

One of our major concerns is that psychologists interested in cognitive interventions have become too accustomed to automatically adopting the well-used concepts of the field: negative and positive self-statements, specific irrational beliefs, and cognitive distortions assumed to be conceptually distinct. In the preceding pages, special attention was paid to the importance of attending more to the *function* of cognitive phenomena than to their content, as illustrated by the constructs of self-statements, irrational beliefs, and cognitive distortions. We have also argued that adaptive functioning may sometimes be a result of the existence of illusions or distorted, self-enhancing appraisals. Thus, the concept of distortion cannot be used interchangeably as a synonym for maladaptive functioning.

The intent of this article was to stimulate thought about constructs frequently used by clinicians and researchers in the cognitive therapy field. We hope that the areas we have dealt with will point to future research directions as well as contribute to the reader's growing awareness of limitations and key issues arising from attempts to make cognition relevant to clinical concerns.

REFERENCES

Abrahms, J. L. Irrational, maladaptive cognitions and behaviors of the super insurance producer. *CLU Journal*, 1979, **33**(3), 34–43.

Alden, L. E., & Safran, J. Irrational beliefs and nonassertive behavior. *Cognitive Therapy and Research*, 1978, **2**, 357–364.

Alloy, L. B., & Abramson, L. Y. Judgment of contingency in depressed and nondepressed students: Sadder but not wiser? *Journal of Experimental Psychology: General*, 1979, **108**, 441–485.

Arnkoff, D. B. Self-statement therapy and belief therapy in the treatment of test anxiety (Doctoral dissertation, Pennsylvania State University, 1979). *Dissertation Abstracts International*, 1980, **40**, 4469B. (University Microfilms No. 80-05970). (a)

Arnkoff, D. B. Psychotherapy from the perspective of cognitive theory. In M. J. Mahoney (Ed.), *Psychotherapy process: Current issues and future directions*. New York: Plenum, 1980. (b)

Bandura, A. Self-efficacy: Toward a unifying theory of behavioral change. *Psychological Review*, 1977, **84**, 191–215.

Beck, A. T. Thinking and depression: I. Idiosyncratic content and cognitive distortions. *Archives of General Psychiatry*, 1963, **9**, 324–333.

Beck, A. T. *Cognitive therapy and the emotional disorders*. New York: International Universities Press, 1976.

Beck, A. T., Laude, R., & Bohnert, M. Ideational components of anxiety neurosis. *Archives of General Psychiatry*, 1974, **31**, 319–325.

Bedrosian, R. C., & Beck, A. T. Principles of cognitive therapy. In M. J. Mahoney (Ed.), *Psychotherapy process: Current issues and future directions*. New York: Plenum, 1980.

Cacioppo, J. T., Glass, C. R., & Merluzzi, T. V. Self-statements and self-evaluations: A cognitive response analysis of heterosocial anxiety. *Cognitive Therapy and Research*, 1979, **3**, 249–262.

Carmody, T. P. Rational-emotive, self-instructional, and behavioral assertion training: Facilitating maintenance. *Cognitive Therapy and Research*, 1978, **2**, 241–253.

Coyne, J. C. A critique of cognitions as causal entities with particular reference to depression. *Cognitive Therapy and Research*, 1982, **6**, in press.

Craighead, L. W. Self-instructional training for assertive-refusal behavior. *Behavior Therapy*, 1979, **10**, 529–542.

Ellis, A. *Reason and emotion in psychotherapy*. New York: Lyle Stuart, 1962.

Ellis, A. *The essence of rational psychotherapy: A comprehensive approach to treatment*. New York: Institute for Rational Living, 1970.

Ellis, A. The basic clinical theory of rational-emotive therapy. In A. Ellis & R. Greiger (Eds.), *Handbook of rational-emotive therapy*. New York: Springer, 1977.

Ellis, A. The theory of rational-emotive therapy. In A. Ellis & J. M. Whiteley (Eds.), *Theoretical and empirical foundations of rational-emotive therapy*. Monterey, California: Brooks/Cole, 1979.

Galassi, J. P., Frierson, H. T., Jr., & Sharer, R. Behavior of high, moderate, and low test anxious students during an actual test situation. *Journal of Consulting and Clinical Psychology*, 1981, **49**, 51–62.

Genest, M., & Turk, D. C. Think-aloud approaches to cognitive assessment. In T. V. Merluzzi, C. R. Glass, & M. Genest (Eds.), *Cognitive assessment*. New York: Guilford, 1981.

Ginsburg, M., Glass, C. R., & Heinssen, R. K., Jr. *A measure of irrational beliefs in heterosocial situations*. Unpublished manuscript, Catholic University of America, 1981.

Glass, C. R., & Arnkoff, D. B. *The effect of cognitive set on thinking processes in four types of problematic situations*. Paper presented at the meeting of the Association for Advancement of Behavior Therapy, New York, November 1980.

Glass, C. R., & Merluzzi, T. V. Cognitive assessment of social-evaluative anxiety. In T. V. Merluzzi, C. R. Glass, & M. Genest (Eds.), *Cognitive assessment*. New York: Guilford, 1981.

Glass, C. R., Merluzzi, T. V., Biever, J. L., & Larsen, K. H. Cognitive assessment of social anxiety: Development and validation of a self-statement questionnaire. *Cognitive Therapy and Research*, 1982, **6**, in press.

Glogower, F. D., Fremouw, W. J., & McCrosky, J. C. A component analysis of cognitive restructuring. *Cognitive Therapy and Research*, 1978, **2**, 209 223.

Goldfried, M. R. Anxiety reduction through cognitive-behavioral intervention. In P. C. Kendall & S. D. Hollon (Eds.), *Cognitive-behavioral interventions: Theory, research, and procedures*. New York: Academic Press, 1979.

Goldfried, M. R., & Kent, R. N. Traditional versus behavioral personality assessment: A comparison of methodological and theoretical assumptions. *Psychological Bulletin*, 1972, **77**, 409–420.

Golin, S., Terrell, F., & Johnson, B. Depression and the illusion of control. *Journal of Abnormal Psychology*, 1977, **86**, 440–442.

Hollandsworth, J. G., Jr., Glazeski, R. C., Kirkland, K., Jones, G. E., & Van Norman, L. R. An analysis of the nature and effects of test anxiety: Cognitive, behavioral, and physiological components. *Cognitive Therapy and Research*, 1979, **3**, 165–180.

Houston, B. K. Dispositional anxiety and the effectiveness of cognitive coping strategies in stressful laboratory and classroom situations. In C. D. Spielberger & I. G. Sarason (Eds.), *Stress and anxiety* (Vol. 4). Washington, D.C.: Hemisphere Publ., 1977.

Jesness, C. F. Comparative effectiveness of behavior modification and transactional analysis programs for delinquents. *Journal of Consulting and Clinical Psychology*, 1975, **43**, 758–779.

Jones, R. G. A factored measure of Ellis' irrational belief system (Doctoral dissertation, Texas Technological College, 1968). *Dissertation Abstracts International*, 1969, **29**, 4379B–4380B. (University Microfilms No. 69-6443).

Kelly, G. A. *The psychology of personal constructs.* New York: Norton, 1955.

Kendall, P. C. Assessment and cognitive-behavioral interventions: Purposes, proposals, and problems. In P. C. Kendall & S. D. Hollon (Eds.), *Assessment strategies for cognitive-behavioral interventions.* New York: Academic Press, 1981.

Kendall, P. C., & Braswell, L. On cognitive-behavioral assessment: Model, measures, and madness. In C. D. Spielberger & J. N. Butcher (Eds.), *Advances in personality assessment.* Hillsdale, New Jersey: Erlbaum, 1982.

Kendall, P. C., Finch, A. J., Jr., & Montgomery, L. E. Vicarious anxiety: A systematic evaluation of vicarious threat to self-esteem. *Journal of Consulting and Clinical Psychology,* 1978, **46**, 997–1008.

Kendall, P. C., & Hollon, S. D. Assessing self-referent speech: Methods in the measurement of self-statements. In P. C. Kendall & S. D. Hollon (Eds.), *Assessment strategies for cognitive-behavioral interventions.* New York: Academic Press, 1981.

Kendall, P. C., Williams, L., Pechacek, T. F., Graham, L. E., Shisslak, C., & Herzof, N. Cognitive-behavioral and patient education interventions in cardiac catheterization procedures: The Palo Alto medical psychology project. *Journal of Consulting and Clinical Psychology,* 1979, **47**, 48–59.

Klass, T. A cognitive analysis of guilt over assertion. *Cognitive Therapy and Research,* 1981, **5**, 283–297.

Klinger, E. *Structure and functions of fantasy.* New York: Wiley, 1971.

Krantz, S., & Hammen, C. The assessment of cognitive bias in depression. *Journal of Abnormal Psychology,* 1979, **88**, 611–619.

Landau, R. J., & Goldfried, M. R. The assessment of schemata: A unifying framework for cognitive, behavioral, and traditional assessment. In P. C. Kendall & S. D. Hollon (Eds.), *Assessment strategies for cognitive-behavioral interventions.* New York: Academic Press, 1981.

Landfield, A. W. Interpretive man: The enlarged self-image. In J. K. Cole & A. W. Landfield (Eds.), *Nebraska Symposium on Motivation* (Vol. 24). Lincoln: University of Nebraska Press, 1977.

Landfield, A. W. Personal construct psychology: A theory to be elaborated. In M. J. Mahoney (Ed.), *Psychotherapy process: Current issues and future directions.* New York: Plenum, 1980.

Lazarus, R. S. Cognitive behavior therapy as psychodynamics revisited. In M. J. Mahoney (Eds.), *Psychotherapy process: Current issues and future directions.* New York: Plenum, 1980.

Lazarus, R. S. The stress and coping paradigm. In C. Eisdorfer, D. Cohen, A. Kleinman, & P. Maxim (Eds.), *Models for clinical psychopathology.* Jamaica, New York: Spectrum, 1981.

Lazarus, R. S., Cohen, J. B., Folkman, S., Kanner, A., & Schaefer, C. Psychological stress and adaptation: Some unresolved issues. In H. Selye (Ed.), *Selye's guide to stress research* (Vol. 1). Princeton, New Jersey: Van Nostrand Reinhold, 1980.

Lazarus, R. S., Kanner, A. D., & Folkman, S. Emotions: A cognitive-phenomenological analysis. In R. Plutchik & H. Kellerman (Eds.), *Emotion: Theory, research, and experience* (Vol. I), *Theories of emotion.* New York: Academic Press, 1980.

Lewinsohn, P. M., Mischel, W., Chaplin, W., & Barton, R. Social competence and depression: The role of illusory self-perceptions. *Journal of Abnormal Psychology,* 1980, **89**, 203–212.

Lohr, J. M., & Bonge, D. *Situational Irrational Cognitions Inventory: A second report.* Paper presented at the 13th Annual Convention of the Association for Advancement of Behavior Therapy, San Francisco, December, 1979.

Lohr, J. M., & Bonge, D. Cross-validation and modification of a measure of irrational beliefs. *Cognitive Therapy and Research*, 1982, **6**, in press.

Lohr, J. M., Brandt, J. A., & Bonge, D. *The Situational Irrational Cognitions Inventory: A preliminary report.* Paper presented at the 11th Annual Convention of the Association for Advancement of Behavior Therapy, Atlanta, December 1977.

Mahoney, M. J. *Cognition and behavior modification.* Cambridge, Massachusetts: Ballinger, 1974.

Mahoney, M. J. *Scientist as subject: The psychological imperative.* Cambridge, Massachusetts: Ballinger, 1976.

Mahoney, M. J. Psychotherapy and the structure of personal revolutions. In M. J. Mahoney (Ed.), *Psychotherapy process: Current issues and future directions.* New York: Plenum, 1980.

Mahoney, M. J., & Arnkoff, D. B. Cognitive and self-control therapies. In S. L. Garfield & A. E. Bergin (Eds.), *Handbook of psychotherapy and behavior change* (2nd ed.). New York: Wiley, 1978.

Mancuso, J. C., & Ceely, S. G. The self as memory processing. *Cognitive Therapy and Research*, 1980, **4**, 1–25.

Meichenbaum, D. *Cognitive-behavior modification: An integrative approach.* New York: Plenum, 1977.

Meichenbaum, D., & Butler, L. Cognitive ethology: Assessing the streams of cognition and emotion. In K. Blankstein, P. Pliner, & J. Polivy (Eds.), *Advances in the study of communication and affect: Assessment and modification of emotional behavior* (Vol. 6). New York: Plenum, 1980. (a)

Meichenbaum, D., & Butler, L. Egocentrism and evidence: Making Piaget kosher. In M. J. Mahoney (Ed.), *Psychotherapy process: Current issues and future directions.* New York: Plenum, 1980. (b)

Meichenbaum, D., & Butler, L. Toward a conceptual model for the treatment of test anxiety: Implications for research and treatment. In I. G. Sarason (Ed.), *Test anxiety: Theory, research, and applications.* Hillsdale, New Jersey: Erlbaum, 1980. (c)

Meichenbaum, D. H., & Cameron, R. *Stress inoculation: A skills training approach to anxiety management.* Unpublished manuscript, University of Waterloo, 1972.

Merluzzi, T. V., Cacioppo, J. T., & Glass, C. R. *Cognitive responses and attentional factors in high and low socially anxious males.* Unpublished manuscript, University of Notre Dame, 1979.

Merluzzi, T. V., & Glass, C. R. *A multidimensional scale for assessing cognitive self-statements in social anxiety.* Unpublished manuscript, University of Notre Dame, 1981.

Merluzzi, T. V., Rudy, T., & Glass, C. R. The information processing paradigm: Implications for clinical science. In T. V. Merluzzi, C. R. Glass, & M. Genest (Eds.), *Cognitive assessment.* New York: Guilford, 1981.

Mischel, W. A cognitive social learning approach to assessment. In T. V. Merluzzi, C. R. Glass, & M. Genest (Eds.), *Cognitive assessment.* New York: Guilford, 1981.

Mischel, W., & Staub, E. Effects of expectancy on working and waiting for larger rewards. *Journal of Personality and Social Psychology*, 1965, **2**, 625–633.

Neimeyer, G. J., & Neimeyer, R. A. Personal construct perspectives on cognitive assessment. In T. V. Merluzzi, C. R. Glass, & M. Genest (Eds.), *Cognitive assessment.* New York: Guilford, 1981.

Neisser, U. *Cognitive psychology.* New York: Appleton, 1967.

Nelson, R. E., & Craighead, W. E. Selective recall of positive and negative feedback, self-control behaviors, and depression. *Journal of Abnormal Psychology*, 1977, **86**, 379–388.

Neuringer, C. Dichotomous evaluations in suicidal individuals. *Journal of Consulting Psychology*, 1961, **25**, 445–449.

Ross, L. The intuitive psychologist and his shortcomings: Distortions in the attribution process. In L. Berkowitz (Ed.), *Advances in experimental social psychology* (Vol. 10). New York: Academic Press, 1977.

Schwartz, G. E. Psychobiological foundations of psychotherapy and behavior change. In S. L. Garfield & A. E. Bergin (Eds.), *Handbook of psychotherapy and behavior change* (2nd ed.). New York: Wiley, 1978.

Schwartz, R. M., & Gottman, J. M. Toward a task analysis of assertive behavior. *Journal of Consulting and Clinical Psychology*, 1976, **44**, 910–920.

Simon, H. A. From substantive to procedural rationality. In F. Hahn & M. Hollis (Eds.), *Philosophy and economic theory*. London and New York: Oxford University Press, 1979.

Sobel, H. Projective methods of cognitive analysis. In T. V. Merluzzi, C. R. Glass, & M. Genest (Eds.), *Cognitive assessment*. New York: Guilford, 1981.

Sollod, R. N., & Wachtel, P. L. A structural and transactional approach to cognition in clinical problems. In M. J. Mahoney (Ed.), *Psychotherapy process: Current issues and future directions*. New York: Plenum, 1980.

Sutton-Simon, K. Assessing belief systems: Concepts and strategies. In P. C. Kendall & S. D. Hollon (Eds.), *Assessment strategies for cognitive-behavioral interventions*. New York: Academic Press, 1981.

Thorpe, G. L., Amatu, H. I., Blakey, R. S., & Burns, L. E. Contributions of overt instructional rehearsal and "specific insight" to the effectiveness of self-instructional training: A preliminary study. *Behavior Therapy*, 1976, **7**, 504–511.

Tosi, D. J. Personal reactions with some emphasis on new directions, application, and research. In A. Ellis & J. M. Whiteley (Eds.), *Theoretical and empirical foundations of rational-emotive therapy*. Monterey, California: Brooks/Cole, 1979.

Tversky, A., & Kahneman, D. Judgment under uncertainty: Heuristics and biases. *Science*, 1974, **185**, 1124–1131.

Velten, E. A laboratory task for induction of mood states. *Behaviour Research and Therapy*, 1968, **6**, 473–482.

Vygotsky, L. S. *Thought and language* (E. Hanfmann & G. Vakar, Eds. and trans.). Cambridge, Massachusetts: MIT Press, 1962. (Originally published, 1934.)

Wallett, D. *Toward an integrated theory of emotion*. Unpublished manuscript, Pennsylvania State University, 1979.

Weisz, J. R., & Stipek, D. J. Competence, contingency, and the development of perceived control. *Human Development*, 1982, **25**, in press.

Wertsch, J. V. The regulation of human action and the given-new organization of private speech. In G. Zivin (Ed.), *The development of self-regulation through private speech*. New York: Wiley, 1979.

Wine, J. Cognitive-attentional theory of test anxiety. In I. G. Sarason (Ed.), *Test anxiety: Theory, research, and application*. Hillsdale, New Jersey: Erlbaum, 1980.

Zajonc, R. B. Feeling and thinking: Preferences need no inferences. *American Psychologist*, 1980, **35**, 151–175.

Zeiss, A. M., Lewinsohn, P. M., & Muñoz, R. F. Nonspecific improvement effects in depression using interpersonal skills training, pleasant activity schedules, or cognitive training. *Journal of Consulting and Clinical Psychology*, 1979, **47**, 427–439.

Think Cognitively: Selected Issues in Cognitive Assessment and Therapy

CAROL R. GLASS AND DIANE B. ARNKOFF[1]

Department of Psychology,
Catholic University of America,
Washington, D.C.

The purposes of this article are to delineate and discuss a number of ideas and issues of more direct relevance to cognitive assessment and therapy. The groundwork for this endeavor is put forth in Arnkoff and Glass (this volume), and we now will pursue some of the implications of directions highlighted in that article. Although we have organized the present article into two major areas, selected issues in cognitive assessment and selected issues in cognitive therapy, there

---

[1] This article was the joint effort of both authors. Order of authorship was determined randomly.

ADVANCES IN COGNITIVE-BEHAVIORAL RESEARCH
AND THERAPY, VOLUME 1

are several themes that run broadly through both sections: fallacies, functions, and frameworks.

The idea of fallacies, or false notions, becomes evident in the discussion of the validity of cognitive assessment techniques and the relationship between cognitive methods and cognitive change. It may be false to assume that our measures really assess what they purport to measure. It may also be false to assume that cognitive change is the exclusive product of cognitive therapy methods or that cognitive methods are only characteristic of a cognitive viewpoint or perspective on change.

The emphasis on function reappears in this article, where it is used in two distinct ways. First, we suggest several interesting approaches to the assessment of the function or meaning of thoughts. Later, we stress the importance of assessing the current mode of functioning in clients and the role of individual differences in determining response to therapeutic interventions.

The final theme, frameworks, refers to the need for organizational schemes and models to guide our efforts in assessment and therapy. With respect to assessment, an understanding of the similarities and differences among measures, and their relative strengths and weaknesses, is crucial to select an approach wisely that is consistent with goals, needs, and theory. We also propose a two-part model of therapy stages and cognitive methods, based on the client's awareness or familiarity with different methods of change and his or her current mode of functioning. After an alliance is established using the client's preferred methods, the therapist can introduce new points of view and methods for dealing with areas of weaker functioning.

The entire article represents an attempt to confront the reader with what we think are some of the more fascinating issues in cognitive assessment and therapy. We have hoped more to be thought provoking than to claim unequivocal access to truth. Hopefully, then, these ideas will be as exciting to the reader as they are to us.

I. ISSUES IN COGNITIVE ASSESSMENT

Although there are a large number of important issues relevant to the practice of cognitive assessment, the limitations of space necessitate a good deal of choice and discretion. We have chosen to narrow our discussion primarily to self-statement assessment, to provide as much depth as possible and to address a topic that may be of interest to both researchers and cognitive therapists. The reader is referred to new volumes by Merluzzi, Glass, and Genest (1981) and Kendall and Hollon (1981b) for a more comprehensive account of cognitive assessment strategies.

For the purpose of this article, we have selected three'issues: an examination of new methodologies for assessment, frameworks for existing measures, and psychometric considerations. Specifically, we begin by returning to a major conceptual focus of the article by Arnkoff and Glass (this volume), but now from the point of view of applications. Two approaches are suggested for the assessment of meaning and function, going beyond typical assessment of content alone. Next, we discuss several dimensions on which methods of self-statement assessment can be organized. This issue underlies and is basic to choosing particular techniques appropriate to the needs of the situation and the questions of interest. Finally, we examine issues of the validity of self-statement assessment. It is suggested that our measures may not be assessing what, on the surface, they appear to be.

A. Assessment of Meaning and Function

The vast majority of the literature on the assessment of thoughts or self-statements has relied on frequencies or response rates of various categories of cognition. Researchers have counted the number of task-oriented thoughts, negative self-referent statements, and so on. Arnkoff and Glass (this volume) speculated that frequencies or categories of self-statements should be seen in the context of individual differences—their meaning and impact on a particular person. The overwhelming focus on descriptions of the content of thought often blinds us to the rich possibilities inherent in the analysis of the *process* or *function* of cognition. Two major approaches for the assessment of the subjective meaning of thoughts are sequential analysis and ratings of impact.

1. Sequential Analysis

The reader who is familiar with the old expression, "You can't see the forest for the trees," has already grasped the basic philosophy underlying sequential analysis. When we focus only on the content of individual thoughts, we are looking at or creating an inventory of the separate trees, and missing the forest, which consists of the interrelationships between individual trees. An examination of the "flow" of thoughts in relation to each other over a period of time is one method to find the "forest" of cognition! In other words, a content analysis examines individual components of thoughts without seeing how they fit together. Sequential analysis, which addresses patterns and interdependency, thus comes much closer to allowing us to understand the process of internal dialogue as well as the function certain thoughts may play in influencing the thoughts immediately following them.

Schwartz and Gottman (1976) attempted a rough assessment of the sequence of thoughts as part of their task analysis of assertive behavior. After completing a structured questionnaire, subjects were given a multiple-choice question and asked to indicate which one of four sequences characterized the pattern of their thoughts: − + (coping), − − (unshaken doubt), + + (unshaken confidence), or + − (giving up). They found that high-assertive subjects endorsed a pattern of "unshaken confidence" more often than did low-assertive subjects. Over the course of cognitive therapy, we might also expect a gradual change from a pattern of "unshaken doubt" to one of "coping": the negative self-statements that previously led only to other maladaptive thoughts come to be used as cues to produce positive, coping self-statements (Meichenbaum, 1977).

Schwartz and Gottman's question relied on a self-reported, *subject-determined* "sequence" analysis that required a certain amount of awareness and inference on the part of each individual subject. The statistical technique of sequential analysis, typically applied to the patterns and interdependency of streams of behavior (Bakeman, 1978; Castellan, 1979; Gottman & Notarius, 1978), has potential utility for the study of the stream of consciousness as well. Data from think aloud procedures (Klinger, 1978) and self-statements elicited in thought-listings (Cacioppo, Glass, & Merluzzi, 1979) can be subjected to sequential analysis. This procedure might also shed light on the relationships between behavior and one's thoughts in a given situation. This technique thus represents an *empirically determined* analysis of patterns of thoughts, and does not rely on inference or subject categorization of process.

To explore the question of whether the overall pattern of thought may yield more information than the content analysis of individual self-statements, an example is in order. Our illustration parallels that given by Notarius (1981), and we are grateful for his permission to present it here. We begin by setting the stage: Let us imagine that we are attempting a replication of Cacioppo *et al.* (1979), who examined the cognitive responses of high and low heterosocially anxious men who anticipated an interaction with an unfamiliar woman. After sitting quietly for 3 minutes, subjects listed the thoughts they had during that period on a special thought-listing form. In Cacioppo *et al.*, judges scored all thoughts into categories of positive (+), negative (−), or neutral/irrelevant self-statements (0), and data were submitted to an analysis of variance after summing the frequency of thoughts in each category.

The results of Cacioppo *et al.* (1979) showed that high heterosocially anxious men, compared to low-anxious subjects, had more negative and fewer positive self-statements. Notarius (1981) goes beyond the analysis of rates of various types of cognitive responses to pose the question, "Does the order in which cognitive self-statements are reported contribute to our understanding of group differences between high and low heterosocially anxious males?" (p. 346). A detailed examination of this example will illustrate the process involved in obtaining an answer to this question.

Sample data for 10 subjects in our hypothetical replication are shown in Table I, grouped separately for high- and low-anxious men.[2] Each string of +, −, and 0 codes represents one subject's temporal sequence of listed thoughts. For example, a subject might have listed two negative thoughts followed by one neutral and three positive thoughts: − − 0 + + +. Note that any given code can be viewed both as an *antecedent* to the code immediately following and as the consequent of the code directly preceding it. In this example, there is one instance in which a 0 occurs as an antecedent to a +, and the same 0 code also represents an instance where 0 follows a − code. The next step is to construct a conditional frequency table (see Table II), showing the frequency with which each code follows every other code. The marginal totals for each row can be easily summed. Thus, the data shown in Table II illustrate that a negative thought is followed by another negative thought 56 times for high-anxious and 15 times for low-anxious subjects.

TABLE I
Fictitious Coded Data from Thought-Listing Procedure

Low heterosocially anxious men	High heterosocially anxious men
Subject 1: − + − + + − 00 −	Subject 31: − + + 0 + − − − + +
Subject 2: 000 − − 0 + − + +	Subject 32: + 00 + − − − + 00
Subject 3: − 00 + + − 0 − + 0	Subject 33: 0 + 0 − 00 − −
Subject 4: + − + + − 0 − + + 0	Subject 34: + + − − 0 + − +
Subject 5: 0 − + 00 + + − − + + +	Subject 35: 00 + + 0 + 0 − − −
.	.
.	.
.	.
.	.

[2] The authors appreciate Cliff Notarius' assistance in conceptualizing the figure and tables.

Carol R. Glass and Diane B. Arnkoff

TABLE II

Contingency Tables of Data Presented in Table I

	Low heterosocially anxious men					High heterosocially anxious men			
	Consequent						Consequent		
	0	+	−				0	+	−
Antecedent 0	31	18	36	85		0	35	29	10	84
+	22	55	40	117		+	23	24	25	72
−	32	44	15	91		−	16	19	56	91

Conditional frequencies

	Consequent					Consequent		
	0	+	−			0	+	−
Antecedent 0	.37	.21	.42		0	.47	.39	.14
+	.19	.47	.34		+	.32	.33	.35
−	.35	.48	.17		−	.18	.21	.62

Conditional probabilities

By dividing each cell by the respective row marginal, the conditional probability of a consequent thought following a specific antecedent thought is obtained; these conditional probabilities are shown at the bottom of Table II. Examination of our fictitious data reveals several interesting differences between high and low heterosocially anxious subjects. For example, the probability of a negative thought, given that a negative thought has just occurred, $p(-/-)$, is .62 for high-anxious but only .17 for low-anxious men. For these low-anxious subjects, a negative thought is most likely followed by a positive thought, $p(+/-) = .44$. This suggests that high heterosocially anxious individuals are caught in a "negative thought cycle," whereas low-anxious subjects tend to react to negative thoughts with a "positive thought" intervention (Notarius, 1981). Meichenbaum and Butler (1980a) have noted, in fact, that thinking processes of high-anxious individuals tend to have an automatic "run-on" nature.

To test whether such patterns occur more frequently than would be predicted by chance, Bakeman (1978) suggests the use of binomial test z-scores. Let us assume that our results on the sequential analysis were indeed significant. Since the frequency of negative thoughts is identical for the two groups, $(f-) = 91$, an analysis of the number of negative thoughts would have led to the conclusion that the groups did not differ!

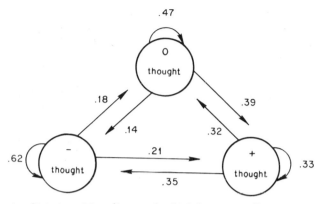

Fig. 1. State transition diagram for high heterosocially anxious men.

With a small number of categories, it is also possible to depict the same conditional probabilities graphically that were presented in tabular form in Table II. A state transition diagram, such as the one shown in Fig. 1, offers an easily discernible portrait of sequential patterns of thoughts for high heterosocially anxious men. We can clearly see the self-defeating pattern of negative thoughts leading to other negative thoughts, while positive thoughts seem to lead with almost equal probability to any of the three thought categories.[3]

A recent study by Henshaw (1978), summarized in Meichenbaum, Henshaw, and Himel (1982), used this methodology to analyze data from a "think aloud" assessment. Henshaw compared the frequencies of six categories of thought statements collected while high- and low-creative individuals worked on various tasks. He also used sequential analysis to compare the patterning of thoughts for the two groups. Following any one of the six categories, high-creative subjects were more likely to emit a *facilitative* statement (controlling attention; positive evaluation of abilities, strategies, and task; positive affect) and less likely to become *silent* than low-creative persons. Following an

---

[3] Our example offers an illustration of an analysis based on a single antecedent. Higher order models are available, however, which can examine sequences in which antecedents consist of the two events immediately preceding a consequent. Additionally, Sackett's (1974) lag sequential analysis allows the researcher to study the pattern of thoughts preceding or following a particular criterion code of interest. For example, if we were interested in positive thoughts, we could compute the conditional probabilities of all other codes occurring one, two, and three positions (lags) prior to and/or following positive thoughts.

instance of *inhibitive* ideation (task-irrelevant thoughts; negative evaluation of ability, strategies and task; negative affect), low-creative subjects were more likely to become silent or to produce another inhibitive
thought than high-creative subjects, and were less likely to emit facilitative mediation or *strategy* statements. Although facilitative statements functioned similarly in both groups, low-creative subjects
showed more debilitated performance following an inhibitive statement than did the high-creative group. The results of this sequential
analysis led Meichenbaum *et al.* (1980) to conclude that the absence
of a problem-solving set (seeing the stressor, task, or situation as a
problem to be solved) is a crucial factor leading to inadequate
performance.

Sequential analysis thus need not capture only the patterning of
cognition, but may serve as a valuable tool for the analysis of complex
interactions between cognition, emotion, and behavior. Meichenbaum
and Butler (1980a) propose the term "cognitive ethology" for the variety of assessment procedures designed to tap cognitive, affective,
and behavioral experience. The goal of such procedures is to "describe
the content, frequency, and patterning of cognitions . . . that may
reflect or engender different affective states and contribute to individual
differences in performance" (p. 144). Lazarus, Kanner, and Folkman
(1980) have also emphasized this interdependent nature of emotional,
motivational, and cognitive processes, since emotion is seen to arise
from *patterns of appraisal* that reflect how a person construes the
actual or anticipated outcome of a transaction.

Finally, several methodological issues must be kept in mind when
using sequential analysis: reliability, specification of questions of interest, and independence (Notarius, 1981).

The question of data reliability is one which is as crucial for sequential analysis as it is for any statistical technique. Just as behavioral
observation data must be reliably coded, data based on cognitive responses must also show a high degree of interrater agreement. Thus,
the utility of the results of the analysis is critically tied to the dis-
tinctiveness and clarity of description of the categories chosen for
coding and the level of training of the raters employed. Notarius (1981)
points out that since the basic unit for analysis is a block of time or
cognitions, reliability for sequential analysis must be estimated for
each time/response block, and not across an entire setting.

Notarius (1981) also urges the experimenter to specify questions of
interest before collecting data, to avoid getting "swamped" by too
much potentially significant information. We would urge researchers
interested in thought sequences to allow theoretical considerations to

guide the formulation of coding systems and the questions asked in the sequential analysis. For example, the analysis of sequences of positive, negative, and neutral codes used in our example was derived from Meichenbaum's (1977) conception of cognitive therapy change; Wine's (1980) theory would suggest looking at sequences coded in other ways, such as on-task and off-task.

Concerns over violations in the assumption of independence are discussed in detail by Bakeman, Cairns, and Applebaum (1979), Castellan (1979), and Notarius, Krokoff, and Markman (1981). Although sequential data may be highly correlated, the exact effects of such violations are still unknown. Notarius et al. (1981) suggest that the binomial z can be confidently used when the number of within-subjects observations (n) is > 30 or the probability values of antecedent–consequent pairs are not extremely skewed (.10–.90). Violations of independence are of greatest concern when data from individual subjects are pooled, and the probability structure of different subjects' responses are significantly nonequivalent.

2. Assessment of Impact

Attempts to assess the impact or evaluation of cognitions represent an alternative to sequential analysis, and may also help to shed light on the question of the function or meaning of thoughts, beliefs, attributions, images, expectations, and other cognitive factors. Knowledge of the impact or belief in a maladaptive thought may represent a "missing link" in understanding why particular cognitions affect emotions and behavior. Similarly, successful or unsuccessful performance or strong affect may influence the strength of such beliefs or evaluations of cognitions.

A recent study by Klass (1981), comparing subjects with low, moderate, and high guilt over assertion, illustrates one interesting strategy for the assessment of the impact of self-statements. In addition to indicating how frequently each self-statement on a structured inventory characterized their thoughts, subjects rated each of the 30 self-statements on a seven-point scale according to its impact on their ability to inhibit or foster refusal in assertive situations. Results of the content/frequency analysis showed that high-guilt subjects more often indicated thoughts emphasizing harm to the other person and individual responsibility than did low-guilt subjects. High-guilt subjects also judged harm and responsibility considerations as having less impact on ability to refuse and were less certain that criticism of others would aid refusal. Klass suggests that this differential sensitivity to negative effects of thoughts may weaken the effect that feedback from new assertive experiences may have on the individual. The degree to which particular thoughts guide action may underlie assertion more than how often they occur.

A similar measure was used by Zeiss, Lewinsohn, and Muñoz (1979) in their study of the effects of different treatments for depression. Clients rated each of 80 positive and 80 negative thoughts on the basis of both frequency and emotional impact (from very disturbing to very pleasant). Unlike the results of Klass (1981), in which frequency and impact covaried, Zeiss et al. found a significant posttherapy decrease in the frequency of negative thoughts, but not their impact. Positive thoughts and impact both increased, although not to a significant degree.

A slightly different approach to the assessment of meaning is offered by Cacioppo et al. (1979). After subjects listed their thoughts in anticipation of the interaction with an unfamiliar woman, they were asked to go back and rate each thought on the same valence dimension that judges later used: favorable toward self, unfavorable toward self, or neither favorable nor unfavorable toward self. Although judges' ratings revealed differences between cognitive responses of high- and low-anxious subjects, subjects' own subjective ratings were not affected by anxiety level. Cacioppo et al. suggest that each group may thus have a unique frame of reference for what constitutes a favorable self-statement. Perhaps, too, different frames of reference lead to individual differences in the meaning or impact of thoughts to subjects.

The strength of an individual's belief in his or her ability to perform a task is also of interest. Bandura (1977) evaluates this factor in his approach to self-efficacy assessment. Subjects not only complete a checklist of whether they can or cannot perform each behavior in a hierarchy, but must also choose a number from 10 to 100 which indicates how confident they are that they could now perform each task.

It is conceivable that, after indicating "I can do that," an individual might be anywhere from slightly to very certain that he or she could behave in that manner. Similarly, we may have said to ourselves at some point, "No way, I can't do that," yet when pressed to give realistic betting odds, would admit that maybe we were not all that convinced of our inabilities. Since the strength of one's self-judged efficacy should be related to intensity and persistence of effort, and thus to level of performance (Bandura, 1980), such beliefs may be very important to assess.

Meichenbaum, Genest, and Turk (1977) addressed this issue in a slightly different way, by employing videotape thought reconstruction with subjects who had undergone a cold-pressor test (submerging arm in a tub of ice water) with the instructions to keep the hand in the water as long as possible. Meichenbaum et al. (1980) report that results of this study showed no differences in the use of potential coping self-statements and images between subjects who tolerated a full 5 minutes of pain and those who dropped out! However, those who did not withdraw appeared to have more of a belief that they *could use* these strategies to cope with the pain, which Meichenbaum et al. liken to Bandura's expectations of personal efficacy. They thus had a stronger belief that such self-statements and images would help them to cope.

At a metacognitive level, it is not enough for the content of cognition to contain potential coping strategies, but the individual must know (1) that these *are* coping strategies, (2) that he or she knows *how* to use them, and (3) that the use of such strategies will *affect* one's ability to handle the situation. This latter factor, then, is perhaps most directly illustrative of the importance of assessing the impact of cognitions.

B. Organization and Procedures of Assessment

The review of a number of recent chapters and presentations (Genest & Turk, 1981; Kendall & Hollon, 1981a; Meichenbaum & Butler, 1980a; Glass, 1980) reveals a convergence in the literature toward establishing a framework for cognitive assessment based on the *procedures* of assessment (the type of measure used, such as interview, questionnaire) and the *target* of assessment (the cognitive factor being assessed, such as self-statements, expectancies, attributions). The interrelationships among cognitive constructs are addressed by Arnkoff and Glass (this volume). In this section, we will focus on models for organizing cognitive assessment procedures on the basis of two major dimensions: the timing and the structure of the methods used. Each of these dimensions will be examined in turn, and brief descriptions of some of the most common measures will be provided.

1. Temporal Dimension

Meichenbaum and Butler (1980a) use a three-category system to organize cognitive assessment procedures temporally according to when they are administered relative to task performance or social interaction. Methods employed *following* performance include questionnaires, thought listing, videotape reconstruction, and interviews, while think aloud and recording private speech are used at a point *accompanying* performance. Finally, Meichenbaum and Butler list measures administered *preceding* performance, including interviews, task-related projectives, and attribution and expectancy questionnaires. (We would suggest that attribution measures might be more clearly classified as following performance, since they seek the individual's perception of the causes of success and failure.) This system offers a clear-cut, parsimonious way to organize a variety of approaches.

Glass (1980) and Genest and Turk (1981) limit their organization of the procedures of cognitive assessment to self-statements and think-aloud approaches, respectively. Instead of focusing on the temporal relationship between cognitive assessment and performance, however, they have chosen to examine the timing of assessment relative to the occurrence of the *thoughts*. As Genest and Turk (1981) point out, all cognitive assessment is retrospective to some extent, since there is a period of time between the experience of the thought and the individual's verbalization or self-report! But some assessment procedures are more able to get at the "flow" of thoughts as they occur, while others are truly more retrospective in nature. Genest and Turk (1981) and Glass (1980) base their organization schemes on a continuum of assessment procedures from concurrent to retrospective.

The most concurrent methods of cognitive assessment involve recording spontaneous private speech, free association, and thinking aloud. Private speech refers to naturalistic speech or verbalized self-instructions that are spontaneous and not intended for a listener. Such self-talk is generally studied in young children, and psychologists who record and code these verbalizations may study thought-related speech as it occurs without intruding into the process.

It is interesting that the free association method used in psycho-analysis is quite similar to approaches such as thinking aloud (Genest & Turk, 1981). In free association, the client is asked to say out loud the thoughts that are passing through his or her mind during the therapy session. Think-aloud procedures involve specific instructions on the part of the experimenter for the subject to engage in ordinary activities or specific tasks and to verbalize his or her stream of con-scious thoughts as soon as they occur. Glass (1980) points out that think-aloud procedures also can be utilized in conjunction with asking subjects to *imagine* they are in a particular situation. For example, Craighead, Kimball, and Rehak (1979) had subjects imagine scenes involving social rejection and asked them to report, "What thoughts are racing through your head?" (p. 387). In this study, based on a scoring system using positive and negative self-referent and positive and negative task-referent statements, the number of negative self-referent statements was found to be significantly correlated with mood scale increases in feelings of anxiety, hostility, and depression.

Random sampling of thoughts and self-monitoring procedures can be seen as slightly less concurrent than the three approaches just discussed. In random thought sampling, subjects are interrupted at random intervals, either by an experimenter or by a portable beeper (Klinger, 1978), and they then record or narrate their most immediate thoughts. The thought sampling approach can be combined with questionnaire assessment if the subject is asked to respond to a rating scale instead of directly reporting the thought. Results of thought sampling thus usually represent in vivo data, but of a less dynamic or continuous nature than those previously discussed. We like Genest and Turk's (1981) analogy that thinking aloud provides a motion picture of conscious events, while thought sampling provides repeated snapshots.

Self-monitoring procedures are similar to those in the behavioral literature, in which individuals are asked to tally or describe the nature of specific cognitions and the situations in which they occur (Beck, Rush, Shaw, & Emery, 1979). Such records are frequently used in the process of cognitive therapy. Once the client understands the concept of automatic thoughts and self-statements, he or she may be given an assignment to "catch" as many thoughts as possible and record them on a special form. Often the client is instructed to record thoughts that involve a common theme, such as rejection, or to record thoughts accompanying increased dysphoria or precipitating environmental events. Beck et al. (1979) cite the case of a depressed woman who exploded in anger at her three children, and then recorded such thoughts as "I'm worse than my mother ever was. I'm not fit to care for my children. They'd be better off if I was dead" (p. 151).

Moving on to assessment that employs increasingly more retrospective procedures, we find videotape thought reconstruction, structured questionnaires, thought listings, and interviews. Videotape thought reconstruction involves videotaping a subject's behavior in an actual or role-played problematic situation. As the videotape is played back, subjects are asked to recall the thoughts (and/or feelings) experienced while in the original situation. Extending the motion picture analogy, this task is similar to the process in which actors and actresses "dub in" a sound track after a movie scene is filmed. This approach is also similar to Kagan's Interpersonal Process Recall (Kagan & Krathwohl, 1967), in which therapists under supervision are videotaped during a therapy session and trained to recall their feelings and thoughts while viewing the videotape. The effects of training and specific prompts on results obtained from videotape-aided thought reconstruction remains an empirical question.

The most structured type of retrospective assessment, self-report inventories or questionnaires, requires subjects to endorse a list of specific, predetermined thoughts. Self-statement inventories or checklists, for example, require individuals to indicate whether they experienced various thoughts or how frequently they occurred. Such questionnaires have been developed for the study of depression (Hollon & Kendall, 1980), creativity (Henshaw, 1978), coping with stressful medical procedures (Kendall, Williams, Pechacek, Graham, Shisslak, & Herzof, 1979), assertiveness (Schwartz & Gottman, 1976), test anxiety (Galassi, Frierson, & Sharer, 1981), and social anxiety (Glass, Merluzzi, Biever, & Larsen, 1982).

A third type of more retrospective procedure, thought listing, was used as an example for the sequential analysis section of this article. Subjects are asked to recall and list everything that went through their minds during the few minutes immediately preceding the assessment. Several scoring dimensions can be extracted from thought listing data, including valence (positive, negative, or neutral/irrelevant) and locus of attention (focus on self, others, situation).

Finally, clinical interviews represent the most retrospective assessment tool. During the therapy session, a cognitively oriented counselor can ask the client to recall a recent situation that was particularly difficult, depressing, or anxiety provoking, and report what he or she was thinking and feeling at that time (Meichenbaum, 1977).

The temporal dimension of the *procedures* of cognitive assessment, primarily self-statement assessment, has thus been organized in two different ways: the temporal occurrence of thoughts relative to performance, and the timing of the verbal report relative to when the thought occurred. Note that both systems, however, yield similar results when the thoughts of interest are those that occur during performance. Those methods categorized as following performance by Meichenbaum and Butler (1980a) (videotape thought reconstruction, questionnaires, thought listing, interviews) are the same four that fall toward the retrospective end of the continuum (Genest & Turk, 1981; Glass, 1980). Those measures considered to accompany performance (private speech, thinking aloud) are also found at the more concurrent pole of the scale.

We would like to suggest that a system tying assessment to the occurrence of thoughts is, in the long run, a more flexible scheme than one tied to performance. It is important to realize that these systems will overlap only when the thoughts of interest are those that occur during performance. But what if the thoughts we are interested in are ones occurring before or after the behavioral action (i.e., self-statements reflective of attributions or outcome expectancy)? It is conceivable that we might want a subject to think aloud and report his or her thoughts in *anticipation* of having to face a stressor, as Cacioppo et al. (1979) did, although the performance-referent system classifies think-aloud as a method that accompanies performance.

Thus, using the thought process of interest as the referent for the temporal dimension is an alternative that allows us to choose assessment procedures on the basis of the type of data desired and the relative advantages and disadvantages of each approach. For example, more concurrent approaches rely less on memory and may reduce problems of forgetting and inaccurate recall.

2. Structural Dimension

In addition to the temporal dimension, the procedures of cognitive assessment can be organized according to the amount of *structure* they provide the client or subject. In other words, how much does the experimenter intrude into the process with specific instructions, probes, questions, or retrieval cues during the report of cognitions (Glass, 1980)? If we return our focus to the assessment of self-statements, the reader will see that the structural dimension can also be conceptualized as a continuum. At the low end, we find spontaneous verbalizations, which are often unobtrusive and thus least reactive, but which run into difficulty if our subjects naturally verbalize only a small and possibly selective proportion of their actual thoughts.

As we add structure, however, we also increase the demand characteristics of the assessment. Even though only a global cue is given to "think aloud," Kendall and Hollon (1981a) suggest that the procedure may have a reactive quality that might influence the actual flow of thoughts. Videotape thought reconstruction adds even more structure to the assessment by presenting subjects with a visual and auditory record of their performance, which may be an important factor in aiding memory and accuracy. However, stopping the tape at prearranged points may present specific demand characteristics for subjects to report a thought, and could result in assessment of post hoc reappraisals (Meichenbaum, 1977) of what subjects guess they could have been thinking. Additionally, there may be reactive effects due to increased self-consciousness in the presence of a videotape camera (Duvall & Wicklund, 1972).

At the most structured end of the scale we find checklists, inventories, and questionnaires with very specific cues for subjects to report on the frequency or occurrence of experimenter-selected thoughts. These highly structured measures thus present subjects with a recognition task more than one of recall (Glass & Merluzzi, 1981). This should facilitate memory but, at the same time, increase the possibility of post hoc reappraisals.

The clinician or researcher must thus choose a cognitive assessment procedure based on his or her goals and questions, and consider the advantages and disadvantages of temporal and structural variations. Issues of discrete event vs continuous sequential assessment, social desirability demands, ease of scoring and administration, the flexibility of the assessment method for use in different settings and across different problem areas, and its openness to idiosyncratic events should also be considered (Glass 1980).

C. Validity of Assessment Techniques

As researchers begin to develop new, creative methods to assess cognitive experience, they must not forget the importance of the traditional psychometric requirements of reliability and validity. Many of these newly developed measures are created for use in a particular cognitive therapy outcome evaluation or group comparison study. These and other measures continue to be used in the literature because they "look" valid, have been used in the past, and have produced some meaningful results, even though sufficient attention has not been paid to questions of validity (Glass & Merluzzi, 1981). At this point, we propose that researchers and clinicians start thinking about the issue of the *construct* validity of the self-statement measures described in the preceding section. We pose the following questions: What are such measures really assessing? Are they really giving us an accurate, veridical measure of subjects' stream of consciousness, internal dialogues, or self-talk? How are questions of discriminant and convergent validity relevant to cognitive assessment?

Meichenbaum and Cameron (1981) have speculated on the meaning of self-reports of cognitive activity. They conclude that the report of no activity may not necessarily indicate the *absence* of thoughts, but rather the inability to describe verbally one's cognitive experience, lack of motivation, or the operation of implicit ("unconscious") rules. On the other hand, the report of a specific cognitive activity does not imply it is really experienced. Meichenbaum and Cameron suggest that some reports may be "confabulated," in that the individual has inferred from behavior what he or she "must have been thinking." This would be more of a problem for retrospective assessment techniques administered at a point after performance or cognitive activity. For example, assume that we were to ask John, a socially anxious individual, to pick up the phone, call up a woman he was attracted to, and ask her out on a date. Our subject dials, but puts down the receiver after two rings. Even though he may not have experienced a particular thought, perhaps a post hoc reappraisal process sets in. Thus, John endorses having had the thought, "I can't do this," on a self-statement inventory. Perhaps he has inferred from his behavior that, since he quit in the middle of the task, this is a likely thought for him to have had at the time.

We think it highly unlikely that subjects who report having certain thoughts "very frequently" on a self-statement inventory really have had *these exact thoughts*. For one thing, much of our actual thought processes (a) are probably highly idiosyncratic, automatic, and non-conscious (Vygotsky, 1934/1962), (b) do not occur in the form of complete sentences, (c) may sometimes rely heavily on imagery and not language, and (d) have probably not been tallied or counted by the individual. So what are subjects really saying when they circle a "5" on such an inventory, indicating on the five-point scale that they had this thought quite often?

There appear to be at least four possibilities:

1. The report of having had a thought "very frequently" may reflect not the frequency but the *impact* or importance of the thought. The subject may read the statement on the questionnaire, feel that it really hits home, and thus infer that he or she must have had that thought frequently. There is certainly a difference between feeling *as if* you have had a thought quite often and actually thinking it (Goldfried, 1980).

2. The endorsement of the item may reflect a *translation* process on the part of subjects, from the idiosyncratic or fragmented actual thoughts to the grammatical complete sentence "English translation" on the inventory. It is as if they may be saying, "I'm aware of having had a thought *like that*, which bears some resemblance to this item on the questionnaire." This implies the presence of some internal clustering or organizational schema, by which the person classifies thoughts or thought fragments as being like certain thoughts but different from others.

3. The self-report may represent the decision that the thought "matches up" with one's self-concept, presentation of self to others, and/or personal construct system. Subjects therefore may be indicating "that's like me" by endorsing the item, or "that's not like me" by not reporting the thought. This raises the interesting question of whether the self-concept of being a failure predisposes an individual to actually *think* negative self-statements or just *report* them. Reporting more negative thoughts than you really experience may reflect a process of distortion without awareness. This brings to mind the body of research showing that depressives distort environmental feedback in a negative direction only at the point of recall and not at the time of immediate

perception (DeMonbreun & Craighead, 1977; Nelson & Craighead, 1977). It would follow that a more concurrent cognitive assessment, which relies less on recall or memory, would reduce the magnitude of such distortion. The degree of distortion could thus be assessed by comparing the results of retrospective approaches with more concurrent techniques.

4. Finally, it may be that subjects are "translating" affective experiences into a language-based self-statement format (M. MacCarthy, personal communication). Although an individual may experience physiological signs of anxiety, such as increased heart rate or sweaty palms, he or she may not be aware at the time of any cognitive activity or specific anxiety-related thoughts. Yet, on a self-statement inventory, the subject may give a high endorsement to the thought, "This sure is scary." The intensity of the emotional experience becomes expressed in thought-related terms, even though no such thoughts were necessarily experienced at the time.

These four hypotheses may also be relevant for other approaches to self-statement assessment, including thought-listings, think-aloud, and thought-sampling. For example, when asked to think aloud, an individual may experience a fragment of thought, but then "translate" it into a more complete verbal means of expression. But techniques that assess the flow of thoughts, at least retrospective measures such as thought listings, raise additional validity concerns. Here, not only do we run into the issue of whether subjects really had these thoughts, but whether they had them in the order in which they were reported! Certainly, such reports bear some approximation to the actual flow of internal dialogue, but it is also highly probable that a lot has been left out of the report or rearranged. There are many "automatic" thoughts of which the individual is not aware or which did not have much impact—thoughts that went in one lobe and out the other, so to speak.

In spite of the important issues we have raised relevant to the construct validity of our measures, we want to reassure the reader that we still believe that data from self-statement assessments are of real value to the researcher or clincian. We may not, with 100% accuracy, be identifying the exact sequence of a person's thoughts, but it is still crucial that he or she chose to report them in that order. Even though reports of self-statements may not ever be totally veridical, people are telling us something meaningful about themselves that reflects differences in more "deep" cognitive structures, schemata, or processes.

We agree with Meichenbaum and Cameron (1981) that, at this point, we need more methodological studies to determine how best to conduct cognitive assessment. Complementary strategies and converging operations to assess cognitive experience are crucial. It is also important not to lose sight of the links between cognition, specific situations, and behavioral performance. We believe that some people will have cognitive patterns that are cross-situationally consistent, but others will not. Within a single individual, certain cognitive experiences may be situation-specific, but others may be linked more to core cognitive styles and belief systems. For example, if Susan has a tendency toward task-irrelevant thinking in test situations, is this a pattern that underlies other evaluative interactions? Are there other potentially anxiety-arousing occasions that do not elicit task-irrelevant thought?

A multitrait–multimethod methodology thus appears quite relevant for issues in cognitive assessment. The validity of different methods for the assessment of self-statements should be examined both in terms of their relationship to other targets of *cognitive* assessment (e.g., beliefs, attributions, schemata) as well as to the assessment of *behavior* and *affect*. A multimodal focus would add to the discriminant and convergent validation of cognitive assessment, and allow for the examination of the cross-situational consistency of cognitive experiences. Since many personality tests (i.e., anxiety trait measures) inquire about cognitive aspects, it would also be important to examine whether cognitive assessments are incrementally valid over personality measures, and, if so, to what extent.

To conclude this section, we would like to quote Mischel (1981), who offers the following evaluation of cognitive assessment:

> Although not exempt from the assessment problems faced by other approaches, cognitive person variables . . . and cognitive assessment generally, may have special appeal to the extent that they are rooted in psychological processes (the generation and encoding of information, the choice of performance alternatives, the self-regulation of goal-directed action). These person variables interface with basic processes of mental functioning rather than describing persons more statically by locating their positions on assessor-supplied trait dimensions. (p. 498)

II. ISSUES IN COGNITIVE THERAPY

In this section, we address issues that arise from making a distinction between cognitive procedures and cognitive change. As we will argue, although change may be conceived as cognitive, there may be several means available to achieve that change. A model will be presented which maintains that the choice of procedures depends on the needs and skills of the client. The role of cognitive procedures in light of this model will be examined. Finally, resistance to change will be discussed. Just as change may be explained cognitively, so resistance may be explained in a cognitive conceptualization of therapy.

A. The Relationship between Cognitive Methods and Cognitive Change

A common assumption is that a therapeutic intervention of a certain type will produce changes of that same type: behavioral methods are assumed to produce behavior change, and cognitive methods are assumed to produce cognitive change. The popularity of cognitive methods may be partly due to the belief that a change in cognitive processes in therapy is desirable.

Arguments and evidence from several sources, however, reveal the problematic nature of assuming an isomorphism between procedure and process (Coyne, 1982). Bandura (1977) argues that a change in self-efficacy expectations is best achieved through behavioral procedures. Empirical evidence of the complex relationship between procedure and process comes from Zeiss et al. (1979), who compared three treatments for depression: interpersonal skills training, pleasant activities treatment, and cognitive training (consisting of a package of several cognitive interventions such as self-monitoring of thoughts, challenging of irrational thoughts, and an adaptation of fixed role therapy). Their assessments included instruments specifically matched to each treatment, such as the Personal Beliefs Inventory, which was designed to measure the type of change expected from the cognitive treatment, and ratings of verbal behavior in a group interaction to measure the type of change expected from the interpersonal skills training. The results were generally consistent in showing that each treatment affected the assessment targets equally; the effects of treatments were general rather than specific to the type of procedure. As the authors conclude, "the label of a therapy does not ensure that the behaviors labeled will be those most directly affected" (p. 436).

We can create a typology of "labels" or methods of clinical intervention. The cognitive methods would include verbal persuasion, Socratic dialogue, self-monitoring of thoughts, and so on. There is no necessary correspondence, however, between these "cognitive" methods and the type of change that would result. Two *different* questions may be involved: What are the effects of cognitive treatments on different aspects of the client's functioning? And, What treatments produce cognitive effects? Both are empirical questions, and both are worthy of investigation.

Empirical examples and anecdotal instances of the sometimes surprising relationship between procedure and process can be found in many forms of therapy. Bandura's evidence of self-evaluation change through behavioral performance has been mentioned (Bandura & Adams, 1977; Bandura, Adams, Hardy, & Howells, 1980). Perhaps others have also had the experience of assigning a client to self-monitor thoughts and finding that the assignment results in a change in overt behavior or affect. For example, a depressed client assigned to monitor self-talk at work may come to therapy the next week and report a striking improvement in mood. In some cases, the sequence may be that the self-monitoring led to insight into a self-defeating pattern, and then to a realization by the client that his or her life is not so hopeless. With other clients, however, the leap from a focus on self-talk to affect seems more direct, as when the client says, "Well, I still have those thoughts, but I don't let them hold me back anymore." Somehow the attention to the cognitive assessment has broken a cognitive-affective chain.

As implied by the previous paragraph, the most appropriate method to achieve a given type of change may vary according to factors such as type of disorder. For example, some phobias seem to be best treated by participant modeling, and depression seems to be modifiable by cognitive therapy. However, Paul's (1967) famous statement of the outcome question says that we must look not only at the specific problem, but also at the characteristics of the client: "What treatment, by whom, is effective for this individual with that specific problem, and under which set of circumstances" (p. 111; see also Kiesler, 1966). Individual differences among clients, beyond differences in disorders, will partly determine the most effective treatment. To date, we have only scattered information on such individual differences, particularly in cognitive therapy.

Though our explicit knowledge about the choice of method based on knowledge of both disorder and individual differences may be scattered, it is clear that successful therapists do use some form of implicit knowledge to guide them. Eclectic therapists label themselves as such because no one approach seems sufficient (Garfield & Kurtz, 1977). One of the attractions of the cognitive perspective may be its flexible combination of verbal and behavioral methods, as well as its easy integration with other techniques (Arnkoff, 1981). Although change may be conceived of ultimately as cognitive process, it is clear that there are various methods to induce change. We would do well to study eclectic therapists to ascertain how they combine information on the disorder and other characteristics of the client in choosing among intervention methods.

B. A Model of Therapy Stages: Client Characteristics and Therapeutic Methods

One client characteristic which may be important in the choice of treatment method is the client's own comfort and familiarity with procedures that are similar to those we employ as "therapy." Clients differ in their familiarity with the various approaches that therapists use. Some clients are highly introspective, coming to therapy with a high regard for self-examination; others are puzzled by such an activity. Clients differ too on their awareness of affect and familiarity with labels for affect; for some clients, an important task is to learn to attach "feeling words" to their experience. Not all clients need to learn control of their affect; some are too tightly controlled when they enter therapy and need to learn affect expression (Bowers, 1980; Mahoney, 1980). Some clients regularly examine and modify thoughts, while for others, the idea that self-talk influences affect and behavior is new and surprising. Knowledge of contingency management also varies greatly, with some clients already adept at self-reinforcement (Perri & Richards, 1977). Virtually all methods used formally in therapy have a counterpart in untutored self-change.

We hypothesize that successful eclectic therapists informally assess their client's familiarity and comfort with various change methods, and use this information to their advantage. It is rare that a client will be equally comfortable with all methods to achieve change. For example, some clients are introspective, but resist taking action based on their self-discoveries. Other clients are "doers," but dislike examining their actions. When a client is uncomfortable with a change method, it is likely that the discomfort is associated less with the method itself than with what the client feels is likely to happen if he or she uses the method. For example, clients may experience fear of loss of control if they are encouraged to express affect. Others may resist examining patterns because of a fear of what they will find out about themselves if they do so. Reluctance to take action to change behaviors may arise from an implicit preference for the current patterns, however problematic, over feeling obliged to do what the client knows he or she "should" do.

The manner in which the therapist uses this information about client style changes, we believe, at different stages of therapy. In the early part of therapy, the therapist strives to build the therapeutic alliance by making use of the client's preferred style—by "speaking the client's language." For therapy to result in significant change, however, it is important in later stages of therapy to help the client to work in uncomfortable or unfamiliar modes. Since the ultimate goal of therapy is to help the client to become self-sufficient in dealing with present and future problems, it is essential to teach clients to help themselves in ways in which they are weak at the outset (Mahoney & Arnkoff, 1978). Some progress can be made by adopting methods that are familiar to the client; such a procedure is probably essential at the beginning of therapy. But maintenance and generalization of change require learning new, perhaps threatening competencies. Therefore, we begin from the client's strengths, but proceed to weaker areas once trust is created.

This model bears some similarity to Carkhuff's (1969) model of phases of helping, which moves from an early emphasis on communication and relationship building to an advanced phase of action. Our model conceives of competencies that the client brings to therapy in somewhat different terms. We are concerned with being explicit about types of competencies and therefore explicit about what type of communication will be necessary early on, and what contrasting mode of action will be necessary later in therapy.

To elaborate, we are proposing that there are, for this purpose, two stages in therapy. In the first stage, rapport and trust are primary. In this first stage the therapeutic alliance is built. The therapist demonstrates understanding of the client's world, and begins to teach his or her own point of view. The client's preferred methods of solving problems are used as a foundation by the therapist at this stage, in order to build the contract necessary for the work to proceed. At the same time, the therapist introduces the client to the therapist's perspective, again taking off from the client's preferred style.

An illustration may clarify the process that takes place at the outset of therapy. Two hypothetical clients will be described who differ in their preferred methods of solving problems. The background and reason for seeking treatment for both clients, however, is the same. Each client is in her late 20s, is recently divorced after a 2-year marriage, and is an attorney with a private law firm. Each is seeking treatment because of difficulty in accomplishing her work to her satisfaction in a reasonable length of time. Both of these clients report spending an inordinate amount of time in the office, with consequent loss of social activities. Yet, each client feels that she is not producing enough and that the work she does produce is not of the quality required to reach her goal of becoming a partner in the law firm.

The first of these two clients, hereafter called Client Number One, is introspective and verbal, and enjoys self-examination to discover patterns and meaning. When such a client comes to therapy, the therapist generally listens closely and reflects the client's concerns and explanations in order to demonstrate understanding. At the same time, the therapist will begin to explain his or her own point of view, translating from the client's vocabulary into the therapist's. The therapist reframes the client's understanding into the therapist's point of view (Watzlawick, Weakland, & Fisch, 1974). A cognitive therapist, for example, will listen carefully to our introspective client's analysis of her perfectionist demands on herself, reflect her ideas, and also take the opportunity to demonstrate the maladaptive conclusion the client has drawn. The therapist may indicate that it certainly sounds like the client saw her parents as demanding a great deal. With such an idea, she indeed might feel driven to succeed. But the therapist would also frame questions about the client's conclusions to lead her to see the missing link in her reasoning: her actions are understandable only if she has also concluded that as an adult, she still must succeed in order to be loved. Her explanation of the problem is on the right tract but incomplete. The therapist thus understands and adopts the client's self-examining methods for dealing with the problem, at the same time taking off from these methods to demonstrate what the therapist will be able to contribute that is new.

The second client will illustrate how the alliance would be created with someone who had a similar problem but different preferred methods for dealing with it. Client Number Two also complains of difficulty in finishing projects. This client, however, is adept at changing her overt actions but uncomfortable in linking behavior to early experience or present beliefs. She hopes to learn new overt activities to help her succeed. The therapist discovers that she has tried self-change procedures that parallel self-reinforcement and stimulus control to keep herself working, but she still has trouble getting the work done on time. In this case, the therapist would initially reflect the client's desire to change her behavior and offer encouragement that the work they would do together would lead to more adaptive behavior. The therapist would also begin to introduce his or her own perspective, this time taking off from the pragmatic, behavior-oriented strength of the client. The therapist would lead the client with questions about what she could be thinking that would result in this behavior. Eventually she would conclude from her behavior that it's *as if* she's thinking that her work will not be good enough. In that case, it's no wonder that the behavior change methods she has tried on herself so far have not been successful. The therapist conveys the message that together they will find new ways to reach her ultimate goal of changing her behavior.

In the early stages of therapy, the goals with each client are to build trust, underscore the client's strengths, and introduce the therapist's perspective. The *means* to these goals will differ according to the presenting problem and individual differences among clients in the strengths and weaknesses they bring to therapy.

Although we have described the alliance-building stages of therapy as if they always occur in one precise fashion, we realize that not every therapist works in exactly the style we have presented. The most graphic exception we can think of is that of Perls, who seemed to dispense altogether with an initial building of rapport in his group demonstrations, except for learning the client's name (e.g., Perls, 1973)! We assume that his abrupt approach was possible because individuals attending his demonstrations were already familiar with his approach, convinced of his effectiveness, or willing to take the word of others that it would be worthwhile to work with him. If the client comes to therapy already familiar with the therapist and his or her techniques, or if the client begins therapy with faith that whatever the therapist suggests will be beneficial, then the foundational rapport-building phases can be modified (or perhaps even dispensed with). By some means or another an alliance must be formed, and we suggest that it generally occurs not before therapy but at the beginning of it.

Change in therapy begins, then, with a foundation built on the client's strengths, or familiar ways of solving problems. We propose, however, that change will be limited if therapy continues in this fashion. Flexible therapists use the therapeutic alliance to push clients beyond the familiar and into the unfamiliar or threatening methods to produce change. Therapy using methods that are too comfortable for the client will eventually reach an impasse.

A study by Shuger and Bebout (1980) provides some empirical support for the idea that working only in modes comfortable for the client has limited therapeutic value. In this study, clients engaged in gestalt and psychoanalytic therapy were assessed on experiential focusing, impulse–affect expression and control, and report of symptoms. One sample was assessed early in therapy and another sample after at least 1 year of therapy. The purpose of the study was to assess differences in clients receiving these two types of therapy. Specifically, clients in later stages of gestalt therapy were hypothesized to show greater impulse expression, while clients in later stages of psychoanalytic therapy were hypothesized to show greater self-control. The results evidenced marked differences between clients in later stages of gestalt therapy and psychoanalytic therapy, but these differences were also present in clients who were just beginning therapy. No significant differences were found between clients in the early and later stages of gestalt therapy; the same was true of clients in psychoanalytic therapy. The authors conclude that when the client chooses the type of therapy that is most appealing, the match of client and therapy "may actually work against therapeutic change by merely reinforcing rather than challenging clients' expectancies and assumptions" (p. 38). While the impact of this study would be greater if one sample of clients had been assessed as they progressed through therapy, the results are nevertheless interesting.

Extrapolating from the Shuger and Bebout study, the eclectic therapist may be able to generate more change than the therapist who adheres to one method of therapy. The methods of the therapist who is a strong adherent to one school of therapy may be very powerful, but the Shuger and Bebout study suggests that the "wrong" people may choose such a therapist—those who really do not need that school's approach! The therapist who is flexible in choice of methods can engage the client in therapy by appealing to the client's preferred ways of dealing with problems, but then can bring in less comfortable methods to take the client farther.

The most appropriate sequence of methods to use, then, clearly depends on the client's strengths and weaknesses. For Client Number One discussed above, who is highly introspective, therapy must move in the direction of behavior change. Assuming that this client is like many introspective individuals, she will have a great deal to learn about behavior change. It is likely, however, that she will easily adopt the therapist's cognitive perspective. She may find it difficult to focus on her behavior, but may resist less if the therapist allows her to use her strength in self-understanding to guide her efforts and examine the changes she makes. Client Number Two described above, however, needs a different sequence of techniques. She can be counted on to translate the learning in therapy to overt action on her own, since that is her primary goal for seeking therapy as well as her strength. In this case the therapist must focus on the understanding of patterns. Like the first client, this client may have little trouble adopting the cognitive perspective, but in this case it will be because the therapist demonstrates its utility for affecting action. An early behavioral success will cement the therapeutic alliance. But for the client to learn the appropriate action to take, the therapist would foster self-examination.

C. Therapy Stages and Cognitive Methods

If the choice of interventions depends on the stage of therapy and client characteristics, the question naturally arises as to when to use cognitive methods. In discussing this question, it is again important to distinguish between the methods and the cognitive viewpoint in therapy. While cognitive *methods* refer to such interventions as self-monitoring of thoughts and Socratic dialogue to uncover maladaptive thinking, the cognitive *viewpoint* is a model of functioning and therapy which focuses on the way a person organizes perception and behavior (e.g., Beck, 1976). Just as the empirical approach is more characteristic of behavior therapy than is any one technique (Kazdin, 1978), so the cognitive viewpoint is more characteristic of cognitive therapy than is any one method. A therapist who gives behavioral homework or uses gestalt techniques can still be practicing cognitive therapy if the techniques are conceptualized in cognitive terms (Arnkoff, 1981).

Since most therapists who do cognitive therapy feel that empirical validation of their procedures is very important, and since they often combine behavioral methods with cognitive methods, this approach has sometimes been called cognitive–behavior therapy. However, we have deliberately chosen to use the terms cognitive therapy and cognitive assessment. This usage reflects our preference for defining cognitive approaches in theoretical rather than in methodological terms. Even though we agree that empirical evaluation is essential, and we use behavioral methods (as well as others), we choose the term cognitive therapy to emphasize its theoretical implications.

A therapist who adopts the cognitive viewpoint will introduce this perspective with virtually all clients early in therapy. The manner in which cognitive constructs are introduced will vary from client to client, as discussed earlier. The therapist uses the client's vocabulary and experiences to illustrate the value of the cognitive viewpoint. This perspective becomes the background for understanding the activities and discoveries of therapy, regardless of the specific techniques used.

The introduction of the cognitive viewpoint, according to this model, would vary according to client characteristics only in the details of the presentation. The use of *methods* that have been labeled cognitive, however, such as self-instructional training or analysis of irrational beliefs, would vary a great deal, depending on the client's familiarity with similar methods. For clients who come into therapy already comfortable with self-examination and an awareness of the importance of beliefs, such as Client Number One discussed above, cognitive methods could be used primarily to draw the client into therapy in the initial stages. A method such as uncovering automatic thoughts would be consistent with the client's expectations, while also providing new learning. By using these techniques in the initial stages of therapy with such a client, the therapist can arrange an early success experience for the client. Later in therapy, according to this model of sequential methods, the therapist would focus on methods less familiar to the client. These methods would range anywhere from behavioral skills training to awareness training, depending on the client's least developed methods of self-change. Cognitive methods could be used as an accompaniment to other methods in later stages of therapy, with the purpose of helping the client understand and consolidate gains. The client might self-monitor her thoughts while trying out a new skill, for example. The skills training would be the central focus, but since self-examination is useful for her, attending to self-talk as well could help her in the resolve to initiate the new behavior.

For a client who is less familiar and comfortable with cognitive methods, such as Client Number Two, the sequence and emphasis would be different. Because the client is unaccustomed to self-examination, an insensitive leap into cognitive methods early in therapy could be counterproductive. For example, Gormally, Varvil-Weld, Raphael, and Sipps (1981) compared a cognitive counseling treatment with skills training for social anxiety. They found an unusually high drop-out rate in the cognitive treatment. Their conclusion from examining the responses of the subjects who dropped out was that the cognitive focus was premature. Subjects who were socially unskilled and who wished to learn skills were dissatisfied with the goals of the cognitive treatment. As one subject said, "I'm looking for a way to start to get to know girls, and not re-evaluating some of the notions in my head." The introduction of cognitive procedures with such a client, then, would initially be tied closely to the client's goals and expectations. Self-monitoring of thoughts, for example, would be proposed as a means to assess the client's specific difficulties and, therefore, the behavior to be changed.

Later in therapy with a person such as Client Number Two, the therapist may choose to focus on cognitive procedures, with the client's action orientation as the background only. Although attention to maladaptive beliefs and thoughts may be painful or difficult for Client

Number Two, it seems vital for her to learn such methods to deal with both present and future problems.

In general, then, the model proposes a sequence of alliance with the client's strengths, followed by a focus on the client's less developed competencies or methods. Adaptive functioning in this model is defined as the ability to choose among a variety of means to solving problems. Successful therapy may therefore involve dealing in multiple modes of intervention, to teach the client a variety of self-change techniques (Meichenbaum & Butler, 1980b). In many cases, though, a plethora of methods may not be necessary. When a client is especially adept at one method of self-change prior to therapy, no direct focus in therapy on that method may be necessary. Clients actively process the material of therapy. The introspective client discussed in this section would be likely to attend to the meaning of change even in a solely behavioral treatment, and the action-oriented client would translate her insight into behavioral terms even with little or no aid in doing so. The active processing by clients may be the reason that studies assessing specific effects of treatments often encounter no differences among treatments, with all treatments resulting in a variety of changes (Arnkoff, 1980; Zeiss et al., 1979). Nevertheless, the best treatment may be one that goes beyond the "train and hope" strategy of generalization (Stokes & Baer, 1977). The best treatment may help the client translate learning from one component of functioning to others.

We have said that therapists make informal assessments of their clients' strengths in preparation for choosing the methods and sequence of therapy. It would certainly be useful to make this process explicit, both to evaluate the model of therapy stages and to aid in planning treatment. To our knowledge, no formal assessment designed for this purpose has been developed. We can offer some suggested starting points, however. The facility in self-examination, which was a strength for Client Number One, may be assessed by a scale such as the private self-consciousness section of the Self-Consciousness Scale (Fenigstein, Scheier, & Buss, 1975). This subscale elicits information about "the extent to which people are aware of the private aspects of themselves" (Buss, 1980, p. 10). Clients who score high on private self consciousness may easily adopt cognitive or analytic techniques early in therapy, but they may also be weaker in behavioral methods or in evocation of affect such as accomplished by gestalt techniques. If a behavioral method is used, the client may "fill in the gaps" of the technique by gaining an understanding of the meaning of the change, without assistance by the therapist. Alternatively, the therapist may choose to make behavioral gains the primary focus, with secondary attention to beliefs or thoughts about the new behavior.

A second type of client strength which would be important is knowledge of behavioral self-control methods. Such naturalistic knowledge has been assessed by Perri and Richards (1977). The structured interviews used in this study could be adapted for assessing clients' knowledge of behavioral self-change methods at the outset of therapy. When a client is already accustomed to using such methods, therapeutic techniques stressing less developed procedures may be the focus of therapy, using the client's behavioral skills as a strength to assist in other types of change.

The cognitive assessment techniques discussed at length earlier in this chapter may be even more crucial in helping us make an explicit assessment of clients' strengths. Thus far, all attention in the literature has been focused on cognitive differences between persons who either exhibit or do not exhibit particular behavioral or emotional disorders. However, clients with similar presenting problems may well show individual differences in their cognitive responses on think-aloud tasks, thought listings, or self-monitoring of thoughts. Such information would assist the therapist in determining the client's current level of familiarity or awareness of his or her maladaptive cognitive processes. For example, some clients coming into therapy for difficulties in social interactions, in that they experience a great deal of anxiety in making friends and conversing with others, may already have easy access to their internal dialogue. They may produce a large number of responses on cognitive assessment measures, readily agree that these responses are quite typical, and report that the reason they're having difficulty is that they "think too much." Other socially anxious clients may respond differently to the cognitive assessment: such clients may have difficulty reporting on their thoughts, seem quite surprised to find that they have recorded the particular thoughts they did, and report that the reason they are having difficulty is that they "aren't very skilled at meeting people." Thus, in addition to assessing clients' actual behavioral skills deficits and/or maladaptive cognitions, therapists need to assess several other factors prior to therapy in order to guide cognitive therapy interventions: (1) clients' own implicit theories of their disorders, (2) their goals for therapy, (3) their expectations of how therapy will help them change, and (4) their familiarity with methods of cognitive change and their own cognitive processes. Cognitive assessment, to the extent that it can aid us in answering these questions, is therefore an integral part of our model of cognitive therapy stages.

D. Resistance to Change

Only brief mention has been made in this article of difficulties the client faces in adopting unfamiliar procedures in therapy. Clearly this discussion would be unrealistic if it ignored resistance. We have every reason to expect at least some resistance in therapy if the work is truly therapeutic. Forging into unknown territory is frightening even with an experienced guide, and the sequential model just presented is predicated on guiding the client into uncomfortable activities.

Kelly (1955) proposes that threat is experienced when the person is aware of a possible change in core structure. Certainly these conditions are precisely the definition of successful therapy. Although resistance is to be expected, a lack of cooperation is not necessarily an indication of smoothly functioning therapy. The therapist must always be open to the possibility that he or she is mistaken in deciding how best to proceed with the client, or has forged ahead without adequate preparation. Just as adaptive behavior for the client consists of flexibility in solving problems, so the same is true for the therapist. Perhaps the therapist can differentiate resistance from a problem created by therapist misjudgment by examining his or her own reactions. If the therapist is frustrated, the client's lack of cooperation may indicate a problem other than normal resistance, such as poor attention to the client's real concerns, or self-defeat on the part of the therapist (Arnkoff, 1981; Beck et al., 1979).

Assuming, however, that the client is uncooperative because of threat rather than because of therapist clumsiness, some guidance on resistance may be found in the cognitive literature. Beck et al. (1979) devote a chapter to therapy with the "difficult" client. Their solutions may be generalized into the directive to "maintain a problem-solving attitude" (p. 298). Naturally, the type of problem solving advocated is consistent with the cognitive viewpoint. As Bedrosian and Beck (1980) say, "these 'obstacles' should be dealt with in the same ways as any other problems: investigate and evaluate the relevant cognitions" (p. 136). Resistance is thus grist for the cognitive therapeutic mill.

By their very nature, some methods may reduce the tenacity of resistance. One is the Socratic dialogue, the judicious use of questions to lead clients to discovery of maladaptive processes by themselves. Beck et al. (1979) advocate questioning as a wise alternative to "disputation and indoctrination" (p. 69). Because clients discover new ideas on their own, resistance may be partially circumvented. The focus on anomalies between the client's model and experience may also serve to reduce resistance. Sollod and Wachtel (1980) address transference in Piagetian terms as a process in which assimilation predominates. "One therapeutic task is to draw the patient's attention to facts which cannot so easily be assimilated into these extant schemata and by so doing encourage accommodation of extant cognitive structures to these facts" (p. 17). Beck's procedure of setting up experiments to demonstrate that the client's assumptions do not hold (1976; Beck et al., 1979) is one means of drawing attention to anomalies that must be accommodated.

Another respect of some cognitive methods that may cut through resistance is their "as if" quality. Earlier, we discussed the uncovering of automatic thoughts as an "as if" procedure: the therapist helps the client examine behavior and feelings to discover that "it's *as if* I were saying these things to myself." The tentative nature of the conclusion may avert threat, since the therapist is not forcing the thoughts down the client's throat. (Our apologies to John B. Watson!) Kelly (1970) makes a similar point with regard to the scientific method: "The nice thing about hypotheses is that you don't have to believe them. This, I think, is a key to the genius of the scientific method. It permits you to be inconsistent with what you know long enough to see what will happen . . . the scientist [can] . . . learn from his experience rather than adhere stubbornly to his professional identity" (pp. 258–259). Such is the nature also of Kelly's fixed role therapy, in which the client temporarily adopts a given identity, merely to see what will happen (1955). The scientific method, adopting an "as if" hypothesis-testing focus, is characteristic of cognitive therapy. Perhaps the client, like the scientist, uses the "as if" framework to learn from experience in cognitive therapy, because there is less pressure to adhere stubbornly to a maladaptive identity.

III. CONCLUSIONS

Throughout this article run the themes of fallacies, functions, and frameworks. We have argued that it is fallacious to assume that our cognitive assessment techniques measure exactly what we intend them to measure; it is essential that we assess the validity of our assessment devices. Further, we have argued that the most promising direction for cognitive assessment may be toward the assessment of the function of cognitive processes, and we have suggested some means for doing so. We applaud the new directions being taken in cognitive assessment, toward unifying frameworks or organizational schemes for assessment.

We see in them the prospect of better guidance in the choice of assessment procedures for both therapy and research, so that we can choose those procedures which best match the specific purpose desired.

Models for choice of therapy technique have been slower to come in the cognitive field than models of assessment, probably because of the assumption that a cognitive rationale requires "cognitive" techniques. Just as it is a fallacy to assume that cognitive assessment measures perform their task as desired, so it is a fallacy to assume that cognitive change techniques are the only or even the best means to achieve cognitive change in all circumstances. As we have argued, a treatment rests more on its guiding principles than on its specific techniques (Mahoney, 1980). Our functional emphasis has led us to propose a rudimentary model of therapy stages based on the competencies or current modes of functioning of the client. Cognitive assessment within this model would therefore require attention to the client's competencies. In planning the timing and choice of cognitive techniques, important assessment targets would be not only the client's cognitive processes, but also the client's understanding of the function these and/or other processes serve in his or her problems. We have suggested an elementary framework emphasizing that the client's strengths are the foundation of treatment, but that he or she must learn to expand competencies and thereby expand experience if therapy is to be successful.

Just as our clients must expand their competencies, it is important for us as clinicians and researchers to expand our own competencies. We are excited by the conceptual activity at the cutting edge of our field. We look forward to both continuing confusion and its outcome, the sharpening of our questions and our skills.

REFERENCES

Arnkoff, D. B. Self-statement therapy and belief therapy in the treatment of test anxiety (Doctoral dissertation, Pennsylvania State University, 1979). *Dissertation Abstracts International*, 1980, **40**, 4469B. (University Microfilms No. 80-05970).

Arnkoff, D. B. Flexibility in practicing cognitive therapy. In C. Emory, S. Hollon, & R. Bedrosian (Eds.), *New directions in cognitive therapy*. New York: Guilford, 1981.

Bakeman, R. Untangling streams of behavior: Sequential analyses of observation data. In G. P. Sackett (Ed.), *Observing behavior Vol. II: Data collection and analysis methods*. Baltimore, Maryland: University Park Press, 1978.

Bakeman, R., Cairns, R. B., & Applebaum, M. Note on describing and analyzing interactional data: Some first steps and common pitfalls. In R. B. Cairns (Ed.), *The analysis of social interactions: Methods, issues, and illustrations.* Hillsdale, New Jersey: Erlbaum, 1979.

Bandura, A. Self-efficacy: Toward a unifying theory of behavioral change. *Psychological Review,* 1977, **84,** 191–215.

Bandura, A. Gauging the relationship between self-efficacy judgment and action. *Cognitive Therapy and Research,* 1980, **4,** 263–268.

Bandura, A., & Adams, N. E. Analysis of self-efficacy theory of behavioral change. *Cognitive Therapy and Research,* 1977, **1,** 287–308.

Bandura, A., Adams, N. E., Hardy, A. B., & Howells, G. N. Tests of the generality of self-efficacy theory. *Cognitive Therapy and Research,* 1980, **4,** 39–66.

Beck, A. T. *Cognitive therapy and the emotional disorders.* New York: International Universities Press, 1976.

Beck, A. T., Rush, A. J., Shaw, B. F., & Emery, G. *Cognitive therapy of depression: A treatment manual.* New York: Guilford, 1979.

Bedrosian, R. C., & Beck, A. T. Principles of cognitive therapy. In M. J. Mahoney (Ed.), *Psychotherapy process: Current issues and future directions.* New York: Plenum, 1980.

Bowers, K. S. "De-controlling" cognition and cognitive control: Toward a reconciliation of cognitive and dynamic therapies. In M. J. Mahoney (Ed.), *Psychotherapy process: Current issues and future directions.* New York: Plenum, 1980.

Buss, A. H. *Self-consciousness and social anxiety.* San Francisco, California: Freeman, 1980.

Cacioppo, J. T., Glass, C. R., & Merluzzi, T. V. Self-statements and self-evaluations: A cognitive response analysis of heterosocial anxiety. *Cognitive Therapy and Research,* 1979, **3,** 249–262.

Carkhuff, R. R. *Helping and human relations* (Vol. 2). New York: Holt, 1969.

Castellan, N. J. The analysis of behavior sequences. In R. B. Cairns (Ed.), *The analysis of social interactions: Methods, issues, and illustrations.* Hillsdale, New Jersey, Erlbaum, 1979.

Coyne, J. C. A critique of cognitions as causal entities, with particular reference to depression. *Cognitive Therapy and Research,* 1982, **6,** in press.

Craighead, W. E., Kimball, W. H., & Rehak, P. J. Mood changes, physiological responses, and self-statements during social rejection imagery. *Journal of Consulting and Clinical Psychology,* 1979, **47,** 385–396.

DeMonbreun, B. G., & Craighead, W. E. Distortion of perception and recall of positive and neutral feedback in depression. *Cognitive Therapy and Research,* 1977, **1,** 311–330.

Duvall, S., & Wicklund, R. A. *A theory of objective self-awareness.* New York: Academic Press, 1972.

Fenigstein, A., Scheier, M. F., & Buss, A. H. Public and private self-consciousness: Assessment and theory. *Journal of Consulting and Clinical Psychology,* 1975, **43,** 522–527.

Galassi, J. P., Frierson, H. T., & Sharer, R. Behavior of high, moderate, and low test anxious students during an actual test situation. *Journal of Consulting and Clinical Psychology,* 1981, **49,** 51–62.

Garfield, S. L., & Kurtz, R. A study of eclectic views. *Journal of Consulting and Clinical Psychology,* 1977, **45,** 78–83.

Genest, M., & Turk, D. C. Think-aloud approaches to cognitive assessment. In T. V. Merluzzi, C. R. Glass, & M. Genest (Eds.), *Cognitive assessment.* New York: Guilford, 1981.

Glass, C. R. Advances and issues in cognitive assessment. In J. P. Galassi (Chair), Current issues and research in cognitive assessment and cognitive-behavioral counseling. Symposium presented at the meeting of the American Psychological Association, Montreal, September 1980.

Glass, C. R., & Merluzzi, T. V. Cognitive assessment of social-evaluative anxiety. In T. V. Merluzzi, C. R. Glass, & M. Genest (Eds.), Cognitive assessment. New York: Guilford, 1981.

Glass, C. R., Merluzzi, T. V., Biever, J. L., & Larsen, K. H. Cognitive assessment of social anxiety: Development and validation of a self-statement questionnaire. Cognitive Therapy and Research, 1982, 6, in press.

Goldfried, M. R. Discussant in P. C. Kendall (Chair), Assessment strategies for cognitive-behavioral interventions. Symposium presented at the meeting of the Association for Advancement of Behavior Therapy, New York, November 1980.

Gormally, J., Varvil-Weld, D., Raphael, R., & Sipps, G. Treatment of socially anxious college men using cognitive counseling and skills training. Journal of Counseling Psychology, 1981, 28, 147–157.

Gottman, J. M., & Notarius, C. I. Sequential analysis of observational data using Markov chains. In T. Kratochwill (Ed.), Strategies to evaluate change in single-subject research. New York: Academic Press, 1978.

Henshaw, D. A cognitive analysis of creative problem-solving (Doctoral dissertation, University of Waterloo, 1978). Dissertation Abstracts International, 1978, 39, 4580B.

Hollon, S. D., & Kendall, P. C. Cognitive self-statements in depression: Development of an automatic thoughts questionnaire. Cognitive Therapy and Research, 1980, 4, 383–395.

Kagan, N., & Krathwohl, D. R. Studies in human interaction: Interpersonal process recall stimulated by videotape. East Lansing, Michigan: Michigan State University, 1967.

Kazdin, A. E. Behavior therapy: Evolution and expansion. The Counseling Psychologist, 1978, 7, 34–37.

Kelly, G. A. The psychology of personal constructs. New York: Norton, 1955.

Kelly, G. A. Behaviour is an experiment. In D. Bannister (Ed.), Perspectives in personal construct theory. New York: Academic Press, 1970.

Kendall, P. C., & Hollon, S. D. Assessing self-referent speech: Methods in the measurement of self-statements. In P. C. Kendall & S. D. Hollon (Eds.), Assessment strategies for cognitive-behavioral interventions. New York: Academic Press, 1981. (a)

Kendall, P. C., & Hollon, S. D. (Eds.), Assessment strategies for cognitive-behavioral interventions. New York: Academic Press, 1981. (b)

Kendall, P. C., Williams, L., Pechacek, T. F., Graham, L. E., Shisslak, C., & Herzof, N. Cognitive-behavioral and patient education interventions in cardiac catheterization procedures: The Palo Alto medical psychology project. Journal of Consulting and Clinical Psychology, 1979, 47, 48–59.

Kiesler, D. J. Some myths of psychotherapy research and the search for a paradigm. Psychological Bulletin, 1966 65, 110–136.

Klass, T. A cognitive analysis of guilt over assertion. Cognitive Therapy and Research, 1981, 5, 283–297.

Klinger, E. Modes of normal conscious flow. In K. S. Pope & J. L. Singer (Eds.), The stream of consciousness. New York: Plenum, 1978.

Lazarus, R. S., Kanner, A. D., & Folkman, S. Emotions: A cognitive-phenomenological analysis. In R. Plutchick & H. Kellerman (Eds.), *Emotion: Theory, research, and experience (Vol. 1): Theories of emotion*. New York: Academic Press, 1980.

Mahoney, M. J. Psychotherapy and the structure of personal revolutions. In M. J. Mahoney (Ed.), *Psychotherapy process: Current issues and future directions*. New York: Plenum, 1980.

Mahoney, M. J., & Arnkoff, D. B. Cognitive and self-control therapies. In S. L. Garfield & A. E. Bergin (Eds.), *Handbook of psychotherapy and behavior change* (2nd ed.). New York: Wiley, 1978.

Meichenbaum, D. *Cognitive-behavior modification: An integrative approach*. New York: Plenum, 1977.

Meichenbaum, D., & Butler, L. Cognitive ethology: Assessing the streams of cognition and emotion. In K. Blankstein, P. Pliner, & J. Polivy (Eds.), *Advances in the study of communication and affect: Assessment and modification of emotional behavior* (Vol. 6). New York: Plenum, 1980. (a)

Meichenbaum, D., & Butler, L. Toward a conceptual model for the treatment of test anxiety: Implications for research and treatment: In I. G. Sarason (Ed.), *Test anxiety: Theory, research, and applications*. Hillsdale, New Jersey: Erlbaum, 1980. (b)

Meichenbaum, D., & Cameron, R. Issues in cognitive assessment: An overview. In T. V. Merluzzi, C. R. Glass, & M. Genest (Eds.), *Cognitive assessment*. New York: Guilford, 1981.

Meichenbaum, D., Genest, M., & Turk, D. C. *A cognitive-behavioral approach to the management of pain*. Paper presented at the 11th Annual Convention of the Association for Advancement of Behavior Therapy, Atlanta, December, 1977.

Meichenbaum, D., Henshaw, D., & Himel, N. Coping with stress as a problem-solving process. In H. W. Krohne & L. Laux (Eds.), *Achievement, stress, and anxiety*. Washington, D.C.: Hemisphere Publ., 1982.

Merluzzi, T. V., Glass, C. R., & Genest, M. (Eds.), *Cognitive assessment*. New York: Guilford, 1981.

Mischel, W. A cognitive social learning approach to assessment. In T. V. Merluzzi, C. R. Glass, & M. Genest (Eds.), *Cognitive assessment*. New York: Guilford, 1981.

Nelson, R. E., & Craighead, W. E. Selective recall of positive and negative feedback, self-control behaviors, and depression. *Journal of Abnormal Psychology*, 1977, **86**, 379–388.

Notarius, C. I. Assessing sequential dependency in cognitive performance data. In T. V. Merluzzi, C. R. Glass, & M. Genest (Eds.), *Cognitive assessment*. New York: Guilford, 1981.

Notarius, C. I., Krokoff, L. J., & Markman, H. J. Analysis of observational data. In E. E. Filsinger & R. A. Lewis (Eds.), *Assessing marriage: New behavioral approaches*. Beverly Hills, California: Sage, 1981.

Paul, G. L. Strategy of outcome research in psychotherapy. *Journal of Consulting Psychology*, 1967, **31**, 109–118.

Perls, F. *The gestalt approach and eye witness to therapy*. New York: Bantam, 1973.

Perri, M. G., & Richards, C. S. An investigation of naturally occurring episodes of self-controlled behaviors. *Journal of Counseling Psychology*, 1977, **24**, 178–183.

Sackett, G. P. *A nonparametric lag sequential analysis for studying dependency among responses in observational scoring systems*. Unpublished manuscript, University of Washington, 1974.

Schwartz, R. M., & Gottman, J. M. Toward a task analysis of assertive behavior. *Journal of Consulting and Clinical Psychology*, 1976, **44**, 910–920.

Shuger, D., & Bebout, J. Contrasts in gestalt and analytic therapy. *Journal of Humanistic Psychology*, 1980, **20**, 22–39.

Sollod, R. N., & Wachtel, P. L. A structural and transactional approach to cognition in clinical problems. In M. J. Mahoney (Ed.), *Psychotherapy process: Current issues and future directions.* New York: Plenum, 1980.

Stokes, T. F., & Baer, D. M. An implicit technology of generalization. *Journal of Applied Behavior Analysis*, 1977, **10**, 349–367.

Vygotsky, L. S. *Thought and language* (E. Hanfmann & G. Vakar, Eds. and trans.). Cambridge, Massachusetts: MIT Press, 1962. (Originally published, 1934.)

Watzlawick, P., Weakland, J., & Fisch, R. *Change: Principles of problem formation and problem resolution.* New York: Norton, 1974.

Wine, J. Cognitive-attentional theory of test anxiety. In I. G. Sarason (Ed.), *Test anxiety: Theory, research, and applications.* Hillsdale, New Jersey: Erlbaum, 1980.

Zeiss, A. M., Lewinsohn, P. M., & Muñoz, R. F. Nonspecific improvement effects in depression using interpersonal skills training, pleasant activity schedules, or cognitive training. *Journal of Consulting and Clinical Psychology*, 1979, **47**, 427–439.

Rule-Governed Behavior: A Potential Theoretical Framework for Cognitive–Behavioral Therapy

ROBERT D. ZETTLE AND STEVEN C. HAYES

Department of Psychology,
University of North Carolina,
Greensboro, North Carolina

73

ADVANCES IN COGNITIVE-BEHAVIORAL RESEARCH
AND THERAPY, VOLUME 1

The emergence and increasingly wide acceptance of cognitively based treatments are major developments in behavior therapy. In recent years there have been the formation of a new journal, *Cognitive Therapy and Research*, and a special interest group within the Association for Advancement of Behavior Therapy devoted to cognitive–behavioral therapy (Dowd, 1978), as well as the appearance of several major books in the area (Beck, Rush, Shaw, & Emery, 1979; Kendall & Hollon, 1979, 1981; Mahoney, 1974; Meichenbaum, 1977).

It is unclear which specific intervention procedures comprise cognitive–behavioral therapy (Wilson, 1978), but one suggested area in common is the commitment to behavioral methodology each reflects (Kendall & Hollon, 1979). Methodological rigor has often distinguished behavior therapy from other treatment approaches. In recent years, however, behavior therapy has increasingly neglected conceptual concerns (Hayes, Rincover, & Solnick, 1980). Cognitive–behavioral therapy, in particular, currently finds itself in the unfortunate position of a methodological movement without a firm conceptual foundation.

Several conceptual frameworks are available within which cognitive–behavioral therapy might be viewed. Among these are methodological behaviorism, Watsonian metaphysical behaviorism, radical behaviorism, mediational S-R theory, and social learning theory (Wilson, 1978). Of these varying conceptual views, social learning theory, with its emphasis on reciprocal determinism (Bandura, 1977) and the causal properties of cognitions, appears to enjoy the highest status among cognitive–behavioral therapists. Generally neglected altogether is the potential contribution that a radical behavioral analysis of cognitive–behavioral therapy might provide.

One reason for the relative neglect of radical behaviorism may be unfamiliarity with its view on private events and confusion over how it differs from other forms of behaviorism as a philosophy of psychology. Contemporary radical behaviorism (e.g., as reflected in the current writings of Skinner, Day, Catania, and others) is often confused with Watsonian behaviorism. For example, radical behaviorism is thought to represent the rejection of feeling, thinking, and other cognitive events (e.g., see Shevrin & Dickman, 1980). In fact, contemporary radical behaviorism incorporates these events *as behavior*—nothing more, but also, nothing less.

It is curious that methodological behaviorism, rather than radical behaviorism, has become a common ground for much of cognitive–behavioral therapy. Methodological behaviorism (as a philosophical position) has emphasized that, for methodological reasons, only publicly observable behavior can be considered as scientifically admissible. We can, however, generate "hypothetical constructs" which we infer based upon public events. Private events are thus relegated to a land of the hypothetical; never directly accessible and never, somehow, on a par with publicly observable organismic activity. Over time, the odious philosophical content of this position has seemingly faded from view for many cognitive–behavioral therapists and the words "methodological behaviorism" have come to mean simply "behavioral methodology," or for some "the scientific method," or even "empiricism."

With "methodological behaviorism" cut loose from its philosophical moorings, many cognitive–behavioral therapists have been left clinging to the flotsam and jetsam of mere empiricism. For these, radical behaviorism may provide an alternative philosophical and methodological vessel.

The fact that radical behaviorism has been so ignored and misunderstood as it applies to cognitive behavior is due in part to radical behaviorists themselves. Much of the applied empirical work done by radical behaviorists has seemingly not required attention to the factors being examined by cognitive therapists.

Due largely to historical factors (Kazdin, 1978) applied work in a radical behavioral tradition has emphasized the manipulation of strong behavioral consequences with severely disturbed populations. Very few adult clinicians, for example, are radical behaviorists. A radical behavioral view of common clinical issues has thus been poorly developed or has been developed in a way that has not led to the needed research (e.g., Skinner's 1957 book on verbal behavior). Presently, it is sadly true that radical behaviorists have "consistently eschewed the analysis and modification of private events" (Wilson, 1978, p. 8).

The present article is a first attempt to provide a framework for cognitive–behavioral therapy (and semantic therapies more generally) in radical behavioral terms. As such, it is both general and speculative. Nevertheless, it is meant to be testable, modifiable, and clinically applicable. It is written in the hopes that cognitive–behavioral therapists might look anew at radical behaviorism as an approach within which to develop their field. It is also hoped that radical behaviorists will begin to study cognitive phenomena in a rigorous manner.

I. RADICAL BEHAVIORISM AND COGNITIVE PHENOMENA

It is not our intent to describe radical behaviorism in detail, but some generalities about cognitive phenomena are warranted. To the radical behaviorist, behavior is regarded as observable organismic activity. Private events are regarded as stimuli or behavior that can be observed by an audience of one. [Public observability is not regarded as essential for scientific analysis (see Skinner, 1945).] Private events are not given special status simply because of the audience size. This does not mean that thoughts do not have special roles to play (the current article argues that they do) but merely that privacy does not establish that status.

Because the position is functional, causal factors are reserved for those that can be shown directly to help predict and control behavior. It is recognized that behavior can influence other behavior and that behavior can influence the environment so as to influence other behavior ("reciprocal determinism"). Nevertheless, *ultimately* all "causes" are restricted to environmental events. Behavioral "causes" are not ultimately acceptable since no one can change behavior without changing its context (e.g., through instructions, drugs, consequences, settings).

Behavioral influences are often thought to be important aspects of an overall causal chain, but for practical reasons the search is never ended until sources of environmental control are established. Note that this concern is as great for public as for private behaviors. The statement "He's a good quarterback because he throws rocks well" is as objectionable as "He's a good quarterback because he avoids anxiety-provoking thoughts." Both may be partially true but both are thought to be dangerously incomplete.

Thoughts and feelings, then, are behavioral phenomena on an equal par with other behaviors. Like all behaviors they can enter into causal sequences, but cannot be accepted as the ultimate cause of other behaviors. If cognitive phenomena control other behavior, the task is to identify the environmental supports for such behavior–behavior relationships.

A concept of critical importance to this task is rule-governed behavior. All behavior is thought to be ultimately contingency shaped, but an important subset of this behavior is rule-governed behavior (Skinner, 1966, 1969, Chapter 6; Zettle, 1980b). Skinner (1969, p. 146) provides an interesting example. An outfielder moves to catch a ball. Following its trajectory, he moves under it and grasps it with his glove. This event is undoubtedly contingency shaped. The outfielder is simply responding, as he has done hundreds of times before, to the effects his behavior has on moving toward the ball. A dog can easily acquire the same behavior in the same way (e.g., in catching frisbees). Contrast this with the ship captain moving to "catch" a descending satellite. The trajectory of the satellite is analyzed in detail. Mathematical models are consulted which take into account a host of factors such as wind speed and drag coefficients. Its place of impact is predicted and approached. This behavior is not controlled solely or directly by the past consequences of trying to catch satellites—it is controlled by *rules*. Unlike ball catching, this activity requires a verbal organism as host.

It is our view that the concept of rule-governed behavior, if expanded somewhat, can incorporate much or all of cognitive and semantic therapy without distorting its basic phenomena. It also points to several mechanisms of change as yet under investigated in the field. In the sections that follow, we will outline the essential characteristics of rule-governed behavior, identify some of its components and functional units, apply this to therapies developed by Ellis, Meichenbaum, and Beck, and point to some mechanisms of psychopathology and its treatment implied by this analysis.

II. DEFINITION OF RULES

Rules have been described by Skinner (1966, 1969) simply as "contingency-specifying stimuli." This definition is somewhat problematic. We are concerned that it is excessively narrow in some respects, and excessively broad in others. It also readily leads to confusion between rules and discriminative stimuli in general. Part of this confusion seems to result from the differing nature of their definitions. Essentially, Skinner's definition of rules as contingency-specifying stimuli is a topographical one whereas discriminative stimuli are defined functionally. Rules that are not followed can be readily distinguished from discriminative stimuli but confusion results when rules are followed.

An example may help clarify the difficulty. Consider a complex operant task which is presented to two different subjects. One subject is merely presented with the task with no further instruction while the second subject is told by the experimenter, "If you perform responses a, b, and c following lights x, y, and z you will be rewarded with money." In time, the behavior of both subjects in the task may appear quite similar if not identical, although the controlling variables would be quite different (Skinner, 1966). The first subject's behavior (setting aside, for the moment, self-generated rules) is under the control of the lights.[1] The behavior of the second subject is under the control of the rule and the lights.

It can be seen that all effective rules are discriminative stimuli, but not all discriminative stimuli are rules. What is crucial here is that rule-governed behavior involves two distinct sets of contingencies. One set of contingencies involves those related directly to the behavior of interest (e.g., the operant task above). The second set is verbal and somewhat independent of the first. This can be seen most readily when the two are in competition. For example, a person may be told "You are supposed to fast today." The effects of fasting itself may never have functioned as a reinforcer, and yet the person may follow the rule, for example, in order to avoid social sanctions for noncompliance.

These dual contingencies are possible only in social organisms that can establish behavior that is effective solely through the mediation of others—that is, in verbal organisms. We will follow Skinner's definition of verbal behavior as "behavior reinforced through the mediation of other persons" (Skinner, 1957, p. 14).

The direct contingencies themselves, even if they are at times complex, are simply the controlling variables. Only verbal organisms can discern and differentially reinforce behavior *because of* its controlling variables. Thus, it is self-awareness, or contingencies about contingencies, that are the essential requirements for rule-governed behavior.

We are ready now to return to the definition. Rule-governed behavior is behavior in contact with two sets of contingencies, one of which includes a verbal antecedent. These verbal antecedents are rules. This definition has several advantages. It makes a clear distinction, as Skinner's does not, between rules and other complex antecedents such as modeling stimuli (e.g., see Skinner, 1969, page 163). Further, it avoids the thorny problem of what it means to "specify" contingencies. It incorporates rules that, while verbal, do not clearly specify contingencies. As will be seen later, Skinner's definition applies most clearly to a subtype of rule-governed behavior proposed in the present system. Finally, it directs attention to the dual contingencies involved in rule-governed behavior.

---

[1] The above example is being offered to illustrate the differential discriminative control of rule-governed behavior versus responding which is merely contingency shaped. As will be discussed later, it is entirely possible that the behavior of the first subject might, in some sense, also be rule-governed in nature, although the relevant rule would be self-generated rather than provided by the experimenter's instructions.

III. COMPONENTS OF RULE-GOVERNED BEHAVIOR

Rule-governed behavior involves verbal antecedents, and different types of verbal behavior relate to different types of rules. To understand this, we will concentrate at first on rules given to a listener by another person (self-rules are much more difficult and will be discussed later). Three steps are involved in this sequence. First, the speaker speaks.[2] The functional units involved have to do with the contingencies surrounding speaking. Second, the form of the verbal behavior itself must be considered. Finally, the listener listens and reacts in some way due to contingencies surrounding listening. Put another way, a complete analysis must incorporate functional units for the speaker, formal aspects of speech, and functional units for the listener.

A. Functional Units of Speaker Behavior

Skinner has developed several separate functional units for the speaker. While many of these units have implications for rule-governed behavior, the most important are *tacts* and *mands*. A tact is a verbal operant in which a response of given form is evoked or strengthened by a particular object or event or their properties (Skinner, 1957, pp. 81–82). Thus, it is under relatively tight stimulus control and is relatively insensitive to changes in states of deprivation or aversive stimulation impinging on the speaker. For example, I may say "that's a chair" when a chair is brought forth. This is probably a tact. It is if its emission is controlled by the chair itself. Importantly, a chair is a chair regardless of my needs or desires at the moment. Note that tacting is not the same as "naming" or "referring to." A tact requires the direct experience or contact with a particular object or event. It is experiental, not inferential. For example, "that's good" is not a tact, although it is a name. A mand, by contrast, is a verbal operant in which the response is under the control of conditions of reinforceability in the speaker (e.g., relevant conditions of deprivation or aversive stimulation) and of antecedents indicating an availability of a relevant consequence (Skinner, 1957, pp. 35–36). For example, a person enters a room and wanting to sit down says "a chair." A chair is

---

[2] It should be noted that "speaker" in the current discussion is synonymous with "rule giver" and "listener" with that of "rule follower." This is being done largely out of convenience and is not meant to imply that the only rules are spoken ones. Obviously, rules can also be presented by the written word, sign language, or other means.

then brought forth by a listener. Note that the mand is reinforced by characteristic listener-mediated consequences.

Each of these units leads to characteristic forms. For example, tacts often look like descriptions (e.g., "that's water"), while mands often look like requests (e.g., "bring me water"). The formal unit is not the functional one but there is some relationship between them. Were there not, different functional units for the speaker would not lead to differential listener behavior.

The listener usually relies very heavily on the form of speech in discerning the contingencies surrounding their reaction to it. Thus, the formal units of speech are the major mode of interchange between a speaker and listener. The speaker speaks because there is a listener and vice versa.

Tangentially, this suggests one reason to study rule-governed behavior. An understanding of the listener should lead to an understanding of the speaker. While the reverse is also true, efforts along these lines have not led to satisfactory behavioral research, particularly because speech is so multiply determined. Unlike research on speaker behavior, investigations of rule-governed behavior allow ready access to the major class of independent variables influencing it, namely, verbal behavior.

B. Functional Units of Listener Behavior

1. Pliance

At least three main functional units can be discerned in the listener. One parallels the mand. We term it *pliance*, drawn from the word compliance. Pliance is rule-governed behavior primarily under the control of apparent speaker-mediated consequences for a correspondence between the rule and the relevant behavior. The rule itself is termed a *ply*. A simple case is as follows. A thief says "Your wallet or your life" and the person hands the thief the wallet, an apparent instance of pliance. Note that, just as we cannot be sure from the description above that the statement is a mand (though it has the common form of one), we cannot be sure that handing over the wallet is pliance. It is pliance only if the listener is under the control of apparent speaker-mediated consequences for following the rule. This can be determined by the sensitivity the behavior shows to variables affecting apparent speaker-mediated consequences such as the ability of the speaker to monitor compliance (e.g., suppose the thief were obviously blind and paralyzed), the ability of the speaker to deliver consequences (e.g., suppose the "gun" is obviously made of chocolate), the importance of the consequences to the listener (e.g., suppose the victim is Superman), and many others (e.g., history, credibility).

2. Tracking

A second unit of rule-governed behavior parallels the tact. We term it *tracking*, to suggest following a path. Tracking is rule-governed behavior under the control of the apparent correspondence between the rule and the way the world is arranged. The rule itself is termed a *track*. A simple case might be the advice "The way to get to Greensboro is to follow I-85." If the listener's behavior is brought under control of the rule because of an apparent correspondence between it and how actually to get to Greensboro, then this is tracking.

Tracking is sensitive to a host of variables affecting the apparent correspondence between the rule and natural contingencies and the importance of that correspondence. For example, tracking is influenced by the listener's history with similar rule givers, the correspondence between the rule and other rules or events in the listener's history, the importance of the consequence implied by the rule, and so on. Note that the speaker does not mediate compliance. Tracking would be as likely to occur if the rule is in a book as if it were given by an actual speaker (assuming similar histories in these two situations).

3. Augmenting

A third unit of rule-governed behavior does not clearly parallel units in the speaker. We term it *augmenting*, to suggest a changed or heightened state of affairs. Augmenting is rule-governed behavior under the control of apparent changes in the capacity of events to function as reinforcers or punishers. The rule is itself termed an *augmental*.

Several different functional units of speaker behavior can serve as augmentals. A particularly obvious one is the *autoclitic*. Autoclitics denote verbal behavior by a speaker which is based upon or depends upon other verbal behavior (Skinner, 1957, p. 315). Autoclitics of particular types are normally manipulated in composing poems and similar literary productions until the final verbal output has a certain emotional impact on the composer (Skinner, 1957, Chap. 14). Much of this effect may result from the ability of words to elicit conditioned emotional responses. A poem that generates a certain emotional reaction in its composer may be expected to have a similar impact on other listeners and thereby alter their capacity to find particular events reinforcing or punishing. An example of an augmental would be an abstract poem that leaves listeners somehow more sensitive to the importance of interpersonal relationships in their lives. The listeners may not be able to tact this relationship. Nevertheless, it may produce changes in behavior.

Augmenting rarely exists in pure form—it is usually mixed with pliance or tracking. Each of these can be affected by augmentals because they each involve implied or specified consequences. An example of how augmentals mix with other units might be the following. An antiabortion appeal is preceded by a song about death. Later the arguments about abortion keep referring to the death of unborn children. The initial augmental may create a state of reinforceability which can increase the behavior change potential of these arguments. The common advice to speakers to first "create a need" is reflective of this process.

It should be noted that other forms of verbal behavior by a speaker can function in the same way. Rather than presenting a song about death prior to an antiabortion appeal, the speaker might try to affect the listener in a similar way by forms resembling a mand (e.g., "I want you to think of death and all it means") or a tact (e.g., "The message which follows will have a greater impact on you if you first think about death and all it means"). Because augmenting is a subtle unit without a clear parallel speaker unit, the primary analysis below will concentrate on pliance and tracking. Augmenting will be discussed periodically throughout the article, however.

There are probably other units of rule-governed behavior, but the three main units above seem most distinct and useful. Note that each definition includes the word "apparent." This is simply to emphasize that rules are antecedent stimuli. The consequences that follow them affect their future value as antecedents, but not their present value. Their present value is determined by the history of the listener.

C. Formal Aspects of Speech and Speaker–Listener Interactions

Although there is a relationship between the speaker, the form of rules, and the listener, this relationship is not direct. Figure 1 shows the possible avenues of interaction between a speaker and a listener considering only mands, tacts, pliance, and tracking. There are eight possible avenues. For example, a speaker may emit a tact, which appears to be a tact, and yet pliance may be produced. Suppose a parent upon reading a thermometer tells a child a tact: "It's cold outside." Though this may be a tact in tact form, it could lead to pliance. The child may put on a jacket, not because it is cold but because what is

Functional unit of verbal behavior for the speaker	Apparent form	Functional unit of rule-governed behavior for the listener
Mand	Mand form	Pliance
Tact	Tact form	Tracking

Time

Fig. 1. An outline of speaker–listener interchanges.

"heard" is "I'm demanding you put on a jacket, or else." This can be understood by examining Fig. 2.

Not only can the rule not fit the form of speech (e.g., a tact form is seen as a ply) but the form of speech may not fit the functional unit of speech.

As suggested in the earlier discussion of augmenting, speakers often deliberately manipulate the form of speech. For example, a parent tells a child "If you act like that, the neighbors won't like it." Though this is in tact form, it may actually be a mand (e.g., "cut it out"). We call these mands "Trojan tacts" because, like the Trojan horse, the tact form conceals their true nature. They are extremely common, and for good reason, as we will show shortly.

To understand such maneuvers, a more detailed analysis of pliance and tracking is necessary. In particular, we need to describe the forms they can take and to account for why rules once followed are later abandoned. Pliance does not necessarily involve doing what one is told. The unit also incorporates doing the opposite, when the controlling variable is the avoidance of control by speaker-mediated consequences. Pliance is probably most often generated by mands in mand

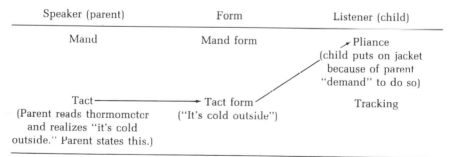

Fig. 2. An example of an interchange between a speaker and a listener. Note that the words "It's cold outside" are a tact from the point of view of the speaker, and a ply from the point of view of the listener.

form. In this situation, speaker-mediated consequences are delivered
for behavior of value primarily to the speaker. If the speaker-mediated
consequences are weak or aversive, the listener may begin to undermine apparent manding. In the present system, this can be termed
counterpliance. It has also been termed reactance (e.g., Brehm, 1966),
and other names. Note that this is a formal, not a functional, subunit.
Counterpliance is still a type of pliance. Society has an investment
in reducing coercive controls through counterpliance (Hayes & Maley,
1977). For example, it is considered "polite" to soften mands by the
use of certain autoclitics (e.g., "please," "if you could"). Hard mands
("I demand this") are very likely to generate counterpliance if the
contingencies allow it.

Tracking can also involve apparently contradictory listener behavior.
Recall that tracking is controlled by the apparent correspondence between the rule and the way the world works. Suppose a listener learns
that whatever a speaker says is usually wrong. The apparent correspondence between the rule and the world may be reversed and tracking may take on an apparently opposite form. An example is provided
by one of our friends who, when playing volleyball, consistently calls
balls that are just inside the line "out." If he shouts "out" everyone
on his team knows to dive for the ball, because it probably is actually
"in."

The conditions generating pliance or tracking also imply conditions
for the termination of control by plys and tracks. Plys should lose
control when the speaker cannot monitor the behavior and cannot or
does not deliver the consequences, when the consequences are weakened relative to others (e.g., by changes in reinforceability), and other
such factors. Tracks should lose control when they are tested and
shown to be inaccurate, when the speaker is shown to be less credible,
when other experiences or rules conflict with the track, when the
consequences specified by the track lose their importance, and so on.
These are summarized in Table I.

This analysis allows us to examine speaker manipulation of forms
of speech, for example, a "Trojan Tact." Suppose a parent tells a child
"If you are good, you'll go to heaven." This apparent tact is probably
really a mand ("I want you to be good"). However, phrased in a more
direct manner, the role of the speaker would be clear. When the parent
is out of sight, why should the child obey? The conditions controlling
pliance are difficult to maintain over long periods of time (see Table
I). For one thing, ideally it requires an ever-present rule giver. God
serves this function of course—one reason religion seems to be socially

TABLE I

Some Examples of Conditions That May Lead to the Abandonment of Control by a Previously Effective Rule

Tracking	Pliance
1. Tested, it is found to be inaccurate	1. The speaker cannot monitor the behavior
2. The rule conflicts with other rules or experiences	2. The speaker does not control relevant consequences
3. The speaker is no longer credible	3. Consequences for other behavior are now more reinforcing than speaker-mediated consequences
4. The consequences specified by the rule are no longer relevant	4. The speaker does not deliver the consequence
5. Consequences for other behavior are now more important than those specified by the rule	

useful. It is no accident that religious commandments are left in clear mand form (e.g., "Thou shalt not . . ."). But mere mortals can ill afford to produce straight pliance when long-term control is desired. If a Trojan Tact generates tracking, the ensuing control is much more likely to be long lasting. The Trojan Tact "If you are good, you'll go to heaven" is untestable (you have to die to do so), and specifies an infinitely large consequence. Thus, the conditions for terminating control are weak. Figure 3 shows the diagram of a successful Trojan Tact. Once this rule is adopted, it may be followed for a long time—perhaps the person's whole life. Unfortunately, too many Trojan Tacts may also eventually undermine tracking. The example of the adolescent who sees all parental advice (even accurate tacts) as mands and then rebels (shows counterpliance) may be a result of this process. This is shown in Fig. 4.

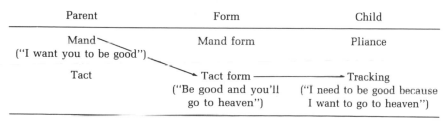

Fig. 3. An example of a successful Trojan Tact.

Parent	Form	Rebellious Child
Mand	Mand form	Pliance ("My parents just don't want me to have fun. I'll be damned if I'm going to stop seeing my friends—I'll show my parents who's boss")
Tact ⟶ ("In my experience, people like that will get others into trouble")	⟶ Tact form ("Son, those friends of yours will get you in trouble")	Tracking

Fig. 4. An example of counterpliance in response to a tact in tact form. Note that Trojan Tacts may encourage this, since the listener may eventually learn not to believe that tact forms are really tacts.

Many strange sequences are explainable in this manner. For instance, sometimes mands are deliberately stated as mands in order to generate tracking! An example is provided in the tale of how Brer Rabbit outwitted Brer Fox (Harris, 1955). When finally caught by Brer Fox, Brer Rabbit pleads: "I don't keer w'at you do wid me, Brer Fox, so you don't fling me in dat brier-patch. Roas' me . . . hang me des ez high as you please, . . . drown me des es deep ez you please, . . . skin me, snatch out my eye-balls, t'ar out my years by de roots, en cut off my legs, but do please, Brer Fox, don't fling me in dat brier-patch" (Harris, 1955, p. 13). Why? Because Brer Fox would find it reinforcing to hurt Brer Rabbit. Any mand contains an implied description about the world, namely, the state of reinforceability in the speaker. Were Brer Rabbit to say, "Rabbits find dat briar patch highly aversive," tracking is unlikely to result because the information is not credible. The aversive stimulation impinging on Brer Rabbit (i.e., being about to be cooked) would be expected to produce manding. By manding the exact opposite of what he wants, credible (but inaccurate) information about how to punish rabbits is given to Brer Fox. Although the actions of Brer Fox appear to be counterpliance to the rabbit's request, they are probably primarily tracking. Had Brer Fox read in a credible book that rabbits hate briar patches, he would have probably done the same thing. This example is shown in Fig. 5. Thus, there is a complex and dynamic relationship between verbal behavior and rule-governed behavior. The effects on the listener account for the behavior of the speaker.

Brer Rabbit	Form	Brer Fox
Mand ⟶	Mand form	Pliance
("Let me free in the briar patch")	("Please don't throw me in the briar patch")	
Tact	Tact form	Tracking
		("Rabbits hate briar patches. I want to do what Brer Rabbit hates")

Fig. 5. An example of deliberately putting a mand in mand form to generate tracking.

IV. SELF-RULES

As already pointed out, rules that come to govern an individual's behavior can be formulated and issued either by himself or by another.[3] The discussion thus far has been limited to instances of rule-governed behavior in which the speaker and listener are separate individuals. In the case of self-rules, the speaker and listener exist in the same skin. This complicates the analysis as the rules involved cannot be directly manipulated. It is especially difficult, for instance, to determine whether a particular self-rule governs behavior, or whether the rule is merely a collateral response. That is, both the rule and the behavior it appears to govern may be controlled by the same variables.

A. Formulation of Self-Rules

There appear to be at least two reasons why an individual whose behavior is already complying with a set of contingencies would formulate rules about these conditions. One reason may be described as being proximal and personal—a person may formulate rules "because he himself can then react more effectively either now or later when the contingency-shaped behavior has weakened" (Skinner, 1969, p. 159). In such instances, the same individual is thus both a rule formulator and rule follower and it is advantageous to specify the variables of which his behavior is a function.

A second account of why individuals formulate "self-rules" is more distal and appeals to the individual's social history. The formulation of rules is verbal behavior in the sense that it has a history of rein-

[3] Throughout the article, masculine pronouns will be used when the sex of the referent noun is ambiguous. This is done merely out of convenience rather than male chauvinism.

forcement exclusively through the mediation of other persons (Skinner, 1957). As Skinner (1969 and elsewhere) has emphasized, "self-awareness" which contributes to the formulation of "self-rules" is a function of one's interaction with a social environment.

As suggested earlier, self-awareness is often a prerequisite for rule-governed behavior. Self-awareness is induced by a verbal community repeatedly questioning its members about behavior they have already engaged in, are currently engaged in, and will engage in, and the variables of which their behavior is a function. The verbal descriptions that are supplied in response to such inquiries may subsequently come to exert control over the speaker's behavior.

The proper formulation of self-rules may be critical in the avoidance of psychopathology. For example, it is common to describe a relationship in ways that are untestable (e.g., "It is horrible not to be loved"). This will be analyzed in more detail shortly. For now, it should be clear that rule formulation is a major area of concern in self-rules.

B. Following of Self-Rules

A definition of rule-governed behavior offered earlier emphasized contact with dual contingencies, one of which is verbal in nature. By definition then, any instances of self-rule-governed behavior must also be affected by these two sets of contingencies. One contingency affecting self-rule-governed behavior is that following one's own rules may permit more efficient responding. The novice poker player may formulate rules of the game such as when to bet or pass on certain hands through the outcomes of his playing. He may subsequently recall these rules in future games and use them to guide his playing in a more efficient way than if he had not formulated any rules but merely allowed his behavior to be shaped by the natural contingencies of gambling. These natural contingencies and the rule both surround the card playing and are the dual contingencies required of rule-governed behavior. An ultimate appeal to social contingencies may be needed to account for many instances of self-rule following.

The verbal community may retrospectively question individuals as to what self-rules they have used to guide their behavior and reinforce individuals for a correspondence between their behavior and their post hoc reports of rules they have followed. Likewise, the verbal community may ask individuals to state rules that they will use in the future to guide their behavior in certain situations and will then consequate a correspondence between verbal and nonverbal behavior.

Thus, even if rules do not lead to natural consequences that capture the behavior (e.g., unlike the card player previously), rule following may still occur due to social consequences. Self-rules which are only verbalized covertly may exert at least some control over behavior for both of these reasons.

Numerous theorists have sought to provide an alternative account of self-rule following by appealing to self-reinforcement (Bandura, 1976; Kanfer, 1970, 1971, 1977; Kanfer & Karoly, 1972; Mahoney, 1974; Thoresen & Mahoney, 1974). To summarize, it has been argued that individuals generate self-rules regarding their behavior and self-reinforce themselves for complying with such rules. It has already been pointed out that public rule givers often socially or otherwise reinforce rule following. Analogously, it has been argued that the same individual as both a rule formulator and follower, socially or otherwise self-reinforces himself for rule following. Radical behaviorists, by contrast, have maintained that the procedure of reinforcing oneself for following self-rules may serve ultimately to cue the type of social and other reinforcement for self-rule following just discussed (Catania, 1975, 1976; Munt, Hayes, & Nelson, 1979; Rachlin, 1974; Rosenfarb, Hayes, & Zettle, 1981; Zettle, 1980b). Accordingly, an appeal to self-reinforcement in an account of why self-rules are followed merely diverts attention away from the ultimate social and other contingencies which must be analyzed in accounting for such behavior.

The allure of self-reinforcement as a variable controlling self-rule following is reduced upon considering an analysis of resolutions and other types of self-rules that are made public. While resolutions, plans, purposive statements, and other similar self-rules may be effective at the covert level as just seen, the power and saliency of social contingencies affecting rule following may be increased whenever such self-rules are made public. Skinner's analyses of resolutions are especially relevant in this regard:

> We prepare aversive stimuli which will control our own future behavior when we make a resolution. This is essentially a prediction concerning our own behavior. By making it in the presence of people who supply aversive stimulation when a prediction is not fulfilled, we arrange consequences which are likely to strengthen the behavior resolved upon. Only by behaving as predicted can we escape the aversive consequences of breaking our resolution. As we shall see later, the aversive stimulation which leads us to keep the resolution may eventually be supplied automatically by our own behavior. The resolution may then be effective even in the absence of other people. (Skinner, 1953, p. 237)

> A "resolution" is a sort of mand upon oneself which masquerades as a tact. *I am not going to smoke for the next three months* is not a response to a future event.

Its value in self-control lies in the fact that it can be made now when appropriate contingencies, possibly involving aversive events, are powerful, whereas "not smoking for three months" requires three months for its execution, during which time the underlying deprivation or aversive stimulation may change. The resolution creates a set of conditions under which smoking is particularly punished (as "breaking a promise") either by the speaker himself or by others. The effect is greater if the resolution is publicly announced or, better, conspicuously posted during the period in which it is in force. (Skinner, 1957, p. 444)

As pointed out by Skinner, once an individual publicly states a rule about his future behavior as in making a resolution, he has made a social commitment. Accordingly, he is placing his self-rule following under the control of social contingencies whereby he may be punished for a discrepancy between his verbal and nonverbal behavior. Private commitments may function similarly. The fact that resolutions under some conditions may be an effective self-control procedure illustrates the dual contingencies surrounding such self-rule following. Resolutions about behavior which would result from natural contingencies are of little value. Their value lies in pitting social contingencies for following such self-rules against those naturally controlling the behavior resolved upon. Using Skinner's example, smoking may again become reinforcing over the course of time in which the resolution is in effect. The fact that smoking does not then occur attests to the power of social contingencies which the resolution establishes.

C. Functional Units of Self-Rule Following

Thus far, the formulation and following of self-rules have been considered with little regard to the form that self-rules may take and the functional units of behavior that they may control. This is a difficult task. Unlike public rules, self-rules do not permit clear distinctions between the rule giver and the rule follower.

Thus, the distinction between pliance and tracking is difficult to assess in self-rule following. For example, the presence of the speaker cannot be manipulated so as to test for pliance. We can, however, see points along the continuum which might be agreed to be instances of self-pliance or self-tracking. Self-tracking occurs when we act as if the rule is to be followed because it is a description of the state of affairs. Self-pliance occurs when we act as if the rule is to be followed simply because it has been formulated. These definitions will be discussed more later, but a self-track might be something like "I think Ann dislikes me. I'll ignore her and that way I won't get hurt." A self-ply might look more like "No matter what happens, I'm never going to talk to a woman again—even if I know she's good for me."

At first glance it would appear as though the type of rule and the type of rule-governed behavior would always be consonant in the case of self-rules: Tacts would generate self-tracking; mands would generate self-pliance. Unfortunately, this is not true and the resultant distortion of self-rule following turns out to be an essential concern of most cognitive therapies. For example, there are several ways that self-rules may be generated which appear to be tacts, but are not. One is an impure tact. An impure tact is verbal behavior that is controlled by a stimulus object or event as well as by consequences relevant to the speaker's current level of deprivation (Skinner, 1957). Impure tacts thus are functionally similar to mands in that they are at least partly controlled by levels of deprivation and aversive stimulation of the speaker. A pure tact, by contrast, is controlled by generalized reinforcement rather than by consequences relating to the speaker's current level of deprivation. Scientific laws provide one example of pure tacts. Another instance of pure tacts may be the probabilities of certain hands in poker paying off which a novice player may eventually formulate. An example of an impure tact might be the socially unskilled person who says "if I tell any girl I meet my troubles and anxieties right away, she'll see I'm honest and will like me more." This may appear to be a description of an actual relationship, but if the rule was formulated in part simply because the person feels better by dumping all his neurotic anxieties right away, then it is impure. The actual contingencies are not those pointed to by the rule—it is under the control of particular states of aversive stimulation or deprivation. Many of the Freudian defense mechanisms (e.g., rationalization) may involve this mechanism.

Another problem occurs when rules are in tact form, but are actually intraverbals. Tacts, recall, require the control by stimulus objects or their properties. Unlike mere naming, tacting requires a direct experiential base. For example, a person may say "It is terrible to be embarrassed." This is not a tact, though it is in tact form. "Terrible" is not a stimulus object or property. It is logically derived (Skinner might call it an "intraverbal"). Thus, many self-rules appear to be tacts, but instead are mere creations of verbal convention. As we will show later, impure tacts and intraverbals can be very destructive when they generate tracking.

Self-augmenting also seems possible. Under certain conditions, speakers may attempt to induce particular emotional changes in themselves as an audience. This may be an effective means of self-control in some instances (Skinner, 1953, pp. 235–236). A woman who is somewhat ambivalent about having an abortion may, for example, repeat to herself poems, songs, or proverbs about death, which makes her "decision" in this matter an easier one to make.

V. RULE-GOVERNED BEHAVIOR AND COGNITIVE–BEHAVIORAL THERAPY

Our preliminary analysis of rule-governed behavior, though not exhaustive, and somewhat speculative, nevertheless provides some insights into current cognitive–behavioral interventions. Several current types of cognitive–behavioral therapy will be examined using this system: rational–emotive therapy (RET) (Ellis, 1962, 1973a,b), cognitive restructuring methods (Goldfried, 1979; Meichenbaum, 1977), and cognitive treatment of depression (Beck *et al.*, 1979). While these particular treatments have sometimes been viewed collectively as examples of rational psychotherapy (Wilson, 1978) or cognitive restructuring therapies (Mahoney & Arnkoff, 1978), sufficient differences exist among their specific methodologies, techniques, and underlying theoretical and conceptual bases to make separate analyses of each meaningful. Indeed, to do otherwise would be to perpetuate a "uniformity" myth (Kiesler, 1966; Meichenbaum, 1977)—the tendency to overlook fundamental differences among particular treatments because of their similarities. An attempt will be made to point out some of these important differences as well as similarities in the three types of cognitive–behavioral therapy we will be considering. Separate analyses will be provided of each treatment as a therapeutic procedure and of its underlying conceptual basis. This appears to be meaningful, since treatment may be effective for reasons unrelated to those specified by a particular theory or view of psychopathology upon which it is based.

VI. RET AND RULE-GOVERNED BEHAVIOR

A. Current Status

Outcome research on RET, with few exceptions (Moleski & Tosi, 1975; Wolfe, 1976), has been limited to unsystematic case studies and experimental analog investigations.[4] In general, RET appears to lead

---

[4] For the purposes of this chapter, RET is regarded as a cognitive–behavioral treatment. We have expressed some reservations about its conceptual and empirical status elsewhere (Zettle & Hayes, 1980).

to significant reductions in anxiety in comparison to attention-placebo and no-treatment control groups, but has been found to be less effective or no more effective than several other available procedures (DiLoreto, 1970; Germer, 1975; Jarmon, 1973; Karst & Trexler, 1970) in the treatment of anxiety. Some research suggests that other cognitive treatment procedures, differing from RET as it is usually practiced, may be more effective than RET in reducing anxiety (Germer, 1975; Kanter, 1976; Meichenbaum, 1972; Meichenbaum, Gilmore, & Fedoravicius, 1971— for a comprehensive review of the RET literature see Zettle & Hayes, 1980).

Despite a limited base of empirical support for its general efficacy, RET appears to be enjoying widespread acceptance as a form of cognitive–behavioral therapy. Gregg (1973) estimated that in excess of 500 therapists practiced RET. Garfield and Kurtz (1976) have more recently reported that 1.75% of a sample of clinical psychologists surveyed gave RET as their prominent therapeutic orientation. In fact, more clinical psychologists endorsed a rational–emotive than a Rogerian orientation.

B. Rational–Emotive Theory

Ellis (1962, 1973a,b) has consistently maintained that maladaptive emotional responses do not result directly from external situations, but are instead caused by irrational beliefs which clients hold about such situations. More specifically, according to Ellis (1973a), clients react to certain events at point A with any number of irrational beliefs, largely consisting of statements of should, ought, or must and often relating to personal worth. It is these responses at point B that, in turn, lead to anxiety and other maladaptive responses at point C. As a therapeutic procedure, RET basically attempts to initiate therapeutic change by replacing these irrational beliefs which are assumed to be the basis of psychopathology with alternative beliefs which are more rational in nature.

What particular thoughts comprise the universe of irrational beliefs appears to be somewhat unclear and arbitrary. In one of his earlier writings, Ellis (1962) listed 11 beliefs that comprise one's potential repertoire of irrational thoughts. More recently, however, several modifications in this original list have been made (Ellis & Harper, 1975).

The origin of irrational beliefs is also unclear. Ellis (1973a) has generally preferred a biological rather than a learning-based account for the origin of irrational beliefs, while other writers (DiGiuseppe, Miller, & Trexler, 1977) have suggested that irrational beliefs are acquired rather than inborn. Assuming that irrational self-statements are acquired, it is also unclear whether they are initially formulated by clients as self-rules, are rules originally issued by others which clients then follow, or are a combination of the two. Phenomenologically, irrational beliefs are self-rules. When irrational beliefs are originally formulated and issued by others, these original rule givers are unlikely to be in a position to exert any direct control over rule following. However, certain kinds of public rules (e.g., tracks) do not require presence of the rule giver. Thus, irrational beliefs are probably composed of both self-rules and public rules.

Irrational Beliefs as Rules

As already suggested, the irrational beliefs enumerated by Ellis may be regarded as rules. Essentially, rational–emotive theory maintains that maladaptive behavior is rule-governed. For the moment, in order to conduct a rule-governed analysis of rational–emotive theory, we will regard this assumption as being valid; an evaluation of its empirical status will be provided in the succeeding section.

The majority of Ellis's irrational beliefs are in mand form. Autoclitics such as "should," "must," and "ought" (which are regarded by Ellis as a defining characteristic of irrational self-verbalizations) are commonly used in conjunction with such mands. Several of Ellis's irrational beliefs are in tact form but do not actually tact the way the world is arranged. A tact, by definition, is experientially based and is therefore testable. Ellis says irrational beliefs "cannot be supported by any empirical evidence" (Ellis, 1973a, p. 57). In other words, they are not experientially based and testable: they are not tacts. Nevertheless, they may resemble tacts and may generate tracking. For instance, an irrational belief such as "It is essential that I be loved by nearly everyone, and if that does not occur it is awful" appears to tact a relationship between an event (not being loved) and its consequences (it's awful). However, "awful" is not an environmental object or event. For this reason, some irrational beliefs are often based on mere verbal convention or social agreement and are likely to be inaccurate and untestable. Nevertheless, clients may respond to irrational beliefs *as if* they were accurate and tested tracks. Recall that tracking is controlled by testing the relationship described, the credibility of the speaker, states of reinforceability, and so on. In this fact lies the destructive potential of tracks that are not tact based. Intraverbals or impure tacts are not experientially based. Thus, they cannot be "tested" in the same way a tact can. Suppose the track "If people don't love me, it's horrible" is followed. How could it ever be tested or disproved? The upset felt when people reject us is real enough, but it isn't "horrible," it is just the upset. "Horrible" is not a tact: it is not an object or property of an object. Given the rule, an upset following rejection is even more likely, and in turn "confirms" the rule. A maladaptive track of this sort is very difficult to abandon, and behavior controlled by irrational beliefs may thus appear insensitive to actual contingencies.

Behavior controlled by irrational beliefs may also be conceptualized in part as pliance. It seems plausible that particular histories of reinforcement for rule following may establish pliance as a response class under the control of rules which share certain formal characteristics—such as the use of "should" and similar autoclitics. If pliance in the past has been mediated through unescapable or unavoidable aversive control, current mands of particular forms may effectively control avoidance behavior (pliance). For example, the rule "Don't ever fail" may be followed so as to avoid the catastrophe that might attend rule breaking. It is as if the rule is followed simply because it has been formulated—it is a type of self-pliance.

This is troublesome when the self-plys are poor rules. Pliance is designed to produce insensitivity to the contingencies ("Just do as I say"). Sometimes this is helpful ("Don't touch a hot stove"); sometimes not. It depends on the situational appropriateness of the particular rule. Most "irrational beliefs" are clearly destructive when they are viewed as plys.

C. Rational–Emotive Therapy

1. Therapeutic Components

Precisely what specific procedures and techniques comprise RET is somewhat unclear based on a reading of Ellis's writings. Following Ellis's (1980) recent attempt to differentiate RET from other cognitive treatments and his (1973b) description of RET as a "cognitive–emotive–behavioristic method of psychotherapy," we will attempt to delineate several of the key therapeutic components which are most relevant for our analysis.

1. Cognitive components. The cognitive emphasis within RET essentially involves discrimination training, whereby clients are taught to differentiate between rational and irrational beliefs. After disputing and debating particular instances of irrational beliefs with clients, the therapist proceeds to instruct the client how logically and empirically to dispute such irrational self-statements and to replace them with ones of a rational nature.

2. Emotive components. The emotive components of RET emphasized by Ellis largely deal with the verbal behavior of rational–emotive therapists toward their clients. In particular, Ellis recommends actively haranguing, persuading, and cajoling clients until they acknowledge irrational beliefs that are assumed to be the basis for their present difficulties.

3. Behavioral components. RET, like many other types of behavioral treatments, incorporates homework assignments in which clients are required to engage in appropriate overt behaviors in situations that they find anxiety provoking. According to Ellis, such homework assignments are instrumental in assisting the client in interrupting and disputing irrational beliefs and are therefore regarded as "motor counterpropagandizing activities."

2. Rational–Emotive Therapist as a Rule Giver

All of the therapeutic components of RET just outlined place primary emphasis on the verbal behavior of rational–emotive therapists in their interactions with clients. While the other cognitive–behavioral approaches to be considered are also primarily "talking therapies" and therefore rely heavily upon verbal interactions between client and therapist as a medium of therapy, the role of the therapist as rule giver appears to be of relatively greater importance in the case of RET. Beck (Beck et al., 1979), for instance, has commented that RET is more didactic in nature than his own cognitive treatment, since RET has the therapist essentially tell clients that irrational beliefs are controlling their behavior and with what rational beliefs they can be replaced.

From the present perspective, RET could be aimed at undermining the formulation and following of inaccurate and untestable tracks, and replacing them with more accurate and testable ones. Many aspects of RET fit in with this analysis, but many others do not. Some rational beliefs which clients are taught appear to be quite similar to those they are designed to replace. A rational belief such as "I'm not worthless if I fail," like its corresponding irrational belief, does not tact any natural contingencies and also must be regarded as untestable. The distinction made between rational beliefs that "can be supported by empirical data and [are] appropriate to the reality that is occurring" and irrational beliefs that "cannot be supported by any empirical evidence" (Ellis, 1973a, p. 57) is thereby undermined. Thus, aspects of RET seem to challenge untestable tracks, but others simultaneously establish them.

The use of emotive components shows a similar pattern: some of it seems behaviorally sensible, some of it is not. As discussed earlier, particular aspects of a speaker's behavior, such as the way and manner in which rules are stated, may be the important discriminative stimuli for rule following by a listener. Ellis encourages therapists to confront clients very directly. These statements may have an augmenting function. An aversive state is created in which clients are motivated to change their own talk. For example, the statement "show me how losing a loved one is awful!" when delivered forcefully may encourage clients to try to answer. Since the irrational statement is not a tact, no evidence can ultimately be brought to bear. Thus, the client may experience the fact that their belief is unsupported—announcing this realization may lead in turn to escape from the confrontation.

Unfortunately, confrontation can have other outcomes. For example, it may model the opposite of the behavior desired in the client. Confrontational therapist verbal behavior consists primarily of mands, not tacts. To the degree that RET results in client behavioral change, it may often involve pliance rather than tracking. The client may, for example, agree that his beliefs are irrational and may try to change, but may never really see their irrationality. Rational–emotive therapy may be replacing maladaptive behavior controlled by one set of plys and untestable tracks with therapeutic behavioral change governed by an alternative set of therapist-formulated plys and untestable tracks. Changes in clients' self-verbalizations may at times be controlled by the mand, "You shouldn't say 'shoulds' to yourself."

Confrontation by the therapist might also result in counterpliance and other attempts by clients to escape or avoid perceived aversive control (e.g., by dropping out). No studies have yet been done on this question. Others have expressed reservations about the effectiveness of this approach. As Mahoney (1974) has observed, "It may be more therapeutic to be gently directive in self-discovery exercises than to beat a client over the head with the salience of his irrationality" (p. 233).

Concerns about the confrontational nature of RET would perhaps be lessened if Ellis in fact behaved quite differently in therapy. However, there is evidence that Ellis essentially engages in the same type of verbal behavior in conducting RET that he recommends in his writings. A recent analysis of 20 initial therapy sessions with Ellis indicated that he spent the greatest percentage of time (36%) engaged in didactic teaching, with lesser amounts devoted to rhetorical questioning of the client (16%) and presentation of concrete examples (12%) (Becker & Rosenfeld, 1976). Additionally, it was noted that many of Ellis's statements contained cursing and forceful language. Presently, no data exist to support this tactic.

The confrontational manner of rational–emotive therapists may serve as an effective screening mechanism, ensuring that clients who continue in treatment are the very type of individuals whose behavior may be most readily controlled by therapist rules. Thus, RET may work (when it does) through two mechanisms. First, the client may abandon untested tracks and seek out new ones which are more accurate and testable. The use of homework may be particularly important in this latter regard. Second, RET may work by adding therapist rules. These may be essentially "irrational" as well, but may control more adaptive responding because the rules themselves are more adaptive. Changes in this case might be more limited, and might account for the equivocal results RET has achieved relative to other cognitive therapies.

VII. COGNITIVE RESTRUCTURING AND RULE-GOVERNED BEHAVIOR

A. Current Status

Another popular cognitive–behavioral modification procedure is cognitive restructuring. Cognitive restructuring procedures, encompassing more specific treatments such as stress inoculation training and systematic rational restructuring, have been found to be effective in a variety of relatively specific, nondebilitating problem areas including test anxiety (Goldfried, Linehan, & Smith, 1978; Holroyd, 1976; Hussian & Lawrence, 1978; Meichenbaum, 1972), speech anxiety (Fremouw & Zitter, 1978; Meichenbaum et al., 1971), and the management of anger (Novaco, 1975, 1976, 1979) and pain (Meichenbaum & Turk, 1976; Turk & Genest, 1979). In addition, as previously pointed out, cognitive restructuring procedures in several studies have been found to be relatively more effective than rational–emotive-based treatments in the reduction of anxiety (Germer, 1975; Meichenbaum et al., 1971).

B. Importance of Self-Statements

Cognitive restructuring procedures seek to reduce anxiety by identifying negative self-statements and replacing them with alternative self-verbalizations more coping in nature (Meichenbaum, 1974, 1977). The results of a recent component analysis (Glogower, Fremouw, & McCroskey, 1978) suggest that knowledge and rehearsal of coping self-statements as replacements for negative thoughts are the primary components contributing to the effectiveness of the procedure. Given the important role that coping self-statements play in the efficacy of cognitive restructuring procedures, our analysis will focus on such coping self-statements and the types of negative self-statements they are designed to replace.

Based on their form, negative self-statements, such as "I'm making a fool of myself" or "My God, am I anxious!," have the appearance of tacts. However, as previously noted in the discussion of irrational beliefs, self-awareness of "making a fool of oneself" or "being anxious" is probably not verbal behavior under the control of environmental objects or events. Rather, negative self-statements generally appear to be verbal behavior under the control of other verbal behavior. For example, a client who, while giving a speech, observes that he has mispronounced a word or that his heart is beating faster than usual may then conclude "I'm making a fool of myself" or "My God, am I anxious." Self-awareness of mispronouncing a word or the activity of one's heart refer to events and therefore can be conceptualized as tacts; the collateral verbal behavior that follows cannot. Therefore, undermining negative self-statements may be aimed at the weakening of untestable tracks.

1. Functions of Coping Self-Statements

Given the finding that negative self-statements may elicit emotional reactions (Rimm & Litvak, 1969; Rogers & Craighead, 1977; Russell & Brandsma, 1974), it seems conceivable that coping self-statements as conditioned emotional stimuli might serve a similar augmenting function in facilitating anxiety-relief. A series of investigations by Meichenbaum and Cameron (1972, 1974), incorporating coping self-statements with anxiety-relief procedures, however, has failed to provide definitive support for this conceptualization. A second function that coping self-statements might serve, in light of attentional interpretations of anxiety (Wine, 1971), is as distractors in diverting attention away from anxiety-eliciting cues. Recent research by Hayes, Hussian, Turner, Anderson, and Grubb (1979), however, suggests that coping self-statements provide therapeutic effects beyond any mere distractive function that they might serve.

Another potential function that coping self-statements might serve is a self-instructional one. This view has been supported by Kanfer, Karoly, and Newman (1975) in comparing the relative effectiveness of different rules in increasing darkness tolerance among children.

Different groups of children who were fearful of the dark were instructed to engage in statements of a neutral nature, ones relating to competence, or statements about the dark itself. Children in the competence group, for instance, were asked to say, "I am a brave boy (girl). I can take care of myself in the dark," whereas subjects in the stimulus group were instructed in statements about the dark itself such as, "The dark is a fun place to be. There are many good things in the dark." The overall results were viewed from a self-control interpretation and indicated that the group instructed in competence statements was superior to the other two groups:

> Thus, the competence group may have shown greater tolerance because the verbal controlling responses represented self-instructions to behave like a brave boy or girl, with the expectation of social approval and self-reinforcement based upon past encouragements to act competently. (Kanfer *et al.*, 1975, p. 257)

If coping self-statements do serve as self-instructions as Kanfer *et al.* suggest, it remains unclear whether they essentially function as plys or tracks. However, the finding that competence statements were more effective than statements about the dark itself and the appeal made to social factors in interpreting this outcome suggest that coping self-statements may often produce pliance rather than tracking. Children in the competence group were essentially instructed to engage in public statements about their behavior ("I can take care of myself in the dark."), while subjects in the factual group were in effect engaging in descriptive statements about the dark itself. The statements of the children in the competence group appear to have served the same function as public resolutions about one's behavior or, alternatively, as mands issued by another speaker. In either case, the behavior of following such rules would be expected to be controlled in part by socially mediated consequences. For this reason, the statements of children in the competence group apparently resulted in pliance. By contrast, the statements of the factual group resemble tacts about the dark and would be expected to result in increased darkness tolerance to the extent that they were found to be accurate. When children tested such tracks by finding out that the dark is not "a fun place to be," the ability of such statements to control behavior could be greatly weakened.

2. Coping Self-Statements as Plys

The possibility that coping self-statements may primarily control pliance rather than tracking was evaluated recently by the authors (Zettle & Hayes, 1979). If coping self-statements are plys, they should be affected by the variables of which pliance is a function. For example, if they are plys the effectiveness of coping self-statements should vary to the degree that both the statements themselves as well as the behaviors to which they make reference are publicly accessible. Both conditions are generally met in clinical cognitive restructuring procedures. In a typical clinical application of coping self-statements, for instance, the therapist may instruct an anxious client to rehearse particular self-statements out loud while subsequently observing his behavior while confronting an anxiety-provoking situation. The therapist can thus monitor the degree to which the client in fact complies with the statement he has made about his behavior. If, on the other hand, coping self-statements function as tracks, their effectiveness should presumably not be affected by whether or not they are stated publicly.

Speech-anxious college students were randomly assigned to either a control group or to one of two experimental groups. Control group subjects received no coping self-statements while subjects in both experimental groups selected a coping self-statement ("I can remain calm and relaxed by taking deep breaths and talking more slowly.") from a bag supposedly (but not actually) containing many different statements. The two experimental groups differed only in the degree to which the coping self-statement which they were to use was apparently made known to the experimenter. Subjects in a social context group were asked to read out loud to the experimenter the coping self-statement they selected. Subjects in a private self-statement group received the same self-statement but merely read it to themselves (and thus believed the experimenter did not know their rule). Social context subjects thus made an overt purposive statement about their behavior during speeches while private condition subjects engaged in the same self-rule but at a completely covert level.

The results may be viewed as providing preliminary support for a rule-governed account of coping self-statements as plys. On self-report measures of speech anxiety, only the social context group showed improvement over the private condition and control groups. More specifically, subjects in the social context group reported feeling less anxious about their speeches and more helped by the procedure than those in the other two groups. The only difference among the groups on behavioral measures indicated that subjects in the social context group had followed the coping self-statement by talking more slowly. The coping self-statement per se had no effect on self-report or behavioral indicants of anxiety as demonstrated by the lack of differences between the private condition and control group. The coping self-statement was effective only when it was made public and thus appears to have functioned as a ply (under the control of the social consequences) rather than a track (under the control of the correspondence between the rule and the way the world is arranged).

3. Coping Self-Statements as Competing Rules

A final possibility is that coping self-statements function by replacing or competing with negative self-statements. There are some data (e.g., see Craighead, Kimball, & Rehak, 1979; Kendall, Williams, Pechacek, Graham, Shisslak, & Herzof, 1979) that suggest that an absence of negative self-statements is more important than the presence of positive self-statements in many clinical problems (see also Kendall & Hollon, 1981). Coping self-statements may work by competing with and replacing negative self-statements in some people. As analyzed earlier, negative thoughts are often destructive rules and clinical benefits from their elimination would be expected.

C. Implications for Treatment

Conceptualizing coping self-statements as plys would appear to have several implications for treatment procedures that incorporate them. Since pliance cannot be mediated by a rule giver unless the behavior to be engaged in is clearly specified, coping self-statements that more closely specify the relevant behavior should result in greater change than others which do so in a vague manner. For instance, a coping self-statement such as, "I can remain calm and relaxed by talking at a steady pace," should be more effective in reducing speech anxiety than one which merely states, "I can remain calm and relaxed." Since pliance also cannot be mediated unless the behavior specified by the rule can be monitored, coping self-statements should be most effective when they are public and when the therapist can directly observe the actions of clients in confronting and interacting with anxiety-provoking situations.

Thus, coping self-statements may operate primarily through the social influence that a therapist exerts over clients. They direct the behavior of clients toward a stimulus situation they might otherwise avoid. It seems probable that exposure by clients to anxiety-eliciting stimuli, which following coping self-statements provides, is of considerable importance in any substantial reductions of anxiety that occur.

If the present analysis of coping statements is correct, this treatment approach should be most successful in relatively minor disorders, susceptible to social influence. Most of the studies to date have examined just such problems. A second implication is that more general disorders of rule formulation would not be treated. Essentially, the therapist is establishing a new set of rules to follow without attacking directly the formulation of self-rules. The effects, therefore, should be relatively specific. Indeed, the literature tends to confirm this (e.g., Hussian & Lawrence, 1978).

VIII. RULE-GOVERNED BEHAVIOR AND THE COGNITIVE TREATMENT OF DEPRESSION

A. Current Status

Perhaps one of the most highly regarded of the cognitive behavior therapies currently in use is Beck's cognitive treatment of depression. Its status can be accounted for by the success it has shown in the treatment of a highly prevalent and potentially life-threatening affective disorder. For instance, outpatient nonbipolar depressives receiving cognitive therapy have demonstrated greater improvement than those treated with antidepressant medication (Rush, Beck, Kovacs, & Hollon, 1977). This effect has been maintained over a 1-year follow-up period (Kovacs, Beck, Rush, & Hollon, 1978). In addition, both acute and chronic depressives have been shown to improve with cognitive therapy, while pharmacological treatment has been primarily successful with chronically depressed clients (Rush, Hollon, Beck, & Kovacs, 1978). Additional outcome research attesting to the efficacy of the cognitive treatment of depression has recently been reviewed by Beck and his associates (Beck *et al.*, 1979; Hollon & Beck, 1979) and will not be detailed here.

B. Cognitive Basis of Depression

According to a cognitive view of depression, this affective disorder is "in part, a consequence of pervasive, negative misconstructions of objective experiences" (Hollon & Beck, 1979, p. 154). In particular, Beck (1967) has argued that depressed clients exhibit what he has labeled "the negative cognitive triad," consisting of a regard for themselves as defeated, deprived, or diseased, for their worlds as full of obstacles preventing the achievement of satisfactions, and for their futures as pessimistic, without any hope of improvement. More specific examples of the negative cognitive triad are detailed by Beck's classification of logical distortions which characterize the thinking of depressed individuals:

> 1. *Selective abstraction* (a stimulus set); forming a conclusion regarding a particular event on the basis of an isolated detail, while ignoring contradictory and more salient evidence.
> 2. *Arbitrary inference* (a response set); drawing a conclusion in the absence of evidence.
> 3. *Overgeneralization* (a response set); extracting a belief or rule on the basis of a particular event and applying that concept in an unjustifiable fashion to other dissimilar situations.
> 4. *Magnification* (a response set); the overestimation of the significance or magnitude of undesirable consequent events.
> 5. *All-or-none thinking* (a response set); the tendency to think in absolute terms. (Hollon & Beck, 1979, pp. 156–157)

According to a cognitive view of depression, such distorted thinking by clients not only results in a depressed affect but also leads to behavioral deficits commonly noted in depressed clients.

1. Problem of Inference

All types of cognitive behavioral treatments maintain that the disorders they deal with to a large degree are cognitively based, or stated somewhat differently, rule-governed. A problematic issue facing cognitive procedures is that clients are sometimes thought to be engaging in particular types of self-statements because their behavior is dysfunctional. Such inferences, however, are derived from the very behavior they attempt to explain.

While all cognitive approaches are affected by this issue, it is less problematic in Beck's approach than in Ellis's or Meichenbaum's. For instance, as already suggested, rational–emotive theory uses a relatively deductive approach to determine the particular irrational beliefs clients may have. The cognitive approach outlined by Beck appears to be more inductive. Particular depressive self-statements which are identified are more a client's "own," rather than inferred beliefs which clients are persuaded to accept as the basis for their present difficulties. On this point, Beck has pointed out several distinctions he draws between his own cognitive approach and a rational–emotive one:

> In cognitive therapy, the process of identification is largely inductive, at least with respect to the individual client. Even though the therapist begins early in treatment to try to generate and to test hypotheses regarding potential assumptions, the evidence for and testing these hypotheses is closely tied to the monitored cognitive and behavioral data presented by the client. Thus, client and therapist

work collaboratively to attempt to identify attitudes or beliefs that run through the client's life. In rational–emotive therapy, the process is one of deduction. Efforts are made to demonstrate to the client that he or she does hold to one or more of the identified universe of irrational beliefs. (Hollon & Beck, 1979, p. 192)

2. Rules and Cognitive Distortions

As we have done throughout this article, we will assume that a cognitive view of depression is basically sound in order to offer a rule-governed account of this perspective. In this regard, the general classes of logical distortions Beck believes characterize the thinking of depressed clients may be conceptualized as disorders in rule formulation and rule following. For instance, errors in selective abstraction, arbitrary inference, and overgeneralization all suggest a tendency by depressive clients to formulate inaccurate and untestable rules. The rules that are formulated may have the form of tacts and clients track them *as if* they specified relationships among events in the environment. The rule following which is generated is insensitive to the natural consequences which are produced.

Some of these types of errors may be especially destructive because the specific type of rule has been successful in the past. For example, some types of selective abstraction or arbitrary inference may have previously fostered socially desirable behaviors such as achievement. Suppose a person followed the self-track "I'm becoming a tremendous success in psychology." In fact, little or no data may have existed to support this statement. Nevertheless, it may have supported the kind of hard work needed to achieve professional recognition. Should such a person enter a deep depression, the same type of rule ("I'm becoming a tremendous failure") may not be terribly maladaptive.

It is known that formerly successful rules are particularly likely to be followed, even when they are no longer functional (e.g., Galazio, 1979). Thus, such disorders of rule formulation may be particularly difficult to treat.

C. Cognitive Treatment of Depression

Beck's cognitive treatment of depression may be viewed as training clients to tact variables controlling their own behavior and subsequently to track such rules. Stated somewhat differently, the attempt is to replace inaccurate and untestable rules which may be contributing to a client's depression with rules that are controlled by events with which clients have direct contact. Behavior subsequently controlled by such rules may be viewed as tracking. It is relatively sensitive to the natural contingencies since they are described in the formulated rules.

D. Therapeutic Components

While Beck prefers to refer to his specific approach to the treatment of depression as cognitive therapy, he has emphasized its incorporation of both cognitive and behavioral components and its differentiation from cognitive–semantic approaches, such as RET, which rely more on semantic or persuasive techniques (Beck, 1964, 1967, 1970).

1. Cognitive Components: Training in Tact-Formulation

Beck has maintained that verbal interactions between client and therapist should be collaborative rather than persuasive and confrontational, as advocated by Ellis. In following such an approach, the therapist avoids issuing mands to clients. This decreases possible client counterpliance and increases the importance of tracking controlled by rules formulated in collaboration with the therapist. Beck, in articulating this general "therapeutic climate" conducive to effective treatment, has stated:

> The basic strategy that underlies interaction between client and therapist is one of *collaborative empiricism*. Client and therapist serve as active collaborators in the identification of problem areas and in the design and execution of tests of the various beliefs. The data generated by these tests, rather than therapist credibility or authority, are relied upon to provide understanding and to produce change. The client is not persuaded to change by the therapist; rather, the evidence generated by the client in unbiased experiments is allowed to speak for itself. (Hollon & Beck, 1979, pp. 180–181)

Such an approach in effect seeks to establish more accurate self-rule formulation in clients. It also appears to be less anxiety-provoking than directly confronting clients with the inappropriateness of their self-statements. Rogers and Craighead (1977) assessed the impact of the degree of discrepancy among the self-statements they employed upon emotional arousal. Degree of discrepancy was "defined as the conceptual distance between a subject's belief about one's self and the belief inherent in the presented self-statement" (Rogers & Craighead, 1977, p. 102). The finding of a significant interaction between the valence of self-statements (positive vs negative) and degree of discrepancy lead Rogers and Craighead (1977) to conclude that:

The skin conductance interaction results support the notion that an incremental modification of self-verbalization would more likely produce attenuation of physiological arousal than would an all-or-none (highly discrepant) approach. The implied relationship is that decreases in autonomic arousal should correspond with subjective feelings of relief. It would thus seem that the method employed by Beck (1976) is less likely to cause undue physiological arousal than is Ellis's technique (p. 115).

Specific cognitive techniques within Beck's approach, such as identifying automatic thoughts and evaluating thought content, constitute training in identifying specific depressive self-statements and formulating more accurate and testable rules. In this regard, Beck has emphasized the necessity of clients being able to "distance" themselves from their beliefs, or stated somewhat differently, being able to observe their own verbal behavior from the perspective of a listener. Over time, self-rules are often not viewed critically by the person formulating them. The usual listener behaviors in a public interaction (e.g., examining the credibility of the statement and the speaker; recognizing that reality and descriptions of it may not always be in harmony; and so on) may be gradually suspended for self-rules. This has several destructive effects. For example, augmenting functions may occur automatically— in a sense, the person-as-listener may become needlessly emotionally invested in a particular view of things. Similarly, obvious impure tacts or intraverbals may be seen as tacts in a way they never would be for others' rules. Distancing allows self-rules to be viewed as behavior of an organism—not as literal reality or as the organism itself.

This process is similar to training in the application of the scientific method, as evidenced by Mahoney's (1974, 1977) advocacy of a "personal science" approach to cognitive therapy. Like scientists, clients are guided by the therapist to reformulate their beliefs as testable hypotheses whose accuracy can then be evaluated through homework assignments. For any such hypothesis to be truly testable, it must attempt to tact a relationship between behavior and other variables. Tacts are the language of experience—of direct contact with the world. Beck's therapy can be thought of as training in tact formulation.

2. Behavioral Components: Training in Tracking

Beck has outlined several behavioral techniques, such as graded task assignment and activity scheduling, that comprise his cognitive therapy for depression. Of primary importance for the current analysis are homework assignments in which clients are essentially given an opportunity to "test out" specific hypotheses they have formulated from their beliefs. This strategy may be conceptualized as providing clients training in tracking. Clients are essentially encouraged to evaluate the accuracy of their rules, once they have been reformulated into testable hypotheses, in determining to what degree they actually specify relevant contingencies. For example, the belief of a depressed executive that "I can't get anything done" may be reformulated into the hypothesis of "Fewer than 50% of new projects I receive are delegated to others within a week of when I receive them." This specific hypothesis can subsequently be confirmed or disconfirmed by the client gathering the relevant data through self-monitoring procedures. Given the likelihood that the client's hypothesis is shown to be inaccurate, more accurate tracks can be formulated in their place. Hollon and Beck (1979) in commenting on this process have observed:

> The explicit *disconfirmation* of stated beliefs by means of direct, self-monitored experiences following from the client's own activities is followed by a discussion of the contingencies involved and the conclusions that can be drawn. Such a procedure involving both enactive and cognitive-symbolic components, is seen as the optimal paradigm for generating cognitive changes and for maximizing the generality of the behavioral procedures. Instead of "getting the client moving," such a combination increases the probability of the client's being able to challenge successfully anticipated nongratification or fantasized incompetence in future situations. Similarly, rather than simply mobilizing the client in the face of negative expectations, the client is trained to evaluate systematically such predictions, putting the beliefs to an unbiased test, eventually learning that it is the negative expectations that are inaccurate. (pp. 184–185)

Given that the skills of tact formulation and tracking that clients acquire through cognitive therapy are likely to be sensitive to and be maintained by the natural contingencies surrounding important behavior, it is not surprising that any treatment gains would generalize and be maintained across time. Beck's approach, in comparison to the approach of Ellis and Meichenbaum, is probably most consistent with the approach implied by the conceptual system developed here.

IX. RULE-GOVERNED BEHAVIOR AND PSYCHOPATHOLOGY

The purpose of the present article is to begin to develop rule-governed behavior as a theoretical framework for considering cognitive–behavioral therapy. There is a danger that the analysis might become a mere post hoc explanation for established techniques. For example, Dollard and Miller's (1950) pioneering effort has been so regarded and its impact was less than its potential as a result. The present analysis, however, could conceivably form the basis of a more general approach to psychopathology and its treatment. While this is extremely speculative, some possible directions can be seen.

A. Mechanisms of Psychopathology

1. Pathological Rule Formulation

One general mechanism of psychopathology according to a rule-governed analysis is dysfunctional rule formulation. The most obvious examples involve self-rules. We are less likely to doubt ourselves than someone else. For this reason, inappropriate self-rules are likely to lead to rule following and maladaptive results.

One common error in rule formulation has been analyzed extensively above: the formulation of self-rules which appear to be based on tacts but are not. These self-rules are often based upon impure tacts or intraverbal behavior. Such rules generally are in tact form and may successfully produce tracking. Tracking under such conditions, however, is "blind" and may often appear insensitive to its natural consequences. Clinical manifestations of self-deception (Knapp, 1980) and rationalization (Zettle, 1980a) provide clear examples.

The destructive effect of tracking nontact rules depends heavily on the specific rule involved. The belief that "everyone loves me" may not be as destructive as "everyone must love me," even though both might be nonexperientially based. (The first statement could be a tact, although it is unlikely.) The tendency to formulate and track nonexperiental (nontact) rules, however, might be a general response class. If so, even harmless self-rules of this sort could be part of a generally maladaptive response pattern.

Other self-rules may function as plys. For example, the statement "I am going to exercise every day for a week" may be followed as if following it was due simply to its being said. In other words, the person may not be able to give reasons for doing it, but seems to be doing it "just because I said I would." Often these are stated publicly, thus engaging possible social consequences. These self-plys can be pathological under some circumstances. Unlike tracking, the whole purpose of pliance is to produce an insensitivity to immediate environmental contingencies. Pliance to public rules is often established when insensitivity is required (e.g., "Junior, don't touch the hot stove"). By adding in speaker-mediated contingencies for rule following, natural contingencies may be overridden. A similar process occurs with self-plys. If this is useful (in the exercise example it may well

be), self-pliance is healthy. But it can be destructive when there is no
need for insensitivity. For example, a person may follow the rule,
"I'm going to be a millionaire no matter what." If this produces emotional and interpersonal carnage, reevaluation of such a goal would
be desirable, but may not occur. Thus, self-plys can be formulated
pathologically if their precise content is destructive.

In addition to self-rules, the formulation of public rules can also be
maladaptive. The verbal behaviors of the pathological liar, psycho-
pathic con artist, sociopathic gang leader, or manipulative histrionic
are examples. Such instances involve separate speakers and listeners
and the rule-following behavior of the listener (e.g., the "easy mark"
or the gang member) may also often be regarded as maladaptive.

2. Pathological Rule Following

There are two types of problems in maladaptive rule following. One
involves "errors in translation" in verbal interactions between particular speakers and listeners. Specific aspects of a speaker's verbal behavior (e.g., tone of voice or use of certain words) may exert incorrect
discriminative control over the listener—it is often difficult to know
what a speaker is "really saying."

The slippage in this system can produce particular listener histories
that will lead to serious difficulties. Since so much of our behavior
is rule governed, any unusual tendencies in discerning and following
rules will radically alter a listener's world. For example, if the listener
is unable to distinguish tacts from mands, possibly as a result of their
historical similarity in form in the listener's world, he might be expected to respond to tacts issued by the speaker as if they were plys
or vice versa. This would be most likely to occur with a specific
speaker (with whom the listener has had this type of history) but
generalization to other speakers might also occur. Such a person may
seem to set up others in an authority role. Some may then follow these
tacts as plys ("passive-dependency"), or attempt to undermine them
("passive-aggressive"). Any disorder in the tendency to interpret others
would certainly have pervasive and profound effects, perhaps leading
to typical patterns of maladaptive behavior which have traditionally
been referred to as "personality disorders." Behaviors denoted by a
personality disorder may resemble traits (e.g., in their cross-situational
consistency) but they may also be conceptualized as a response class
under the control of aspects of rules that are pervasive and part of all
interpersonal interactions. Thus, a single core difficulty could have
quite general effects.

Even if rules are accurately discerned, a second type of problem is possible: they may be followed pathologically. For example, a person whose pliance has consistently been achieved through highly aversive means or to serve the whims of the speaker, may tend later to show counterpliance in response to reasonable plys. The rebellious individual with "difficulty relating to authority" is an example. Similarly, a person exposed to an inconsistent or unpredictable environment may never learn to follow tracks well. The lower class individual who does not stay in school because "school doesn't really help you get a job—that's just jive" may be an example.

Similar difficulties can occur with self-rules. Inability to show proper self-pliance or tendencies to show self-counterpliance are common. For example, a person with a weight problem may say, "I won't eat for three more hours" and immediately be overwhelmed by hunger, unable to think of anything but food, and finally, give in and eat. This kind of self-defeating behavior may amount to a kind of self-counterpliance, quite similar to its public form. Others are simply unable to make commitments to themselves and to follow them. This lack of self-pliance can be destructive when some insensitivity to immediate contingencies is needed in order to come under the control of more remote consequences. Persons with this difficulty are commonly said to be impulsive, untrustworthy, self-destructive, or lacking in self-control.

B. Mechanisms of Therapeutic Change

1. Formulating "Tactful" Tracks

As we have suggested, maladaptive tracking appears typically to result when the rules involved are not tacts. Accordingly, a general strategy for therapeutic change is to encourage clients to replace formulations about their behavior and its consequences which are intraverbals or impure tacts (e.g., "That's terrible!," "God, am I anxious!," "I can't do anything right!"), with formulations that are restricted to tacts (e.g., "I received an F on my exam," "My palms are sweaty," "I completed three reports on time"). Any behavior controlled by such "tactful" tracks is apt to be more flexible and sensitive to its actual consequences. Such a strategy seems to underlie the success of Beck's cognitive treatment of depression and may be a major mechanism involved in insight-oriented psychotherapies (Zettle, 1980a), or in growth-oriented interventions such as est (cf. Baer & Stolz, 1978).

Other available treatments focus on instructing speakers to formulate tacts, as opposed to mands and intraverbals, in their interactions with certain listeners. "Communication training" for couples in marital therapy and Parent Effectiveness Training, for instance, may be conceptualized as employing this general strategy.

2. Formulating Plys

Behavior therapists have long emphasized the importance of proper client goal-setting both for oneself and others. Issues such as specificity, immediacy, and discernibility in goals set may amount to training in proper ply formulation. These dimensions allow the individual to know when a ply has been met. In the case of self-plys, this may begin to expose the individual to the natural consequences of doing (or not doing) what you say you are going to do. These consequences may then capture and support self-pliance. In the case of public plys it may allow the individual to experience a more predictable world and may increase the likelihood of pliance.

Other aspects of ply formulation are also important. Every ply implies a state of reinforceability in the speaker. The rule itself should be in contact with the actual reinforcers. For example, the statement "I'm going to be a millionaire" is presumably based upon the apparent beneficial aspects of being rich. In fact, these aspects may not be reinforcers for a given individual. For that person, such a rule may not be desirable. Plys can also specify behavior not in the person's repertoire (or capable of becoming so). People with "unrealistic standards" show this pattern.

3. Rule Following

The treatment of disorders of rule following is not well advanced. Difficulties occur in two areas: failure to discern rules accurately and failure to follow rules. Errors in discerning rules are extraordinarily difficult to treat because the therapist's own verbal behavior is also likely to be misunderstood. One case occurs when tacts produce pliance or counterpliance. In such instances, the client may believe that the therapist has some personal stake in advice being offered. Some therapist strategies in this case might include (a) avoiding all statements in mand form (including autoclitics such as "must"), (b) discussing the potential confusion itself, (c) encouraging self-testing of apparent tacts, (d) encouraging more self-rule formulation and following, especially "tactful" tracks, (e) avoiding obvious differential reinforcement from the therapist for rule following (i.e., use "unconditional positive regard"), and (f) manding behavior opposite that desired, as in "paradoxical intention" (Frankl, 1960).

At times mands (perhaps in tact form) may produce tracking. This is likely to be reflected in things such as excessively moralistic behavior or in extreme conformity. In this case, confrontation might be useful, especially if it is paradoxical, so as to break down mand rule following. Training in self-rule formulation and following may also be helpful.

Disorders of rule following include such things as (a) showing excessive counterpliance to plys, (b) showing little or no pliance, (c) failing to track adaptive rules, and (d) tracking destructive rules. All of these can involve either public or self-rules. The general strategy in each case might be to arrange conditions in which a better history of successful rule following can be built. For example, the person showing little or no pliance may need at first to be in a restrictive environment in which pliance can be produced in response to reasonable demands. Gradually, social controls could be loosened as the successful results of pliance begin to take hold. Some group homes, or even organizations such as Synanon, can be thought of in this light. Unfortunately, no concrete advice can be offered in these areas because so little is known. The general outlines of an approach based on this analysis are clear, however.

This article has attempted to argue that behaviorists should attend to the concept of rule-governed behavior and explore the potential relevance of Skinner's (1957) analysis of verbal behavior to the therapeutic environment. In our view, a more thorough understanding of rule-governed behavior in particular, and verbal behavior more generally, may help provide solutions to several thorny clinical problems and may expand the scope of behavior therapy. Areas such as personality disorders or psychological growth have hardly been touched by behaviorists—the present analysis suggests ways in which we may begin. Finally, the present analysis may offer an alternative conceptual framework for cognitive–behavioral therapy and semantic therapy more generally. Whether such a bold statement is justified will depend on future empirical and conceptual work on the concept of rule-governed behavior.

REFERENCES

Baer, D. M., & Stolz, S. B. A description of the Erhard seminars training (est) in the terms of behavior analysis. *Behaviorism*, 1978, **6**(1), 45–70.

Bandura, A. Self-reinforcement: Theoretical and methodological considerations. *Behaviorism*, 1976, **4**(2), 135–155.

Bandura, A. *Social learning theory*. New York: Prentice-Hall, 1977.

Beck, A. T. Thinking and depression: II. Theory and therapy. *Archives of General Psychiatry*, 1964, **10**, 561–571.

Beck, A. T. *Depression: Clinical, experimental, and theoretical aspects*. New York: Harper, 1967.

Beck, A. T. Cognitive therapy: Nature and relation to behavior therapy. *Behavior Therapy*, 1970, **1**, 184–200.

Beck, A. T. *Cognitive therapy and the emotional disorders*. New York: International Universities Press, 1976.

Beck, A. T., Rush, A. J., Shaw, B., & Emery, G. *Cognitive therapy of depression*. New York: Guilford, 1979.

Becker, I. M., & Rosenfeld, J. G. Rational emotive therapy—a study of initial therapy sessions of Albert Ellis. *Journal of Clinical Psychology*, 1976, **32**, 872–876.

Brehm, J. W. *A theory of psychological reactance*. New York: Academic Press, 1966.

Catania, A. C. The myth of self-reinforcement. *Behaviorism*, 1975, 3(2), 192–199.

Catania, A. C. Self-reinforcement revisited. *Behaviorism*, 1976, **4**(2), 157–162.

Craighead, W. E., Kimball, W. H., & Rehak, P. J. Mood changes, physiological responses, and self-statements during social rejection imagery. *Journal of Consulting and Clinical Psychology*, 1979, **47**, 385–396.

DiGiuseppe, R. A., Miller, N. J., & Trexler, L. D. A review of rational-emotive psychotherapy outcome studies. *The Counseling Psychologist*, 1977, **7**, 64–72.

DiLoreto, A. D. A comparison of the relative effectiveness of systematic desensitization, rational-emotive and client-centered group psychotherapy in the reduction of interpersonal anxiety in introverts and extroverts (Doctoral dissertation, Michigan State University, 1969). *Dissertation Abstracts International*, 1970, **30**, 5230A–5231A. (University Microfilms No. 70-9521).

Dollard, J., & Miller, N. E. *Personality and psychotherapy: An analysis in terms of learning, thinking, and culture*. New York: McGraw-Hill, 1950.

Dowd, E. T. *Cognitive Behavior Therapy Newsletter. Association for Advancement of Behavior Therapy*, 1978, **1**(1).

Ellis, A. *Reason and emotion in psychotherapy*. Secaucus, New Jersey: Stuart, 1962.

Ellis, A. *Humanistic psychotherapy*. New York: McGraw-Hill, 1973. (a)

Ellis, A. Rational-emotive therapy. In R. Corsini (Ed.), *Current psychotherapies*. Itasca, Illinois: Peacock, 1973. (b)

Ellis, A. Rational-emotive therapy and cognitive behavior therapy: Similarities and differences. *Cognitive Therapy and Research*, 1980, **4**(4), 325–340.

Ellis, A., & Harper, R. A. *A new guide to rational living*. New York: Prentice-Hall, 1975.

Frankl, V. E. Paradoxical intention: A logotherapeutic technique. *American Journal of Psychotherapy*, 1960, **14**, 520–535.

Fremouw, W. J., & Zitter, R. E. A comparison of skills training and cognitive restructuring-relaxation for the treatment of speech anxiety. *Behavior Therapy*, 1978, **9**, 248–259.

Galizio, M. Contingency-shaped and rule-governed behavior: Instructional control of human loss avoidance. *Journal of the Experimental Analysis of Behavior*, 1979, **31**, 53–70.

Garfield, S. L., & Kurtz, R. Clinical psychologists in the 1970's. *American Psychologist*, 1976, **31**, 1–9.

Germer, W. A. Effectiveness of cognitive modification, desensitization, and rational-emotive therapy in the treatment of speech anxiety (Doctoral dissertation, University of Texas at Austin, 1975). *Dissertation Abstracts International*, 1975, **36**, 907B–908B. (University Microfilms No. 75-16, 674).

Glogower, F. D., Fremouw, W. J., & McCroskey, J. C. A component analysis of cognitive restructuring. *Cognitive Therapy and Research*, 1978, **2**(3), 209–223.

Goldfried, M. R. Anxiety reduction through cognitive-behavioral intervention. In P. C. Kendall & S. D. Hollon (Eds.), *Cognitive-behavioral interventions: Theory, research, and procedures*. New York: Academic Press, 1979.

Goldfried, M. R., Linehan, M. M., & Smith, J. L. The reduction of test anxiety through rational restructuring. *Journal of Consulting and Clinical Psychology*, 1978, **46**, 32–39.

Gregg, G. The rational therapist: Epictetus, not Freud. *Psychology Today*, 1973, **1**(2), 61.

Harris, J. C. *The complete tales of Uncle Remus*. Boston, Massachusetts: Houghton-Mifflin, 1955.

Hayes, S. C., Hussian, R. W., Turner, A., Anderson, N., & Grubb, T. *The nature, effect, and generalization of "coping statements" in the treatment of clinical anxiety: Alternating treatments design*. Paper presented at the meeting of the Association for Advancement of Behavior Therapy, San Francisco, December 1979.

Hayes, S. C., & Maley, R. F. Coercion: Legal and behavioral issues. *Behaviorism*, 1977, **5**(2), 87–95.

Hayes, S. C., Rincover, A., & Solnick, J. V. The technical drift of applied behavior analysis. *Journal of Applied Behavior Analysis*, 1980, **13**, 275–285.

Hollon, S. D., & Beck, A. T. Cognitive therapy of depression. In P. C. Kendall & S. D. Hollon (Eds.), *Cognitive-behavioral interventions: Theory, research, and procedures*. New York: Academic Press, 1979.

Holroyd, K. A. Cognition and desensitization in the group treatment of test anxiety. *Journal of Consulting and Clinical Psychology*, 1976, **44**, 991–1001.

Hussian, R. W., & Lawrence, P. S. The reduction of test, state, and trait anxiety by test-specific and generalized stress inoculation training. *Cognitive Therapy and Research*, 1978, **2**(1), 25–37.

Jarmon, G. J. Differential effectiveness of rational-emotive therapy, bibliotherapy, and attention-placebo in the treatment of speech anxiety (Doctoral dissertation, Southern Illinois University, 1972). *Dissertation Abstracts International*, 1973, **33**, 4510B. (University Microfilms No. 73-6217).

Kanfer, F. H. Self-regulation: Research, issues, and speculations. In C. Neuringer & J. L. Michael (Eds.), *Behavior modification in clinical psychology*. New York: Appleton, 1970.

Kanfer, F. H. The maintenance of behavior by self-generated stimuli and reinforcement. In A. Jacobs & L. B. Sachs (Eds.), *The psychology of private events*. New York: Academic Press, 1971.

Kanfer, F. H. The many faces of self-control, or behavior modification changes its focus. In R. B. Stuart (Ed.), *Behavioral self-management: Strategies, techniques, and outcomes*. New York: Brunner/Mazel, 1977.

Kanfer, F. H., & Karoly, P. Self-control: A behavioristic excursion into the lion's den. *Behavior Therapy*, 1972, **3**, 398–416.

Kanfer, F. H., Karoly, P., & Newman, A. Reduction of children's fear of the dark by competence-related and situational threat-related verbal cues. *Journal of Consulting and Clinical Psychology*, 1975, **43**(2), 251–258.

Kanter, N. J. A comparison of self-control desensitization and rational restructuring for the reduction of interpersonal anxiety (Doctoral dissertation, State University of New York at Stony Brook, 1975). *Dissertation Abstracts International*, 1976, **36,** 3611B. (University Microfilms No. 76-792, 392).

Karst, T. O., & Trexler, L. D. Initial study using fixed-role and rational-emotive therapy in treating public-speaking anxiety. *Journal of Consulting and Clinical Psychology*, 1970, **34,** 360–366.

Kazdin, A. E. *History of behavior modification: Experimental foundations of contemporary research.* Baltimore, Maryland: University Park Press, 1978.

Kendall, P. C., & Hollon, S. D. (Eds.). *Cognitive-behavioral interventions: Theory, research, and procedures.* New York: Academic Press, 1979.

Kendall, P. C., & Hollon, S. D. (Eds.). *Assessment strategies for cognitive-behavioral interventions.* New York: Academic Press, 1981.

Kendall, P. C., Williams, L., Pechacek, T. F., Graham, L. E., Shisslak, C., & Herzof, N. Cognitive–behavioral and patient education interventions in cardiac catheterization procedures: The Palo Alto medical psychology project. *Journal of Consulting and Clinical Psychology*, 1979, **47,** 48–59.

Kiesler, D. Some myths of psychotherapy research and the search for a paradigm. *Psychological Record*, 1966, **65,** 110–136.

Knapp, T. Psychoanalysis, behavior analysis, and self-deception. In S. C. Hayes (Chair), *The baby and the bathwater: Radical behavioral interpretations of traditional clinical phenomena.* Symposium presented at the meeting of the Association for Advancement of Behavior Therapy, New York 1980.

Kovacs, M., Beck, A. T., Rush, A. J., & Hollon, S. D. *Comparative efficacy of cognitive therapy and pharmacotherapy in the treatment of depressed outpatients: A 12-month follow-up.* Unpublished manuscript, University of Pittsburgh, 1978.

Mahoney, M. J. *Cognition and behavior modification.* Cambridge, Massachusetts: Ballinger, 1974.

Mahoney, M. J. Personal science: A cognitive learning therapy. In A. Ellis & R. Grieger (Eds.), *Handbook of rational psychotherapy.* New York: Springer, 1977.

Mahoney, M. J., Arnkoff, D. B. Cognitive and self-control therapies. In S. L. Garfield & A. E. Bergin (Eds.), *Handbook of psychotherapy and behavior change* (2nd ed.). New York: Wiley, 1978.

Meichenbaum, D. H. Cognitive modification of test anxious college students. *Journal of Consulting and Clinical Psychology*, 1972, **39,** 370–380.

Meichenbaum, D. H. *Cognitive behavior modification.* Morristown, New Jersey: General Learning Press, 1974.

Meichenbaum, D. H. *Cognitive-behavior modification: An integrative approach.* New York: Plenum, 1977.

Meichenbaum, D. H., & Cameron, R. *An examination of cognitive and contingency variables in anxiety relief procedures.* Unpublished manuscript, University of Waterloo, 1972.

Meichenbaum, D. H., & Cameron, R. The clinical potential of modifying what clients say to themselves. *Psychotherapy: Theory, Research, and Practice*, 1974, **11,** 103–117.

Meichenbaum, D. H., Gilmore, J. B., & Fedoravicius, A. Group insight versus desensitization in treating speech anxiety. *Journal of Consulting and Clinical Psychology*, 1971, **36,** 410–421.

Meichenbaum, D. H., & Turk, D. The cognitive-behavioral management of anxiety, anger, and pain. In P. O. Davidson (Ed.), *The behavioral management of anxiety, depression, and pain.* New York: Brunner/Mazel, 1976.

Moleski, R., & Tosi, D. J. Comparative psychotherapy: Rational-emotive therapy versus systematic desensitization in treating speech anxiety. *Journal of Consulting and Clinical Psychology*, 1976, **44**, 309–311.

Munt, E. D., Hayes, S. C., and Nelson, R. O. *The effects of immediate environmental factors on a self-reinforcement procedure designed to improve reading comprehension skill.* Paper presented at the meeting of the Association for Advancement of Behavior Therapy, San Francisco, December 1979.

Novaco, R. W. *Anger control: The development and evaluation of an experimental treatment.* Lexington, Massachusetts: Heath, 1975.

Novaco, R. W. Treatment of chronic anger through cognitive and relaxation controls. *Journal of Consulting and Clinical Psychology*, 1976, **44**, 681.

Novaco, R. W. The cognitive regulation of anger and stress. In P. C. Kendall & S. D. Hollon (Eds.), *Cognitive-behavioral interventions: Theory, research, and procedures.* New York: Academic Press, 1979.

Rachlin, H. Self-control. *Behaviorism*, 1974, **2**, 94–107.

Rimm, D. C., & Litvak, S. B. Self-verbalization and emotional arousal. *Journal of Abnormal Psychology*, 1969, **74**, 181–187.

Rogers, T., & Craighead, W. E. Physiological responses to self-statements: The effects of statement valence and discrepancy. *Cognitive Therapy and Research*, 1977, **1**, 99–119.

Rosenfarb, I., & Hayes, S. C., & Zettle, R. D. *Public versus private goal-setting and self-reinforcement of academic behavior.* Paper presented at the meeting of the Association for Behavior Analysis, Milwaukee, May 1981.

Rush, A. J., Beck, A. T., Kovacs, M., & Hollon, S. D. Comparative efficacy of cognitive therapy versus pharmacotherapy in outpatient depressives. *Cognitive Therapy and Research*, 1977, **1**, 17–37.

Rush, A. J., Hollon, S. D., Beck, A. T., & Kovacs, M. Depression: Must pharmacotherapy fail for cognitive therapy to succeed? *Cognitive Therapy and Research*, 1978, **2**, 199–206.

Russell, P. L., & Brandsma, J. M. A theoretical and empirical integration of the rational-emotive and classical conditioning theories. *Journal of Consulting and Clinical Psychology*, 1974, **42**, 389–397.

Shevrin, H., & Dickman, S. The psychological unconscious: A necessary assumption for all psychological theory? *American Psychologist*, 1980, **35**, 421–434.

Skinner, B. F. The operational analysis of psychological terms. *Psychological Review*, 1945, **52**, 270–277.

Skinner, B. F. *Science and human behavior.* New York: Free Press, 1953.

Skinner, B. F. *Verbal behavior.* New York: Appleton, 1957.

Skinner, B. F. An operant analysis of problem solving. In B. Kleinmuntz (Ed.), *Problem-solving: Research, method, and theory.* New York: Wiley, 1966.

Skinner, B. F. *Contingencies of reinforcement: A theoretical analysis.* New York: Appleton, 1969.

Thoresen, C. E., & Mahoney, M. J. *Behavioral self-control.* New York: Holt, 1974.

Turk, D. C., & Genest, M. Regulation of pain: The application of cognitive and behavioral techniques for prevention and remediation. In P. C. Kendall & S. D. Hollon (Eds.), *Cognitive-behavioral interventions: Theory, research, and procedures.* New York: Academic Press, 1979.

Wilson, G. T. Cognitive behavior therapy: Paradigm shift or passing phase? In J. P. Foreyt & D. P. Rathjen (Eds.), *Cognitive behavior therapy: Research and application.* New York: Plenum, 1978.

Wine, J. Test anxiety and direction of attention. *Psychological Bulletin*, 1971, **76**(2), 92–104.

Wolfe, J. L. Short-term effects of modeling/behavior rehearsal, modeling/behavior rehearsal-plus-rational therapy, placebo, and no treatment on assertive behavior (Doctoral dissertation, New York University, 1975). *Dissertation Abstracts International*, 1975, **36**, 1936B–1937B. (University Microfilms No. 75-22, 937).

Zettle, R. D. Insight: Rules and revelations. In S. C. Hayes (Chair), *The baby and the bathwater: Radical behavioral interpretations of traditional clinical phenomena.* Symposium presented at the meeting of the Association for Advancement of Behavior Therapy, New York, 1980. (a)

Zettle, R. D. *The role of rule-governed behavior in clinical phenomena.* Unpublished manuscript, University of North Carolina at Greensboro, 1980. (b)

Zettle, R. D., & Hayes, S. C. *The effect of social context on the impact of coping self-statements.* Unpublished manuscript, University of North Carolina at Greensboro, 1979.

Zettle, R. D., & Hayes, S. C. Conceptual and empirical status of rational-emotive therapy. In M. Hersen, R. M. Eisler, & P. M. Miller (Eds.), *Progress in behavior modification* (Vol. 9). New York: Academic Press, 1980.

On Facing the Generalization Problem: The Study of Self-Regulatory Failure

DANIEL S. KIRSCHENBAUM AND
ANDREW J. TOMARKEN

Department of Psychology,
University of Wisconsin,
Madison, Wisconsin

ADVANCES IN COGNITIVE-BEHAVIORAL RESEARCH
AND THERAPY, VOLUME 1

The face of failure, like Medusa's, is not easily confronted. Instead of resolutely brandishing polished shields à la Perseus, we lesser mortals often combat our failures by blaming others or extenuating circumstances (e.g., Stevens & Jones, 1976), devaluing the sources of unfavorable evaluations (e.g., Jacobs, 1977), and avoiding the situations associated with failures (e.g., Duval & Wicklund, 1972). In view of our oftentimes cowardly response to failure, it is indeed heartening to observe the recently accelerated interest in "the generalization problem" in clinical psychology, that is, the failure of most therapies to produce behavior change that generalizes over time and across settings (e.g., Goldstein & Kanfer, 1979; Karoly & Steffen, 1980; Kazdin & Wilson, 1978; Stokes & Baer, 1977).

Despite increased concern about the generalization problem, the amount of empirical attention to it pales in comparison to its scope and importance. For example, even though the long-term efficacy of psychotherapies has been seriously questioned for three decades (e.g., Eysenck, 1952; Baer, Wolf, & Risley, 1968; Ford & Urban, 1963; Goldstein, Heller, & Sechrest, 1966), the pace of follow-up research remains both slow and relatively constant (LaDouceur & Auger, 1980). More specifically, LaDouceur and Auger noted that only 25% of the behavior therapy outcome studies published since 1963 included follow-ups of 6 months or longer. Since researchers evaluate behavior therapies more often than other therapies (Hoon & Lindsley, 1974; Kazdin, 1980; Smith & Glass, 1977), this finding is particularly disconcerting.

At least three other factors, aside from reluctance to confront failure, have contributed to the relative dearth of studies of long-term outcomes. First, it is very difficult to conduct good follow-up studies. The sheer duration of long-term research mitigates against doing it. Practical considerations, including delays in educational reinforcement for graduate students and the increasingly restrictive publish-or-perish mandate for academicians, undoubtedly lower the probability of attempting follow-up studies (LaDouceur & Auger, 1980). In addition, the forbidding requirements for conducting maximally useful follow-up studies make them enormously expensive on several dimensions. Stokes and Baer (1977) and Mash and Terdal (1980) stressed that most extant follow-ups have assessed far less than an ideal amount both in terms of time and effects. Not only are follow-ups of extended durations desirable, but, follow-ups that directly and continually measure both target behaviors and contexts are needed to describe fully the process of generalization (see, also, Hall, 1980; Kazdin & Wilson, 1978).

Three other, perhaps more fundamental, factors impede progress on the generalization problem. Although these factors will be examined in more detail in subsequent sections, it is important to introduce them here. First, clinical researchers may underestimate the pervasiveness of the generalization problem because, like all human judges, we tend to use faulty heuristics or judgment rules (for reviews see Arkes, 1981; Nisbett & Ross, 1980). The remaining factors are limitations in both conceptualization and research on the generalization problem (Goldstein, Lopez, & Greenleaf, 1979; Stokes & Baer, 1977; Wildman & Wildman, 1980). Failure to maintain and extend therapeutic changes following therapy has been viewed by researchers and theorists as primarily due to a passive type of extinction or forgetting (e.g., generalization decrement theory of extinction, Kimble, 1961, pp. 293–302; fading or disuse theories of forgetting, Hall, 1966, pp. 590–592). In other words, the process of failing to generalize behavior change, according to this perspective, involves the individual as an unfortunate victim of inadequate learning rather than an active participant in the process of generalization failure. More broadly, acquisition and generalization phases may well function as distinct entities, with their own sets of principles and ground rules. Thus, extant conceptualizations of generalization seem incomplete and relatively limited in scope accounting, in part, for the restricted range of studies that has been undertaken to explore the generalization problem.

In an attempt to expand the types of empirical investigations conducted on the generalization problem, which is the major purpose of this article, first we will review previous conceptualizations and research. Then, we will present recent theorizing and a new viewpoint, the study of self-regulatory failure, which emphasizes the active role of individuals in the failure to generalize behavior change. Finally, we will describe four directly relevant research domains and conclude by attempting to integrate this conceptual and empirical work.

I. THE GENERALIZATION PROBLEM: PRIOR CONCEPTUALIZATIONS AND RESEARCH

The concepts surrounding the generalization problem include maintenance, stimulus generalization, response generalization, transfer of training (positive and negative), forgetting (remembering, memory), and extinction (resistance to extinction). In an attempt to join Stokes and Baer in their "sidestep" of the controversies concerning terminology, we prefer their parsimonious definition of generalization: "the occurrence of relevant behavior under different, nontraining conditions (i.e., across subjects, settings, people, behaviors, and/or time) without the scheduling of the same events in those conditions as had been scheduled in the training conditions" (p. 350). This definition implies that at some point therapy (training) stops and the potential for generalization begins. Precisely identifying this transition may be impossible (Mash & Terdal, 1980). Nonetheless, in most instances the termination of therapy is discernible at least as a just-noticeable-difference in the type and quality of contact between the therapist(s) and clients (target population, subjects, patients) [cf. Kanfer & Goldstein's (1980) definition of therapy, pp. 2–3].

Based on reviews of the generalization literature, several writers attempted to help clinicians promote generalization by providing lists of suggestions (Hunt & Matarazzo, 1973, included four suggestions; Stokes & Baer, 1977, listed seven items; Wildman & Wildman, 1980, listed 16 items) while others described principles (e.g., Goldstein et al., 1979; Marholin & Touchette, 1979). Still other writers reviewed selected concepts in the literature of relevance to increasing generalization ranging from dispositional variables (e.g., Kanfer, 1979; Karoly, 1980) to promising clinical procedures (e.g., Fishman & Lubekin, 1980; McPeak, 1979; Sherman & Levine, 1979) to ecological or setting events (e.g., Price, 1979; Winett & Neale, 1980).

To summarize and integrate this diverse array of information, we will use a behavioral equation (cf. Kanfer & Phillips, 1970):

$$p(\text{Generalization}) = f(\text{Stimulus} \times \text{Organism} \times \text{Response} \times \text{Consequence})$$

This equation suggests that the probability of generalization is determined by a complex *interaction* of elements including stimulus variables, dispositional and biological characteristics of the organism, response variables, and environmental consequences. To summarize the extant generalization literature, first we will briefly review the most promising findings pertaining to each of these elements. Following the review, an evaluation section will point to some key weaknesses in the literature and, thereby, accentuate the importance of searching for new approaches to the generalization problem.

A. Stimulus Variables

A large body of literature in the areas of transfer of training (e.g., Underwood, 1951; Thorndike & Woodworth, 1901) and operant conditioning (e.g., Ferster & Skinner, 1957) indicates that properties of stimuli affect generalization. If a stimulus reliably elicits a response and if reinforcement reliably follows the stimulus–response pairing, the stimulus acquires control of the response (see Marholin & Touchette, 1979). Therapists use the facilitative aspects of stimulus control to their advantage by keeping their offices or the setting of the intervention relatively constant. In the early stages of therapy this approach maximizes the impact of the new experiences provided in therapy by intensifying the therapist's reinforcing capability (cf. Goldfried, 1980). Paradoxically, however, this kind of stimulus control also magnifies the contrasts between the in-therapy and extra-therapy environments. Thus, the new behaviors acquired through therapy, perhaps ranging from overt behaviors such as new social skills to new covert behaviors such as improved self-perceptions, may be less likely to occur in the presence of the rather different stimuli in extra-therapy settings.

For certain problem behaviors limiting the range of stimuli that elicit certain responses can facilitate generalization whereas, more commonly, extending the range of eliciting stimuli promotes generalization (see Kanfer & Grimm, 1977). For example, many behavioral excesses, such as addictive behaviors, require placing relatively permanent limits on the number and type of eliciting stimuli to encourage generalized reduction in problem behavior. Research on controlled drinking (Sobell & Sobell, 1976) and some recent studies on obesity illustrate this point (Carroll & Yates, 1981; Paulsen, Lutz, McReynolds, & Kohrs, 1976). In the latter studies, obese clients were taught to control the stimuli that elicit eating by, for example, eating in only one place in their homes and only at certain regular times, and doing nothing else while eating. These procedures contributed to more weight loss in stimulus control groups at long-term (6 + month) follow-ups in both studies.

For many target behaviors, particularly "behavioral deficits" (Kanfer & Grimm, 1977), extending the range and type of stimuli associated with new behavioral repetoires facilitates generalization. Several writers (e.g., Marholin & Touchette, 1980; Stokes & Baer, 1977) have suggested methods and principles for doing this: (1) *Multiple Therapists.* Use many different therapists to conduct the treatment program to prevent a single individual from inadvertently serving as a controlling (limiting) stimulus. Stokes and Baer (1977) cogently argued that training with sufficient, rather than maximum, numbers of therapists is more cost-effective. Illustratively, Stokes, Baer, and Jackson (1974) found that training by one therapist failed to produce any generalized use of greeting responses by three of four retarded subjects whereas the addition of a second therapist in training occasioned generalization for all subjects to more than 20 people. (2) *Multiple Settings.*

Use multiple settings when conducting interventions to prevent a particular setting from exerting excessive stimulus control. This principle encourages use of in vivo therapies (Sherman & Levine, 1979), homework assignments for practicing and shaping behavior change in the natural (extra-therapy) environment (Kanfer, 1980), behavioral rehearsal or role playing, and incorporating actual elements (e.g., significant others) from the natural environment into the training sessions. Evidence supporting utilization of multiple settings includes the general superiority of in vivo versus office-based treatments for a variety of problems in living (e.g., Linden & Wright, 1980; see reviews by Sherman, 1979; Sherman & Levine, 1979). (3) Planned Extra-therapy Stimulus Control. Especially when modifying behaviors or behavioral sequences of very low probability, "planting" controlling stimuli in exta-therapy settings may promote generalization. Both objects and people can serve as effective prompts in this regard. For example, Stokes and Baer (1976) taught two learning disabled children several word-recognition skills while teaching one of them to serve as a peer-tutor. Neither child generalized newly learned skills across settings until they were reunited, at which point generalization increased markedly (see also Johnston & Johnston, 1973; Redd, 1970). In a similar vein, Rabin and Marholin (1978) demonstrated that a light associated with training later facilitated generalization of a severely retarded man's rate of work across time and settings (see also Page, Iwata, & Neef, 1976).

B. Organismic Variables

In recent years large numbers of behaviorally oriented psychologists have begun focusing on the role of organismic variables, including self-generated private events, as mediators of behavior change (e.g., Bandura, 1969, 1977a; Kanfer, 1977; Kanfer & Phillips, 1970; Kendall & Hollon, 1979; Mahoney, 1974, 1977). A vast array of dispositional and self-regulatory concepts, in addition to a few biological variables, have been discussed as particularly relevant to the problem of generalization of therapeutic changes. Although three formal theories that integrate several crucial self-elements will be presented in Section II (Bandura, 1977b; Kanfer, 1971; Marlatt & Gordon, 1980), it is important in the present context to highlight the range of organismic variables that has been considered to date.

Following Mischel (1973), Staats (1975), and others (e.g., Kanfer & Karoly, 1972), Karoly (1980) described several dozen organismic variables that have demonstrated some potential as mediators of generalized behavior change. Table I groups many of the concepts discussed by Karoly under labels of five interrelated psychotherapeutic "tasks." Several of the concepts in Table I have also been discussed by other writers in terms of their impact on generalization. For example, Goldstein *et al.* also cite a variety of findings in experimental psychology showing that providing subjects with "general principles" (e.g., memorization techniques, labels, rules, advance organizers, learning sets) improved generalization with diverse tasks (e.g., memorization of poetry, dart shooting, mathematics tasks). In a more clinical vein, Kanfer (1979) summarized several studies documenting improved generalization for interventions that enhanced internal attributions for success, taught cognitive skills, increased perceptions of control and choice, and, improved coping and problem-solving skills.

One set of findings deserves special emphasis here because of its relative omission in analyses of the generalization problem. The influence of biological organismic variables on generalization has not been fully considered in the literature despite the fact that biology does affect generalization of therapeutic effects for many problem behaviors. Most obviously, as noted by Karoly (1980), the capacity of the person to learn [cf. Mischel's (1973) "cognitive construction competencies"] can affect initial behavior change and generalization. Limitations in cognitive skill development, determined genetically as well as environmentally (Jensen, 1980), clearly influence learning of the abstract cognitive mediators of generalization previously described (e.g., problem solving, planning).

Within the area of generalized change in addictive behaviors, biological variables play another type of important, and often underestimated, role. Several studies of alcoholism, smoking, and obesity underscore this point. Cannon, Baker, and Wehl (1981) conducted a 1-year follow-up to assess the relative effects of emetic and shock aversion conditioning procedures as treatment adjuncts for reducing alcoholism. They found that regardless of group assignment, heart rate response to alcohol assessed prior to treatment was the best predictor of abstinence rates at 6 and 12 months posttreatment (e.g., the R^2 population estimate of effect size at 12 months—the R^2 expected in replication—accounted for 31% of the variance). Thus, among subjects who received a substantial treatment regimen, heart rate elevation to alcohol correlated with long-term success. Not only do these findings support the use of conditioning-based interventions, but they imply that the ability to develop physiological sensitivities to the taste of alcohol should be studied more directly as a means to promote generalization of therapeutic effects (cf. Solomon, 1977).

TABLE I

Some Concepts within Karoly's (1980) Open-Task Cognitive Social-Learning View of Psychotherapy Processes[a]

I. Readiness for problem recognition	II. Decision, commitment, and motivational arousal	III. The acquisition of cognitive and instrumental skills
Attentional style	Goals	Motivation to learn
Mode of emotional modulation	Self-evaluation	Ability to learn
Repression-sensitization	Goal-setting	Developmental and contextual readiness to process and perform
Preparatory set	Cognitive dissonance	Characteristic reaction to success/failure
Physiological state	Self-relevant feedback	Plans
Cognitive–perceptual factors	Perception of internal states	Self-instruction
Attitudinal factors	Information processing	Age
Ability factors	Evaluative dimensions	Self-guiding speech
Discriminated self-awareness	Originality	Fear of success
Selective attention to self	Personal standard	
Positive/negative self-monitoring	Referential performance standard	
State/trait anxiety	Valuation of activity	
Social anxiety	Performance attribution	
Introversion–extroversion	Self-applied consequences	
Frustration tolerance	Proficiency expectation	
Subjective/objective self-awareness	Personal history dimensions	
Self-efficacy	Achievement motivation	
Differential self-focus	Hot cognitions	
	Self-perception	
	Persistence	
	Value-expectancies	
	Commitment	
	Need for social approval	

IV. Maintenance processes: Memory and self-regulation
  Selective recall of outcomes
  Optimism–pessimism
  Ego involvement
  Memory control strategies (coding, storage, organization retrieval)
  Self/task orientation
  Self-reinforcement style

V. Transfer processes: Situation appraisal and problem solving
  Psychological climate
  Social pressure
  Interpersonal conflict
  Negative emotional–interpersonal state
  Recognition of high-risk situations
  Profile of proficiency
  Cognitive coping skills (e.g., positive thinking)
    Alternative thinking
    Means–end thinking
    Consequential thinking
    Causal thinking

[a] Karoly (1980) defines and discusses each of these concepts as they pertain to the generalization of therapeutic behavior change. Reprinted with permission.

Leventhal and Cleary (1980) recently summarized research on smoking. They noted that the psychological and biological approaches to the problem "are often presented as antagonistic . . . [whereas] actually, the two approaches are complimentary" (p. 387). Leventhal and Cleary describe nicotine fixed-effect, nicotine regulation, and multiple regulation models. The latter approach incorporates findings showing that the smoker's "brain is in the bladder" with the opponent-process theory of motivation to help explain how cravings are conditioned and maintained.

The role of biology in obesity is more insidious than in other addictive problems. Many people, including a large number of professionals, have developed erroneously simplistic views of the causes of obesity and the variables that maintain it (Mahoney, 1975; Rodin, 1981; Wooley, Wooley, & Dyrenforth, 1979). Perhaps part of the reason for these widespread misconceptions lies in the ease with which we can develop our own "folk-wise" implicit theories about this phenomenon (see Arkes, 1981; Nisbett & Ross, 1980). Contrary to many people's beliefs, biological variables exert a powerful force that seriously impedes obese individuals from maintaining weight loss. Among the physiological factors involved in the refractory nature of obesity are permanently enlarged fat cells, a process that can occur at any age; higher basal levels of insulin which increases hunger pains, food consumption, and fat storage; and lowered basal metabolism as a direct function of dieting (see Rodin, 1981; Wooley et al., 1979). On a more optimistic note, both biological and psychological methods are being developed to counteract this physiological press against maintenance of weight loss effectively, for example, exercise as a means to reset metabolic changes induced by dieting (Donahoe, Lin, Keesey, & Kirschenbaum, 1981) and changing actual types of foods consumed and meal patterning (Rodin, 1979, 1981).

C. Response Variables

In the preceding section we noted that certain *types* of responses (e.g., attributional and attentional responses, coping skills, problem solving and planning skills) can facilitate generalization under some conditions. Aside from considering targeting these types of responses (Stokes & Baer, 1977), at least three other principles describe more general characteristics of responses that affect generalization.

First, the availability of responses subsequent to termination of therapy (and in extra-therapy settings more generally) may depend on the extent to which the responses were practiced, even overlearned, during therapy (Goldstein et al., 1979). Evidence from experimental psychology supports this contention (e.g., Mandler, 1954) as do some outcome studies (e.g., Bednar & Weinberg, 1970; Jeffrey & Wing, 1979; Weissberg, Gesten, Rapkin, Cowen, Davidson, Flores de Apodaca, & McKim, 1981).

A second response principle pertains to the notion of Baer et al. (1968) of "behavioral traps." Baer et al. (1968) suggested that natural contingencies often do not seize upon or "trap" changed behavior, thereby failing to maintain it. Accordingly, they recommended that "generalization should be programmed rather than expected or lamented" (p. 97). One method to program generalization described by Stokes and Baer (1977) is to select carefully for training those responses that have a greater likelihood of becoming trapped or to modify environmental contingencies (hopefully to produce permanent changes) to increase trapping. For example, a relative abundance of behavioral traps may account, in part, for the relative ease of modifying the social behaviors of withdrawn children (cf. Lorion, Cowen, & Caldwell, 1974) and, more generally, the adjustment of children with relatively minor behavior problems (cf. Durlak, 1980). An additional example of an especially clever means to increase behavioral trapping was provided by Seymour and Stokes (1976). These investigators taught delinquent girls how to recruit their own reinforcement successfully. The girls prompted staff members to attend to appropriate behaviors by saying things like "Am I working well?" which, in turn, maintained those appropriate behaviors.

A third means to increase generalization involves defining target behaviors, broadly and inclusively, as response classes. Response classes are integrated sets of responses; the modification of one of the responses affects others within the same class. For example, Stokes and Baer (1977, pp. 356–357) cite studies by Sherman and his associates showing response generalization within classes of both motor and verbal behaviors (see also Wildman & Wildman, 1980).

D. Environmental Consequences

Extrapolating primarily from basic research on extinction and forgetting, researchers have had some success in extending generalization by manipulating aspects of environmental consequences. One of the more widely recommended procedures (e.g., Hunt & Matarazzo, 1973; O'Leary & Wilson, 1975) is to provide "booster sessions," aperiodic meetings following the formal completion of training. Underlying principles supporting the logic of booster sessions are traceable to the classic experiments on the beneficial effects of "relearning" on memory (forgetting) curves (Ebbinhaus, 1885); research on increased resistance to extinction due to partial reinforcement (Humphreys, 1939); studies of increased responding under variable and "thinned" schedules of reinforcement (Ferster & Skinner, 1957); as well as others (see Kimble, 1961). Both phone call and in-person boosters have led to improved generalization over time in studies on obesity (e.g., Kingsley & Wilson, 1977), alcoholism (e.g., Stojiljkovic, 1969), smoking (e.g., Dubren, 1977), and nail biting (Spevak & Richards, 1980).

Related to booster sessions, some researchers have used "schedule thinning" (i.e., changing from continuous to partial reinforcement or increasing the number of responses required for reinforcement or increasing the variability of the reinforcement). Schedule thinning increased the generalization over time (Kazdin & Polster, 1973) and across settings (Whitman, Mercurio, & Caponigri, 1970) of newly acquired social responses by retarded subjects. In a study improvement experiment with college students, Richards, Perri, and Gortney (1976) found that increasing the intervals between treatment sessions resulted in improved generalization of effects over time (course exam performance assessed at 5 weeks posttreatment). Several other related procedures have also promoted generalized change in a few studies. For example, researchers used delayed reinforcement and reinforcement of rather loosely defined response sets to improve generalization (see reviews by Marholin, Siegel, & Phillips, 1976; Stokes & Baer, 1977).

In addition to altering the schedule of reinforcement, changing the type of reinforcement from more obvious, discrete, tangible reinforcers to more subtle, naturally occurring, social reinforcers can increase generalized change in behavior. Consistent with some of the research on intrinsic motivation (Deci, 1975), Marholin et al. (1976) noted that Nolan, Mattis, and Holliday (1970) found that "those children who had been gradually faded from food to social reinforcers were found to exhibit additional improvements in behavior, beyond the changes in target behaviors, compared to children who had not been graduated to social reinforcement at the termination of the treatment period" (p. 311). Another concept related to type of reinforcement concerns the administrator of rewards. Consistent with the earlier discussions of organismic and response variables, generalization may be enhanced by encouraging self-reward and by developing more potent behavioral traps. Involvement of significant others in the behavior change enterprise is perhaps the most frequently recommended method to increase behavioral trapping (e.g., Hall, 1980; Stokes & Baer, 1977). Recent evidence supports this idea, even with such refractory problems as obesity (e.g., Brownell, Heckerman, Westlake, Hayes, & Monti, 1978; Weisz & Bucher, 1980).

E. Evaluation: Toward New Directions in Generalization Conceptualizations and Research

The number and diversity of suggestions and positive findings in the preceding description of the generalization literature suggests at least a glimmer of hope regarding the long-term efficacy of therapeutic interventions. A variety of concepts, principles, and recommendations provide some empirically grounded guidelines for improving the generalization of therapeutic effects. Unfortunately, closer scrutiny of this literature reveals key conceptual and empirical limitations.

The single most obvious unifying concept that seems to underlie most of the extant generalization research is that failure to generalize therapeutic behavior change is caused by extinction or forgetting. Thus, researchers utilized a variety of methods to cue target behaviors in extra-therapy settings (stimulus control), increase response "strength" in acquisition (e.g., practice; overlearning), and modify reinforcement contingencies to blur the discriminability between treatment phases and termination (e.g., booster sessions, schedule thinning). Most explicitly, when studying rate of relapse over time researchers often note the resemblance between the resulting function and "a negatively accelerating curve, typical of the 'extinction' or 'forgetting' curves found in the learning literature" (Hunt & Matarazzo, 1973, p. 107). Indeed, the similarity between the typical relapse curves and a classic negatively accelerating extinction/forgetting curve is uncanny and, therefore, conceptually seductive (see Fig. 1).

The obvious similarities of the curves in Fig. 1 probably encouraged researchers to invoke the "representativeness" heuristic (Kahneman & Tversky, 1973). Thus, researchers may have thought that the usual methods of modifying extinction and forgetting curves should help modify the usual generalization curve. Unfortunately, these "usual methods" were derived primarily from animal studies designed to test extant theories of extinction and forgetting (see Kimble, 1961). Since organismic (or dispositional) factors presumably exert less influence on animals than humans, these methods deemphasize potentially vital organismic variables. They also fail to accentuate the differences between acquisition and generalization. Behavior in generalization may follow very different rules than behavior in acquisition. In support of

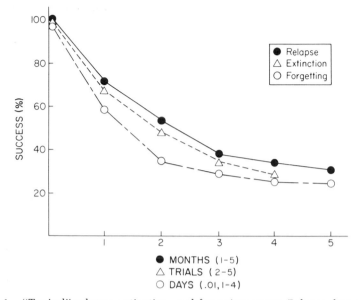

Fig. 1. "Typical" relapse, extinction, and forgetting curves. Relapse data obtained from Hunt *et al.* (1971); extinction data from Hovland (1936); and forgetting data from Ebbinhaus (1885).

this latter viewpoint, the following close inspection of some of the more widely used generalization strategies reveals marked inconsistencies in efficacy.

1. *Limited Efficacy of Generalization Strategies*

As noted in Section I,D, many clinicians and researchers use booster sessions to promote generalization. This procedure is very closely allied to extinction-based conceptualizations of the generalization problem. As mentioned previously, booster sessions can facilitate generalization (e.g., Kingsley & Wilson, 1977; Spevak & Richards, 1980). Unfortunately, the majority of the relevant investigations reveal no additive effects of booster session on generalized behavior change.

The smoking treatment studies that examined the long-term efficacy of booster sessions revealed significantly improved abstinence rates in a 4-week follow-up study (Dubren, 1977) and in separate reports of 1- and 2-year follow-ups in a second investigation (Colletti & Kopel, 1979; Colletti & Stern, 1980). On the other hand, four other investigations showed that booster sessions did not significantly improve long-term smoking cessation relative to comparison and control procedures (Colletti & Supnick, 1980; Elliot & Denney, 1978; Kopel, 1974; Relinger, Bornstein, Bugge, Carmody, & Zohn, 1977). Furthermore, several factors qualify the findings of studies that indicated some benefits attributable to booster sessions. Dubren's (1977) data were based solely on uncorroborated self-report provided by subjects who participated impersonally; television and telephone served as the only source of therapist–client contact for these subjects. In addition, 6 of the 29 subjects who were assigned to the booster treatment in the Dubren study (telephone call-in for taped "reinforcement" messages) reported that they never utilized the booster. Unfortunately, the smoking data for these 6 subjects were still included in data analyses; the $p < .05$ difference between "booster" and control groups in proportion of subjects who remained abstinent at follow-up is, therefore, uninterpretable. In the follow-up studies reported by Colletti and his associates, their most successful booster treatment (called the "self-monitoring group") included 4 weeks of posttreatment "positive feedback" provided via telephone by therapists and an additional 3 months of weekly contacts (Colletti & Kopel, 1979). This group maintained abstinence significantly better than only one of the two additional groups that had not received the 4 weeks of posttreatment contact (Colletti & Kopel, 1979; Colletti & Stern, 1980).

Paralleling the generally disappointing findings on the efficacy of booster sessions for smoking reduction, the obesity literature includes at least five controlled studies that revealed no substantial increment in generalization due to booster sessions (Ashby & Wilson, 1977; Beneke & Paulsen, 1979; Hall, Hall, Borden, & Hanson, 1975; Wilson & Brownell, 1978; Perri, Stalonas, Twentyman, Toro, & Zastowny, 1980). In three studies, however, booster sessions led to some improvement in sustained weight reduction (Hall et al., 1975; Hall, Bass, & Monroe, 1978; Kingsley & Wilson, 1977). Unfortunately, once again, the "positive" findings were weak and inconsistent. For example, Hall et al. (1975) found that booster sessions improved maintenance of weight loss only for a subgroup of the participants who received booster sessions, those who received the boosters from the same therapist they worked with during treatment; Kingsley and Wilson (1977) found significant booster effects only at 3- and 6-month follow-ups and not at 9- and 12-month follow-ups.

The inconsistencies in efficacy and the generally minimal results observed for booster sessions is similar to the level of effectiveness of several other generalization strategies suggested by traditional learning theories. For example, fading contact between therapists and clients appeared to produce no increment in generalization in studies of smoking reduction (Relinger et al., 1977), weight reduction (Beneke & Paulsen, 1979), and study improvement (Richards & Perri, 1978).

2. Organismic Variables and Limitations in Efficacy of Self-Regulatory Training

One of the limitations of the passive extinction/forgetting analogy may account, in part, for these disappointing results. The suggestions and principles of generalization reviewed under stimulus, response, and consequence subheadings (i.e., most of the literature on generalization typically deemphasized the importance of organismic variables). As noted earlier, attributions, perceptions of choice, and a variety of other dispositional and biological factors clearly mediate generalization of behavior change. At present, however, many of these variables have merely been noted as possible factors to be considered (e.g., Karoly, 1980). Specific principles for how to use them to promote generalization are only just beginning to emerge.

The most sophisticated integration of organismic variables with respect to their impact on generalization are models of self-regulation and related processes (e.g., Bandura, 1977b; Kanfer, 1971, 1977; Marlatt & Gordon, 1980). Among the studies that formed the basis for these models are a large number of attempts to improve generalization. Unfortunately, these studies, like those based on extant learning/memory theories, relied on a very logical but relatively simplistic conceptualization of the generalization problem: If people learn how to regulate their own behavior more effectively (in the relative absence of external constraints), then they should generalize behavior changes established in therapy more readily than those who do not learn such self-regulatory skills (see Bandura, 1969; Kanfer & Phillips, 1970; Thoresen & Mahoney, 1974). The original proponents of this "power to the person" view of self-regulatory skill development did not advance their ideas as panaceas. Rather, they suggested that such processes hold great promise for helping many people at least some of the time under some conditions. Nevertheless, many clinical researchers and practitioners, strongly encouraged by some early impressive results (e.g., Stuart, 1967), tested the limits of training self-regulatory skills to enhance generalization. Unfortunately, the following brief selective review will show, again, that something more is needed to attack the generalization problem thoroughly.

Many of the investigators who have studied treatments for obesity consider the self-regulatory training approach to be the best one currently available (e.g., Mahoney & Mahoney, 1976). In this treatment, clients typically plan their caloric expenditures and meals, keep track of their eating and related behaviors, use stimulus control principles to narrow the cues that elicit eating, and self-reward for effective execution of these new eating habits (e.g., Mahoney & Mahoney, 1976; Stalonas, Johnson, & Christ, 1978; Stuart, 1967). Self-regulatory treatments appear at least as effective, and generally more so, than more traditional dietary, nutritional, social pressure, and pharmacological approaches in the short-run, that is, during treatment (Brightwell & Sloan, 1977; Leon, 1976; Stunkard & Mahoney, 1976). However, lack of control of "nonspecific" factors such as treatment credibility, client expectancies, and extra-therapy attention call even this conclusion into question (Stalonas, Kirschenbaum, & Zastowny, 1981). Moreover, results of long-term follow-ups indicate very little evidence for the efficacy of this approach with regard to generalization of effects over time (Stunkard & Penick, 1979). For example, Stunkard and Penick (1979) found that their self-regulatory intervention compared to a traditional approach (diet, nutrition education, medication, supportive group therapy) produced greater weight loss at posttreatment and 1-year follow-up. This group difference disappeared at 5-year follow-up (mean weight loss of the self-regulatory group = 11.7 pounds vs 12.1 for traditional treatment at 5 years posttreatment; at pretreatment these clients were 78% overweight, i.e., approximately 100 pounds overweight). A 5-year follow-up of the Stalonas et al. (1978) study similarly indicated significant weight gain in all four groups that had received a self-regulatory treatment (Stalonas, Perri, Kerzner, Twentyman, & Johnson, 1980). A similarly disappointing relapse trend was noted in eight 1-year follow-up studies summarized by Stunkard and Penick (1979) and in several more recent long-term follow-ups (e.g., Beneke & Paulsen, 1979; Gottestam, 1979; Israel & Saccone, 1979; Collins, Wilson, & Rothblum, 1980).

The results of follow-ups of self-regulatory treatments for smoking reduction and the improvement of study behaviors again resemble the obesity literature in many respects. Leventhal and Cleary (1980) summarized the smoking literature, including self-regulatory interventions and concluded: "success rates for different therapies are not markedly different; it is simply better to do something than nothing . . . Whereas most backsliding occurs within 6 months, it continues with inexorable force for 12 months till there is a residual of quitters and smoking reducers of 10% to 25% of the pretherapy base level although figures of 35% to 45% are occasionally reported" (p. 374) (see also Elliott & Denney, 1978; Lando, 1978).

In a recent review of the literature on improving study behaviors, Kirschenbaum and Perri (1981) concluded that multicomponent interventions, particularly those that incorporated self-regulatory training, produced the best outcomes even in the relatively few long-term follow-up studies. However, they also noted several rather important inconsistencies in efficacy. For example, Greiner and Karoly's (1976) information + self-monitoring + self-reward group did not differ from controls in exam scores; and Richards and Perri's (1978) study skills + self-control + faded contact groups did not improve on any measures (including exam and GPA assessments posttreatment and GPA at 1-year follow-up) relative to controls. More recently, Kirschenbaum, Malett, Humphrey, and Tomarken (1982b) found that a group of volunteers that had received an intensive 11-week self-regulatory, supportive interactional, and study skills intervention (the "Daily Plans/High Grade" group) showed an initial elevation of GPA at posttreatment and then a significant linear decline over a 1-year follow-up assessment. The resulting 1-year follow-up GPA was nominally lower than controls.

3. Where Do We Go from Here? Toward the Study of Self-Regulatory Failure

Despite the integration of important organismic variables such as self-monitoring and self-consequation (Karoly, 1980), self-regulatory training apparently does not guarantee generalization. Perhaps this disheartening conclusion is attributable to the fact that, in one important respect, approaches to improved generalization based on self-regulatory training are very similar to those based on nonmediational procedures. Both self-regulatory training and booster sessions and virtually all of the extant methods for "improving" generalization rely on *assumptions* about what people actually do in extra-therapy settings: that certain common forgetting or extinction processes, that is, relatively passive responses to altered environmental contingencies, predominate. But, what do we really know about the variables that become activated during generalization? Are we remedying a problem before we understand its nature? Is it not possible that certain shifts in attention or attribution or expectancies or some other dispositional variables reliably precipitate failure to generalize? Current knowledge includes very little information, for example, about which organismic variables, both dispositional and biological sorts, people utilize during the generalization process. Therefore, perhaps training in self-regulatory skills fails to enhance generalization because it, just like use of booster sessions and related nonmediational techniques, ignores the organismic variables that become focal during generalization.

The study of self-regulatory failure directs attention to "what people actually do to fail at self-regulation" (Kirschenbaum, 1976, p. 3). It uses empirical evidence from diverse literatures and self-regulatory models to formulate hypotheses and integrate potentially vital dispositional variables. Specifically, the term *"self-regulatory failure" describes all processes by which individuals fail to generalize desired behavior changes over time and across settings, in the relative absence of immediate external constraints* (cf. Kirschenbaum, 1976; Kirschenbaum & Karoly, 1977; Tomarken & Kirschenbaum, 1982). Thus, the study of self-regulatory failure is a search for self-regulated components or elements that actively prevent or inhibit generalization of behavior change (cf. Marlatt & Gordon, 1980).

A graphic illustration may clarify where this search begins. Figure 2 presents a hypothetical curve that closely resembles the long-term follow-up data available for many treatments of addictive disorders (e.g., Hunt, Barnett, & Branch, 1971; Israel & Saccone, 1979; McFall & Hammen, 1971). As shown in the figure, baseline often precedes substantial behavior change during intervention (e.g., weight loss, smoking cessation) followed by some generalization over time subsequent to therapy (cf. Brightwell & Sloan, 1977). The box labeled "self-regulatory failure" suggests that at some identifiable point following termination of therapy, the failure process begins. Unfortunately, then it typically proceeds with an "inexorable force" (Leventhal & Cleary, 1980). The components of that inexorable force may well include certain key changes in dispositional variables regulated by the individual (e.g., changes in attribution, attention, self-evaluation) as well as environmental influences. By studying what people do and think about within the self-regulatory failure box depicted in Fig. 2, we may learn a great deal about how to help others more effectively struggle to generalize.

A heuristic base from which the study of self-regulatory failure may proceed is found in several models of self-regulation and related processes. Section II describes three models and their implication for self-regulatory failure. While we readily acknowledge the salience of several other conceptualizations (e.g., Abramson, Garber, & Seligman, 1980; Hall, 1980; Leventhal & Johnson, 1982; Miller, Gallanter, & Pribram, 1960; Solomon & Corbit, 1973), the following models appear most clearly related to self-regulatory failure.

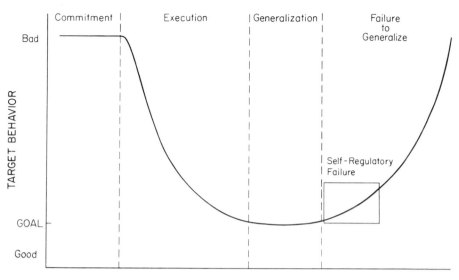

Fig. 2.   Hypothetical depiction of change in self-regulated behavior over time—from the commitment phase through failure to generalize.

II. SELF-REGULATORY FAILURE: THREE RELEVANT THEORETICAL MODELS

A. A Closed Loop (or Negative Feedback) Model of Self-Regulation

Kanfer (1971) integrated a diverse array of information to formulate a cybernetic model of self-regulation (cf. Miller *et al.*, 1960). Later elaborations of this view by Kanfer and Karoly (Kanfer, 1980; Kanfer & Karoly, 1972; Karoly, 1977) provide an interesting account of when self-regulation starts and what occurs during self-regulation.

With regard to definitions of key terms, Kanfer and Karoly (1972) described self-regulation as "the processes by which an individual alters or maintains his behavioral chain in the absence of immediate external supports" (p. 406). Self-control is viewed as a special case of self-regulation in which the person emits a controlling response to decrease the probability of a formerly high probability behavior (e.g., the dieter does something to resist eating a piece of cake for the long-term payoff of weight loss; the hero does something that gets him/her to tolerate the immediate threat of gunfire in order to save a comrade). Thus, self-regulation does not necessarily involve a conflict between short- and long-term consequences. It applies to situations in which people merely attempt, without substantial external supports, to improve their skills in academic, social, athletic, and other contexts.

The first of four major stages in Kanfer's and Karoly's recent conceptualizations of the closed loop model of self-regulation is *problem recognition* (Karoly, 1977). During this phase the person becomes aware that his or her normal patterns of behaving have been interrupted or no longer produce their usual effects. Sometime after acknowledging the existence of a problem, perhaps after more closely observing the target behaviors (Kanfer, 1971), a *commitment* or decision point phase ensues. This is the time when people decide to initiate a behavior change process. The commitment to change or promise is described as a verbal operant (Kanfer & Karoly, 1972) subject to manipulation by a variety of consequences (e.g., reinforcement history for making promises; explicitness required in the commitment; criteria established for behavior change). After committing to change, a person undergoes an execution or *extended self-regulation* phase. During this execution phase individuals first *self-monitor*, i.e., systematically observe their target behaviors (discriminate their occurrence from nonoccurrence and perhaps record frequencies of occurrence). The level of performance of target behaviors noted in self-monitoring is then compared to the standards established in the commitment phase, i.e., *self-evaluation* occurs. Finally, self-rewards are allocated if the self-evaluation was favorable and self-punishment is presumed to follow unfavorable self-evaluations. This chain of events, from self-monitoring through *self-consequation* (self-reward or self-punishment), establishes the negative feedback loop because self-reward presumably maintains the target behavior whereas self-punishment requires the individual to change his or her responding.

According to the model, when deliberate extended self-regulation operations (self-monitoring, self-evaluation, self-consequation) cease, then "self-regulation becomes irrelevant as an explanatory construct" (Karoly, 1977, p. 220). Karoly (1977) suggests that *habit reorganization* can label the fourth and final phase of the model to describe the management of the target behavior after it has reached satisfactory levels of performance. Of course, if during habit reorganization the target behavior becomes problematic once again, the entire closed loop should become initiated again in the problem recognition phase (cf. Kanfer, 1971).

Although the model does not explicitly describe elements of self-regulatory failure, by inference it suggests several potentially important elements. During habit reorganization the person may fail to recognize (discriminate) the reemergence of the problem. The insidious nature of some problems, such as alcoholism and weight control, may increase the likelihood of activating this mechanism in self-regulatory failure. On the other hand, for many problem behaviors the habit reorganization phase may never be reached (see Kanfer, 1980, p. 343). For example, in extending self-control over eating, studying, and related effortful activities, competing or conflicting demands from both physiological and other motivational sources may never completely desist. Therefore, generalization of self-regulation in some cases probably requires relatively permanent execution of self-monitoring self-evaluation, and self-consequating operations. In these cases, factors that contribute to the discontinuation of self-monitoring, self-evaluation, and self-consequation presumably comprise elements of self-regulatory failure.

B. Self-Efficacy Theory

Bandura (1977b) suggested that behavioral outcomes are a joint function of "efficacy expectations" and "outcomes expectations." He defined an efficacy expectation as the conviction that one can successfully execute a particular behavior. Outcome expectations are judgments of the extent to which the particular behavior, once performed, will accomplish certain outcomes. While emphasizing the importance of efficacy and outcome expectancies as determinants of outcomes, Bandura took care to indicate that expectancies alone do not produce desired outcomes. He noted, for example, that in self-regulation, self-consequation delivered contingent upon self-evaluation, serves an important role as a source of incentives (cf. Kanfer, 1971). Furthermore, Bandura observed that response capability, or ability to execute skilled behavior, also determines outcomes.

Concerning generalized behavior change, Bandura (1977, p. 194) indicated that appropriate skills and incentives are needed. In addition, "efficacy expectations are a major determinant of . . . how long [people] will sustain effort in dealing with stressful situations." "Strong" efficacy expectations and "generalized" expectations resist extinction and apply in diverse contexts, respectively. According to the theory, development of these types of efficacy expectations proceeds most efficiently by successfully accomplishing challenging things and then attributing those accomplishments to one's own skills (e.g., Bandura & Barab, 1973; Bandura, Jeffrey, & Gajdos, 1975). In addition, modeling, verbal persuasion, and emotional reactions can affect the strength and generality of efficacy expectations, thereby, affecting generalization of behavior change.

Apparently, generalized behavior change is expected to follow from strong generalized efficacy expectations that had been carefully established in therapy. Such expectations should help people confront the stressors associated with continuing effortful behavior change despite physiological pressures and a reduction in reinforcement from the therapist. It follows the theory, therefore, to suggest that lowered strength and generality of efficacy expectations may comprise an important aspect of self-regulatory failure. Based on the logic and data described by Bandura, the factors that may lower perceived self-efficacy include (a) experiencing failures, particularly repeated failures, and attributing them to deficits in personal skills (cf. Weiner, 1972); (b) observing failures, of relevance to one's own target behavior, in people who differ widely in personal characteristics; (c) receiving persuasive communication from others that reinforces personal responsibility for failures; (d) attributing increased physiological arousal to personal inadequacies; (e) observing a declining rate of improvement; (f) perceiving a decline in the difficulty of emitting target behaviors; and (g) developing the perception that one's coping skills are inadequate or clearly situation specific.

C. A Cognitive–Behavioral Model of the Relapse Process

Marlatt and Gordon (1980) presented an account of some of the possible causes of failure to generalize behavior change over time for persons who voluntarily terminate the use of a substance such as alcohol, cigarettes, or narcotic drugs (see also Marlatt, 1978b). Some aspects of the model also apply to any relapse from behavior change. Marlatt and Gordon define relapse as "any discrete violation of an imposed rule or set of rules governing the rate or pattern of consumption behaviors" (p. 413). Therefore, this model applies to many attempts to generalize behavior change including, for example, failure to maintain dietary restrictions and failure to abstain from undesirable sexual practices.

Marlatt and Gordon's model posits a sequence of five factors or stages that culminate in an increased probability of relapse. First, the person encounters a *high risk situation*. These are situations that are often associated with relapses and that challenge an individual's "sense of control" (e.g., interpersonal conflict; experience of a strong physiologically linked urge; social pressure). Second, in the face of a high-risk situation, the person emits *no coping response*. The person may not recognize the need for such a response or she or he may possess inadequate coping skills. After failing to attempt to cope with the high-risk situation, for whatever reason, *decreased efficacy expectations* and *increased positive outcome expectations* for the effects of relapsing may ensue (cf. Bandura, 1977b). In other words, people may attribute their failures to cope to their own inadequacies (deceased efficacy expectations) while, concurrently, selectively recalling the positive attributes of the target behavior/substance (positive outcome expectancies for relapse). The additive effect of the high-risk situation, lack of coping response, and alteration in expectations may result in the fourth phase of the model—*initial reuse of the substance* (i.e., initial relapse). The chain of relapsing can then accelerate in the final phase of the model. Specifically, an *abstinence violation effect* and the *perceived effects of the substance* can combine to increase greatly the probability of continued relapsing. The abstinence violation effect consists of the arousal of cognitive dissonance (Festinger, 1964), i.e., a negative emotional drive state resulting from the discrepancy between behavior (relapse) and cognitions ("I am an abstainer."). This dissonant drive state is presumed to motivate changes in cognitions or behavior to reduce the discrepancy, such as increased relapsing with concomitant changes in perceptions ["I am a nonabstainer (drunk, smoker, drug addict, overeater)."]. Another postulated component of the abstinence violation effect is to attribute the relapse to a personal failing or weakness, as opposed to attributing it to external causes. The pleasant sensations or effects resulting from the relapse then are strong reinforcers of the person's decreased efficacy expectations and attribution of personal weakness, according to the model.

Marlatt and Gordon's cognitive–behavioral model clearly applies to self-regulatory failure. Extrapolating from their model, people may engage in self-regulatory failure by (a) experiencing, perhaps through selective exposure, high-risk situations; (b) omitting coping responses when confronting high-risk situations; (c) decreasing their efficacy expectations; (d) increasing their expectations of the benefits available from relapsing; (e) engaging in an initial relapse or countertherapeutic behavior; (f) perceiving inconsistencies between their countertherapeutic actions and self-perceptions; (g) attributing countertherapeutic behavior to personal weakness; and (h) enjoying the consequences of the countertherapeutic behavior.

D. Summary

Table II lists the elements of self-regulatory failure suggested by each of the three models. All of the models emphasize covert events (e.g., self-evaluation). On the other hand, several of the proposed elements are readily observable behavioral or situational events or covert events

TABLE II

Elements of Self-Regulatory Failure Suggested by Kanfer's Closed Loop Model of Self-Regulation, Bandura's Self-Efficacy Theory, and Marlatt and Gordon's Cognitive–Behavioral Relapse Model

Closed loop model	Self-efficacy theory	Cognitive–behavioral relapse model
Failure to recognize (discriminate) the reemergence of the problem	Lowered perceived self-efficacy via	Exposure to high-risk situations
Discontinuation of self-monitoring	Failure, particularly repeated failure, attributed to personal inadequacies	Omission of coping responses when confronting high-risk situations
Discontinuation of self-evaluation	Observation of relevant failures in others	Lowered efficacy expectations
Discontinuation of self-consequation	Reinforcement from others for internal attributions of failure	Expectation of favorable outcomes from relapsing
	Attribution of physiological arousal to personal inadequacies	Initial relapse
	Observation of a declining rate of improvement	Internal attributions for initial relapse
	Perception of decreased difficulty of emitting target behaviors	Experience of pleasant consequences from relapsing
	Perception of one's coping skills as inadequate or situation specific	

with obvious behavioral correlates. Specifically, observable elements are some of Marlatt and Gordon's high-risk situations, initial relapses, and omission of coping responses; Bandura's failure experiences and social reinforcement for internal attributions; and Kanfer's discontinuation of self-monitoring, self-evaluation, and self-consequation.

The distinction between observable and covert elements of self-regulatory failure deserves special emphasis with respect to recent analyses of such covert behaviors (e.g., Kazdin, 1978; Lang, 1978; Nisbett & Ross, 1980; Wong & Weiner, 1981; Wortman & Dintzer, 1978). The observable elements are subject to direct experimental inquiry without undue concern about reactivity (cf. Shuller & MacNamara, 1976). For example, we can study people who complete a therapy program and observe whether those who fail to generalize behavior change, compared to those who succeed, spend more time in high-risk situations, exhibit relapse behaviors, omit behavioral coping responses under stress, and discontinue self-monitoring. In contrast, investigations of many covert events must rely on indirect assessments and reactive questionnaires (see Kazdin, 1978; Kendall & Hollon, 1981; Lang, 1981; Wortman & Dintzer, 1978). Thus, for example, several recent experiments used open-ended response formats, instead of the usual series of specific rating scales, to investigate attributions. They found that some subjects either failed to make attributions (Diener & Dweck, 1978; Hanusa & Schultz, 1977) or they made many fewer and very different attributions than expected based on prior theorizing and research (Harvey, 1981; Wong & Weiner, 1981).

We do not wish to suggest that lowered efficacy expectations, changes in perceptions about the difficulty of emitting target behaviors, internal attributions for failures, and related covert behaviors are not active ingredients of self-regulatory failure. However, the results of relevant research which rely exclusively on self-reports must be considered very cautiously in view of the preceding evidence. Speculations about these covert elements must similarly await rigorous, behaviorally anchored, experimentation (see Kendall, 1981).

Given appropriate skepticism about many of the theoretically derived elements of self-regulatory failure, it may prove heuristic and parsimonious to describe the confluence between the models. Marlatt and Gordon's model suggests that selective exposure to high-risk situations or failure to avoid those situations could set the stage for failure to generalize. It seems plausible to argue that part of self-regulatory failure is inadequate planning of activities, misrecognition of potentially problematic situations, and underestimation of the riskiness of certain situations. Such cognitive behaviors culminate in the first element of self-regulatory failure derived from the closed loop model: failure to recognize the reemergence of the problem. The next step in self-regulatory failure noted in the relapse model also resembles aspects of self-regulatory failure suggested by the closed loop model. Omission of coping responses in Marlatt and Gordon's approach may include disengagement from self-monitoring, self-evaluation, and self-consequation as indicated by the closed loop model. In fact, self-monitoring and self-consequation are widely considered types of coping responses (Meichenbaum, 1975; Peterson & Shigetomi, 1981).

The remainder of the suggested elements of self-regulatory pertain to Bandura's description of self-efficacy theory. These elements include a variety of self-reactions that accentuate personal failures and attributions of personal responsibility for those failures (cf. Abramson et al., 1980; Weiner, 1979). Both self-efficacy theory and the cognitive–behavioral relapse model also indicate that changing perceptions of the target behavior itself and its modification contribute to self-regulatory failure (e.g., developing the belief that control of the target behavior is an easy thing to do—Bandura; anticipating the positive consequences of failing to modify the target behavior—Marlatt & Gordon). Perhaps the latter set of elements may precede or follow some of the self-regulatory failure behaviors suggested by the closed loop model. Thus, for example, decreased strength and generality of self-efficacy expectations may precede or follow decreased self-monitoring.

Most of the suggested elements of self-regulatory failure derived from the three models reviewed here have not been subjected to empirical scrutiny. On the other hand, four areas of research pertain directly to these and related ideas concerning self-regulatory failure, studies of: successful vs unsuccessful self-regulators, the relapse process, self-monitoring in self-regulatory failure, and self-attention and related research in social and experimental psychology. Sections III A–D will review each of these research domains to continue the search for active ingredients in self-regulatory failure. In the final section of the article (Section IV), we will summarize the key research findings and attempt to integrate them with the suggestions derived from the closed loop, self-efficacy, and cognitive–behavioral relapse models.

III. SELF-REGULATORY FAILURE: FOUR RESEARCH DOMAINS

A. Successful vs Unsuccessful Self-Regulators

Since relatively few people show generalization of self-regulated (and externally regulated) behavior change, a number of researchers have attempted to identify which type of person is most likely to generalize behavior change following various interventions (i.e., dispositional variables that predict success). The underlying belief in this approach is that we can increase the efficiency of our therapies by finding ideal matches between the intervention and the person (e.g., Rozensky & Bellack, 1976; Tobias & MacDonald, 1977). In searching for predictors of success and failure, researchers often include a wide array of dispositional and demographic variables as well as occasional behavioral and biological factors. Then, the predictors are correlated with outcomes. Alternatively, researchers compare extreme groups such as successful self-regulators versus unsuccessful self-regulators in, for example, investigations of weight control, smoking reduction, and study improvement.

The study of successful versus unsuccessful self-regulation may reveal active elements of self-regulatory failure. Presumably certain behaviors emitted by unsuccessful self-regulators not only differentiate them from their more successful counterparts but also *cause* them difficulties in substaining and extending changes initiated in therapy. However, the differences between successful and unsuccessful self-regulators identified either correlationally or by comparisons of extreme groups must be considered correlates of self-regulatory failure rather than causal agents. In other words, we cannot assume that even the differences found between extreme groups are the essential or active agents that cause them to be different (McFall, 1976). Differences observed between successful and unsuccessful self-regulators may correlate with other unassessed variables or may be limited to the types of assessments utilized. Despite these qualifications, the following brief review will show that the study of successful versus unsuccessful self-regulators has produced a number of potential elements of self-regulatory failure that coincide with some theoretical predictions and that deserve further study regardless of their relationship to extant theories.

Three papers provide a description of successful versus unsuccessful self-regulation assessed across several problem behaviors using a standard assessment modality (Marlatt & Kaplan, 1972; Perri & Richards, 1977; Rozensky & Bellack, 1974). Marlatt and Kaplan asked college students to report on their New Year's resolutions at the beginning of a new year and then to indicate, on self-report questionnaires, their successfulness in maintaining the resolutions over a 3-month period. The most interesting finding was that commitment to different types of goals seemed to affect reports of generalized behavior change. Students who promised to change rather specific behaviors (e.g., "physical health: desired changes in physique, habits related to health matters [other than losing weight]'') more frequently reported breaking their self-imposed contracts than students who had established more general goals (e.g., heterosexual relationship changes; changes in personal traits). Of course, the self-report assessment qualifies the findings. Since the more general behaviors are subject to increased distortions, for example, barnum effects (Snyder, Shenkel, & Lowery, 1977), it seems likely that some of the "successes" reported by subjects on these dimensions were attributable to the malleability of perceptions of behavior change. Also, the types of habits associated with the specific behaviors are notoriously refractory (e.g., smoking reduction). On the other hand, perhaps the specificity of plans to change these behaviors was so narrow as to limit the ability of the subjects to exercise choices about how and when to change them, thereby decelerating maintenance of self-regulatory behaviors (Kirschenbaum, Humphrey, & Malett, 1981; Kirschenbaum, Tomarken, & Ordman, 1982).

Rozensky and Bellack (1974) compared 12 successful self-regulators to 12 unsuccessful self-regulators in a laboratory assessment of self-reinforcement style. The successful self-regulators were college student volunteers who reported self-directed weight losses of at least 15 pounds or self-directed smoking cessation within a year of the conduct of the experiment. Unsuccessful subjects tried but failed to change these problem behaviors.

Using a verbal recognition memory task, subjects were asked to memorize 30 nonsense syllables quickly and then identify those syllables during a subsequent presentation of 30 sets of syllables. Subjects also pressed one button which lit a lamp if they believed they accurately identified a syllable ("positive self-reinforcement"), a second button if they believed that they erred ("self-punishment"), or no buttons if they were unsure of the accuracy of their performance.

Rozensky and Bellack found that despite nonsignificant differences in accuracy of performance, the unsuccessful self-regulators self-rewarded less and self-punished more than their successful peers. Although the authors did not report information about the appropriateness of the self-reinforcement patterns of the two groups, it appears from their Table I that the unsuccessful group more appropriately consequated their own performance. In other words, the relatively low level of self-reinforcement and relatively high level of self-punishment exhibited by the unsuccessful group more closely resembled actual performance ($\bar{X}$ = 44% accuracy).

Rozensky and Bellack's findings present unsuccessful self-regulators as individuals whose behavior closely resembles behaviors exhibited by depressed individuals (Beck, 1967; Alloy & Abramson, 1979; Lewinsohn, Mischel, Chaplin, & Barton, 1980). Depressives, like the Rozensky–Bellack unsuccessful self-regulators, show greater accuracy in estimating their performance on a variety of tasks (Alloy & Abramson, 1979; Lewinsohn *et al.*, 1980) and yet, concurrently, fail to exhibit generosity in self-consequation patterns (Kirschenbaum, 1976; Lobitz & Post, 1979; Rehm, 1977). This relatively pessimistic self-view also resembles the lower efficacy expectations Bandura posited as a core element in self-regulatory failure. Also, lowered rates of self-reinforcement were described as a potentially important self-regulatory failure process according to the closed loop model. Whether or not these behaviors actually become activated in self-regulatory failure, of course, remains an unanswered empirical question.

Perri and Richards (1977) conducted structured interviews with samples of college students (ns = 12) who had either changed successfully or failed to change successfully one of four problems: smoking reduction, weight control, study improvement, and heterosocial behavior improvement. Two requirements determined subject selection: (1) one of the four problem behaviors was a serious problem, for example, 20 cigarettes per day for 6 months; and (2) a concerted self-initiated effort was maintained for at least 1 week. Furthermore, successful subjects had to report substantial behavior change and maintenance of change over a period of several months prior to the interview. Dramatic differences between groups on measures of change in problem behaviors (e.g., successful smokers reduced mean cigarette consumption by 27 cigarettes per day compared to a 4 cigarette per day mean reduction by unsuccessful smokers), suggested that the researchers successfully employed their selection criteria.

In lengthy structured interviews subjects were queried about subjective feelings concerning the behavior change enterprise and methods of change utilized. The interviews were reliable according to both interobserver and intraobserver ratings of audiotapes. The consistent findings across problem behaviors indicated that the unsuccessful, compared to the successful, self-regulators reported (a) lower initial commitment to change, (b) lower standards for change, and (c) less frequent and less consistent use of self-regulatory (e.g., self-monitoring, self-reward) and related procedures (e.g., problem solving strategies). Subsequent partial replications and extensions of this work by Perri, Richards, and their associates provided corroborative evidence for the latter result. Perri, Richards, and Schultheis (1977) found that another sample of unsuccessful, compared to successful, smokers (ns = 24) reported relatively infrequent use of only a few self-regulatory techniques. Similarly, Heffernan and Richards (1981) found that unsuccessful studiers used fewer techniques (including self-monitoring, stimulus control, planning, and self-reward) with less consistency than their more successful counterparts [see also positive associations between numbers of techniques utilized and success for alcoholics (Littman, Eiser, Ranson, & Oppenheimer, 1979), weight regulators (Sjoberg & Persson, 1979), and ex-smokers (Baer, Fereyt, & Wright, 1977)].

Although their studies relied primarily on self-reports and on college student populations, Perri, Richards, and their associates conducted theoretically meaningful interviews meticulously and reliably. Consistent with Marlatt and Kaplan (1972), their intriguing results suggest that behaviors in the decisional or commitment phase of self-regulation (Kanfer & Karoly, 1972) may influence self-regulatory failure (cf. Seidner & Kirschenbaum, 1980). Low self-reported desire to change, despite the recognition of a problem and some efforts to change it, may decrease maintenance of requisite self-regulatory behaviors over time. A reduction in self-regulatory behaviors may also be mediated by lowered efficacy expectations as indicated by the relatively low standards for change reported by the unsuccessful self-regulators.

The remaining studies in the successful/unsuccessful literature pertaining to self-regulation vary markedly in methodology and target behaviors. Thus, they provide less direct information about self-regulatory failure than that available in the preceding studies. A review of some representative studies will show, nonetheless, that this approach yields some very interesting findings of relevance to self-regulatory failure.

Two recent reviews of the predictors of success/failure in weight reduction reached rather similar conclusions. Weiss (1977) and Cooke and Meyers (1980) reviewed predictor variables including age, age of onset, sex of subject, social class, personality (e.g., anxiety, depression, MMPI profile, body image, adjustment), self-regulatory style, social variables, weight history, and eating style. Both reviewers indicated that most variables did not consistently predict outcomes. However, the reviewers agreed that self-regulatory style (as studied by Bellack and associates) is perhaps the most promising predictor of success/failure. Furthermore, Cooke and Meyers cited some recent work by Mahoney, Rogers, Straw, and Mahoney (1977) suggesting that "cognitive ecology" may affect self-regulatory failure.

Regarding self-regulatory style, Bellack and his associates conducted a series of studies with overweight individuals that extended their earlier laboratory findings. Most relevant to self-regulatory failure, Bellack, Glanz, and Simon (1976) used a priori assessments of self-regulatory style and found that low self-reinforcers compared to high self-reinforcers (identified via a time estimation task) failed to lose as much weight or maintain as much weight loss over a 5-month follow-up of a self-regulatory intervention [cf. similar effects noted in treatment studies by Rozensky & Bellack (1976) and Carroll, Yates,& Gray (1980)].

B. K. Mahoney *et al.*'s study of "cognitive ecology" found that persons who reported a tendency to use excessive discouraging self-talk lost less fat than those who used more encouraging self-statements. In two related studies, induction procedures designed to enhance both efficacy and outcome expectancies (e.g., showing weight control clients that they can increase their tolerance of ice water by using self-monitoring and self-reinforcement procedures) increased maintenance of weight loss subsequent to self-regulatory interventions at a 3-month follow-up (Steffen & Myszak, 1978) and at a 22-month follow-up (Stalonas, Kirschenbaum, & Zastowny, 1981). It is noteworthy that the improvements in the latter studies were based on comparisons to groups that received identical self-regulatory interventions without the induction procedures. Finally, there is evidence in the obesity literature that *lack* of involvement by significant others in the maintenance of behavior change may precipitate self-regulatory failure perhaps by increasing exposure to stressors or high-risk situations (Cooke & Meyers, 1980; see also Pearce, LeBow, & Orchard, 1981).

The success/failure literature with regard to smoking reduction includes several findings resembling those in the obesity literature. For example, both Perri et al. (1977) and Baer et al. (1977) found evidence that failure to use a variety of self-regulatory techniques (e.g., self-monitoring, self-reward) may contribute to self-regulatory failure. Also, significant others were again implicated as increasing exposure to "high-risk" situations (Marlatt, 1978b; Shiffman, 1981). In a related vein, Pomerleau, Adkins, and Pertschuk (1978) found that smokers who relapsed had smoked more frequently in response to situations that upset them compared to nonrelapsers (cf. Leon & Chamberlain, 1973). Perhaps affect-oriented smokers use smoking to cope with various stressors. Thus, after they quit smoking, the stress associated with a relatively large number of situations may intensify due to a reduction in coping responses. According to Marlatt and Gordon's (1980) model, therefore, the probability of relapse should increase for these individuals.

Three additional studies deserve special attention because of their direct relevance to the self-regulatory failure mechanisms suggested by the self-efficacy and the cognitive–behavioral relapse models. Blittner, Goldberg, and Merbaum (1978) compared no-treatment controls to a stimulus control group and a stimulus control group that also received bogus personality test feedback. During a total of 28 biweekly individual meetings, therapists provided subjects in the latter group with information that should have increased the strength of their efficacy and outcome expectancies. Specifically, therapists repeatedly told them that they were specially selected for the treatment because the battery of psychological tests (including group Rorchachs administered twice) consistently showed that "they had strong willpower and great potential to control and conquer their desires and behavior. Thus it was quite certain that during the course of treatment they would completely stop smoking" (p. 555). Although the authors did not assess the effects of the manipulation on expectancies, the latter intervention should have enhanced efficacy and outcome expectancies via verbal persuasion (cf. Bandura, 1977a). As self-efficacy theory would predict, the groups without the "efficacy enhancement" failed to generalize behavior change over time compared to the "efficacy enhancement group" at several follow-up points.

In one of the only studies designed explicitly to assess the applicability of the self-efficacy and the cognitive–behavioral relapse models to generalized behavior change, Candiotte and Lichtenstein (1981) studied predictors of relapse with 78 smokers. Prior to, during, and subsequent to the administration of several different treatments, subjects completed 48-item questionnaires which provided an index of strength of efficacy expectations. Both microanalyses for individual data and multiple regression for group data revealed very clear correspondence between strength of efficacy expectations at termination of treatment and relapse during the first 3 months following treatment. For example, the shrunken Rs were .57 for the regression of whether subjects relapsed on efficacy state ($p < .001$) and .69 for amount of time taken before relapse on efficacy state ($p < .0001$). This evidence impressively supports self-efficacy theory, by showing that lowered strength of efficacy expectations may actively contribute to self-regulatory failure.

Two additional studies provided some support for the importance of inadequate coping responses in self-regulatory failure as posited by the cognitive–behavioral relapse model. Chaney, O'Leary, and Marlatt (1978) conducted a 1-year follow-up subsequent to a treatment study for alcoholism. A large number of demographic variables (e.g., age, marital status, drinking problem duration) and several indices of coping response skill when confronting high-risk situations assessed at posttreatment were used as predictors in multiple regression analyses. Latency of response to problematic situations (one index of coping skill) predicted 1-year outcomes as well or better than any other variable. For example, latency of emitting coping responses accounted for

53% of the variance in predicting number of days abstinent. Although measures of degree of skill in coping responses and duration of coping responses did not predict long-term outcomes, it appears that failing to respond to descriptions of high-risk situations quickly and readily predicted self-regulatory failure. This finding coincides with predictions derived from the cognitive–behavioral model of relapsing. Slow responding to a test of coping skill may correlate with decreased probability of actually utilizing coping responses when confronting high-risk situations subsequent to the termination of treatment (cf. Perri & Richards, 1977). Thus, decreased readiness to utilize coping responses may serve as an active element in self-regulatory failure.

Littman et al. (1979) also studied alcoholic "survivors" and relapsers over a 6-month posttreatment follow-up period. Littman et al. used a stepwise discriminant analysis to examine responses of their groups to a detailed questionnaire. They found that use of coping behaviors, particularly cognitive self-talk strategies such as "stopping to examine motives," most clearly differentiated survivors from relapsers. Also supportive of the cognitive–behavioral relapse model, another discriminating factor was that relapsers viewed more situations as high in risk. Finally, relapsers perceived themselves as less physiologically dependent than did survivors, perhaps reflecting increased self-blame (or lowered self-efficacy) rather than blaming the physical factors for the problem.

The final study in this grouping, Nash (1976), again implicates emotionality in self-regulatory failure (see also Gormally, Rardin, & Black, 1980). Nash (1976) examined differences between people who discontinued involvement in a weight loss program prior to reaching their goals compared to those who continued throughout the program (N = 187). Reminiscent of the Pomerleau et al. (1978) study with affect-oriented smokers, Nash found that people who dropped out early in the program, during the first 4 of 24 sessions, had indicated in a pretreatment questionnaire that emotionality was a more important factor in their eating behavior compared to people who dropped out late in the program or those who continued. Furthermore, people who had previous experience with weight loss programs (i.e., previous failures) dropped out more readily than those who had not been involved with previous treatments (see parallel findings in Gormally et al., 1980, p. 185; cf. Bandura, 1977a).

Summary

Correlational evidence from studies on successful versus unsuccessful self-regulators suggests several things about self-regulatory failure and the various models of self-regulation. First, several of the studies revealed variables (primarily cognitive factors) that may become activated during self-regulatory failure. In other words, certain responses to environmental events or responses to one's own behavior may contribute to self-regulatory failure. The variables implicated in self-regualtory failure by these studies were (a) overly specific goals (Marlatt & Kaplan, 1972), (b) infrequent self-reinforcement (Bellack et al., 1976; Carroll et al., 1980; Rozensky & Bellack, 1974, 1976; Mahoney et al., 1977), (c) weak or low outcome expectancies (Blittner et al., 1978; Perri & Richards, 1977; Perri et al., 1977; Steffen & Myszak, 1978; Stalonas et al., 1981), (d) lowered strength of efficacy expectations, for example, following repeated experiences perceived as failures (Candiotte & Lichtenstein, 1981; Gormally et al., 1980; Nash, 1976), (e) inadequate use of a variety of coping and self-regulatory skills (Baer et al., 1977; Candiotte & Lichtenstein, 1981; Chaney et al., 1978; Littman et al., 1979; Perri & Richards, 1977; Perri et al., 1977; Sjoberg & Persson, 1979), and (f) failing to avoid or selectively exposing oneself to stressful situations (Cooke & Meyers, 1980; Pomerleau et al., 1978; Nash, 1976).

This evidence provides some support for each of the theoretical models presented earlier in addition to suggesting several other mechanisms that may contribute to self-regulatory failure. Decreased self-reinforcement would contribute to self-regulatory failure according to the closed loop model. Similarly, exposure to high-risk, emotionally charged, situations, lowered efficacy and altered outcome expectancies, and failure to use coping responses are the kinds of self-regulatory failure mechanisms proposed by self-efficacy and cognitive–behavioral relapse models. In addition, however, the findings suggest at least two other processes that may function in self-regulatory failure. Use of overly specific standards for behavior change and rather slow or rigid use of a restricted number of coping and self-regulatory skills may also reduce generalization of behavior change.

In concluding this section, several methodological qualifications of the data base require discussion. First, we must reemphasize that the correlational foundations of these studies indicate that their results may suggest hypotheses and assist in testing theoretical predictions but they cannot tell us what people actually do during self-regulatory failure. Successful self-regulators may differ from less successful self-regulators on a host of variables but perhaps only a few (as yet unidentified?) behavioral differences cause self-regulatory failure. Some of the differences between these groups may have been caused by their differential success in self-regulation. Furthermore, many of the present findings derive from post hoc self-reports about the causes of behavior. While self-perceptions clearly determine behavior in important ways (e.g., Bandura, 1977a, 1977b; Mahoney, 1974), these reports often fail to correspond to overt or physiological responses (Lang, 1971; Nisbett & Ross, 1980). Also, the issues under investigation, success vs failure, often cause specific changes in self-perception that do not correspond to external events (e.g., Garber & Seligman, 1980). Thus, we must move closer to studying behavioral and stylistic patterns, assessed by a variety of response systems, that people actually use during self-regulatory failure, if we hope to understand them more clearly and completely. The studies reviewed in the following subsections begin taking that next step.

B. The Relapse Process

Recall that Marlatt and Gordon (1980) defined relapse as violation of rules governing rate or pattern of consumption behaviors. Thus, studies of the process of violating behavioral rules describe self-regulatory failure when the rule violation occurs in the relative absence of external constraints and when it prevents the generalization of therapeutic behavior change. Since many relapses are self-regulated and decrease generalization, we will examine the studies in this important, albeit nascent, field of inquiry (Chaney et al., 1978; Candiotte & Lichtenstein, 1981; Marlatt, 1978b; Marlatt & Gordon, 1980; Sjoberg & Johnson, 1978; Sjoberg & Persson, 1979; Sjoberg & Samsonowitz, 1978; Sjoberg, Samsonowitz, & Olsson, 1978; Lichtenstein, Antonuccio, & Rainwater, 1982; Shiffman, 1981).

Marlatt and his associates used structured interviews and carefully executed content analyses to categorize precipitants of relapses. In the first study, Marlatt (1973, reported in Marlatt, 1978a) interviewed male alcoholics who relapsed following an aversive conditioning treatment. The interviewers asked about the parameters of the first relapse episode including time of day, description of the situation, presence or absence of others, and self-reported feelings. He found that relapse situations were reliably assigned to four major types: (a) frustration and inability to express anger (29%), (b) social pressure to drink (23%), (c) intrapersonal temptation to drink (21%), and (d) intrapersonal negative emotional state (10%).

In a subsequent study, in which 40 alcoholics were followed-up for 1 year after social skills treatment or comparison/control procedures (Chaney et al., 1978), Marlatt's (1973/1978a) interview technique was again used to identify relapse situations. The four situational categories again described most of the high-risk situations. However, according to our calculations, the rank ordered frequencies of the four types of situations in Chaney et al. (1978) did not correlate with the findings of Marlatt (1973/1978a), $\tau = .55$, $p > .15$ (one-tailed): intrapersonal negative emotional states (43%), social pressure (17%), frustration/anger (15.5%), and intrapersonal temptation (15.5%).

Differences in subject populations, duration of follow-up, and treatment procedures employed may account for the inconsistencies noted across the first two studies in the series by Marlatt and his associates. Despite these inconsistencies, the results suggest that interpersonal factors may contribute rather strongly to creating high-risk situations and that certain kinds of emotional states may also affect self-regulatory failure more than others. Additional data consistent with these conclusions were reported by Marlatt and Gordon (1980) in a more elaborate study. These authors used an expanded 12-category scoring procedure to evaluate first relapse episodes reported by 70 alcoholics, 35 smokers, and 32 heroin addicts within 90 days following the termination of various types of treatments. They found considerable similarity across problem behaviors. Once again social factors, particularly those described as social pressure (e.g., direct encouragement from others to relapse, observation of others who are using the substance) and interpersonal conflict, accounted for a substantial number of the high-risk situations (more than 33% for all problem behaviors). They also found that negative emotional states, including frustration, anger, guilt, depression, sadness, grief, worry, and boredom, accounted for approximately one-third of all high-risk situations. Finally, Marlatt and Gordon's data indicated that the vast majority of their smokers and alcoholics followed either their first or second relapse episode with full resumption of their former habits. Thus, as suggested by Marlatt and Gordon, the initial relapse may feature prominently in self-regulatory failure. Self-reactions (e.g., lowered efficacy expectations—"That proves I can't do it!") plus physiological consequences may well contribute to the deleterious effects of the initial relapse.

In another programatic effort to study the relapse process, Sjoberg and his associates conducted a series of unstructured interviews with smokers (Sjoberg & Johnson, 1978; Sjoberg & Samsonowitz, 1978), alcoholics (Sjoberg et al., 1978), and obese individuals (Sjoberg & Persson, 1979). Sjoberg and Persson summarized their anecdotal findings as supporting their dynamic view of the course of relapsing. Although the terminology differs considerably from Marlatt and Gor-

don's, a resemblance emerges in some of the central ideas and predictions. Specifically, Sjoberg and associates' "theory" assumes that:

> Conflicts may create demands on mental energy which in turn is taken from the
> resources available to the cognitive system. When the cognitive system is drained
> of these resources, it becomes much weaker and more primitive, thus giving rise
> to distorted and low quality reasoning and judgments. The narrow perspective,
> typically found in volitional breakdowns, . . . stem(s) from properties of wish
> content due to strong needs. The theory thus predicts that breakdowns will occur
> under emotional stress and that they will be preceded by distorted reasonings and
> a narrow perspective. (Sjoberg & Persson, 1979, p. 349)

Sjoberg et al., paralleling Marlatt et al., noted that reports of conflicts
and emotional distress commonly occur during self-regulatory failure.
Furthermore, Sjoberg et al. associate these conflicts and distress responses with distorted judgments. While Marlatt and Bandura emphasize distortions in self-perceptions as crucial in self-regulatory failure, Sjoberg et al. view logical errors concerning the target behavior
as perhaps more central (e.g., "An extra sandwich now helps me eat
less later;" "It's my vacation—I must relax;" "I have already lost a lot
this week."). Other differences between the viewpoints concern Sjoberg's use of rather vague dynamic postulates (e.g., mental energy,
strong needs) compared to the more operationally and conceptually
specific elements postulated by Bandura and Marlatt. In addition, it
should be accentuated that Sjoberg and associates relied on impres-
sions during interviews, instead of highly structured (publically available) interview protocols and reliable content analyses, to formulate
their view of the relapse process.

   Three additional studies with smokers provide further data about
the relapse process. In the previously described study by Candiotte
and Lichtenstein (1981), a group of 24 subjects agreed to participate
in 5 weeks of intensive data gathering following treatment. Of the 12
subjects in this group who relapsed during the 5 weeks posttreatment,
11 declined to continue their self-monitoring of cigarette smoking behavior, mood, and self-efficacy. Interestingly, these 11 subjects stopped
their self-monitoring "either just prior to or at the same time as they
experienced their relapse episode." During subsequent phone calls,
"many of these subjects indicated that the data collection had become
extremely aversive and they couldn't handle it anymore!" The discontinuation of self-monitoring is an element of self-regulatory failure
clearly predicted by the closed loop model. The aversive reaction to
self-monitoring may precede discontinuation of self-monitoring. Thus,

this affective reaction may be another element of self-regulatory failure consistent with, but not predicted by, the closed loop model (Kirsch-enbaum & Karoly, 1977).

Candiotte and Lichtenstein's analysis of the relapse data for all 44 subjects in their sample who eventually relapsed was also very con-sistent with self-efficacy and cognitive–behavioral relapse models. Relapsers had lower posttreatment self-efficacy than nonrelapsers and they reported negative affect and lowered "confidence" following their first relapse episode. In addition, 49% of the relapsers reported no effort at coping responses following their first cigarette whereas 100% of the people who smoked at least once but then remained abstinent (n = 8), reported using some coping response following their smoking episode.

Lichtenstein et al. (1982) used structured interviews and the Marlatt and Gordon (1980) coding system to investigate the relapse process of another group of smokers. Their 84 subjects had quit smoking for a median period of 5 weeks and were interviewed within a year of the relapse (median − 22 weeks postrelapse). Their findings, and those they cited from a study of 64 smokers by Cummings, Gordon, and Marlatt (1980), although differing in some categories from Marlatt and Gordon's data, again indicated that negative emotional states, social pressure, and interpersonal conflicts accounted for most of the high-risk situations. Additional descriptive analyses provided by Lichten-stein et al. (interrater agreement ranged from 76 to 96%) suggested the following as additional high-risk factors: the presence of other people— particularly smokers, relaxing/recreating (versus working, reading, or watching TV); and drinking alcohol. It is also noteworthy that un-pleasant affect preceded the relapse (44%) twice as often as pleasant affect (22%); 43% of the subjects reported not thinking about smoking during the relapse (cf. closed loop predictions); 39% of the subjects reported no coping responses subsequent to the first cigarette (cf. cog-nitive–behavioral relapse predictions); and the first relapse episode was followed by a rapid resumption of smoking ($\overline{X}$ cigarettes smoked on the following day = 7.5). Finally, although Marlatt and his asso-ciates and Lichtenstein et al. note that physiological factors seem less central to relapse than anticipated, Lichtenstein et al. actually found that 95.5% of the subjects reported continued cravings in at least some circumstances and nearly half of these people reported relatively con-stant or strong cravings. Of course some aspects of the cravings may be cognitive, but physiological factors are probably implicated by these findings.

The final smoking study of relapse relied on an innovative procedure to evaluate relapse "crises." Shiffman (1981) established a well-publicized "Stay-Quit Line" in Los Angeles, California, a telephone counseling service for ex-smokers undergoing relapse episodes. He gathered data, of the sort collected by the other relapse researchers, by having the telephone counselors ask a series of specific questions. Of the 183 interviews with ex-smokers used in the study, 15 were recorded and rated reliably (77–100%) by all three interviewers. This procedure resulted in a sample of people who had been abstinent for a median of 10 days, 39% of whom had smoked approximately one cigarette on the same day as the call or within a few days of the call. Thus, these individuals were actively struggling to prevent self-regulatory failure, especially in view of the data indicating that one or two cigarettes is usually followed, almost immediately, by full-blown resumption of smoking (Marlatt & Gordon, 1980; Lichtenstein et al., 1982).

Shiffman's data generally coincide with the other reports describing the relapse process for smokers. Affective states again appeared to play a major role with negative states accounting for more than twice as many crises as positive affect. Situational precipitants again appeared to include the presence of other smokers and consumptive behavior (including alcohol). In addition, and somewhat contrary to the emphases of previous writers in this area, Shiffman found that more than half of the callers reported a variety of physical symptoms associated with the relapse crises, including achiness, nausea, headache, and irritability. Furthermore, Shiffman explicitly excluded tallies of "cravings" which he seemed to have assumed occurred in all of the crises. Finally, he found that failure to use coping responses significantly and substantially increased the probability of relapsing. Twice as many callers who reported not using coping responses were among the 39% of the sample who had actually relapsed prior to calling compared to the callers who used some coping responses (e.g., reviewing reasons for quitting, leaving the high-risk situation).

Summary

Research on the relapse process certainly adds detailed descriptions of potentially crucial processes in self-regulatory failure. Specifically, these findings suggest the following as elements in self-regulatory failure: (a) single relapse episodes (Candiotte & Lichtenstein, 1981; Marlatt & Gordon, 1980; Lichtenstein et al., 1982); (b) negative emotional states (Candiotte & Lichtenstein, 1981; Chaney et al., 1978; Cummings et al., 1980; Marlatt, 1973/1978a; Marlatt & Gordon, 1980; Sjoberg and associates, 1978, 1979; Lichtenstein et al., 1982; Shiffman, 1981);

(c) positive emotional states (Lichtenstein et al., 1982; Shiffman, 1981); (d) interpersonal conflicts and pressures (all of the references cited above except Candiotte & Lichtenstein, 1981); (e) temptations, cravings, biologically related variables (Chaney et al., 1978; Marlatt, 1973/1978a; Marlatt & Gordon, 1980; Lichtenstein et al., 1982; Shiffman, 1981); (f) coping skills deficits (Candiotte & Lichtenstein, 1981; Chaney et al., 1978; Lichtenstein et al., 1982; Shiffman 1981); (g) lowered efficacy expectations and related distortions in self-judgment (Candiotte & Lichtenstein, 1981; Sjoberg and associates, 1978, 1979); (h) decreased self-monitoring (Candiotte & Lichtenstein, 1981; Lichtenstein et al., 1982); and (i) exposure to such high-risk situations as the presence of other smokers and consumption of alcohol (all references above except Candiotte & Lichtenstein, 1981; Sjoberg and associates, 1978, 1979).

These findings again support many of the predictions derived from the closed loop model, self-efficacy theory, and the cognitive–behavioral relapse model. Particularly impressive were the potency of single relapse episodes, exposure to certain high-risk situations, inadequacies in use of coping skills immediately prior to relapse, and low efficacy expectations. These finding were obtained by Candiotte and Lichtenstein (1981) and Shiffman (1981). They are also especially interesting because the former research was prospective rather than retrospective and because both studies gathered considerable data almost concurrently with actual relapse episodes. As such they add substantially to the construct validity of the relapse process (and self-regulatory failure) as it was proposed by the three theoretical models.

Two issues emerge from the relapse studies that deserve additional commentary. First, many of the researchers deemphasized the role of physiological variables. Perhaps they thought it crucial to do this to accentuate the oftentimes neglected role of social, situational, and dispositional factors in relapsing in addictive disorders. Nonetheless, it should be clearly noted that many of the emotional states described by relapsers in interviews (e.g., Marlatt & Gordon, 1980) in addition to direct indicators of physiological cravings and discomfort (e.g., Shiffman, 1981) suggest that physiological variables may contribute substantially to the self-regulatory failure of addictive disorders (see also Cannon et al., 1981; Rodin, 1981). Second, many of the findings in the present set of studies, as in the prior research on success/failure, are based on self-reports obtained by asking specific sets of questions. The question that remains focal is, What do people actually do during self-regulatory failure? Distortions in self-reports are quite common (Nisbett & Ross, 1980; Snyder et al., 1977) and the particular types of distortions that emerge may follow from the types of questions asked (Kazdin, 1978; Lang, 1978). Thus, even though decreased strength of efficacy expectations (Candiotte & Lichtenstein, 1981) or low self-reports of general motivation (McFall & Hammen, 1971) predict self-regulatory failure, we do not know how these expectations affect behavioral elements of self-regulatory failure. Similarly, reports of decreased self-monitoring (Lichtenstein et al., 1982) provide less convincing evidence of the role of decreased self-monitoring than witnessing the unwillingness of people to continue self-monitoring as they fail to maintain a desired behavior change (Candiotte & Lichtenstein, 1981). In the following section, we describe the results of studies that more directly examine elements of self-regulatory failure, that is, the conditions under which people decrease self-regulatory behaviors.

C. Self-Monitoring in Self-Regulatory Failure

The closed loop model of self-regulation suggests that self-monitoring, the process of systematically gathering information about a target behavior, is "an essential prerequisite for the proper application of self-regulation" (Kanfer, 1970). As we noted previously, many refractory behaviors (e.g., the addictions) probably require relatively permanent (lifetime?) self-regulation. Thus, according to the closed loop model, factors causing substantially reduced self-monitoring comprise elements of self-regulatory failure (Kirschenbaum, 1976).

Research on self-monitoring supports Kanfer's assertion that self-monitoring is necessary for self-regulation. Three studies, using diverse subject populations and settings, showed that self-regulated behavior change occurred when self-monitoring was activated and failed to occur when self-monitoring was discontinued (Broden, Hall, & Mitts, 1971; Gottman & McFall, 1972; Hendricks, Thoresen, & Hubbard, 1974). Several clinical investigations supply additional corroborative evidence. Maletzky (1974) gave nondemand instructions to five clients by informing them, prior to their use of wristcounters to self-monitor, that "counting their behavior would assist therapists in understanding their problems, but that counting would not necessarily decrease unwanted behaviors" (p. 108). Frequency of skin scratching, fingernail biting, disruptive hand-raising in class, facial tics, and inappropriate standing in class declined dramatically during self-monitoring, a process which clients typically noted as important in cueing their active alteration of problem behaviors. Furthermore, the fact that 11 of 12 of Candiotte and Lichtenstein's (1981) smokers discontinued self-monitoring as they relapsed also supports the claim that self-monitoring is necessary in self-regulation and that discontinuation of self-monitoring may contribute to self-regulatory failure (see also Carrol et al., 1980; Stalonas et al., 1981).

While self-monitoring may be a necessary condition for self-regulation, it is not a sufficient condition. Many studies reveal little or no effects attributable to self-monitoring (see reviews by Kazdin, 1974a; McFall, 1977; Nelson, 1977). Studies on the conditions under which self-monitoring does change behavior (i.e., the reactivity of self-monitoring), however, again underscore the vital role of self-monitoring in self-regulation. Recall that self-monitoring, as defined in the closed loop model, systematically provides information about a target behavior that is important enough to disrupt the flow of normal activities (Kanfer, 1971, 1980). Thus, the model indicates that self-monitoring should impact most when it provides useful information about important target behaviors. Consistent with this view, self-monitoring more reactively changes behavior when it provides salient information (e.g., Ashby & Wilson, 1977; Richards, Anderson, & Bakor, 1078) about target behaviors that are considered important (e.g., Cavior & Marraboto, 1976; Kazdin, 1974b)—important enough to want to change them (e.g., Komaki & Dore-Boyce, 1978; McFall & Hammen, 1971).

Given the seemingly vital role of sustained self-monitoring in the maintenance of self-regulation, we must discover the conditions under which self-monitoring decreases or ceases. A process related to sustained self-monitoring has been investigated by several researchers (Duval & Wicklund, 1972; Horan, Baker, Hoffman, & Shute, 1975; Mischel, Ebbesen, & Zeiss, 1973; Roth & Rehm, 1980). These investigators examined factors that influenced selective attention to information about oneself. Selectively attending to certain self-aspects or target behaviors is the initial stage of self-monitoring, that is, the process of discriminating or recognizing the fact that the target behavior occurred (Kanfer, 1971; Nelson & Hayes, 1981). Thus, factors that decrease attention to important self-aspects may predict reductions in sustained self-monitoring over time and across situations. The findings in this literature indicate, therefore, that the following factors may decrease self-monitoring: experiencing failure (Mischel et al., 1973; cf. also Candiotte & Lichtenstein, 1981; Lichtenstein et al., 1982); and accentuating the aversive aspects of failure by having dispositional characteristics oriented toward observing failure (Mischel et al., 1973; Roth & Rehm, 1980) or by focusing on personal liabilities associated with failure (Duval & Wicklund, 1972; Horan et al., 1975; Roth & Rehm, 1980).

Two additional studies (Kirschenbaum & Karoly, 1977; Tomarken & Kirschenbaum, 1982) examined the effects of focusing on failures and successes as potentially active determinants of self-regulatory failure (cf. also Kirschenbaum, Ordman, Tomarken, & Holtzbauer, 1982). Kirschenbaum and Karoly used a paradigm (Mahoney, Moore, Wade, & Moura, 1973) in which volunteer subjects were invited to work on mathematics problems in preparation for graduate school admissions tests. Ninety-six students were assigned to groups in which they either focused on their failures by self-monitoring their inaccurate problem solving (negative self-monitoring), self-recorded accurate problem solving (positive self-monitoring), did not self-record but received the same kind of immediate performance feedback as the self-monitors (performance feedback), or did not self-record or receive immediate feedback (control). Stratified random assignment, based on performance on a math pretest, controlled for variance attributable to ability. Subjects received either difficult (35% accuracy level) or relatively simple (65% accuracy level) math problems to work on during three 15-minute problem-solving periods. During 10-minute free time periods, in-between problem-solving periods, subjects were encouraged to observe their problem-solving activities on a videotape monitor (problem cards and scratch work—with no feedback in any group).

According to predictions derived from the closed loop model of self-regulation, activation-arousal theories of motivation, and several relevant studies (including research on selective attention to the self), negative self-monitoring was expected to cause self-regulatory failure (e.g., lowered performance, decreased self-observation during free time periods) when the task was difficult but positive self-monitoring was expected to occasion self-regulatory failure when the task was relatively simple. Negative self-monitoring actually lowered performance compared to performance feedback and control groups under both levels of task difficulty. However, negative self-monitors also increased self-observation over time when the task was simple whereas positive self-monitors showed the predicted decline in self-observation—even when compared to the equally accurate problem solvers in the performance feedback group. On the other hand, all groups in the high difficulty condition evidenced self-regulatory failure to a considerable extent. Compared to low-task difficulty subjects, high-task difficulty subjects self-evaluated less favorably, self-consequated less favorably, reported higher anxiety, and self-observed somewhat less ($p < .10$).

The results of the Kirschenbaum and Karoly study reinforce the earlier assertion that failure experiences and accentuated reactions to failure may precipitate self-regulatory failure. The repeated experience with very difficult problems (i.e., failure to perform) resulted in negative self-reactions and disengagement from the task (highly significant declines in self-observation over trials for all groups). "The course of this disengagement process was unaltered even when subjects were fitted with experimental 'rose-colored glasses' (i.e., instructed to positively self-monitor)" (p. 1124). In addition, however, focusing on positive aspects of behavior also produced self-regulatory dysfunctioning in the low-difficulty condition. Perhaps when self-regulated tasks become highly overlearned, routine, or automatic (e.g., during extended self-regulation or in the habit reorganization phases), positive self-focusing may actively contribute to self-regulatory failure.

To examine the role of both positive and negative self-monitoring in self-regulatory failure more completely, Tomarken and Kirschenbaum (1982) replicated and extended certain aspects of the previous study. To assess sustained self-regulatory behavior more naturalistically, we encouraged the volunteer subjects (n = 66) to return for two additional sessions over a 2-week interval (the final session included work with a math tutor) In addition, we used a lower level of math difficulty (from 71 to 85% accuracy) to approximate more closely the state of overlearning or task mastery required by activation-arousal theories of motivation (cf. Korman, 1974). In accord with predictions, positive self-monitoring again produced self-regulatory failure. Relative to negative self-monitors, positive self-monitors performed less accurately, spent somewhat less time in self-observation (p < .10), wrote fewer notes to themselves during self-observation, and failed to attend as many extra sessions (see Fig. 3). In addition, when compared to performance feedback subjects, positive self-monitors (but not negative self-monitors) self-observed less.

The results of these two studies are consistent with several other findings in the self-monitoring literature by indicating that differential self-monitoring interacts with level of mastery to affect performance and persistence (e.g., Gottman & McFall, 1972; Litrownik & Freitas, 1980; Wade, 1974; see Kirschenbaum & Karoly, 1977). Additionally, since positive self-monitors selectively attended to positive outcomes, while negative self-monitors attended to negative outcomes, or failures, these findings can also be compared to those from studies assessing the effects of success and failure on performance. Indeed, the parallels are striking. Just as negative self-monitoring compared unfavorably to positive self-monitoring in a low-mastery, high-anxiety context, the actual *experience* of failure, relative to success, has sometimes impaired the performance of individuals who had a previous history of failure (Lazarus & Ericksen, 1952), low expectancies for success (e.g.,

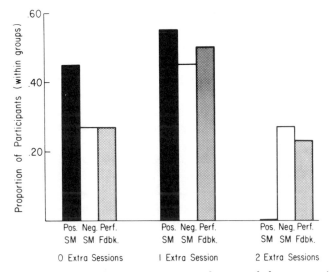

Fig. 3. Proportions of self-monitoring groups that attended extra sessions in the Tomarken and Kirschenbaum study. Pos. SM, Positive self-monitors; Neg. SM, negative self-monitors; Perf. Fdbk., performance feedback. From Tomarken and Kirschenbaum (1982).

Diener & Dweck, 1978, 1980; Shrauger & Rosenberg, 1970), and high levels of anxiety (e.g., Mandler & Sarason, 1952; Wiener & Schneider, 1971). Similarly, the finding that positive self-monitoring occasioned self-regulatory dysfunctioning in a high-mastery context corresponds to the evidence that success, relative to failure, may impair the performance of those with a prior history of success (Lazarus & Ericksen, 1952), expectations for continued success (e.g., Halisch & Heckhausen, 1977; Rijsman, 1974), and low levels of negative affect (e.g., Weiner, 1966; Weiner & Schneider, 1971) (see also Wortman & Brehm, 1975). These parallels strongly suggest that selective attention to successes and failures may have the same effects on self-regulation as the actual experience of success and failure (Tomarken & Kirschenbaum, 1982). In so doing, they indicate that models of self-regulation should more explicitly represent selective attention.

Research on the effects of task mastery on naturally occurring forms of selective attention leads to a similar conclusion. The evidence indicates that individuals often selectively attend to negative information about the self and/or evaluate themselves more negatively than is objectively warranted. This occurs when they have previously failed (e.g., Moore, Underwood, Heberlein, Doyle, & Litzkie, 1979; Postman & Brown, 1952), negative expectancies for success (e.g., Diener &

Dweck, 1980; Silverman, 1964), and heightened negative affect (e.g., Clark & Arkowitz, 1975; Holroyd, Westbrook, Wolf, & Badhorn, 1978). This literature has also shown that success experience, positive expectancies, and low levels of anxiety can result in a selective focus upon positive self-aspects and overly favorable self-evaluations (for reviews, see Bower, 1981; Shrauger, 1975; Wine, 1980). In short, it appears that low-mastery contexts often elicit covert negative self-monitoring, while high-mastery contexts can produce covert positive self-monitoring. Consider these data in light of the evidence that negative self-monitoring debilitates performance in low-mastery contexts, and that positive self-monitoring results in impairments in high-mastery situations. These findings suggest that the attentional styles spontaneously elicited by high- and low-mastery contexts may function as active elements of self-regulatory failure. For this reason, interventions designed to alter these naturally occurring forms of selective attention may reduce self-regulatory dysfunctioning. Finally, this evidence indicates that findings obtained in studies examining the effects of differential self-monitoring may generalize to contexts in which the individual is not explicitly engaged in self-monitoring.

Summary

Taken together, the preceding studies reveal that potentially active elements of self-regulatory failure are susceptible to direct experimental investigation. Specifically, these findings indicate that self-monitoring is necessary for self-regulation. However, it also appears that the beneficial effects of self-monitoring are conditional upon both the valence of target behaviors to which individuals attend and the level of task-mastery. Several studies, including those on selective attention (e.g., Mischel et al., 1973; Candiotte & Lichtenstein, 1981) and differential self-monitoring (e.g., Gottman & McFall, 1972; Kirschenbaum & Karoly, 1977) suggest that failures and the accentuation of failure experiences via negative self-monitoring, can disrupt generalized self-regulation when the target behavior is poorly mastered. Conversely, positive self-monitoring may disrupt self-regulation at high levels of task-proficiency (e.g., Tomarken & Kirschenbaum, 1982; Wade, 1974). The evidence that the effects of differential *attention* to success and failure parallel those of differential *experience* with success and failure (e.g., Lazarus & Ericksen, 1952; Halisch & Heckhausen, 1977) also indicates that selective attention and differential self-monitoring may be central elements in self-regulatory failure. Further support for this conclusion is provided by research showing that low-mastery contexts often lead to covert negative self-monitoring, and

that high-mastery contexts can result in covert positive self-monitoring
(e.g., Bower, 1981; Moore et al., 1979). This latter evidence indicates
that the naturally occurring attentional styles elicited by these contexts
may predispose individuals to self-regulatory dysfunctioning.

D. Self-Attention and Related Research in Social and Experimental Psychology

1. Self-Attention

a. Duval and Wicklund's Theory of Objective Self-Awareness.   Duval
and Wicklund (1972) proposed that we attend to either the external
environment or ourselves. They argued that attention to the self increases when stimuli (e.g., mirrors; review of our personal history)
remind us of our object-like nature. Self-evaluation is then posited as
the natural reaction to self-attention. Unfortunately, since self-evaluation often proves unfavorable and, therefore, aversive, withdrawal
from the self-attentive state typically follows self-attention and self-
evaluation, according to Duval and Wicklund. They further suggested
that we adjust our behavior to the standard used in self-evaluation
only when escape from self-attention becomes impossible.

b. Carver's Cybernetic Model of Self-Attentional Processes.   Carver
(1979) reformulated Duval and Wicklund's theory of objective self-
awareness by suggesting an alternative reaction to self-attention. Carver
argued that self-attention in the presence of a salient standard, rather
than causing withdrawal from continued self-attention, typically ini-
tiates a test-operate-test negative feedback loop (cf. Kanfer, 1971; Kanfer & Karoly, 1972). Like Kanfer's self-monitoring plus self-evaluation
phases, self-attention is the test or comparison phase of this loop.
Carver posited that if the test or self-attentive phase reveals an incon-
gruity between current behavior and a standard (i.e., unfavorable self-
evaluation in Kanfer's model), an operate phase ensues during which
the individual alters behavior to match the standard. In most cases,
self-attention (test) is expected to alternate with behavioral adjustments
(operate) until the behavior conforms to the standard. When the desired
match occurs, individuals disengage (exit) the self-regulatory feedback
loop. However, expectancies, affect, and other factors may interfere
with this self-regulatory loop. For example, Carver (1979) indicated
that negative "outcome expectancies" (i.e., beliefs that one cannot
appropriately alter the behavior, see p. 1273) disengage the process
whereas positive outcome expectancies maintain it.

Carver's model, like Kanfer's, suggests that a process of orienting
to the self triggers a feedback loop of self-regulation when people

notice discrepancies between their standards and behaviors. As described in an earlier section, a variety of studies of direct relevance to Kanfer's closed loop model support the assertion that self-monitoring is a necessary condition for self-regulation. Considerable evidence from the self-attention literature also corroborates this vital assumption.

In a particularly convincing demonstration, Diener and Wallbom (1976) found that mirror-induced self-attention reduced the proportion of college students who cheated on an achievement test from 71 to 7% ($p < .001$). Self-attention in the presence of a salient standard also reduced cheating in children (Beaman, Klantz, Diener, & Swanson, 1979); decreased physical aggression (e.g., Carver, 1975; Scheier, Fenigstein, & Buss, 1974); increased prosocial behavior (e.g., Wegner & Schaefer, 1978; Gotay, 1977); heightened conformity to an equity norm (e.g., Greenberg, 1980; Gibbons, Wicklund, & Rosenfeld, 1979); and improved performance and persistence on a variety of tasks (Carver, Blaney, & Scheier, 1979b; McDonald, 1980; Slapion & Carver, 1981; Wicklund & Duval, 1971; Carver & Scheier, 1979). Additional findings show that self-attention generally cues more careful and complete introspection. Specifically, self-attentive subjects more actively assessed their abilities in several studies (e.g., Carver & Blaney, 1977a, 1977b; Carver, Blaney, & Scheier, 1979a) and more frequently compared their behavior to salient standards in a recent experiment (Carver & Scheier, 1979). Other studies have found that expectancy manipulations only significantly affected behavior when subjects were self-attentive (e.g., Carver et al., 1979a, 1979b; Kuhl, 1981; Steenbarger & Aderman, 1979). Furthermore, individuals made self-attentive via mirrors and those who were dispositionally high in "private self-consciousness" (Fenigstein, Scheier, & Buss, 1975) produced longer (Turner, 1978b) and more accurate self-reports (e.g., Pryor, Gibbons, Wicklund, Fazio, & Hood, 1977; Turner, 1978a; Borden & Pryor, 1981); were more cognizant of their transient affective (e.g., Scheier, 1976; Scheier & Carver, 1977) and physiological states (Pennebaker & Skelton, 1978; Scheier, Carver, & Gibbons, 1979); and were more likely to read first person content into incomplete or ambiguous verbal material (e.g., Carver & Scheier, 1978; Wegner & Giuliono, 1980).

Self-attention apparently increases self-evaluative processes and stimulates self-regulated behavior change under many circumstances. These findings again suggest that some form of self-attention may be a necessary condition for self-regulation (cf. Broden et al., 1971; Gottman & McFall, 1972; Kanfer, 1971). Thus, factors that reduce sustained self-attention may become activated in self-regulatory failure. In addition, just as positive self-monitoring increased self-regulatory failure

(Kirschenbaum & Karoly, 1977: Tomarken & Kirschenbaum, 1982), under some conditions self-attention may well contribute to self-regulatory failure (cf. Carver, 1979; Duval & Wicklund, 1972). Therefore, to explore further potential elements of self-regulatory failure suggested by self-attention research, we will examine factors in this literature that have been shown to decrease self-attention and persistence.

c. *Factors That Decrease Self-Attention and Persistence.* At least two conditions appear to cause individuals to avoid sustained self-attention. First, failure followed by the perception that the failure cannot be changed through subsequent behavioral adjustments appears to motivate escape from sustained self-attention (Duval, Wicklund, & Fine, 1972; Gibbons & Wicklund, 1976; Gur & Sackeim, 1979; Steenbarger & Aderman, 1979). For example, in the Steenbarger and Aderman study, subjects were told that they performed very poorly on an initial test of "intelligence and creativity." Those subjects who were led to believe that they should not improve on a subsequent test lest a waiting room that contained a self-attentional stimulus (mirror) after a short period of time compared to subjects who were led to expect improvements in performance on the subsequent test (cf. Duval et al., 1972). Second, directing one's attention to things other than oneself also diminished self-attention in several studies. Specifically, explicit redirection of attention to stimuli in the immediate environment produced effects directly opposite to those associated with increased self-attention in studies of dissonance reduction (Allen, 1965), attribution of blame for negative outcomes (Duval & Wicklund, 1972, Experiments 1, 2, and 3), self-esteem (Ferris & Wicklund, cited in Wicklund, 1975), and disinhibition of behaviors in social contexts (Diener, 1978, 1979). For example, in three experiments Duval and Wicklund (1972) asked subjects to apportion responsibility for a negative outcome between themselves and another possible perpetrator. Some subjects squeezed a handgrip (Experiment 1) or rotated a turntable (Experiments 2 and 3), while controls did not engage in physical activities when apportioning blame. In each experiment, attribution of blame to the self was diminished with physical activity.

Regarding persistence, the evidence suggests that self-attention can decrease persistence when people (a) expect to fail, (b) experience excessive negative affect, and (c) expect to continue succeeding at tasks directly relevant to those which they already mastered. Concerning the first of these three conclusions, many studies, in fact 18 of 20 in a recent review (Tomarken & Kirschenbaum, 1982a), support the assertion that self-attention debilitates performance and persistence in individuals who expect to fail (e.g., Brockner, 1979; Carver et al., 1979b; Scheier, Carver, & Gibbons, 1981). For example, Carver et al.

(1979b) exposed subjects to an initial failure experience. Subjects then undertook a second task which ostensibly measured the same intellectual skill as "assessed" by the first task, and were either told to expect to do quite well or quite poorly on the second task. As anticipated, negative expectancies plus self-attention reduced persistence on the second task. Similar debilitation of persistence and performance accompanied self-attention in studies that used subjects with chronic negative expectancies (e.g., Carver et al., 1979a), exposed subjects to extensive prior failure (e.g., Kuhl, 1981), or used a very difficult task (e.g., Duval & Friedan, 1979).

Some of the detrimental effects of expecting to fail on persistence may be attributable to a heightened and excessive negative state induced by self-attention. Self-attention clearly increases negative affect for those with negative expectancies (e.g., Carver et al., 1979b; Steenbarger & Aderman, 1979). More generally, self-attention often intensifies the experience of emotion. For example, self-attention has intensified feelings of anxiety (Carver et al., 1979b; Scheier et al., 1981), anger (Scheier, 1976), and sympathy (Scheier, Carver, Schulz, Glass, & Katz, 1978). Since affective states and cognitive processes are somewhat independent (e.g., Zajonc, 1980), it seems plausible to suggest that negative expectancies and negative affective states may function both independently and interactively to disrupt self-regulation when people are self-attentive. The study of Scheier et al. (1981) most clearly illustrates how negative affect, exacerbated by self-attention, may function in self-regulatory failure. These investigators found that very fearful snake phobics who were made self-attentive not only experienced more anxiety but also withdrew earlier from their approach attempts compared to a similar group of non-self-attentive snake phobics (see also Carver & Blaney, 1977a, 1977b; Carver et al., 1979b).

It should be added that the two conditions promoting debilitation enumerated above are highly consistent with the evidence that negative self-monitoring results in self-regulatory dysfunctioning under low-mastery conditions (e.g., Gottman & McFall, 1972; Kirschenbaum & Karoly, 1977). As noted earlier, both negative expectancies (e.g., Diener & Dweck, 1980) and negative affect (e.g., Holroyd et al., 1978) often result in selective attention to negative self-aspects. Since self-attention heightens awareness of whatever dimensions of the self are most salient at the time (Carver, 1979), it may actively promote negative self-monitoring in low-mastery contexts, that is, contexts often associated with negative expectancies and negative affect. Thus, perhaps similar mechanisms account for the performance debilitation incurred by both negative self-monitoring and heightened self-attention under low-mastery conditions.

The final conclusion about the conditions under which self-attention decreases persistence contradicts Carver's (1979) assertion about the beneficial effects of combining self-attention and positive expectancies. Some evidence suggests that when people self-attend after succeeding and expecting to continue succeeding, on well-mastered tasks, decreased persistence may follow (Brockner, 1979; McDonald, 1980). Brockner's subjects first received either success or failure feedback on a "social insight test" (top tenth vs bottom twentieth percentile) and then completed a simple concept formation task (e.g., $\overline{X}$ performance for "success" subjects = 81% accuracy). Both tasks were described as parts of one experiment on "problem solving," thereby, presumably increasing the relevance of the false success/failure feedback to the second task. The data generally indicated that following the success feedback, subjects who were dispositionally high in self-attention and those who were made self-attentive through experimental manipulation made more errors in the second task. Unfortunately, the specific statistical comparisons needed to test these effects were not reported. Similar findings were obtained by McDonald (1980). McDonald's subjects also first received either success or failure feedback (top or bottom tenth percentile) on a creativity test. Then subjects were either made self-aware or not while they completed a "similar but not identical" creativity test which merely required writing as much as they wanted to in response to a Thematic Apperception Test card, that is, an easily mastered task very similar to those used by Liebling and Shaver (1973), Carver and Scheier (1979), and others in the self-attention literature. McDonald, unlike Brockner (1979), actually assessed the perceived relevance of the two tasks. McDonald's subjects, as would be expected for Brockner's subjects also, believed that the two tasks were highly related. Thus, their prior feedback should have induced a highly relevant expectancy for performance in the second task. Most importantly, the subjects who had received the (relevant) success feedback and then became self-aware in the second task persisted significantly less ·in the second task than participants in the other groups.

If Brockner's and McDonald's subjects had not previously succeeded at a relevant and easily mastered task, several findings suggest that self-attention may have increased, not decreased, persistence on the second task (Liebling & Shaver, 1973; Slapion & Carver, 1981; Wicklund & Duval, 1971; Carver & Scheier, 1979). The evidence concerning the effects of success and positive expectancies on attention (e.g., Postman & Brown, 1952; Moore et al., 1979) further indicates that self-attention may impair high-mastery task performance after positive feedback because individuals selectively attend to positive self-aspects under the circumstances. If so, the evidence that positive self-monitoring similarly impairs performance in high-mastery circumstances once again provides a direct correspondence between the self-attention and self-monitoring literatures.

While it is presently unclear why selective attention to favorable outcomes promotes debilitation under high-mastery circumstances, Tomarken and Kirschenbaum (1981) have suggested that its effects may be mediated by an illusion of control (e.g., Alloy & Abramson, 1979; Langer, 1975). This proposal is based upon two sources of evidence. First, high-mastery contexts promote overly high expectancies and perceptions of control. Second, covert positive self-monitoring appears to encourage overconfidence. In support of these assertions, Alloy and Abramson (1979) found that nondepressed people overestimated their degree of control of the outcomes in a task when they received a high frequency of successful trials (see also Koriat, Lichtenstein, & Fischoff, 1980; Langer & Roth, 1976). Additionally, individuals susceptible to this illusion made contingency estimates that were uncorrelated with their actual degree of control, but highly correlated with the number of successful trials experienced (see also Jenkins & Ward, 1967; Nisbett & Ross, 1980; Smedslund, 1963). This later finding suggests that subjects were selectively attending to positive outcomes. If in fact positive self-monitoring promotes the development of this illusion, overconfidence may occasion self-regulatory dysfunctioning by leading individuals to reduce inappropriately effort expenditure below the level necessary for successful performance. Overconfidence may also decrease the individual's effortful responding because it results in lowered positive affect after success (e.g., Atkinson & Raynor, 1974; Kukla, 1978) and a preference for other, more difficult tasks (e.g., Buckert, Meyer, & Schmalt, 1979; Sigall & Gould, 1977; Trope, 1979).

With regard to elements of self-regulatory failure, research on self-attention clearly highlights the importance of the interaction between attentional foci, expectancies, affect, and perhaps other dimensions. Focusing attention on oneself when anticipating failure or when experiencing negative affect or after experiencing repeated successes may actively contribute to self-regulatory failure under certain conditions. Research on deindividuation and task mastery provides additional information about attentional focusing and expectancies concerning performance that will further clarify how these elements may become activated.

2. Deindividuation

Several authors (e.g., Diener, 1977; Ziller, 1964; Zimbardo, 1970) have conceptualized deindividuation as a state of non-self-attention, that is, an internal psychological phenomenon characterized by the absence of self-consciousness and self-evaluation. Diener (1977, 1979, 1980) proposed a model of deindividuation consisting of three major premises:

1. Self-awareness is prevented when the group, not individuals, become the focus of attention and is perceived as a whole unit. . . .
2. Lack of attention to one's own behavior and lack of awareness of one's self as a distinct entity are the crucial cognitive factors comprising deindividuation.
3. A lack of self-regulation results from deindividuation and is comprised of several facets: (a) lack of self-monitoring and retrieval of norms; (b) lack of self-reinforcement; and (c) lack of foresight, planning, and other types of linear sequential processing. Since self-regulation is minimal or eliminated, the deindividuated person is more susceptible to the influence of immediate stimuli, emotions, and motivations. (Diener, 1980).

Although two studies in the deindividuation literature failed to strongly support Diener's model (Diener, 1976; Diener, Dineen, Endresen, Beaman, & Fraser, 1975), four more recent investigations provided corroborative evidence (Diener, 1979; Diener, Lusk, DeFleur, & Flax, 1980; Prentice-Dunn & Rogers, 1980; Diener, 1978). In all of the latter studies, attention to membership within a group was correlated with decreased self-attentiveness and increased antinormative behavior. For example, Diener (1979) compared "deindividuated," "non-self-aware," and "self-aware" groups. Pairs of deindividuated subjects participated with six confederates in a creative series of warm-up activities which were designed to increase group cohesion greatly (e.g., the group was called by a name; the group sang, danced, and engaged in nonverbal activities together). Pairs of non-self-aware subjects also participated in group activities with six confederates but their groups did not have names and the activities were not oriented to developing group cohesion but merely to have a group of people doing the same things at the same times (e.g., listen to music and rating its qualities; writing essays on abstract topics). The groups that included the pairs of self-aware subjects engaged in activities which emphasized the uniqueness of each participant (e.g., rating how music matched their personalities; writing essays about their uniqueness). As expected, in "creativity tests" following the group activities, the deindividuated group engaged in significantly more disinhibited behavior than the other groups (e.g., "finger painting" with their noses; sucking liquids from baby bottles; listing obscenities). A self-report measure of "self-consciousness" summed for all subjects also correlated negatively with disinhibited behavior, consistent with Diener's proposal that lack of self-awareness (attentiveness) results in antinormative behavior.

Diener's model adds to proposed elements of self-regulatory failure derived from Kanfer's model, related research, and studies on self-attention. More specifically, Diener's model and research suggests that within a social context, attending to oneself as part of a group may decrease self-attention and contribute to self-regulatory failure. This notion coincides with the self-attentional proposition that we typically direct our attention in an essentially dichotomous fashion: to ourselves or to other things. It also supports findings indicating that attending to other people or to the external environment can decrease self-attention and, thereby, affect self-regulatory failure under some conditions (e.g., Duval & Wicklund, 1972).

Our earlier review of research on the relapse process suggests another mechanism of self-regulatory failure described in Diener's model and related research. Most studies of relapse situations (e.g., Pomerleau et al., 1978; Shiffman, 1981), like the deindividuation work, featured social factors in high-risk situations (e.g., parties, drinking with others, restaurants, being around others who exhibit the problematic behavior). It seems very plausible to suggest that directing attention to one's membership in these "high-risk" groups may result in decreased monitoring of the target behavior, and, ultimately, self-regulatory failure.

3. Well-Mastered Tasks

At several points, we have referred to findings showing that people often selectively attend to favorable outcomes when performing well-mastered behaviors (e.g., Diener & Dweck, 1980; Moore et al., 1979). Interestingly, some evidence actually suggests that people pay very little attention to any aspect of their behavior when they engage in extremely easy or overlearned tasks. Kimble and Perlmutter's (1970) integration of findings on the development of skillful motor behavior provides evidence consistent with this notion. According to these authors, when first learning to perform unfamiliar motor acts, individuals must continually monitor their responses and compare them to an "image" which has initiated them (see Grant, 1968). At this initial stage, the image functions very much like a behavioral standard in the cybernetic models of self-regulation proposed by Carver (1979) and Kanfer (1971). Specifically, it is said to guide responses and to provide a stop or "exit" mechanism allowing individuals to proceed to other behaviors once their current responses match it. However, as Kimble and Perlmutter (1970) note, evidence suggests that after mastering the motor act, there ensues an opposite trend toward decreased monitoring of responses and less frequent comparisons of behavior to the image.

Schneider and Schiffrin's work (1977; Schiffrin & Schneider, 1977) parallels that of Kimble and Perlmutter (1970) in showing that attentiveness to ongoing behavior varies inversely with degree of task mastery. These authors found that individuals forced to detect complex or novel stimuli engage in *controlled processing*. This search strategy has two major characteristics: it is highly demanding of attentional capacity, and it is a terminating comparison process in which individuals compare external stimuli to a prototype stored in memory. In contrast, when individuals master detection tasks through the consistent mapping of stimuli to responses, they engage in *automatic processing*. This method of search demands neither conscious attention nor voluntary control and, once initiated, tends to run to completion automatically.

Schank and Abelson (1977) have similarly suggested that high levels of competency or familiarity result in lowered self-attention for individuals performing more complex social behaviors. According to these authors, when the individual is acquiring a skill, he engages in *plan processing*. At these times, after dividing a complex behavioral sequence into its constituent parts, the individual actively monitors and regulates his performance on each component. In contrast, *script processing* ensues once the individual has attained a high level of task proficiency. In these cases, formerly small units of behavior are chunked together to form coherent scripts, which the individual can perform freed of the necessity of conscious attention.

The notion that increased mastery results in decreased self-attention also is a central tenet of Langer's (1978, 1979) theory of human *mindlessness*. According to Langer, mindlessness occurs when the individual *thinks* that he or she has been actively monitoring and regulating his behavior, when in fact he or she has been performing automatically according to well-learned and highly general scripts. Langer further speculates that the individual is most likely to be mindless when engaged in highly familiar routinized activities.

In several studies, Langer and her associates have shown that individuals become mindlessly inattentive to their behaviors in high-mastery situations (Langer, Blank, & Chanowitz, 1978; Langer & Imber, 1980; Langer & Newman, 1979; Miransky & Langer, 1978). In Langer and Imber's research, for instance, individuals who had earlier received no practice, moderate practice, or extensive practice with a task were asked to list the task components necessary for successful performance. As predicted, the overpracticed group listed fewer elements than the moderately practiced group, and as many components as the no-practice group. Several experiments also suggest that information seeking, as well as the kind of information processing assessed in the Langer *et al.* mindlessness studies, declines dramatically with increases in the familiarity of the stimuli in the environment (e.g., Berlyne, 1960, 1965; Pyszczynski & Greenberg, 1981; cf. also Smith & Miller, 1978.

While decreased self-attention associated with performing well-mastered tasks may be adaptive in some contexts (Kimble & Perlmutter, 1970; Langer & Weinman, 1981), the evidence reviewed earlier clearly indicates that such inattention to one's behavior may play an active role in self-regulatory failure. Cybernetic models of self-regulation suggest that such inattention to self precipitates disengagement from sustained self-regulation by decreasing self-evaluative other processes. Langer (1978, 1979) recently suggested another mechanism by which inattention to well-mastered behaviors may prove detrimental to sustained behavior change. Specifically, she argued that such inattention may result in an "illusion of incompetence":

> Expertise is attained by successfully ignoring more and more of the particulars of the task in question. With repeated experience, the components of the task drop out. The result of complete mastery, then, is that individuals are often in the position of knowing that they can perform the task without knowing the steps required to accomplish its performance. When circumstances lead these people to question their ability to perform that task successfully (e.g., perhaps even a single question from someone, "Are you sure you can do it?") they may be unsure that they can, because they cannot supply as evidence the steps involved that are necessary to do it. Thus, for tasks over which people should feel most confident, they may be most unconfident. (Langer, 1977, p. 307)

The illusion of incompetence, that is, the unconfident belief in one's ability to perform a well-mastered task when questioned about it, appeared to affect behavior in several studies (Langer & Benevento, 1978, Experiments 1, 2; Langer & Imber, 1980, Experiments 1,2).

In each study, after attaining a high level of mastery on an initial task, subjects performed a different task together with another subject. On this second task, either one of the pair was the "assistant," and the other was the "boss," or neither subject was so labeled. In the final phase, subjects once again worked on the initial task. In each case, subjects given the pejorative label, "assistant," subsequently performed worse on the original task than those in other conditions, and only about half as well as they did earlier. These performance decrements were not obtained with "moderate" instead of high-mastery subjects or with high-mastery subjects who were also directed to attend to task components.

4. Summary

Research on self-attention, deindividuation, and task mastery clearly supports and extends some of the key propositions about self-regulatory failure obtained from previous theorizing and research. Both Kanfer's and Carver's models of self-regulation, and related research on self-monitoring and self-attention, indicate that some form of self-attentive process appears necessary for self-regulation. Thus, factors that decrease sustained self-attention may contribute to self-regulatory failure. The present review produced three such factors: (a) self-attention following failure experiences accompanied by the perception that continued failure is unavoidable or unchangeable (e.g., Duval *et al.*, 1972; Steenbarger & Aderman, 1979); (b) directing attention to the environment (e.g., Duval & Wicklund, 1972)—especially to groups in which one is a member (e.g., Diener, 1979); and (c) repeatedly engaging in well-mastered behavioral sequences (e.g., Kimble & Perlmutter, 1970; Langer, 1978). The first two of these factors, once again, point to the following as potentially important elements of self-regulatory failure: accentuating failure experiences and/or difficult task constraints (cf. Bandura, 1977b), and exposing oneself to high-risk situations involving groups of people (cf. Marlatt & Gordon, 1980; Shiffman, 1981).

Research on self-attention and persistence parallel findings in the self-monitoring literature in revealing those circumstances under which heightened self-attention debilitates performance and persistence. Self-attention plus negative expectancies for success (e.g., Carver *et al.*, 1979b), negative affect (e.g., Scheier *et al.*, 1981), and sustained performance of well-mastered behaviors (e.g., McDonald, 1980) has occasioned deficits in performance and/or persistence. These findings coincide with the evidence showing that negative self-monitoring debilitates self-regulation in low-mastery contexts while positive self-monitoring impairs self-regulated performance in high-mastery situations (e.g., Kirschenbaum & Karoly, 1977; Tomarken & Kirschenbaum, 1982). In fact, several findings on the effects of expectancies (e.g., Diener & Dweck, 1980) and affect (e.g., Holroyd *et al.*, 1978) on self-attention suggest a direct linkage between the self-monitoring and self-attention literatures with regard to self-regulatory failure (Tomarken & Kirschenbaum, 1982a): Heightened self-attention may exacerbate naturally occurring tendencies to negatively self-monitor in low-mastery contexts and positively self-monitor in high-mastery contexts.

IV. SUMMARY AND CONCLUSIONS

People often fail to maintain and extend changes initiated in therapy. In grappling with this disheartening fact, researchers have slowly but steadily investigated variables that enhance generalization in clinical contexts. Indeed some promising procedures emerged in our review of this literature. A consideration of stimulus, organismic, response, and consequence elements revealed some success with increased generalization through multiple therapists, multiple settings, planned extra-therapy stimulus control, teaching "general principles," self-regulatory skills training, overlearning, training responses that were likely to become "trapped" by natural contingencies, booster sessions, schedule thinning, and several other methods. Unfortunately, closer inspection of the efficacy of two of the most widely used of these procedures, booster sessions and self-regulatory training, showed very substantial limitations in their effectiveness. Furthermore, inadequacies in the conceptual foundations of this literature were also evident in the review. We traced the conceptual origins of most of the procedures to passive theories of extinction and forgetting which blurred the distinction between acquisition and generalization and almost totally ignored the vital role of organismic variables in the generalization process. More importantly, assumptions about what causes problems in generalization, rather than empirical scrutiny of the process of failing to generalize, generated most of the procedures that have been tested in the literature.

We advocated the study of self-regulatory failure as a means of broadening the empirical and conceptual foundations of work on the generalization problem in clinical psychology. Self-regulatory failure was defined as "all processes by which individuals fail to generalize desired behavior changes over time and across settings, in the relative absence of external constraints." This approach integrates a variety of seemingly key organismic variables by relying on models of self-regulatory processes and related research to generate testable hypotheses about what people actually do during the process of failing to generalize behavior change.

To describe extant knowledge of self-regulatory failure, first we reviewed three of the most relevant conceptual models. The elements of self-regulatory failure suggested by Kanfer's closed loop model of self-regulation, Bandura's self-efficacy theory, and Marlatt and Gordon's cognitive–behavioral model of the relapse process are summarized in Table II. Although the models all stressed certain covert elements (e.g., self-evaluation), several behavioral and otherwise observable events were also suggested (e.g., exposure to high-risk situations, discontinuation of self-monitoring). We indicated that recent evidence pertaining to the inaccuracy and reactivity of assessing certain complex self-reports (e.g., attributions) suggests cautious examination of many of the proposed covert elements of self-regulatory failure. Given appropriate skepticism, particularly regarding covert elements, primary ingredients of self-regulatory failure suggested by the models included (a) exposure to high-risk situations, (b) omission of coping responses, (c) disengagement from self-monitoring, (d) accentuation of personal failures by attributing them to one's own inadequacies (i.e., low efficacy expectations), and (e) changing perceptions of the target behavior (perceived difficulty managing it and its effects).

To explore these elements and enumerate other potential contributors to self-regulatory failure further, we then reviewed four relevant research domains. The first literature compared successful to unsuccessful self-regulators. This evidence revealed correlates, not causes, of self-regulatory failure that generally coincided with many of the suggested elements derived from the theoretical models. All of the elements proposed based on this literature review and the reviews of the remaining three research areas appears in Table III. The two ingredients from the successful/unsuccessful literature that were not apparent from the models were use of overly specific standards for behavior change and slow or rigid use of a restricted number of coping and self-regulatory skills.

The second literature reviewed was research on the relapse process. This research directly focused on factors associated with failure to maintain changes in target behaviors. As shown in Table III, most of the suggested elements of self-regulatory failure derived from this literature again coincided with many of the proposals from the theoretical models. The importance of single relapse episodes, exposure to high-risk situations, inadequacies in coping responses, and low efficacy expectations was highlighted particularly by two innovative studies that gathered data prospectively (Candiotte & Lichtenstein, 1981) and during relapse crises (Shiffman, 1981). We also noted that many of the authors in this literature deemphasized seemingly important physiological factors. Furthermore, since this research primarily utilized self-reports, without corroboration from others or from behavioral observations, the findings must be interpreted with caution.

Research on self-monitoring in self-regulation, while relying on several studies with nonclinical problems, also supported several suggestions from the theoretical models. Specifically, this research emphasizes the role of self-monitoring in self-regulatory failure (see Table III). Consistent with the closed loop model, self-monitoring ap-

TABLE III

Elements of Self-Regulatory Failure Suggested by Research on Successful vs Unsuccessful Self-Regulators, the Relapse Process, Self-Monitoring in Self-Regulatory Failure, and Self-Attention and Related Research

Successful vs unsuccessful self-regulators	The relapse process	Self-monitoring in self-regulatory failure	Self-attention and related research
Use of overly specific standards in self-evaluation	Initial relapse episode	Discontinuation of self-monitoring	Discontinuation of self-attention
Infrequent self-reinforcement	Negative emotional states	Positive self-monitoring of well-mastered behaviors	Self-attention + failure + perception that failure is unchangeable
Low outcome expectations	Positive emotional states	Negative self-monitoring of poorly mastered target behaviors	Attention directed to non-self-aspects of the environment (including deindividuation)
Low efficacy expectations	Interpersonal conflicts and pressures		Repeated engagement in well-mastered behaviors
Inadequate use of a variety of self-regulatory and coping skills	Biological cravings		Self-attention + low efficacy and outcome expectations
Exposure to stressful situations	Coping skills deficits		Self-attention + sustained performance of well-mastered behaviors
	Low efficacy expectations and related distortions of judgment		
	Decreased self-monitoring		
	Exposure to high-risk situations		

peared necessary for generalized self-regulation. Both accentuating failure via negative self-monitoring and accentuating success via positive self-monitoring may contribute to self-regulatory failure under different circumstances.

The fourth body of research also underscored the role of self-attentive processes, such as self-monitoring, in self-regulatory failure. Studies on self-attention, deindividuation, and task mastery again showed that focusing on failures and focusing on successes may disrupt generalized self-regulation under different task constraints (see Table III). This research also demonstrated that lowered efficacy expectations and heightened negative affect may contribute to self-regulatory failure when people attend to aspects of their own behavior.

One method of integrating the elements of self-regulatory failure suggested by all four research domains is to examine Table III and determine which elements appear in more than one column. The first two areas reviewed and the last two domains overlapped considerably. Certainly part of this clustering is attributable to shared method variance. The successful/unsuccessful literatures used clinical populations and self-reports. The latter researches used largely nonclinical populations and behavioral indices. Despite these important differences between the two clusters, the more common suggestions derived from these studies clearly resemble the five central ideas extracted from the theoretical models. Specifically, major elements of self-regulatory failure derived from the successful/unsuccessful and the relapse literatures are (a) exposure to high-risk situations, (b) coping skills deficits, (c) low efficacy expectations (i.e., accentuation of personal failures), and (d) initial relapse episodes. Continuing the list by including elements suggested by the self-monitoring and self-attention literatures: (e) discontinuation of self-attentive processes, (f) self-attention + accentuation of failures (via negative self-monitoring or low efficacy and outcome expectancies) when the target behavior has been poorly mastered, and (g) self-attention + accentuation of successes (via positive self-monitoring or repeated success experiences) when the target behavior has been well mastered. Three of the six elements suggested by empirical findings (high-risk situations, coping skills deficits, and discontinuation of self-monitoring) are identical to three of the five elements derived from the three models reviewed previously. The remaining ideas from the research literature represent qualifications or extensions of the remaining suggestions extracted from theory.

Certainly the overlap between theory and research suggests that researchers can harness diverse methodologies to study self-regulatory failure. We can study clients in the process of struggling to generalize behavior change or nonclients who may alter key self-attentive or coping behaviors in response to experimental manipulations in the laboratory. Some of our earlier commentaries indicate that we advocate continued investigations of behavioral processes of self-regulatory failure, particularly analyses of the behavior of clinical populations during their struggles to generalize (see the "self-regulatory failure" box in Fig. 2).

In addition to encouraging continued investigation, the overlapping points in the present literature also tell us something important about what people do during self-regulatory failure. Viewing confluent elements suggested by relevant theoretical models and research, a unified picture emerges of the process of self-regulatory failure. Of course this picture remains quite tentative, given the relative paucity of research. It is also subject to qualifications due to variations in dispositional factors and types of target behaviors. Nonetheless, the present literature describes self-regulatory failure as a process of dismantling *self-regulated obsessive–compulsive behaviors.*

A. Self-Regulatory Failure and Obsessive–Compulsive Self-Regulation

To describe how self-regulatory failure resembles a process of dismantling obsessive–compulsive self-regulation, we must first define obsessive–compulsive behavior. Rachman and Hodgson (1980) view obsessions as repetitive thoughts, images, or impulses that are unwanted and difficult to control; compulsions are similarly defined as repetitive stereotyped unwanted overt behaviors (see also McFall & Wollersheim, 1979). The confluent points in the theories and, more persuasively, in the diverse sources of empirical evidence reviewed in this article suggest that generalized self-regulation may well require obsessive–compulsive self-regulation, despite the negative connotations ("neurotic" "disorder") of the term obsessive–compulsive.

The pervasiveness of factors that impede generalized self-regulation suggests that counterbalancing these factors may require a radical solution, such as obsessive–compulsive self-regulation. "High-risk situations" repeatedly identified in the relapse literature include almost all aspects of people's usual cognitive behavioral repertoires or habits and situations commonly encountered in everyday life. For example, both negative and positive affective states have been associated with relapsing as have the presence of other people engaged in such commonplace activities as eating and drinking alcohol. In addition to a host of common situational and cognitive states (e.g., lowered self-efficacy expectations), many self-regulators must also fight a nearly incessant battle with their own physiology (see Cannon *et al.*, 1981; Wooley *et al.*, 1979; Donahoe *et al.*, 1981; Rodin, 1979; Shiffman, 1981).

To combat these seemingly inexorable forces (Leventhal & Cleary, 1980) people may have to engage in behaviors that are antagonistic to the elements of self-regulatory failure identified in this article. Thus, they probably have to maintain self-attention, self-monitoring, and other self-regulated coping responses—continually. Certain cognitive foci may be required to ensure the maintenance of these self-regulatory behaviors. For example, helpful cognitive strategies seem to include those that do not accentuate personal failures when managing difficult target behaviors and those that do not accentuate personal successes when target behaviors become tedious, redundant, or well mastered.

We are suggesting that the term "obsessive–compulsive" aptly describes the manner in which cognitive–behavioral self-regulatory strategies probably have to be applied to prevent self-regulatory failure for most of the people most of the time. We have described the successful self-regulator as an individual who engages in intensive repetitive and perhaps stereotyped sets of overt and covert behaviors that are very difficult to control from the perspective of his or her cognitive–behavioral repertoire and, for some target behaviors, of his or her physiology. Interestingly, successful self-regulators engage in repetitive "well-mastered" behaviors without falling prey to the disengagement from the task often associated with that behavioral pattern (see Section III,D,3).

Despite the logic of the present account, there remains something unsettling about describing successful self-regulators as "obsessive–compulsives." Most empirically based models of the etiology of obsessive–compulsive behaviors suggest that causative factors include overly stringent and quite peculiar socially derived behavioral standards which produce, in addition to obsessive–compulsive "rituals," dysphoric moods and feelings of being driven to do something against one's will (see McFall & Wolersheim, 1979; Rachman & Hodgson, 1980). Furthermore, obsessive–compulsive disorders are quite rare, involve very irrational and consuming cognitive–behavioral patterns, and remain quite refractory despite decades of clinical work, theorizing, and research (Rachman & Hodgson, 1980).

Unlike the usual clincial picture of obsessive–compulsive disorders, we believe that obsessive–compulsive self-regulation is not pathological or unmanageable. While this conceptualization strays from the classic image of the obsessive–compulsive cleaner or checker, the intensity of the involvement with the target behavior seemingly required to prevent self-regulatory failure justifies the usage of the term obsessive–compulsive. Furthermore, anecdotal evidence and the literature we presented on successful vs unsuccessful self-regulators show that successful self-regulators often behave in accord with the present description. For example, successful self-regulators use many more cognitive–behavioral techniques and use them much more often than unsuccessful self-regulators (e.g., Baer et al., 1977; Perri & Richards, 1977). Close observation of most successful self-regulators provides anecdotal corroboration of this finding and also suggests a certain "peculiarity" in the style of successful self-regulators that resembles the ritualistic behavior characteristic of clinical obsessive–compulsives. For example, many successful weight losers do such seemingly irrational things as towel off their steaks to reduce calories, put saccharin in coffee drunk even while indulging in a (rare) dessert, and exercise every week (or every day) despite adverse physical or weather conditions.

Evidence from two additional sources suggests that obsessive compulsive behaviors are not necessarily pathological and can, under some conditions, prove adaptive. First, Rachman and de Silva (1978) conducted three exploratory studies to contrast "abnormal" and "normal" obsessions. They found that 84% of a large nonclinical sample of a diverse group of people reported some obsessive thoughts or impulses. These obsessions mirrored those reported by a small clinical sample in many important respects (e.g., content, relationship with mood, meaningfulness, ability of neutralizing behavior to reduce discomfort). Second, research on sports psychology illustrates the adaptive potential of obsessions. Studies with gymnasts (Mahoney & Avener, 1977), racketball players (Meyers, Cooke, Cullen, & Liles, 1979), golfers (Kirschenbaum & Bale, 1980), and wrestlers (Gould, Weiss, & Weinberg, 1981) indicate that persistent thinking or daydreaming about a sport is clearly associated with improved outcomes. For example, Mahoney and Avener (1977) found that frequency of thoughts about their sport in "everyday situations" correlated significantly ($r = .78$, $p < .01$) with performance among gymnasts who were attempting to qualify for the 1976 United States Olympic Team. In a similar vein, Kirschenbaum and Bale (1980) found that better golf scores among university level golfers were positively correlated ($r = .69$, $p < .05$) with the "obsessive" factor of Nideffer's (1976) Test of Attentional and Interpersonal Style. Thus, even though highly successful athletes often appear obsessed with their sport, such an orientation may produce important dividends in competition. Taking the sports analogy one step further, perhaps appropriate descriptors for the process of successful generalization of self-regulated behavior change should include both obsessive–compulsive and "olympic self-regulation" (particularly with regard to addictive target behaviors).

B. Clinical Recommendations

Notwithstanding the usual caveat about the tentativeness of the present description and the concomitant need for additional research, we can conclude by cautiously offering two sets of clinical recommendations. First, *therapists may assist their clients to generalize self-regulated behavior change by reducing the frequency and intensity of cognitive and environmental high-risk situations* (cf. Marlatt & Gordon, 1980). Improving clients' ability to recognize high-risk situations is a logical first step. This could include reviewing various categories of high-risk situations with the client and developing detailed descriptions of especially problematic situations for him or her based on a comprehensive behavioral assessment. Practicing a variety of coping responses until they are overlearned (cf. Goldstein et al., 1979) in the context of specific high-risk situations should also prove quite useful (e.g., Chaney et al., 1978; cf. Marlatt & Gordon, 1980; Lichtenstein et al., 1982). In addition to improved coping skills, more effective support systems may assist clients in confronting high-risk situations. Research along these lines shows promise with a variety of support groups, for example, spouses (e.g., Brownell et al., 1978; Pearce et al., 1981), families (e.g., McPeak, 1979), and co-workers (e.g., Price, 1979; Winett & Neale, 1979).

A second and more novel suggestion is that *therapists could help clients develop obsessive–compulsive self-regulatory behaviors. Clients probably need to learn how to attend to their target behaviors continually, systematically, and comfortably without letting perceptions of difficulty levels, redundancy, or self-efficacy deter them.* Developing simple and appropriately valenced planning and self-monitoring systems may help in this regard (e.g., Kirschenbaum et al., 1982a, 1982b, 1982c). In addition, several methods of enhancing and maintaining strong positive efficacy expectations revealed in Bandura's (1977b) self-efficacy theory and in research on induction strategies (e.g., Blittner et al., 1978; Steffen & Myszak, 1978) may facilitate sustained self-regulation. For example, prior to beginning the behavior change process it may be useful to demonstrate the potency of the interventions in a "mini-experiment" (see Steffen & Myszak, 1978; Stalonas et al., 1981) and to encourage internal attributions for the observed effects. Finally, research and theorizing on the etiology and maintenance of obsessive–compulsive behaviors, particularly studies concerning checkers, may provide additional and, perhaps surprisingly, useful directions for both clinical practice and research pertaining to self-regulatory failure (see Rachman & Hodgson, 1980).

REFERENCES

Abramson, L. Y., Garber, J., & Seligman, M. E. P. Learned helplessness in humans: An attributional analysis. In J. Garber & M. E. P. Seligman (Eds.), *Human helplessness: Theory and applications.* New York: Academic Press, 1980.

Alloy, L. B., & Abramson, L. Y. Judgment of contingency in depressed and nondepressed students: Sadder but wiser? *Journal of Experimental Psychology: General,* 1979, **108,** 441–485.

Arkes, H. R. Impediments to accurate clinical judgment and possible ways to minimize their impact. *Journal of Consulting and Clinical Psychology,* 1981, **49,** 323–330.

Ashby, W. A., & Wilson, T. Behavior therapy for obesity: Booster sessions and long-term maintenance of weight loss. *Behaviour Research and Therapy,* 1977, **15,** 451–463.

Atkinson, J. W., & Raynor, J. O. *Motivation and achievement.* New York: Wiley, 1974.

Baer, D. M., Wolf, M. M., & Risley, T. R. Some current dimensions of applied behavior analysis. *Journal of Applied Behavior Analysis,* 1968, **1,** 91–97.

Baer, P. E., Foreyt, J. P., & Wright, S. Self-directed termination of excessive cigarette use among untreated smokers. *Journal of Behavior Therapy and Experimental Psychiatry,* 1977, **8,** 71–74.

Bandura, A. *Principles of behavior modification.* New York: Holt, 1969.

Bandura, A. *Social learning theory.* New York: Prentice-Hall, 1977. (a)

Bandura, A. Self-efficacy: Toward a unifying theory of behavioral change. *Psychological Review,* 1977, **84,** 191–215. (b)

Bandura, A., & Barab, P. G. Processes governing disinhibitory effects through symbolic modeling. *Journal of Abnormal Psychology,* 1973, **82,** 1–9.

Bandura, A., Jeffrey, R. W., & Gajdos, E. Generalizing change through participant modeling with self-directed mastery. *Behaviour Research and Therapy,* 1975, **13,** 141–152.

Beaman, A. L., Klentz, B., Diener, E., & Svanum, S. Self-awareness and transgression in children: Two field studies. *Journal of Personality and Social Psychology,* 1979, **37,** 1835–1846.

Beck, A. T. *Depression: clinical, experimental, and theoretical aspects.* New York: Harper, 1967.

Bednar, R. L., & Weinberg, S. L. Ingredients of successful treatment programs for underachievers. *Journal of Counseling Psychology,* 1970, **17,** 1–7.

Bellack, A. S., Glanz, L. M., & Simon, R. Self-reinforcement style and covert imagery in the treatment of obesity. *Journal of Consulting and Clinical Psychology,* 1976, **44,** 490–491.

Beneke, W. M., & Paulsen, B. K. Long-term efficacy of a behavior modification weight loss program: A comparison of two follow-up maintenance strategies. *Behavior Therapy,* 1979, **10,** 8–13.

Berlyne, D. E. *Conflict, arousal and curiosity.* New York: McGraw-Hill, 1960.

Berlyne, D. E. *Structure and direction in thinking.* New York: Wiley, 1965.

Blittner, M., Goldberg, J., & Merbaum, M. Cognitive self-control factors in the reduction of smoking behavior. *Behavior Therapy*, 1978, **9**, 553–561.

Borden, M. A., & Pryor, J. B. *Decreasing and increasing self-report validity by response shaping and self-focusing*. Paper presented at the meeting of the Midwestern Psychological Association, Detroit, 1981.

Bower, G. H. Mood and memory. *American Psychologist*, 1981, **36**, 129–148.

Brightwell, D. R. One year follow-up of obese subjects treated with behavior therapy. *Diseases of the Nervous System*, 1976, **37**, 593–594.

Brightwell, D. R., & Sloan, C. L. Long-term results of behavior therapy for obesity. *Behavior Therapy*, 1977, **8**, 898–905.

Brockner, J. The effects of self-esteem, success-failure, and self-consciousness on task performance. *Journal of Personality and Social Psychology*, 1979, **37**, 1732–1741.

Broden, M., Hall, R. V., & Mitts, B. The effect of self-recording on the classroom behavior of two eighth grade students. *Journal of Applied Behavior Analysis*, 1971, **4**, 191–199.

Brownell, K. D., Heckerman, C. L., Westlake, R. J., Hayes, S. C., & Monti, P. M. The effect of couples training and partner cooperativeness in the behavioral treatment of obesity. *Behaviour Research and Therapy*, 1978, **16**, 323–333.

Buckert, U., Meyer, W., & Schmalt, H. Effects of difficulty and diagnosticity on choice among tasks in relation to achievement motivation and perceived ability. *Journal of Personality and Social Psychology*, 1979, **37**, 1172–1178.

Candiotte, M. M., & Lichtenstein, E. Self-efficacy and relapse in smoking cessation programs. *Journal of Consulting and Clinical Psychology*, 1981, **49**, 648–658.

Cannon, D. S., Baker, T. B., & Wehl, C. K. Emetic and electric shock alcohol aversion therapy: Six- and twelve-month follow-up. *Journal of Consulting and Clinical Psychology*, 1981, **49**, 360–368.

Carroll, L. J., & Yates, B. T. Further evidence for the role of stimulus control training in facilitating weight reduction after behavior therapy. *Behavior Therapy*, 1981, **12**, 287–291.

Carroll, L. J., Yates, B. T., & Gray, J. Predicting obesity reduction in behavioral and nonbehavioral therapy from client characteristics: The self-evaluation measure. *Behavior Therapy*, 1980, **11**, 189–197.

Carver, C. S. Physical aggression as a function of objective self-awareness and attitudes toward punishment. *Journal of Experimental Social Psychology*, 1975, **11**, 510–519.

Carver, C. S. A cybernetic model of self-attention processes. *Journal of Personality and Social Psychology*, 1979, **37**, 1251–1281.

Carver, C. S., & Blaney, P. H. Avoidance behavior and perceived arousal. *Motivation and Emotion*, 1977, **1**, 61–73. (a)

Carver; C. S., & Blaney, P. H. Perceived arousal, focus of attention, and avoidance behavior. *Journal of Abnormal Psychology*, 1977, **86**, 154–162. (b)

Carver, C. S., Blaney, P. H., & Scheier, M. F. Focus of attention, chronic expectancy, and responses to a feared stimulus. *Journal of Personality and Social Psychology*, 1979, **37**, 1186–1195. (a)

Carver, C. S., Blaney, P. H., & Scheier, M. F. Reassertion and giving up: The interactive role of self-directed attention and outcome expectancy. *Journal of Personality and Social Psychology*, 1979, **37**, 1859–1870. (b)

Carver, C. S., & Scheier, M. F. Self-focusing effects of dispositional self-consciousness, mirror presence, and audience presence. *Journal of Personality and Social Psychology*, 1978, **36**, 324–332.

Carver, C. S., & Scheier, M. F. *The self-attention-induced feedback loop and human motivation: A control-systems analysis of social facilitation.* Unpublished manuscript, University of Miami—Coral Gables, 1979.

Cavior, N., & Marabotto, C. M. Monitoring verbal behaviors in a dyadic interaction. *Journal of Consulting and Clinical Psychology,* 1976, **44,** 68–76.

Chaney, E. F., O'Leary, M. R., & Marlatt, G. A. Skill training with alcoholics. *Journal of Consulting and Clinical Psychology,* 1978, **46,** 1092–1104.

Clark, J. V., & Arkowitz, H. Social anxiety and self-evaluation of interpersonal performance. *Psychological Reports,* 1975, **13,** 321–331.

Colletti, G., & Kopel, S. A. Maintaining behavior change: An investigation of three maintenance strategies and the relationship of self-attribution to the long-term reduction of cigarette smoking. *Journal of Consulting and Clinical Psychology,* 1979, **47,** 614–617.

Colletti, G., & Kopel, S. A. *Maintaining behavior change: An investigation of three maintenance strategies and attributional processes in the long-term reduction of cigarette smoking.* Unpublished manuscript (extended report of Colletti & Kopel, *Journal of Consulting and Clinical Psychology,* 1979, **47,** 614–617), State University of New York at Binghamton, 1979.

Colletti, G., & Stern, L. Two-year follow-up of a nonaversive treatment for cigarette smoking. *Journal of Consulting and Clinical Psychology,* 1980, **48,** 292–293.

Colletti, G., & Supnick, J. A. Continued therapist contact as a maintenance strategy for smoking reduction. *Journal of Consulting and Clinical Psychology,* 1980, **48,** 665–667.

Collins, R. L., Wilson, G. T., & Rothblum, E. *The comparative efficacy of cognitive and behavioral approaches in weight reduction.* Paper presented at the meeting of the Association for Advancement of Behavior Therapy, New York, November, 1980.

Cooke, C. J., & Meyers, A. Assessment of subject characteristics on the behavioral treatment of obesity. *Behavioral Assessment,* 1980, **2,** 59–70.

Cummings, C., Gordon, J. R., & Marlatt, G. A. Relapse: Prevention and prediction. In W. R. Miller (Ed.), *The addictive behaviors: Treatment of alcoholism, drug abuse, smoking, and obesity.* Oxford: Pergamon, 1980.

Deci, E. L. *Intrinsic motivation.* New York: Plenum, 1975.

Diener, C. I., & Dweck, C. S. An analysis of learned helplessness: Continuous changes in performance strategies and achievement cognitions following failure. *Journal of Personality and Social Psychology,* 1978, **36,** 451–463.

Diener, C. I., & Dweck, C. S. An analysis of learned helplessness: II. The processing of success. *Journal of Personality and Social Psychology,* 1980, **39,** 940–952.

Diener, E. Effects of prior destructive behavior, anonymity, and group presence on deindividuation and aggression. *Journal of Personality and Social Psychology,* 1976, **33,** 497–507.

Diener, E. Deindividuation: Causes and consequences. *Social Behavior and Personality,* 1977, **5,** 143–155.

Diener, E. *Causal factors in disinhibition by deindividuation.* Unpublished manuscript, University of Illinois, 1978.

Diener, E. Deindividuation, self-awareness, and disinhibition. *Journal of Personality and Social Psychology,* 1979, **37,** 1160–1171.

Diener, E. Deindividuation: The absence of self-awareness and self-regulation in group members. In P. B. Paulus (Ed.), *The psychology of group influence.* Hillsdale, New Jersey: Erlbaum, 1980.

Diener, E., Dineen, J., Endresen, K., Beaman, A. L., & Fraser, S. C. Effects of altered responsibility, cognitive set, and modeling on physical aggression and deindividuation. *Journal of Personality and Social Psychology,* 1975, **31,** 328–337.

Diener, E., Lusk, R., DeFour, D., & Flax, R. Deindividuation: Effects of group size, density, number of observers, and group member similarity on self-consciousness and disinhibited behavior. *Journal of Personality and Social Psychology,* 1980, **39,** 449–459.

Diener, E., & Wallbom, M. Effects of self-awareness on antinormative behavior. *Journal of Research in Personality,* 1976, **10,** 107–111.

Donahoe, P., Lin, D., Keesey, R. E., & Kirschenbaum, D. S. *Exercise for weight reduction: Beyond burning calories—a metabolic advantage.* Paper presented at the meeting of the Association for Advancement of Behavior Therapy, Toronto, November 1981.

Dubren, R. Self-reinforcement by recorded telephone messages to maintain nonsmoking behavior. *Journal of Consulting and Clinical Psychology,* 1977, **45,** 358–360.

Durlak, J. A. Comparative effectiveness of behavioral and relationship group treatment in the secondary prevention of school maladjustment. *American Journal of Community Psychology,* 1980, **8,** 327–340.

Duval, S. & Freidan, G. *Objective self-awareness, task complexity and performance.* Unpublished manuscript, University of Southern California, 1979.

Duval, S., & Wicklund, R. A. *A theory of objective self-awareness.* New York: Academic Press, 1972.

Duval, S., Wicklund, R. A., & Fine, R. L. Avoidance of objective self-awareness under conditions of high and low intra-self discrepancy. In S. Duval & R. A. Wicklund, *A theory of objective self-awareness.* New York: Academic Press, 1972.

Ebbinhaus, H. *Memory: A contribution to experimental psychology.* (1885) (Translated by H. A. Ruger & C. E. Bussenius, 1913). New York: Dover, 1964.

Elliott, C. H., & Denney, D. R. A multiple-component treatment approach to smoking reduction. *Journal of Consulting and Clinical Psychology,* 1978, **46,** 1330–1339.

Ewart, C. K. Self-observation in natural environments: Reactive effects of behavior desirability and goal-setting. *Cognitive Therapy and Research,* 1978, **2,** 39–56.

Eysenck, H. J. The effects of psychotherapy: An evaluation. *Journal of Consulting Psychology,* 1952, **16,** 319–324.

Fenigstein, A., Scheier, M. F., & Buss, A. H. Public and private self-consciousness: Assessment and theory. *Journal of Consulting and Clinical Psychology,* 1975, **43,** 522–527.

Ferster, C. B., & Skinner, B. F. *Schedules of reinforcement.* New York: Appleton, 1957.

Festinger, L. *Conflict, decision, and dissonance.* Stanford, California: Stanford University Press, 1964.

Fishman, S. T., & Lubetkin, B. S. Maintenance and generalization of institutional behavior modification programs. In P. Karoly & J. J. Steffen (Eds.), *Improving the long-term effects of psychotherapy: Models of durable outcome.* New York: Gardiner, 1980.

Ford, D. H., & Urban, H. B. *Systems of psychotherapy.* New York: Wiley, 1963.

Garber, J., & Seligman, M. E. P. (Eds.). *Human Helplessness: Theory and applications.* New York: Academic Press, 1980.

Gibbons, F. X., & Wicklund, R. A. Selective exposure to the self. *Journal of Research in Personality,* 1976, **10,** 98–106.

Gibbons, F. X., Wicklund, R. A., & Rosenfield, D. *Self-focused attention and prosocial behavior.* Unpublished manuscript, University of Texas, Austin, 1979.

Goldfried, M. R. Toward the delineation of therapeutic change principles. *American Psychologist*, 1980, **35**, 991–999.

Goldstein, A. P., Heller, K., & Sechrest, L. B. *Psychotherapy and the psychology of behavior change.* New York: Wiley, 1966.

Goldstein, A. P., & Kanfer, F. H. *Maximizing treatment gains: Transfer enhancement in psychotherapy.* New York: Academic Press, 1979.

Goldstein, A. P., Lopez, M., & Greenleaf, D. O. Introduction, In A. P. Goldstein & F. H. Kanfer (Eds.), *Maximizing treatment gains: Transfer enhancement in psychotherapy.* New York: Academic Press, 1979.

Gormally, J., Rardin, D., & Black, S. Correlates of successful response to a behavioral weight control clinic. *Journal of Counseling Psychology*, 1980, **27**, 179–191.

Gotay, C. C. *Helping behavior as a function of objective self-awareness and salience of the norm of helping.* Unpublished doctoral dissertation, University of Maryland, 1977.

Gottestam, K. G. A three-year follow-up of a behavioral treatment for obesity. *Addictive Behaviors*, 1979, **4**, 179–183.

Gottman, J. M., & McFall, R. M. Self-monitoring effects in a program for potential high school dropouts: A time series analysis. *Journal of Consulting and Clinical Psychology*, 1972, **39**, 273–281.

Grant, D. A. Adding communication to the signaling property of the CS in classical conditioning. *Journal of General Psychology*, 1968, **79**, 147–175.

Greenberg, J. Attentional focus and locus of performance causality as determinants of equity behavior. *Journal of Personality and Social Psychology*, 1980, **38**, 579–585.

Greiner, J. M., & Karoly, P. Effects of self-control training on study activity and academic performance: An analysis of self-monitoring, self-reward, and systematic planning components. *Journal of Counseling Psychology*, 1976, **23**, 495–502.

Gur, R. C., & Sackeim, H. A. Self-deception: A concept in search of a phenomenon. *Journal of Personality and Social Psychology*, 1979, **37**, 147–169.

Halisch, F., & Heckhausen, H. Search for feedback information and effort regulation during task performance. *Journal of Personality and Social Psychology*, 1977, **35**, 724–733.

Hall, J. F. *The psychology of learning.* Philadelphia, Pennsylvania: Lippincott, 1966.

Hall, S. M. Self-management and therapeutic maintenance: Theory and research. In P. Karoly & J. J. Steffen (Eds.), *Improving the long-term effects of psychotherapy: Models of durable outcome.* New York: Gardner, 1980.

Hall, S. M., Bass, A., & Monroe, J. Follow-up strategies in obesity treatment. *Addictive Behaviors*, 1978, **3**, 139–147.

Hall, S. M., Hall, R. G., Borden, B. L., & Hanson, R. W. Follow-up strategies in the behavioral treatment of overweight. *Behavior Research and Therapy*, 1975, **13**, 167–172.

Hanusa, B. H., & Schulz, R. Attributional mediators of learned helplessness. *Journal of Personality and Social Psychology*, 1977, **35**, 602–611.

Harvey, D. M. Depression and attributional style: Interpretations of important personal events. *Journal of Abnormal Psychology*, 1981, **90**, 134–142.

Heffernan, T., & Richards, C. S. Self-control of study behavior: Identification and evaluation of natural methods. *Journal of Counseling Psychology*, 1981, **28**, 361–364.

Hendricks, C. G., Thoresen, C. E., & Hubbard, D. R. *Effects of behavioral self-observation on elementary teachers and students.* Stanford Center for Research and Development, Memorandum No. 121, 1974.

Holroyd, K. A., Westbrook, T., Wolf, M., & Badhorn, E. Performance, cognition, and physiological responding in test anxiety. *Journal of Abnormal Psychology*, 1978, **87**, 442–451.

Hoon, P., & Lindsley, O. R. A comparison of behavior and traditional therapy publication activity. *American Psychologist*, 1974, **29**, 694–697.

Horan, J. J., Baker, S. B., Hoffman, A. B., & Shute, R. E. Weight loss through variations in the coverant control paradigm. *Journal of Consulting and Clinical Psychology*, 1975, **43**, 68–72.

Howland, C. I. Inhibition of reinforcement and phenomena of experimental extinction. *Proceedings of the National Academy of Sciences*, 1936, **22**, 430–433.

Humphreys, L. G. Generalization as a function of the method of reinforcement. *Journal of Experimental Psychology*, 1939, **25**, 361–372.

Hunt, W. A., Barnett, L. W., & Branch, L. G. Relapse in addiction programs. *Journal of Clinical Psychology*, 1971, **27**, 455–456.

Hunt, W. A., & Matarazzo, J. D. Three years later: Recent developments in the experimental modification of smoking behavior. *Journal of Abnormal Psychology*, 1973, **81**, 107–114.

Israel, A. C., & Saccone, A. J. Follow-up effects of choice of mediator and target of reinforcement on weight loss. *Behavior Therapy*, 1979, **10**, 260–265.

Jacobs, M. A comparison of publicly delivered and anonymously delivered verbal feedback in brief personal growth groups. *Journal of Consulting and Clinical Psychology*, 1977, **45**, 385–390.

Jeffrey, R. W., & Wing, R. R. Frequency of therapist contact in the treatment of obesity. *Behavior Therapy*, 1979, **10**, 186–192.

Jenkins, H. M., & Ward, W. C. Judgements of contingency between response and outcome. *Psychological monographs*, 1965, **79**, (1, Whole No. 594).

Jensen, A. R. *Bias in mental testing*. New York: Free Press, 1980.

Johnston, J. M., & Johnston, G. T. Modification of consonant speech-sound articulation in young children. *Journal of Applied Behavior Analysis*, 1973, **5**, 233–246.

Kahneman, D., & Tversky, A. On the psychology of prediction. *Psychological Review*, 1973, **80**, 237–251.

Kanfer, F. H. Self-monitoring: Methodological limitations and clinical applications. *Journal of Consulting and Clinical Psychology*, 1970, **35**, 148–152.

Kanfer, F. H. The maintenance of behavior by self-generated stimuli and reinforcement. In A. Jacobs & L. B. Jachs (Eds.), *The psychology of private events*. New York: Academic Press, 1971.

Kanfer, F. H. The many faces of self-control, or behavior modification changes its focus. In R. B. Stuart (Ed.), *Behavioral self-management: Strategies, techniques, and outcomes*. New York: Brunner-Mazel, 1977.

Kanfer, F. H. Self-management: Strategies and tactics. In A. P. Goldstein & F. H. Kanfer (Eds.), *Maximizing treatment gains: Transfer enhancement in psychotherapy*. New York: Academic Press, 1979.

Kanfer, F. H. Self-management methods. In F. H. Kanfer & A. P. Goldstein (Eds.), *Helping people change* (2nd ed.). Oxford: Pergamon, 1980.

Kanfer, F. H., & Goldstein A. P. Introduction. In F. H. Kanfer & A. P. Goldstein, (Eds.), *Helping people change* (2nd ed.). Oxford: Pergamon, 1980.

Kanfer, F. H., & Grimm, L. G. Behavioral analysis: Selecting target behaviors in the interview. *Behavior Modification*, 1977, **1**, 7–28.

Kanfer, F. H., & Karoly, P. Self-control: A behavioristic excursion into the lion's den. *Behavior Therapy*, 1972, **3**, 398–416.

Kanfer, F. H., & Phillips, J. S. *Learning foundations of behavior therapy*. New York: Wiley, 1970.

Karoly, P. Behavioral self-management in children: concepts, methods, issues, and directions. In M. Hersen, R. M. Eisler, & P. M. Miller (Eds.), *Progress in behavior modification* (Vol. 5). New York: Academic Press, 1977.

Karoly, P. Person variables in therapeutic change and development. In P. Karoly & J. J. Steffen (Eds.), *Improving the long-term effects of psychotherapy: Models of durable outcome.* New York: Gardner, 1980.

Karoly, P., & Steffen, J. J. *Improving the long-term effects of psychotherapy: Models of durable outcome.* New York: Gardner, 1980.

Kazdin, A. E. Self-monitoring and behavior change. In M. J. Mahoney & C. E. Thoresen (Eds.), *Self-control: Power to the person.* Monterey, California: Brooks/Cole, 1974. (a)

Kazdin, A. E. Reactive self-monitoring: The effects of response desirability, goal-setting, and feedback. *Journal of Consulting and Clinical Psychology,* 1974, **42,** 704–716. (b)

Kazdin A. E. Conceptual and assessment issues raised by self-efficacy theory. *Advances in Behaviour Research and Therapy,* 1978, **1,** 177–185.

Kazdin, A. E. Fictions, factions, and functions of behavior therapy. *Behavior Therapy,* 1980, **10,** 629–654.

Kazdin, A. E., & Polster, R. Intermittent token reinforcement and response maintenance in extinction. *Behavior Therapy,* 1973, **4,** 386–391.

Kazdin, A. E., & Wilson, G. T. *Evaluation of behavior therapy: Issues, evidence, and research strategies.* Booton, Massachusetts: Ballinger, 1970.

Kendall, P. C. Assessment and cognitive-behavioral interventions: Purposes, proposals, and problems. In P. C. Kendall & S. D. Hollon (Eds.), *Assessment strategies for cognitive-behavioral interventions.* New York: Academic Press, 1981.

Kendall, P. C., & Hollon, S. D. (Eds.). *Cognitive-behavioral interventions: Theory, research, and procedures.* New York: Academic Press, 1979.

Kendall, P. C., & Hollon, S. D. Assessing self-referent speech: Methods in the measurement of self-statements. In P. C. Kendall & S. D. Hollon (Eds.), *Assessment strategies for cognitive-behavioral interventions.* New York: Academic Press, 1981.

Kimble, G. A. *Hilgard and Marquis' conditioning and learning.* New York: Appleton, 1961.

Kimble, G. A., & Perlmuter, L. C. The problem of volition. *Psychological Review,* 1970, **77,** 361–384.

Kingsley, R. G., & Wilson, G. T. Behavior therapy for obesity: A comparative investigation of long-term efficacy. *Journal of Consulting and Clinical Psychology,* 1977, **45,** (2), 288–298.

Kirschenbaum, D. S. When self-regulation fails: Tests of some preliminary hypotheses. (Doctoral dissertation, University of Cincinnati, 1975). *Dissertation Abstracts International,* 1976, **36,** (9-B), 4692.

Kirschenbaum, D. S., Humphrey, L. L., & Malett, S. D. Specificity of planning in adult self-control: An applied investigation. *Journal of Personality and Social Psychology,* 1981, **40,** 941–950.

Kirschenbaum, D. S., & Karoly, P. When self regulation fails: Tests of some preliminary hypotheses. *Journal of Consulting and Clinical Psychology,* 1977, **45,** 1116–1125.

Kirschenbaum, D. S., Malett, S. D., Humphrey, L. L., & Tomarken, A. J. Specificity of planning and the maintenance of self-control: One year follow-up of a study improvement program. *Behavior Therapy,* 1982, in press. (a)

Kirschenbaum, D. S., Ordman, A. M., Tomarken, A. J., & Holtzbauer, R. Effects of differential self-monitoring and level of mastery on sports performance: Brain power bowling. *Cognitive Therapy and Research,* 1982, in press. (b)

Kirschenbaum, D. S., & Perri, M. G. Improving academic competence in adults: A review of recent research. *Journal of Counseling Psychology,* 1982, in press.

Kirschenbaum, D. S., Tomarken, A. J., & Ordman, A. M. Specificity of planning and choice applied to adult self-control. *Journal of Personality and Social Psychology,* 1982, in press. (c)

Komaki, J., & Dore-Boyce, K. Self-recording: Its effects on individuals high and low in motivation. *Behavior Therapy,* 1978, **9,** 65–72.

Kopel, S. A. The effects of self-control, booster sessions, and cognitive factors on the maintenance of smoking reduction. (Doctoral dissertation, University of Oregon, 1974). *Dissertation Abstracts International,* 1974, **35B,** 4182. (University Microfilms No. 75–3895,67).

Koriat, A., Lichtenstein, S., & Fischhoff, B. Reasons for confidence. *Journal of Experimental Psychology: Human Learning and Memory,* 1980, **6,** 107–118.

Korman, A. K. *The psychology of motivation.* New York: Prentice-Hall, 1974.

Kuhl, J. Motivational and functional helplessness: The moderating effect of state versus action orientation. *Journal of Personality and Social Psychology,* 1981, **40,** 155–170.

Kukla, A. An attributional theory of choice. In L. Berkowitz (Ed.), *Advances in experimental social psychology* (Vol. 11). New York: Academic Press, 1978.

LaDouceur, R., & Auger, J. Where have all the follow-ups gone? *The Behavior Therapist,* 1980, **3,** 10–11.

Lando, H. A. Toward a clinically effective paradigm for the maintenance of nonsmoking. *Behavior Therapy,* 1978, **9,** 666–668.

Lang, P. J. The application of psychophysiological methods to the study of psychotherapy and behavior modification. In A. E. Bergin & S. L. Garfield (Eds.), *Handbook of psychotherapy and behavior change.* New York: Wiley, 1971.

Lang, P. J. Self-efficacy theory: Thoughts on cognition and unification. *Advances in Behaviour Research and Therapy,* 1978, **1,** 187–192.

Langer, E. J. The illusion of control. *Journal of Personality and Social Psychology,* 1975, **32,** 311–328.

Langer, E. J. Rethinking the role of thought in social interaction. In J. H. Harvey, W. Ickes, & R. F. Kidd (Eds.), *New directions in attribution research* (Vol. 2). Hillsdale, New Jersey: Erlbaum, 1978.

Langer, E. J. The illusion of incompetence. In L. Perlmutter & R. Monty (Eds.), *Choice and perceived control.* Hillsdale, New Jersey: Erlbaum, 1979.

Langer, E. J., & Benevento, A. Self-induced dependence. *Journal of Personality and Social Psychology,* 1978, **36,** 886–893.

Langer, E. J., Blank, A., & Chanowitz, B. The mindlessness of ostensibly thoughtful action: The role of placebic information in interpersonal interaction. *Journal of Personality and Social Psychology,* 1978, **36,** 635–642.

Langer, E. J., & Imber, L. G. When practice makes imperfect: Debilitating effects of overlearning. *Journal of Personality and Social Psychology,* 1979, **37,** 2014–2024.

Langer, E. J., & Newman, H. The role of mindlessness in a typical social psychological experiment. *Personality and Social Psychology Bulletin,* 1979, **5,** 295–298.

Langer, E. J., & Roth, J. Heads I win, tails it's chance: The illusion of control as a function of the sequence of outcomes in a purely chance task. *Journal of Personality and Social Psychology,* 1975, **32,** 951–955.

Langer, E. J., & Weinman, C. When thinking disrupts intellectual performance: Mindfulness on an overlearned task. *Personality and Social Psychology Bulletin,* 1981, in press.

Lanzetta, J. T., & Driscoll, J. M. Effects of uncertainty and importance on information search in decision making. *Journal of Personality and Social Psychology*, 1968, **4**, 479–486.

Lazarus, R. S., & Ericksen, C. W. Effects of failure stress upon skilled performance. *Journal of Experimental Psychology*, 1952, **43**, 100–105.

Leon, G. R. Current directions in the treatment of obesity. *Psychological Bulletin*, 1976, **83**, 557–578.

Leon, G. R., & Chamberlain, K. Emotional arousal, eating patterns, and body image as differential factors associated with varying success in maintaining a weight loss. *Journal of Abnormal Psychology*, 1973, **40**, 474–480.

Leventhal, H., & Cleary, P. D. The smoking problem: A review of the research and theory in behavioral risk modification. *Psychological Bulletin*, 1980, **88**, 370–405.

Leventhal, H., & Johnson, J. E. Laboratory and field experimentation: Development of a theory of self-regulation. In P. Wooldridge, R. Leonard, & M. Skipper (Eds.), *Nursing research*. St. Louis, Missouri: Mosby, 1982, in press.

Lewinsohn, P. M., Mischel, W., Chaplin, W., & Barton, R. Social competence and depression: The role of illusory self-perceptions. *Journal of Abnormal Psychology*, 1980, **89**, 203–212.

Lichtenstein, E., Antonuccio, D. O., & Rainwater, G. *The resumption of cigarette smoking: A situational analysis of retrospective reports*. Manuscript under review, University of Oregon, 1982.

Liebling, B. A., & Shaver, P. Evaluation, self-awareness, and task performance. *Journal of Experimental Social Psychology*, 1973, **9**, 298–306.

Linden, W., & Wright, J. Programming generalization through social skills training in the natural environment. *Behavioural Analysis and Modification*, 1980, **4**, 239–251.

Litman, G. K., Eisler, J. R., Rawson, N. S. B., & Oppenheim, A. N. Differences in relapse precipitants and coping behavior between alcohol relapsers and survivors. *Behaviour Research and Therapy*, 1979, **17**, 89–94.

Litrownik, A. J., & Freitas, J. L. Self-monitoring in moderately retarded adolescents: Reactivity and accuracy as a function of valence. *Behavior Therapy*, 1980, **11**, 245–255.

Lobitz, W. C., & Post, R. D. Parameters of self-reinforcement and depression. *Journal of Abnormal Psychology*, 1979, **88**, 33–41.

Lorion, R. P., Cowen, E. L., & Caldwell, R. A. Problem types of children referred to a school based mental health program. *Journal of Consulting and Clinical Psychology*, 1974, **42**, 491–496.

McDonald, P. J. Reactions to objective self-awareness. *Journal of Research in Personality*, 1980, **14**, 250–260.

McFall, R. M. *Behavioral training: A skill-acquisition approach to clinical problems*. Morristown, New Jersey: General Learning Press, 1976.

McFall, R. M. Parameters of self-monitoring. In R. B. Stuart (Ed.), *Behavioral self-management: Strategies, techniques, and outcomes*. New York: Brunner/Mazel, 1977.

McFall, R. M., & Hammen, C. L. Motivation, structure, and self-monitoring: The role of nonspecific factors in smoking reduction. *Journal of Consulting and Clinical Psychology*, 1971, **37**, 80–86.

McPeak, W. R. Family therapies. In A. P. Goldstein & F. H. Kanfer (Eds.), *Maximizing treatment gains: Transfer enhancement in psychotherapy*. New York: Academic Press, 1979.

Mahoney, B. K., Rogers, T., Straw, M., & Mahoney, M. J. *Results and implications of* a problem-solving treatment for obesity. Paper presented at the meeting of the Association for Advancement of Behavior Therapy, Atlanta, December 1977.

Mahoney, M. J. Cognition and behavior modification. Cambridge, Massachusetts: Ballinger, 1974.

Mahoney, M. J. The obese eating style: Bites, beliefs, and behavior modification. Addictive Behaviors, 1975, 1, 47–53.

Mahoney, M. J. Reflections on the cognitive learning trend in psychotherapy. American Psychologist, 1977, 32, 5–13.

Mahoney, M. J., & Mahoney, K. Permanent weight control. New York: Norton, 1976.

Mahoney, M. J., Moore, B. E., Wade, T. C., & Moura, N. G. M. The effects of continuous and intermittent self-monitoring on academic behavior. Journal of Consulting and Clinical Psychology, 1973, 41, 65–69.

Maletzky, B. M. Behavior recording as treatment: A brief note. Behavior Therapy, 1974, 5, 107–112.

Mandler, G. Transfer of training as a function of degree of response overlearning. Journal of Experimental Psychology, 1954, 47, 411–417.

Mandler, G., & Sarason, S. A study of anxiety and learning. Journal of Abnormal and Social Psychology, 1952, 47, 166–173.

Marholin, D., II, Siegel, L. J., & Philips, D. Treatment and transfer: A search for empirical procedures. In M. Hersen, R. M. Eisler, & P. M. Miller (Eds.), Progress in behavior modification (Vol. 3). New York: Academic Press, 1976.

Marholin, D., II, & Touchette, P. E. The role of stimulus control and response consequences. In A. P. Goldstein & F. H. Kanfer (Eds.), Maximizing treatment gains: Transfer enhancement in psychotherapy. New York: Academic Press, 1979.

Marlatt, G. A. A comparison of aversive conditioning procedures in the treatment of alcoholism. Paper presented at the meeting of the Western Psychological Association, Anaheim, CA, 1973. Reported in G. A. Marlatt, Craving for alcohol, loss of control, and relapse: A cognitive-behavioral analysis. In P. E. Nathan, G. A. Marlatt, & T. Lobert (Eds.), Alcoholism: New directions in behavioral research and treatment. New York: Plenum, 1978. (a)

Marlatt, G. A. Craving for alcohol, loss of control, and relapse: A cognitive-behavioral analysis. In P. E. Nathan, G. A. Marlatt, & T. Loberg (Eds.), Alcoholism: New directions in behavioral research and treatment. New York: Plenum, 1978. (b)

Marlatt, G. A., & Gordon, J. R. Determinants of relapse: Implications for the maintenance of behavior change. In P. O. Davidson & S. M. Davidson (Eds.), Behavioral medicine: Changing health lifestyles. New York: Brunner/Mazel, 1980.

Marlatt, G. A., & Kaplan, B. Self-initiated attempts to change behavior: A study of New Year's resolutions. Psychological Reports, 1972, 30, 123–131.

Mash, E. J., & Terdal, L. G. Follow-up assessments in behavior therapy. In P. Karoly & J. J. Steffen (Eds.), Improving the long-term effects of psychotherapy: Models of durable outcome. New York: Gardner, 1980.

Masters, J. C., & Santrock, J. W. Studies in the self-regulation of behavior: Effects of cognitive and affective events. Developmental Psychology, 1976, 12, 334–348.

Meichenbaum, D. Self-instructional methods. In F. H. Kanfer & A. P. Goldstein (Eds.), Helping people change: A textbook of methods. Oxford: Pergamon, 1975.

Miller, G., Galanter, E., & Pribram, K. Plans and the structure of behavior. New York: Holt, 1960.

Miransky, J., & Langer, E. J. Burglary (non)prevention: An instance of relinquishing control. Personality and Social Psychology Bulletin, 1978, 4, 399–405.

Mischel, W. Toward a cognitive social learning reconceptualization of personality. *Psychological Review*, 1973, **80**, 252–283.

Mischel, W., Ebbesen, E. B., & Zeiss, A. R. Selective attention to the self: Situational and dispositional determinants. *Journal of Personality and Social Psychology*, 1973, **27**, 129–142.

Moore, B., Underwood, B., Heberlein, P., Doyle, L., & Litzkie, K. Generalization of feedback about performance. *Cognitive Therapy and Research*, 1979, **3**, 371–380.

Nash, J. D. *Curbing dropout from treatment for obesity.* Paper presented at the meeting of the Association for Advancement of Behavior Therapy, New York, December, 1976.

Nelson, R. O. Assessment and therapeutic functions of self-monitoring. In M. Hersen, R. M. Eisler, & P. M. Miller (Eds.), *Progress in behavior modification*, Vol. 5. New York: Academic Press, 1977.

Nelson, R. O., & Hayes, S. C. Theoretical explanations for reactivity in self-monitoring. *Behavior Modification*, 1981, **5**, 3–14.

Nisbett, R. E., & Ross, L. *Human inference: Strategies and shortcomings in social judgement.* New York: Prentice-Hall, 1980.

Nisbett, R. E., & Wilson, T. D. Telling more than we know: Verbal reports on mental processes. *Psychological Review*, 1977, **84**, 231–259.

Nolan, J. D., Mattis, P. R., & Holliday, R. C. Long-term effects of behavior therapy: A 12-month follow-up. *Journal of Abnormal Psychology*, 1970, **76**, 88–92.

O'Leary, K. D., & Wilson, G. T. *Behavior therapy: Application and outcome.* New York: Prentice-Hall, 1975.

Page, T. J., Iwata, B. A., & Neef, N. A. Teaching pedestrian skills to retarded persons: Generalization from the classroom to the natural environment. *Journal of Applied Behavior Analysis*, 1976, **9**, 433–444.

Paulsen, B. K., Lutz, R. N., McReynolds, W. T., & Kohrs, M. B. Behavior therapy for weight control: Long-term results of two programs with nutritionists as therapists. *American Journal of Clinical Nutrition*, 1976, **29**, 880–888.

Pearce, J. W., LeBow, M. D., & Orchard, J. Role of spouse involvement in the behavioral treatment of overweight women. *Journal of Consulting and Clinical Psychology*, 1981, **49**, 236–244.

Pennebaker, J. W., & Skelton, J. A. Psychological parameters of physical symptoms. *Personality and Social Psychology Bulletin*, 1978, **4**, 524–530.

Perri, M. G., & Richards, C. S. An investigation of naturally occurring episodes of self-controlled behaviors. *Journal of Counseling Psychology*, 1977, **24**, 178–183.

Perri, M. G., Richards, C. S., & Schultheis, K. R. Behavioral self-control and smoking reduction: A study of self-initiated attempts to reduce smoking. *Behavior Therapy*, 1977, **8**, 360–365.

Perri, M. G., Stalonas, P. M., Jr., Twentyman, C. T., Toro, P. A., & Zastowny, T. R. *Making behavioral treatment for obesity last: An evaluation of social support interventions.* Paper presented at the meeting of the Association for Advancement of Behavior Therapy, New York, November 1980.

Peterson, L., & Shigetomi, C. The use of coping techniques to minimize anxiety in hospitalized children. *Behavior Therapy*, 1981, **12**, 1–14.

Pomerleau, O., Adkins, D., & Pertschuk, M. Predictors of outcome and recidivism in smoking cessation treatment. *Addictive Behaviors*, 1978, **3**, 64–70.

Postman, L., & Brown, D. R. The perceptual consequences of success and failure. *Journal of Abnormal and Social Psychology*, 1952, **47**, 213–221.

Prentice-Dunn, S., & Rogers, R. W. Effects of deindividuating situational cues and aggressive models on subjective deindividuation and aggression. *Journal of Personality and Social Psychology*, 1980, **39**, 104–113.

Price, R. H. The social ecology of treatment gains. In A. P. Goldstein & F. H. Kanfer (Eds.), *Maximizing treatment gains: Transfer enhancement in psychotherapy*. New York: Academic Press, 1979.

Pryor, J. B., Gibbons, F. X., Wicklund, R. A., Fazio, R. H., & Hood, R. Self-focused attention and self-report validity. *Journal of Personality*, 1977, **45**, 514–527.

Pyszczynski, T. A., & Greenberg, J. Role of disconfirmed expectancies in the instigation of attributional processing. *Journal of Personality and Social Psychology*, 1981, **40**, 31–38.

Rabin-Bickelman, E., & Marholin II, D. Programming generalization of treatment effects: A stimulus control procedure. *Journal of Behavior Therapy and Experimental Psychiatry*, 1978, **9**, 277–282.

Rachlin, H. *Introduction to modern behaviorism* (2nd ed.). San Francisco, California: Freeman, 1976.

Rachman, S. J., & Hodgson, R. J. *Obsessions and compulsions*. New York: Prentice-Hall, 1980.

Redd, W. H. Generalization of adult's stimulus control of children's behavior. *Journal of Experimental Child Psychology*, 1970, **9**, 286–296.

Rehm, L. P. A self-control model of depression. *Behavior Therapy*, 1977, **8**, 787–804.

Relinger, H., Bornstein, P. H., Bugge, I. D., Carmody, T. P., & Zohn, C. J. Utilization of adverse rapid smoking in groups: Efficacy of treatment and maintenance procedures. *Journal of Consulting and Clinical Psychology*, 1977, **45**, 245–249.

Richards, C. S., Anderson, D. C., & Baker, R. B. The role of information feedback in the relative reactivity of self-monitoring and external observations. *Behavior Therapy*, 1978, **9**, 687.

Richards, C. S., & Perri, M. G. Do self-control treatments last: An evaluation of behavioral problem-solving and faded counselor contract as treatment maintenance strategies. *Journal of Counseling Psychology*, 1978, **25**, 376–383.

Richards, C. S., Perri, M. G., & Gortney, C. Increasing the maintenance of self-control treatment through faded counselor contract and high information feedback. *Journal of Counseling Psychology*, 1976, **23**, 405–406.

Rijsmon, J. B. Factors in social comparison of performance influencing actual performance. *European Journal of Social Psychology*, 1974, **4**, 279–311.

Rodin, J. Current status of the internal-external hypothesis for obesity: What went wrong? *American Psychologist*, 1981, **36**, 361–372.

Rodin, J. *Obesity theory and behavior therapy: An uneasy couple?* Paper presented at the meeting of the Association for Advancement of Behavior Therapy, San Francisco, December 1979.

Roth, D., & Rehm, L. P. Relationships among self-monitoring processes, memory, and depression. *Cognitive Therapy and Research*, 1980, **4**, 149–158.

Rozensky, R. H., & Bellack, A. S. Behavior change and individual differences in self-control. *Behaviour Research and Therapy*, 1974, **12**, 267–268.

Rozensky, R. H., & Bellack, A. S. Individual differences in self-reinforcement style and performance in self- and therapist-controlled weight reduction programs. *Behaviour Research and Therapy*, 1976, **14**, 357–364.

Schank, R. C., & Abelson, R. P. *Scripts, plans, goals, and understanding*. Hillsdale, New Jersey: Erlbaum, 1977.

Scheier, M. F. Self-awareness, self-consciousness, and angry aggression. *Journal of Personality*, 1976, **44**, 627–644.

Scheier, M. F., & Carver, C. S. Self-focused attention and the experience of emotion: Attraction, repulsion, elation, and depression. *Journal of Personality and Social Psychology*, 1977, **35**, 625–636.

Scheier, M. F., Carver, C. S., & Gibbons, F. X. Self-directed attention, awareness of bodily states, and suggestibility. *Journal of Personality and Social Psychology*, 1979, **37**, 1576–1588.

Scheier, M. F., Carver, C. S., & Gibbons, F. X. Self-focused attention and reactions to fear. *Journal of Research in Personality*, 1981, in press.

Scheier, M. F., Carver, C. S., Schulz, R., Glass, D. C., & Katz, I. Sympathy, self-consciousness, and reactions to the stigmatized. *Journal of Applied Social Psychology*, 1978, **8**, 270–282.

Scheier, M. F., Fenigstein, A., & Buss, A. H. Self-awareness and physical aggression. *Journal of Experimental Social Psychology*, 1974, **10**, 264–273.

Schneider, W., & Shiffrin, R. M. Controlled and automatic human information processing: I. Detection, search, and attention. *Psychological Review*, 1977, **84**, 1–66.

Seidner, M. L., & Kirschenbaum, D. S. Behavioral contracts: Effects of pretreatment information and intention statements. *Behavior Therapy*, 1980, **11**, 689–698.

Seymour, F. W., & Stokes, T. F. Self-recording in training girls to increase work and evoke staff praise in an institution for offenders. *Journal of Applied Behavior Analysis*, 1976, **9**, 41–54.

Sherman, A. R. In vivo therapies for phobic reactions, instrumental behavior problems, and interpersonal and communication problems. In A. P. Goldstein & F. H. Kanfer (Eds.), *Maximizing treatment gains: Transfer enhancement in psychotherapy.* New York: Academic Press, 1979.

Sherman, A. R., & Levine, M. P. In vivo therapies for compulsive habits, sexual difficulties, and severe adjustment problems. In A. P. Goldstein & F. H. Kanfer (Eds.), *Maximizing treatment gains: Transfer enhancement in psychotherapy.* New York: Academic Press, 1979.

Shiffman, S. M. *Relapse following smoking cessation: A situational analysis.* Unpublished manuscript, UCLA, 1981.

Shiffrin, R. M., & Schneider, W. Controlled and automatic human information processing: II. Perceptual learning, automatic attending, and a general theory. *Psychological Review*, 1977, **84**, 127–190.

Shrauger, J. S., Responses to evaluation as a function of initial self-perceptions. *Psychological Bulletin*, 1975, **82**, 581–596.

Shrauger, J. S., & Rosenberg, S. E. Self-esteem and the effects of success and failure feedback on performance. *Journal of Personality*, 1970, **38**, 404–417.

Shuller, D. Y., & McNamara, J. R. Expectancy factors in behavioral observation. *Behavior Therapy*, 1976, **7**, 519–527.

Sigall, H., & Gould, R. The effects of self-esteem and evaluator demandingness on effort expenditure. *Journal of Personality and Social Psychology*, 1977, **35**, 12–20.

Silverman, I. Self-esteem and differential responsiveness to success and failure. *Journal of Abnormal and Social Psychology*, 1964, **69**, 115–119.

Sjoberg, L., & Johnson, T. Trying to give up smoking: A study of volitional breakdowns. *Addictive Behaviors*, 1978, **3**, 149–164.

Sjoberg, L., & Persson, L. A study of attempts by obese patients to regulate eating. *Addictive Behaviors*, 1979, **4**, 349–359.

Sjoberg, L., & Samsonowitz, V. Success and failure in trying to quit smoking. *Scandinavian Journal of Psychology*, 1978, **19**, 205–212.

Sjoberg, L., Samsonowitz, V., & Olsson, G. Volitional problems in alcohol abuse. *Goteberg Psychological Reports*, 1978, **8**, No. 5.

Slapion, M. J., & Carver, C. S. Self-directed attention and facilitation of intellectual performance among persons high in test anxiety. *Cognitive Therapy and Research*, 1981, **5**, 115–121.

Smedslund, J. The concept of correlation in adults. *Scandinavian Journal of Psychology*, 1963, **4**, 165–173.

Smith, E., & Miller, F. Limits on perception of cognitive processes: A reply to Nisbett and Wilson. *Psychological Review*, 1978, **85**, 355–362.

Smith, M. L., & Glass, G. V. Meta-analysis of psychotherapy outcome studies. *American Psychologist*, 1977, **32**, 752–760.

Snyder, C. R., Shenkel, R. J., & Lowrey, C. R. Acceptance of personality interpretations: The "Barnum Effect" and beyond. *Journal of Consulting and Clinical Psychology*, 1977, **45**, 104–114.

Sobell, M. B., & Sobell, L. C. *Behavioral treatment of alcoholic problems*. New York: Plenum, 1976.

Solomon, R. L. An opponent-process theory of acquired motivation. IV: The affective dynamics of addiction. In J. Maser & M. Seligman (Eds.), *Psychopathology: Experimental models*. San Francisco, California: Freeman, 1977.

Solomon, R. L., & Corbit, J. D. An opponent-process theory of motivation: II. Cigarette smoking. *Journal of Abnormal Psychology*, 1973, **81**, 158–171.

Spevak, P. A., & Richards, C. S. Enhancing the durability of treatment effects: Maintenance strategies in the treatment of nail-biting. *Cognitive Therapy and Research*, 1980, **4**, 251–258.

Staats, A. W. *Social behaviorism*. Homewood, Illinois: Dorsey, 1975.

Stalonas, P. M., Jr., Johnson, W. G., & Christ, M. Behavior modification for obesity: The evaluation of exercise, contingency management, and program adherence. *Journal of Consulting and Clinical Psychology*, 1978, **46**, 463–469.

Stalonas, P. M., Jr., Kirschenbaum, D. S., & Zastowny, T. R. *Specific effects of "nonspecific" factors in behavior therapy for obesity*. Paper presented at the meeting of the Association for Advancement of Behavior Therapy, Toronto, November 1981.

Stalonas, P. M., Jr., Perri, M. G., Kerzner, A. B., Twentyman, C. T., & Johnson, W. G. *Do self-control treatments last? A 5-year follow-up of behavioral treatment for obesity*. Paper presented at the meeting of the Association for Advancement of Behavior Therapy, New York, November 1980.

Steenbarger, B. N., & Aderman, D. Objective self-awareness as a nonaversive state: Effect of anticipating discrepancy reduction. *Journal of Personality*, 1979, **47**, 330–339.

Steffen, J. J., & Myszak, K. A. Influence of pretherapy induction upon the outcome of a self-control weight reduction program. *Behavior Therapy*, 1978, **9**, 404–409.

Stevens, L., & Jones, E. E. Defensive attribution and the Kelley cube. *Journal of Personality and Social Psychology*, 1976, **34**, 809–820.

Stojiljkovic, S. Conditioned aversion treatment of alcoholics. *Quarterly Journal of Studies in Alcohol*, 1969, **30**, 900–904.

Stokes, T. F., & Baer, D. M. Preschool peers as mutual generalization-facilitating agents. *Behavior Therapy*, 1976, **7**, 549–556.

Stokes, T. F., & Baer, D. M. An implicit technology of generalization. *Journal of Applied Behavior Analysis*, 1977, **10**, 349–368.

Stokes, T. F., Baer, D. M., & Jackson, R. L. Programming the generalization of a greeting response in four retarded children. *Journal of Applied Behavior Analysis*, 1974, **7**, 599–610.

Stuart, R. B. Behavioral control of overeating. *Behaviour Research and Therapy*, 1967, **5**, 357–365.

Stunkard, A. J., & Mahoney, M. J. Behavioral treatment of the eating disorders. In H. Leitenberg (Ed.), *Handbook of behavior modification*. New York: Prentice-Hall, 1976.

Stunkard, A. J., & Penick, S. B. Behavior modification in the treatment of obesity. *Archives of General Psychiatry*, 1979, **36**, 801–806.

Taylor, S. E., & Fiske, S. T. Salience, attention, and attribution: Top of the head phenomena. In L. Berkowitz (Ed.), *Advances in experimental social psychology* (Vol. 10). New York: Academic Press, 1978.

Thoresen, C. E., & Mahoney, M. J. *Behavioral self-control*. New York: Holt, 1974.

Thorndike, E. L., & Woodworth, R. S. The influence of improvement in one mental function upon the efficiency of other functions. *Psychological Review*, 1901, **8**, 247–261.

Tobias, L. L., & McDonald, M. L. Internal locus of control and weight loss: An insufficient condition. *Journal of Consulting and Clinical Psychology*, 1977, **45**, 647–653.

Tomarken, A. J., & Kirschenbaum, D. S. Self-regulatory failure: Accentuate the positive? *Journal of Personality and Social Psychology*, 1982, in press.

Tomarken, A. J., & Kirschenbaum, D. S. *Self-awareness and self-regulation*. Manuscript in preparation, University of Wisconsin, Madison, 1982. (a)

Trope, Y. Uncertainty-reducing properties of achievement tasks. *Journal of Personality and Social Psychology*, 1979, **37**, 1505–1518.

Turner, R. G. Consistency, self-consciousness and the predictive validity of typical and maximal personality measures. *Journal of Research in Personality*, 1978, **12**, 117–132. (a)

Turner, R. G. Effects of differential request procedures and self-consciousness on trait attributions. *Journal of Research in Personality*, 1978, **12**, 431–438. (b)

Underwood, B. J. Associative transfer in verbal learning as a function of response similarity and degree of first-list learning. *Journal of Experimental Psychology*, 1951, **42**, 44–53.

Wade, T. C. Relative effects on performance and motivation of self-monitoring correct and incorrect responses. *Journal of Experimental Psychology*, 1974, **77**, 245–248.

Wegner, D. M., & Giuliano, T. Arousal-induced attention to the self. *Journal of Personality and Social Psychology*, 1980, **38**, 719–726.

Wegner, D. M., & Schaefer, D. The concentration of responsibility: An objective self-awareness analysis of group size effects in helping situations. *Journal of Personality and Social Psychology*, 1978, **36**, 147–155.

Weiner, B. The role of success and failure in the learning of easy and complex tasks. *Journal of Personality and Social Psychology*, 1966, **3**, 339–344.

Weiner, B. *Theories of motivation: From mechanism to cognition*. Chicago, Illinois: Rand McNally, 1972.

Weiner, B. A theory of motivation for some classroom experiences. *Journal of Educational Psychology*, 1979, **71**, 3–25.

Weiner, B., & Schneider, K. Drive versus cognitive theory: A reply to Boor and Harmon. *Journal of Personality and Social Psychology*, 1971, **18**, 258–262.

Weiss, A. R. Characteristics of successful weight reducers: A brief review of predictor variables. *Addictive Behaviors*, 1977, **2**, 193–201.

Weissberg, R. P., Gesten, E. L., Rapking, B. D., Cowen, E. L., Davidson, E., Flores de Apodaca, & McKim, B. Evaluation of a social-problem-solving training program for suburban and inner-city third-grade children. *Journal of Consulting and Clinical Psychology*, 1981, **49**, 251–261.

Weisz, G., & Bucher, B. Involving husbands in treatment of obesity—Effects on weight loss, depression, and marital satisfaction. *Behavior Therapy*, 1980, **11**, 643–650.

Whitman, T. L., Mercurio, J. R., & Caponigri, V. Development of social responses in two severely retarded children. *Journal of Applied Behavior Analysis*, 1970, **3**, 139–147.

Wicklund, R. A. Objective self-awareness. In L. Berkowitz (Ed.), *Advances in experimental social psychology* (Vol. 8). New York: Academic Press, 1975.

Wicklund, R. A., & Duval, S. Opinion change and performance facilitation as a result of objective self-awareness. *Journal of Experimental Social Psychology*, 1971, **1**, 319–342.

Wildman, R. W. II, & Wildman, R. W. Maintenance and generalization of institutional behavior modification programs. In P. Karoly & J. J. Steffen (Eds.), *Improving the long-term effects of psychotherapy: Models of durable outcome*. New York: Gardner, 1980.

Wilson, G. T., & Brownell, K. Behavior therapy for obesity: Including family members in the treatment process. *Behavior Therapy*, 1978, **9**, 943–945.

Wine, J. D. Cognitive-attentional theory of test anxiety. In I. G. Sarason (Ed.), *Test anxiety: Theory, research, and applications*. Hillsdale, N.J.: Erlbaum, 1980.

Winett, R. A., & Neale, M. S. Modifying settings as a strategy for permanent preventive behavior change: Flexible work schedules. In P. Karoly & J. J. Steffen (Eds.), *Improving the long-term effects of psychotherapy: Models of durable outcome*. New York: Gardner, 1980.

Wong, P. T. P., & Weiner, B. When people ask 'why' questions, and the heuristics of attributional search. *Journal of Personality and Social Psychology*, 1981, **40**, 650–663.

Woodworth, R. S., & Schlosberg, H. *Experimental psychology* (rev. ed.). New York: Holt, 1956.

Wooley, S. C., Wooley, O. W., & Dyrenforth, S. R. Theoretical, practical, and social issues in behavioral treatments of obesity. *Journal of Applied Behavior Analysis*, 1979, **12**, 3–25.

Wortman, C. B., & Brehm, J. W. Responses to uncontrollable outcomes: An integration of reactance theory and the learned helplessness model. In L. Berkowitz (Ed.) *Advances in experimental social psychology* (Vol. 8). New York: Academic Press, 1975.

Wortman, C. B., & Dintzer, L. Is an attributional analysis of the learned helplessness phenomena viable?: A critique of the Abramson-Seligman-Teasdale reformulation. *Journal of Abnormal Psychology*, 1978, **87**, 75–82.

Zajonc, R. B. Feeling and thinking: Preferences need no inferences. *American Psychologist*, 1980, **35**, 151–175.

Ziller, R. C. Individuation and socialization: A theory of assimilation in large organizations. *Human Relations*, 1964, **17**, 341–360.

Zimbardo, P. G. The human choice: Individuation, reason, and order versus deindividuation, impulse, and chaos. In W. J. Arnold & D. Levine (Eds.), *Nebraska Symposium on Motivation*. Lincoln, Nebraska: University of Nebraska Press, 1970.

Social Problem Solving
in Adults

THOMAS J. D'ZURILLA
Department of Psychology,
State University of New York,
Stony Brook, New York

ARTHUR NEZU[1]
Division of Psychological Services,
Fairleigh Dickinson University,
Teaneck, New Jersey

[1] Present address: 139 Temple Avenue, Hackensack, New Jersey 07601.

ADVANCES IN COGNITIVE-BEHAVIORAL RESEARCH
AND THERAPY, VOLUME 1

I. INTRODUCTION

Social problem solving (SPS) refers to the process whereby an individual identifies or discovers effective means of coping with problematic situations encountered in day-to-day living. More specifically, D'Zurilla and Goldfried (1971) have defined SPS as "a behavioral process . . . which (a) makes available a variety of potentially effective response alternatives for dealing with a problematic situation, and (b) increases the probability of selecting the most effective response from among these various alternatives" (p. 108). This process is viewed as a special form of social learning. As Gagné (1966) has observed: "The solving of a problem is an event which needs to be classified, so far as the individual's behavior is concerned, as an act of learning . . . [since] . . . the observed events in problem solving comprise a change in human performance, and this in turn leads us to infer a change in human capability" (p. 140). SPS is also considered a general coping strategy whose goal is the discovery of a *wide range* of effective behavior, and, thus, can be expected to contribute to the facilitation and maintenance of *general* social competence.

After reviewing problem-solving theory and research from several different fields and identifying the most socially relevant work, D'Zurilla and Goldfried (1971) proposed a model of SPS that consists of the following five skills or operations: (a) general orientation (i.e., problem-solving "set"), (b) problem definition and formulation, (c) generation of alternatives, (d) decision making, and (e) verification (i.e., evaluation of solution outcome in real life). Although these skills are conceptualized as primarily cognitive in nature, they may involve certain overt activities as well, such as information seeking, behavior rehearsal, and self-monitoring activities.

An SPS model similar to D'Zurilla and Goldfried's (1971) has been presented by Spivack and Shure (Spivack & Shure, 1974; Spivack, Platt, & Shure, 1976). According to these investigators, effective SPS involves the following abilities: (a) the ability to recognize and appreciate the wide range of possible problematic situations which one might encounter in the social environment, (b) the capacity to generate possible solutions to interpersonal problems, (c) the ability to specify the step-by-step means that are necessary in order to successfully solve a problem, (d) the ability to understand and evaluate the consequences and implications of one's actions, and (e) the awareness of the motivational factors involved in one's actions and the actions of others. Although there are some minor differences in wording, classification, and emphasis, these skills are all included in the five stages of the D'Zurilla and Goldfried model.

As in any other research area in psychology, there is a certain amount of confusion in the literature on SPS due to the use of somewhat different terminology and the failure to define concepts and distinguish between dissimilar albeit overlapping concepts adequately. For example, Spivack et al. (1976) use the term "interpersonal cognitive problem solving" to describe their approach. We prefer the less cumbersome term "social problem solving" for two main reasons. First, we would like to emphasize our concern with the solving of problems in the real-life social setting (often referred to as "problems in living") without limiting our scope strictly to interpersonal problems. Many of the important problems in living with which an individual must cope may be described more accurately as personal or intrapersonal problems (e.g., financial pressures, study problems, vocational indecision, etc.). Second, as mentioned above, although the SPS process is mainly cognitive, it may not always be entirely cognitive in nature. For example, to define a problem adequately, it may be necessary for the problem solver actively to seek out important facts and information from various sources. Similarly, before making a decision, the problem solver might seek information concerning the consequences of different alternatives, or even "test out" different alternatives using behavior rehearsal. Overt behavior in the form of behavioral observation and record keeping may also be involved in the verification stage of problem solving, where the solution outcome is evaluated.

Confusion also results from the failure of some investigators to distinguish clearly between the concepts of problem solving, solution implementation, and behavioral competence. While these are overlapping concepts, they cannot be treated as though they were one and the same. According to D'Zurilla and Goldfried's (1971) conceptualization, "problem solving" is a process of discovery (i.e., finding an effective solution), whereas "solution implementation" refers to the performance of the chosen solution response. The role of solution implementation in the problem-solving process is to provide data for the verification step—i.e., evaluation of the solution outcome in the real-life setting.

The concept of "behavioral competence" has been defined as the "effectiveness or adequacy with which an individual is capable of responding to various problematic situations which confront him" (Goldfried & D'Zurilla, 1969, p. 161). This concept is clearly the broadest of the three, encompassing a wide range of coping behaviors and social skills which have been learned and maintained through a variety of different social-learning processes, including problem solving, modeling, direct verbal instruction, and instrumental learning. Thus, it is clear that problem-solving performance is only one of several forms of behavioral competence.

Failure to distinguish between the above three concepts can result in the confounding of problem-solving variables with other social-learning variables, adding confusion and ambiguity to the study of the relationship between SPS and social or behavioral competence. One example of such confusion is evident in the "observational" or behavioral approach to the study of SPS in children recently proposed by Krasnor and Rubin (1981) and strongly supported by Butler and Meichenbaum (1981). After discussing some of the problems with self-report and laboratory approaches to the study of cognitive problem-solving processes, these investigators argued that a more useful and valid approach to the study of SPS would be to focus on observable behavior in the natural environment. In their procedure, goal-directed coping behaviors are observed in the real-life setting and coded into various types of "strategies" (for example, persistence, flexibility), and "goals" (for example, object transfer, attention). An attempt is then made to infer underlying cognitive problem-solving variables from these data, which are assessed in future subjects by using the same behavioral-observation methods.

Although this observational approach is ideal for the study of *behavioral competence*, the main problem with it as an approach to the study of *SPS* is that it confuses problem-solving performance with other forms of behavioral competence which are not mediated by problem-solving thinking in the particular situation focused on. Cognitive problem-solving variables cannot be inferred when none actually exists. Moreover, a strict observational approach to SPS does not provide a means of identifying and accounting for the possible effects on coping performance of such non-problem-solving factors as performance skill deficits, emotional inhibitions, and motivational deficits. These and other problems associated with different approaches to the assessment of SPS will be discussed further later in this article.

In the sections that follow, we will discuss (a) problem-solving research and developments in cognitive–behavioral therapy which are related to the *process* of SPS, (b) research on the relationship between SPS skills and psychopathology, (c) problems involved in attempting to assess SPS, and (d) studies on the outcomes of SPS training programs with a variety of different populations. We will limit our discussion to SPS with *adults* for two reasons. First, several recent excellent reviews on SPS with children are available elsewhere (see Butler & Meichenbaum, 1981; Kendall, Pellegrini, & Urbain, 1981; Krasnor & Rubin, 1981; Urbain & Kendall, 1980). Second, it is important to treat the research on SPS with children separately from that with adults because of the limits on the generalizability of results and conclusions between the two populations due to the major differences in relevant subject characteristics (for example, stage of cognitive development, social-skill development), degree of external control of behavior, and research and training methods.

II. THE SOCIAL PROBLEM-SOLVING PROCESS

In this section we will discuss some recent research and clinical developments related to the five stages of the D'Zurilla and Goldfried (1971) SPS model. We have made two modifications in the labeling of these stages. First, to emphasize that the main function of the first stage is to orient the individual appropriately to problems in living, we are now labeling this stage *Problem Orientation* instead of the previous General Orientation. Second, we are relabeling the fifth stage *Solution Implementation and Verification* to stress the point made earlier that solution implementation is not a separate component of the SPS process but, instead, is part of the verification procedure—i.e., assessment of the solution outcome.

It should also be emphasized at this point that the five stages of this model are not conceptualized as five separate, independent sets of specific cognitive abilities. The five stages are organized as presented because each represents a different skill or operation having a distinct function or purpose in the SPS process. The assumption is that this way of organizing the SPS process is most logical and useful for both research and training. The basic specific cognitive abilities underlying the SPS process may overlap considerably from stage to stage. Some examples of these basic abilities are objective thinking, systematic thinking, logical thinking, matching ability, causal thinking (i.e., ability to identify cause–effect relationships), and perspective taking (i.e., ability to appreciate the point of view of others in a particular situation). When we speak of SPS *abilities* here, however, we will usually be referring to the more general ability to perform each of the five SPS operations, and not to these specific, underlying abilities.

The order in which the stages are presented should not be taken to imply that real-life problem solving usually proceeds, or should proceed, in an orderly sequence beginning at step one and terminating at step five. The order represents a logical sequence of steps for training purposes and systematic application. In actual practice, however, movement back and forth from one stage to another is expected to be the rule rather than the exception. The problem solver exits from the system only when a satisfactory solution is found (including the possible strategy: "Go get help"), or it is determined that the problem is insoluble and must be accepted as is.

A. Problem Orientation

The purpose of this stage is to (a) reduce or at least distract attention from negative emotional states and thoughts (self-statements) that are likely to disrupt SPS thinking, and (b) focus instead on the stimulus determinants of these negative responses and on self-statements which are likely to facilitate effective problem-solving behavior. To achieve this purpose, the problem solver must adopt a "problem-solving set" consisting of four important components: (a) the identification or recognition of a problematic situation when one occurs, (b) acceptance of the view that problems in living are normal and inevitable, and that problem solving is a viable means of coping with them, (c) "perceived control"—i.e., the expectation that one is *capable* of solving a particular problem effectively, and (d) the set to "stop and think" when confronted with a problem instead of responding "automatically" with habits based on previous experience in similar situations.

It is only when the problem solver recognizes the problem and attends to the relevant information that he can prepare to deal effectively with it. To understand how problem recognition usually occurs it is helpful to consider the A–B–C framework that Ellis (1962, 1977) uses in his rational–emotive approach to psychopathology and therapy. The "A" refers to some activating stimulus event or experience in life (for example, a man is rejected three times in a row when he asks a certain woman for a date). "B" refers to the individual's thoughts and perceptions regarding this experience (for example, "I can't stand to be rejected," "I must be a real loser"). The "C" represents the emotional and behavioral consequences of A and B (for example, confusion, depression, withdrawal, less frequent asking for dates in the future).

The individual's first concern is usually with the emotional and behavioral responses at point C. Instead of labeling C as "the problem," and dwelling on these responses, one should use them as cues for attending to and recognizing the *situation* which might be causing them. For effective problem solving, the most relevant information concerning the nature of the problem is likely to be found in A and/ or B. In his Rational–Emotive Therapy (RET), Ellis (1977) tends to focus on the identification of problems at point B involving distorted or irrational beliefs. However, it is also possible that the main problem might be found at point A (for example, being too aggressive in his approach to the woman, an obstacle presented by a third person, such as another man with whom the woman is involved or a mother who disapproves of the person's profession). Once the right problem is recognized and attended to, the individual can then begin to deal with it in a concrete manner.

Ellis and other rational-behavior therapists (Ellis, 1962; Ellis & Grieger, 1977) have long argued that an accepting, problem-solving-oriented approach to problems in living (i.e., disappointment, frustration, conflict, failure, etc.) is a necessary condition for effective functioning. They have maintained that emotional disturbance and self-defeating behavior often result from a tendency to view these problems as highly threatening or tragic events which happen only to people who are abnormal, inadequate, bad, or unlucky. Some support for their hypothesis has come from recent studies in which the thought processes of individuals who cope well when "stressed" were compared with those of individuals who usually perform poorly under stressful conditions (for example, pressure of gymnastic competition, Mahoney & Avener, 1977; anger-provoking situations, Meichenbaum, Henshaw, & Himel, 1979; interpersonal confrontation, Schwartz & Gottman, 1976; medical stress, Kendall, Williams, Pechacek, Graham, Shisslak, & Herzoff, 1979). After reviewing these studies, Meichenbaum et al. (1979) concluded that a common characteristic associated with effective coping performance was the adoption of an appropriate "problem-solving set." The more competent individuals tended to accept the stress situation and view it positively as a challenge or "problem-to-be-solved," whereas the less effective individuals were more likely to perceive the situation negatively as a threat or aversive experience.

The most important component of problem orientation could very well be the "perception of control," or the belief that one is *capable* of solving a given problem effectively. This concept is similar to Bandura's (1977b) "self-efficacy," which refers to the conviction or expectation that one will be able to perform a particular coping behavior successfully. According to Bandura, expectations of personal efficacy affect both the *initiation* of coping behavior and its *persistence* in the face of obstacles and aversive experiences. Bandura also differentiates efficacy expectations from outcome expectations. The latter is defined as the expectation that a given coping behavior will lead to a certain outcome. In problem-solving terms, outcome expectations would refer to a person's ability to anticipate the consequences of certain solution alternatives, which is an important ability in the decision-making stage. As Bandura points out, perceived control or self-efficacy can be learned through four different sources of information: performance accomplishments, modeling, verbal instruction, and physiological states (for example, a reduction in anxiety in a particular situation leads to greater self-efficacy). In SPS training, modeling and verbal instruction might be used at first to facilitate problem-solving attempts, after which successful problem-solving performance and reduced anxiety or apprehension in response to problems should act as a powerful reinforcer for expectations of control.

To proceed to the other stages of SPS the problem solver must learn to inhibit the tendency to respond impulsively and "automatically" with habits based on previous experience and, instead, to "stop and think." After finding that psychiatric patients did poorly on a test of SPS ability when compared to a group of normal subjects, Platt and Spivack (1974) also found that the normals were more likely to include in their responses to hypothetical problems the idea that one should *think* before acting, whereas the patients showed more concern with the taking of immediate action. A similar difference between "good" and "poor" problem solvers in a normal college student population was reported many years ago by Bloom and Broder (1950).

A recent study comparing the thought processes of high- versus low-creative subjects on a creative problem-solving task has also provided support for the importance of problem-orientation variables (Henshaw, 1979). Using a "think aloud" procedure, Henshaw found that high-creative subjects emitted significantly more facilitative, problem-oriented statements (i.e., task-oriented statements, statements expressing acceptance and positive feelings about the challenge, positive evaluations of one's ability), and significantly less negative, inhibitive statements (i.e., task-irrelevant statements, statements expressing negative feelings about the task, negative evaluations of one's ability). Henshaw also found that high-creative subjects were significantly more likely to follow an inhibitive statement with a facilitative or creative statement, whereas the low-creative subjects tended to follow an inhibitive statement with either silence or another inhibitive statement.

A method that is likely to be quite useful for training and practice in the use of the problem-orientation operation is the self-instructional method of Meichenbaum (1977). Designed to improve coping performance and interject thought where behavior had been too impulsive, this method involves training individuals to (a) identify negative, inhibitive self-statements in a problematic situation, and (b) replace them with facilitative, problem-solving-oriented self-verbalizations. Studies on the effects of training in the specific problem-orientation package presented here are lacking; however, studies by Meichenbaum and other investigators offer evidence that self-instructional training focusing on problem-solving-oriented self-statements significantly enhances coping performance in a variety of problematic situations, including creative problem solving (Meichenbaum, 1975), intellectual problem solving (Meichenbaum & Cameron, 1973), and anxiety-related situations (Holroyd, 1976; Meichenbaum, Gilmore, & Fedoravicius, 1971). In addition to these findings, Bandura (1977b) has reported results which demonstrate that self-efficacy expectations are, in fact, significantly related to superior coping performance in stress situations. These results all strongly suggest that the problem-orientation stage is likely to play a major role in SPS performance.

B. Problem Definition and Formulation

This operation is probably the most important one in the SPS process but it is also the most difficult and complex. Its purpose is to assess the problem and identify a realistic goal or objective for problem solving. The role of this process in SPS is comparable to the role of assessment in behavior therapy. A complete, accurate, clinical assessment facilitates the selection of appropriate therapy techniques and contributes to the evaluation of therapeutic outcome. Similarly, in SPS a well-defined problem is likely to facilitate the generation of relevant solutions, improve decision-making effectiveness, and contribute to the accuracy of solution verification. There are four components to this operation: (a) seeking all available facts and information about the problem, being careful to describe these facts to oneself in clear, specific, concrete terms, (b) differentiating relevant from irrelevant information, and objective facts from unverified inferences, assumptions, and interpretations, (c) identifying the factors or circumstances that are making the situation "problematic" (for example, threat, frustration, etc.), and (d) setting a realistic problem-solving goal (i.e., specifying the desired outcome).

The first two components stress objectivity and specificity. The aim is to obtain as much accurate, factual information as possible and avoid having to deal with information that is highly subjective, inaccurate, or distorted. However, not all information required for effective SPS is directly observable. The problem solver must often rely on "processed" information based upon his judgments, inferences,

valuations, assumptions, and other interpretations. The difficulty with
this information is that it is often subject to distortion. When the
definition of a problem is based upon information that is inaccurate
or distorted, then the problem solver is dealing with a pseudo-problem
rather than a real problem. The pseudo-problem is insoluble because
the solution chosen to deal with it is likely to be inappropriate for the
problematic situation as it exists in reality. For example, the man in
our previous example who was rejected when he asked a certain
woman for a date may infer that she is avoiding him because he is
not manly enough and then decide to approach her more aggressively.
If this inference is incorrect and the woman is really *afraid* of aggressive men, then his "solution" is sure to fail and he will be rejected
once again.

In connection with his cognitive theory of depression, Aaron Beck
(1967, 1970) has discussed some common errors in information processing that could result in pseudo-problems. Knowledge of these
mistakes might help a problem solver to avoid making them.

1. *Arbitrary inference.* This distortion is illustrated in the example
described above. A person draws a conclusion, usually about the motives, feelings, or other underlying characteristics of others or himself,
without sufficient facts to support it and rule out alternative
interpretations.

2. *Selective abstraction.* This error has also been referred to as
"cognitive deficiency" (Beck, 1970). A person attends to certain selected facts and information in a situation and makes an assumption
based upon these facts while ignoring or disregarding other relevant
information. For example, a baseball player focuses on his own errors
in a ball game and assumes that the loss was his fault when, in fact,
several other players made more costly errors. A problem solver often
makes this type of error when attempting to judge the relevancy of
information in a problematic situation.

3. *Overgeneralization.* A problem solver often makes assumptions
about the general characteristics of people or situations within a given
class when defining a problem. A serious mistake would be to draw
a sweeping conclusion about *all* people or situations within the same
class on the basis of a single, often trivial, event. A woman who is
taken advantage of sexually by a man concludes: "All men are pigs!"

4. *Magnification and minimization.* Magnification occurs when an
individual exaggerates the value, intensity, or significance of an event.
A man who gets rejected by one woman considers the rejection a
"catastrophe" which "proves" that he is inadequate. Minimization,

on the other hand, refers to the opposite mistake of inappropriately devaluing or reducing the significance of an event. A woman minimizes the danger of walking down a particular lonely street at night, or a worker fails to recognize the significance of his habit of coming to work late.

In addition to the above cognitive distortions, there is another type of mistake individuals often make in defining problems that is related to causal and consequential thinking (i.e., identifying cause–effect relationships, anticipating the consequences of behavior). This error involves overestimation or underestimation of the probability that a particular effect will follow a certain prior event, or that particular consequences will follow certain behaviors. When this error occurs, pseudo-problems may again be created. For example, consider a student who greatly overestimates the likelihood of failing an exam following a given amount of study time. If the student does not have any more study time available, he may perceive a problem where none exists in reality. Another example is an employee who greatly underestimates his chances of getting a raise if he were to ask the boss for one. He may try to figure out what more he can do to impress the boss when it is not really necessary to do so. It should also be emphasized at this point, however, that when an individual responds in a given situation on the basis of misinformation or misconceptions, he may indeed create a *real* problem for himself because his behavior may turn out to be inappropriate or maladaptive.

Most of the cognitive distortions discussed above can also disrupt performance in later SPS stages. For example, inaccurate prediction of the likely consequences of a given behavior can also be a costly mistake in the decision-making stage. In order to avoid cognitive distortions, the problem solver must clearly differentiate between objective or observable facts and information which is based on his or someone else's judgments, inferences, or interpretations. The problem solver should accept and utilize the latter information only when there are enough objective facts to confirm the validity of that information. Since this decision itself requires a judgment, the problem solver can only hope to minimize his errors, not eliminate them entirely.

Assuming that the problem solver is dealing with relevant and accurate information, he then attempts to use this information to *formulate* or conceptualize the problem. This formulation component is designed to help the individual "understand" the problem so that he will be better able to identify appropriate objectives as well as generate relevant solution alternatives. According to D'Zurilla and Goldfried

(1971), a situation is considered to be "problematic" when "no effective response alternative is immediately available to the individual confronted with the situation" (p. 108). Any novel or unfamiliar situation is likely to be problematic for an individual; however, certain problematic situations are likely to have a greater impact on social competence than others because (a) they are more difficult to solve (i.e., the problem is complex and/or the number of effective solutions is very limited) and (b) the consequences of inaction or ineffective coping are more serious (i.e., prolonged emotional distress, creation of new problems). These critical problematic situations can usually be classified into one of the following four categories:

1. *Aversion.* Aversive problematic situations involve the presence (or threat) of negative or punishing stimulation. For example, a person who has been spending money foolishly is now being threatened frequently with legal action by creditors because of payments that are past due. An example at a more general community level is a university that is confronted with the problem of an increasing number of robberies on campus.

2. *Loss of Reinforcement.* In this type of situation, a change in the environment has resulted in the loss or absence of expected reinforcement. A freshman college student who had always passed his examinations in high school has now failed to pass two exams in a row in college.

3. *Frustration.* These problematic situations involve the presence of some obstacle or obstacles preventing a person (couple, group) from attaining some desired goal. A couple would like to go away by themselves for a "special" weekend but they cannot find anyone who can take in their two young teenage daughters for the weekend.

4. *Conflict.* Two types of conflict problematic situations can be identified: *interpersonal*-conflict situations and *personal*-conflict situations. In an interpersonal-conflict situation, one person (some people) in a relationship (couple, family, community) has behavior expectations that conflict with those of the other person (people) in the relationship. Husband and wife differ regarding their preferred sexual activities. College roommates disagree about the playing of music while studying. In a personal-conflict situation, an individual is faced with conflicting stimulus demands originating from the environment and/ or himself. A father's two young children are both playing in concerts on the same evening and both want very much for him to attend. A student sees a number of other students cheating during an important examination. Knowing that he is in competition with these other stu-

dents for a good grade, the student is strongly tempted to cheat also, but at the same time his conscience is telling him that it would be wrong.[2]

Formulation of the problem leads to the specification of a problem-solving goal (i.e., description of the desired outcome). The major objective in all problematic situations is to alter the situation so that it is no longer problematic. However, there is also an important secondary objective: to maximize other positive consequences (positive reinforcement) and minimize negative consequences (punishment). Without the latter objective, the problem solver may fail to maximize his effectiveness and minimize the likelihood of creating new problems for himself. The problem-solving goal should describe exactly what changes are desired in the problematic situation (i.e., behavior changes, reinforcements, aversive events or obstacles to be removed, etc.) and, if possible, what specific other consequences are desired and which ones are to be avoided.

The problem-solving goal is important because it provides direction for generating alternatives as well as criteria or performance standards to be used in evaluating alternatives in the decision-making and solution-verification stages. The two most important considerations in setting the problem-solving goal are (a) that it be stated in concrete, behavioral terms, and (b) that it be realistic and attainable. Stating the goal or desired outcome in concrete, behavioral terms helps the problem solver to identify relevant, appropriate solutions as well as to evaluate accurately solution effectiveness. An unrealistic or unattainable goal would have a serious negative effect on these operations. The effect would be to change the situation from a soluble problem to an insoluble one, where it would be impossible to find a "satisfactory" solution.

Nezu and D'Zurilla (1981a,b) have recently conducted two experiments designed to assess more specifically the significance of the problem-definition-and-formulation stage in the overall problem-solving process. In the first experiment, the investigators studied the effects of training in problem-definition-and-formulation skills on decision-making effectiveness. Three groups of college student subjects were given different levels of instruction in problem definition and formulation (PDF): (a) specific training in PDF, (b) general guidelines for PDF, and (c) no instruction in PDF. Half of the subjects in each group

---

[2] For a further discussion of conflict situations, social skills, and psychopathology, see Phillips (1978).

were also given special training in D'Zurilla and Goldfried's (1971) utility model of decision making and the other half were given no instruction in this decision-making method. After training, the subjects were presented with eight socially oriented test problems (for example, how to avoid a fight with a friend, how to reduce the number of robberies in the dorms), along with a list of possible solutions for each, varying in degree of effectiveness. The subjects were asked to choose the best solution for each problem. The main hypothesis of the study was confirmed: the subjects who were given the specific training in PDF skills did significantly better on the decision-making task than the subjects who received no training. When only the subjects who did *not* receive training in the decision-making method were considered, it was found that specific training in PDF also resulted in significantly better decision making than simply teaching the general guidelines for PDF, and the latter resulted in significantly better decisions than not providing any guidelines at all for PDF. In addition to these results for PDF, the study also found that subjects who were given training in decision making chose more effective solutions than subjects who received no training in decision making.

In the second experiment, the investigators studied the effects of training in PDF on the generation-of-alternatives process. College student subjects were again divided into three groups representing different levels of instruction in PDF as described above. In this experiment, however, half of the subjects in each group were trained to generate alternatives according to the "quantity" principle (i.e., "quantity-breeds-quality") (see Osborn, 1963) and the other half were given no instruction in the application of this principle. After training, the subjects were asked to generate solutions for one of two socially oriented test problems. Problem-solving goals were set by the experimenters for both problems so as to ensure common objectives for guiding the generation of alternatives for all subjects. The main hypothesis was confirmed: the subjects who were given the specific training in PDF produced solutions that were judged to be significantly more effective than those produced by the subjects who received no training. When only the subjects who did *not* receive instruction in the quantity principle were considered, it was found that specific training in PDF also resulted in significantly better solutions than simply teaching the general guidelines for PDF. However, in this study no significant differences were found between the group that received general guidelines for PDF and the group that received no instruction in PDF. In addition to these results for PDF, the study also found that the subjects who received instruction in the use of the quantity principle produced significantly better solutions than those who did not receive "quantity" instructions.

An inspection of the data for these two studies suggests that a ceiling effect may have been responsible for the failure to obtain a significant difference between the two levels of training in PDF when subjects also received instruction in decision making or the quantity principle. Presented in written form, the experimental problems were only moderately difficult and ambiguous to begin with. In addition, the subjects were all normal college students who would be expected to have relatively good SPS skills. This notion was confirmed by the fact that the subjects who received no training at all performed in the moderately effective range in both studies. The instruction in decision making and the quantity principle added another significant increment to performance, leaving very little room for the further improvement required to demonstrate a significant difference between the two levels of training in PDF. Future studies should focus on more vaguely defined and difficult problems, possibly using a simulated problematic situation rather than the written format, and subject populations with greater deficits in SPS ability.

C. Generation of Alternatives

The function of this stage is to make available as many solution alternatives as possible and to maximize the likelihood that the "best" solution will be among these alternatives. To accomplish this purpose, the method of brainstorming (Osborn, 1963; Parnes, 1967) and the strategy-tactics procedure have been recommended (see D'Zurilla & Goldfried, 1971).

The brainstorming method is based primarily on two general principles: (a) deferment of judgment and (b) quantity-breeds-quality. According to the "deferment" principle, more high-quality solution responses will be generated if the person defers evaluation of his responses until a later time in the problem-solving sequence—i.e., the decision-making stage. In applying this principle, the problem solver is encouraged to "avoid criticism" and "let go of your imagination." The "quantity" principle suggests that the more solution alternatives a person produces, the more good quality ideas he will come up with, thus increasing the likelihood that the "best" solution will be discovered. Two basic rules in the application of this principle are "generate as many responses as possible" and "combine and improve responses to make additional, new solution responses." These brainstorming rules are designed to facilitate the retrieval of a wide range of responses from one's behavioral repertoire while reducing inhibitive factors that may limit one's potential for creative or inventive thinking.

The assumption behind the strategy-tactics procedure is that the probability of finding the "best" solution will be increased when the problem solver considers a variety of different general approaches to the problem, instead of thinking only in terms of specific, concrete actions. In this procedure, the term "strategy" refers to a general course of action or plan that describes *what* a person intends to do in a given problematic situation, whereas the term "tactics" refers to the specific means or steps that describe exactly *how* the strategy can be implemented. There are two variations of the strategy-tactic procedure. In the first variation, the problem solver first generates as many strategies as possible using the four brainstorming rules, then conducts a rough screening of these strategies and eliminates any that are obviously irrelevant, inferior, or impracticable, and finally generates alternative tactics or means for implementing each of the remaining strategies, once again following the brainstorming rules. In the decision-making stage of SPS, all of these specific tactics are evaluated in attempting to decide on the best solution. In the second variation of the strategy-tactic procedure, the problem solver first generates as many strategy-level solutions as possible and then moves to the decision-making stage to evaluate these general approaches and choose the best strategy or strategy combination to serve as the "solution plan." The problem solver then returns to the generation-of-alternatives stage to generate alternative tactics for implementing this solution plan, after which he returns to decision making to select the final, specific solution.

The second variation of the strategy-tactics procedure simplifies the decision-making operation and makes it more efficient since fewer specific tactics or means must be evaluated. Instead of evaluating specific tactics for *all* strategies generated, only the alternative means for the "solution plan" are evaluated. However, this approach is likely to be effective only when the problem solver is familiar enough with the strategy alternatives to permit an accurate evaluation of these solutions at a more general level. When the problem solver is dealing with strategies that are novel or unfamiliar and there is uncertainty regarding effective implementation, then the second procedure would probably be more effective since it requires a detailed evaluation of all solution alternatives at a specific, concrete level.

In a recent study by D'Zurilla and Nezu (1980) the above generation-of-alternatives principles were investigated. One hundred undergraduate students were divided randomly into four experimental groups and one control group. The first experimental group received instruction in the application of "deferment," "quantity," and "strategy-tactics" (first variation). The second group was given instruction in deferment and quantity, but not strategy-tactics. The third group was given instruction in quantity and strategy-tactics, but not deferment. The fourth group received instruction only in the quantity principle. The fifth group, the control group, was not instructed in any of the generation-of-alternative principles. The subjects in this group were simply told to "solve the problem." After the initial instructions, all subjects were asked to solve two socially oriented test problems.

The results showed that the solutions produced by the four experimental groups were judged to be significantly more effective than those produced by the control group which received no instruction in the three generation-of-alternatives procedures. However, there were no significant differences between any of the experimental groups. Since the quantity principle was the only common one across all experimental groups, it was concluded that this principle was primarily responsible for increasing the likelihood of high-quality solution responses, and that neither the deferment principle nor the strategy-tactics procedure added significantly to these effects. The significant difference found in this study between the group that received instruction in the quantity principle and the control group, which received no instruction in "quantity," was later replicated in the study discussed earlier on the effects of problem definition and formulation on the generation-of-alternatives process (Nezu & D'Zurilla, 1981b).

It would be premature to conclude on the basis of the above findings that the deferment principle and the strategy-tactics procedure are of no value for the generation of alternatives. In the design of the above study, only the quantity principle was assessed independently. The deferment principle and the stategy-tactics procedure were evaluated *in combination* with the quantity principle to determine whether they would add significantly to the effects of "quantity." However, since the quantity principle alone increased performance to nearly ceiling level, there was very little room left for significant improvement by adding either "deferment" or "strategy-tactics." If the deferment principle and the strategy-tactics procedure were assessed independently, it is possible that a significant effect might have been found. This possibility is suggested by the results of the Nezu and D'Zurilla (1981b) study described earlier which used the same kinds of test problems and the same type of subject population. The design of this study permitted an assessment of the quantity principle and training in problem definition and formulation independently as well as in combination. The results showed that each procedure was effective when evaluated independently, but that the combination did not add significantly to the effects of either procedure alone.

D. Decision Making

The purpose of this stage is to evaluate the available solution alternatives and select the "best" or most effective one. In the D'Zurilla and Goldfried (1971) model, decision making is based upon the utility model of human choice, where the effectiveness of a given alternative is based upon the *value* and *likelihood* of anticipated consequences. Thus, in SPS, individuals faced with the task of choosing among a list of possible alternatives are expected to select the one that appears to have the best chance of altering the situation so that it is no longer problematic, while at the same time maximizing other positive consequences and minimizing negative ones.

As an aid in identifying important consequences, four categories are considered: short term, long term, personal (i.e., effects on oneself), and social (i.e., effects on others). Regarding the short-term and long-term categories, the decision maker must consider not only the immediate consequences of each solution, but their possible long-range implications as well. Within the personal category, the specific consequences to be considered include time required, amount of effort, personal/emotional costs vs gains, consistency with morals, ethics, and other values, and physical well being. In the social category, specific consequences include effects on family, friends, and the community, reputation and standing in the community, and other socioeconomic costs vs gains. In estimating the likelihood of particular consequences, there are two considerations. One is the likelihood of a particular course of action producing a particular effect on the individual or the social environment in question. The second is the likelihood that the individual confronted with the problem will be capable of implementing the particular solution adequately. This requires an assessment by the problem solver of his own personal assets and liabilities (e.g., skills, inhibitions, skill deficits), and of the possible obstacles and resources in the social environment as well. At this point, the problem solver must be careful to avoid the errors in estimating the probabilities of particular effects or consequences which were discussed earlier.

After considering the above guidelines and anticipating positive and negative consequences for each of the alternatives, the problem solver must then compare the expected overall outcome of each alternative with the desired outcome specified as the problem-solving goal in the problem-definition-and-formulation stage, and choose the alternative for which the expected overall outcome most closely matches the problem-solving goal. As pointed out earlier, if the problem-solving goals are unrealistic, then the decision-making task becomes more difficult, if not impossible. This is because the problem solver would have difficulty finding an alternative that could realistically be expected to produce the desired outcome.

Nezu and D'Zurilla (1979) investigated the effects of training in the above decision-making model on the ability of subjects to make effective decisions when asked to choose the best solution from among a list of alternative solutions to socially oriented test problems. College student subjects were divided into three groups: (a) specific training in decision making (DM), where subjects were given instruction in the details of the model, (b) utility rule only, where subjects were simply taught the general definition of decision making based upon a utility approach, and (c) no instruction in decision making. After training, the subjects were presented with 12 socially oriented test problems and a list of possible solutions for each, varying in degree of effectiveness. The subjects were asked to choose the best solution for each problem. The results showed that the subjects who were given the specific training in DM made choices that were judged to be significantly more effective than those made by the other two groups of subjects. No significant difference was found between the subjects who were simply taught the utility rule and the subjects who received no instruction at all in DM. The results also showed that not only did the subjects who were given specific training in DM *average* more effective solutions than the other subjects, but as a group they selected a greater *number* of superior solutions as well. The significant difference in this study between the group that received the specific training in the decision-making model and the group that received no instruction in decision making was later replicated in the study discussed earlier on the effects of training in problem definition and formulation on decision making (Nezu & D'Zurilla, 1981a).

E. Solution Implementation and Verification

The major function of this stage is to verify the efficacy of the chosen solution in real life. At this point in the SPS process, the problem has been "solved" *symbolically,* which is an important accomplishment, but its effectiveness in dealing with the real-life problematic situation has not yet been established. The only way to verify the solution objectively is to implement the solution and evaluate the outcome. This procedure incorporates methods of *behavioral assessment* (i.e., self-recording, self-rating, and behavioral observation *in vivo*) (see Ciminero, Calhoun, & Adams, 1977) and *self-control* (self-monitoring, self-evaluation, self-reinforcement) (Bandura, 1971; Kanfer, 1970). The process can be described in four steps: (a) performance, (b) observation, (c) evaluation, and (d) reinforcement.

The *performance* step involves the implementation of the solution in the real-life problematic situation. It was emphasized previously that this problem-solving performance is likely to be influenced by factors other than SPS ability, including specific skill deficits, emotional inhibitions, and motivational deficits. The second step, *observation,* implies measurement of the solution outcome at some level and not simply attending to the solution consequences. If the solution involves an attempt to change one's own behavior, then *self-recording* or *self-rating* might be involved. For example, to deal with a financial problem, a person's solution might involve the preparation of a strict budget. To evaluate the outcome, the person might keep a record of the amount of money spent and what it was spent for. On the other hand, if the solution involves an attempt to influence someone else's behavior, then that behavior would be observed and recorded. Parents who are attempting to solve the problem of their young teenage daughter staying out too late every night might keep a record of the time she comes in each night. Ratings would be used when it would be difficult or impossible to record the actual frequency of the behavior in question. For example, when emotional behavior is involved, such as sexual satisfaction, a couple might rate the degree of their sexual pleasure during each sexual experience.

In the *evaluation* step, the problem solver compares the observed outcome with the desired outcome specified during the problem-definition-and-formulation stage (i.e., the problem-solving goal). If the "match" is satisfactory, then the problem solver moves to the final step, namely, *reinforcement,* where he rewards himself for a "job well done." This reward may simply be a positive self-statement (for example, "I'm proud of myself, I handled that very well"), or it might be some more tangible reward, such as purchasing some desired object or engaging in some enjoyable activity. In addition to self-reward, perhaps the most powerful reinforcement of all is likely to come from the positive solution outcome itself, which might involve events such as the reduction of aversive stimulation, the occurrence of positive social reinforcement, the removal of an obstacle to a desired goal, or the resolution of a conflict. This reinforcement step is critical for SPS not only because it reinforces effective problem-solving performance, but also because it strengthens perceived-control or self-efficacy expectations, which are so very important for future problem-solving efforts.

What happens if the "match" between the observed outcome and the problem-solving goal is *not* satisfactory? In this event, the problem solver must attempt to determine whether the source of the difficulty is in (a) the problem-solving process or (b) the performance of the solution response. If it is in (a), he can go back to one or more of the previous stages and attempt to work out an alternative solution that might be more effective. If it is in (b), however, he might try to improve his performance by rehearsing skills, applying anxiety-reduction procedures, or attempting to provide himself with incentives, depending upon what factor or factors might be interfering with his performance. If the individual cannot succeed after attempting these various corrective strategies, then the best "solution" might be to seek help from someone who might either be more familiar with the particular problem confronting him, or more adequately trained to assess the situation and provide appropriate recommendations.

Earlier it was pointed out that the setting of unrealistic goals during the problem-definition-and formulation stage could have negative consequences for the other stages in the SPS process. These negative effects are nowhere more serious than in the solution-implementation-and-verification stage. If an individual's goals or standards are unrealistically high or strict, it may be impossible for him to achieve a satisfactory "match" between the observed outcome of his solution behavior and his performance standards. As a result, instead of terminating the problem-solving process and rewarding himself for a job well done, the problem solver may become lost in obsessive and compulsive problem-solving behavior which goes nowhere. In order to avoid this difficulty, the problem solver must be careful to set realistic goals initially, and then avoid an overly strict adherence to these standards, or an insistence on finding the "perfect match" when evaluating the solution outcome. In direct support of this position, behavior therapists have warned about the negative consequences of unrealistic and overly strict performance standards in the application of self-control procedures (Rimm & Masters, 1979), and cognitive therapists have long argued that perfectionistic goals and expectations can have serious negative emotional consequences (Ellis, 1962; Ellis & Grieger, 1977).

There are no empirical studies at present on the importance of this solution-implementation-and-verification stage in the SPS process. However, studies are not needed to show that SPS would merely be an interesting symbolic exercise if the solution was not implemented and evaluated in the real-life setting. Nor are studies required to demonstrate the fact that solution implementation alone cannot establish or reinforce SPS effectiveness without the assessment and self-control procedures involved in the verification process. Thus, the evidence supporting the role of behavioral assessment and self-control procedures in behavioral intervention can also be used as support for the role of solution verification in SPS (see O'Leary & Wilson, 1980; Rimm & Masters, 1979).

III. SOCIAL PROBLEM SOLVING AND PSYCHOPATHOLOGY

Over the past 15 years we have seen a growing recognition of the need to broaden our conceptualization of psychopathology to include the view that emotional problems and maladaptive behavior may often result from deficiencies in the skills and abilities that define general social competence (Bandura, 1969; D'Zurilla & Goldfried, 1971; Phillips, 1978). Following from this viewpoint has been a broadening of the objectives of clinical-intervention approaches in recent years. Programs have been moving from the narrow base of attempting to reduce or eliminate specific emotional problems and maladaptive behaviors to enhancing an individual's overall effectiveness in dealing with his total social environment. Thus far, the results of this competence or "coping-skills" approach to clinical intervention have been very promising (see Goldfried, 1980). If we view SPS as an important component of social competence, we can hypothesize that (a) some forms of psychopathology and maladjustment might be casually related to deficiencies in SPS skills, and (b) training in SPS skills might be an effective clinical-intervention approach.

The relationship between cognitive problem-solving skills and psychopathology has been investigated in a series of studies conducted by Spivack, Platt, Shure, and their associates at the Hahnemann Community Mental Health/Mental Retardation Center in Philadelphia (see Spivack et al., 1976). These studies have produced some very interesting results and have served as an important impetus for research on the effects of training in SPS skills on social competence and psychopathology. On the other hand, due to various methodological problems which we will discuss below, the results are often ambiguous and difficult to interpret and the validity of many of the conclusions is questionable.

Most of the Hahnemann group's studies have focused on the "means–ends ability" in SPS—i.e., "the ability to orient oneself to and conceptualize the step-by-step means of moving toward a goal" (Spivack *et al.*, 1976, p. 83). This ability is described by Spivack *et al.* as incorporating the recognition of obstacles that must be overcome, the provision of alternative strategies to prevent or overcome these obstacles, and a sensitivity to the idea that a solution may take time to carry out and may at times be a complicated process.

In the SPS model of D'Zurilla and Goldfried (1971), the basic elements of the means–ends ability extend across three stages of the model: problem definition and formulation, generation of alternatives, and decision making. In the problem-definition-and-formulation stage, the problem solver chooses his own problem-solving goal and identifies the various obstacles that may be present to make the situation problematic. In the generation-of-alternatives stage, the problem solver generates various possible *strategies* for achieving the goal, as well as *specific means* of implementing the different strategies. Depending on the particular requirements of the problem, this stage may involve the generation of relatively complex solutions, including various combinations of strategies and specific means put together in step-by-step fashion to form a coherent plan of action. Then, in the decision-making stage, the problem solver considers the most relevant solutions and decides on the best course of action for solving the problem or achieving the problem-solving goal. This decision is based upon a careful evaluation of the likely consequences of the different courses of action, including obstacles and other cost factors such as time and effort.

To assess the means–ends ability, the Hahnemann group developed a method that they have called *Means–Ends Problem Solving* (MEPS) (Platt & Spivack, 1975). The MEPS involves the written or verbal presentation of a series of story stems which depicit situations in which a need is aroused in a protagonist at the onset of the story, and is satisfied by him at the conclusion. The means by which the protagonist achieves the goal is left out. The subject is required to complete the story by filling in those events that might have enabled the protagonist to achieve his goal of satisfying the need. The dependent measures include *relevant means, enumerations, obstacles, time,* and *relevancy scores.* "Relevant means" are the discrete, effective steps that allow the hero of the story to achieve his goal. "Enumerations" are elaborations or specific examples of a more basic means. "Obstacles" measure the recognition of possible obstacles blocking the attainment of the goal. The "relevancy score" is obtained by calculating the ratio of total relevant means to total irrelevant means plus no means. "Irrelevant means" are those that are judged to be ineffective for the particular situation in question. "No means" are responses that are merely repetitions of the story, value judgments, or "accidental" solutions.

Using the MEPS as their main dependent measure, the Hahnemann investigators have compared the performance of various disturbed and maladjusted groups of subjects to that of "normal" matched controls. They found deficits in MEPS performance in groups such as impulsive adolescents in a residential treatment facility (Spivack & Levine, 1963), adolescent psychiatric patients (Platt, Spivack, Altman, Altman, & Peizer, 1974), heroin addicts (Platt, Scura, & Hannon, 1973), and adult psychiatric patients (Platt & Spivack, 1972a, 1973). In addition to these studies, the Hahnemann group also conducted two studies relating MEPS performance to adjustment level *within* patient groups. In one study with psychiatric patients, a higher level of premorbid social competence was found to be associated with a greater number of means and higher relevancy scores (Platt & Spivack, 1972b). In the second study, it was found that male psychiatric patients who obtained low scores on the MEPS also had MMPI profiles that were more clearly psychotic than those of patients who obtained high MEPS scores (Platt & Siegel, 1976). In all of the above studies, the significant results were based primarily on the relevant-means and relevancy scores.

Several investigators outside the Hahnemann group have done similar studies using the MEPS with noninstitutionalized subjects which generally support the findings reported above. Appel and Kaestner (1979) found significant differences in MEPS performance between a group of narcotic drug abusers judged to be in "poor" standing in an outpatient rehabilitation program and a group judged to be in "good" standing. Gotlib and Asarnow (1979) found highly significant differences on several MEPS measures between depressed and nondepressed college students and between depressed and nondepressed clients at a counseling center. In the same study, these investigators also found significant correlations between MEPS measures and scores on the Beck Depression Inventory (Beck, 1967), which provides another test of the relationship between MEPS performance and degree of psychopathology.

In all of the above studies conducted by the Hahnemann group, performance on the MEPS was described as *interpersonal* problem solving, since all of the MEPS stories focused on interpersonal goals (for example, dating and making friends). None of the stories involved negative emotional states, such as anxiety or depression. Siegel and Platt (1976) hypothesized that maladjustment should be related not only to interpersonal problem solving but also to *emotional* problem solving, or the ability to cope effectively with one's own negative affect. In order to investigate this hypothesis, they prepared several MEPS stories in which the protagonist experienced and was required to deal with feelings of anxiety, depression, or threat to self-esteem. Two of these emotionally oriented MEPS stories were then administered along with two interpersonal stories to a group of adolescent psychiatric patients, a group of adult psychiatric patients, and two appropriate control groups matched on age and education. These control groups consisted of adult hospital employees and high school sophomores.

The results showed initial significant differences on both types of problem-solving measures between the patient and control groups in both the adolescent and adult samples. However, after differences in IQ between patient and control groups were controlled for, only the differences on the interpersonal measure held up. On the basis of these results, the investigators concluded that (a) the relationship between IQ and emotional problem solving is stronger than the relationship between IQ and interpersonal problem solving, and (b) interpersonal problem solving is an important factor in behavioral adjustment, whereas emotional problem solving is not. In the study by Appel and Kaestner (1979), which compared the MEPS performance of narcotic drug abusers in "good" and "poor" standing in a drug rehabilitation program, similar emotional and interpersonal MEPS stories were administered to the subjects. The results were consistent with Siegel and Platt's findings: significant differences in MEPS performance were found only on the interpersonal measure.

The validity of the above results and conclusions concerning emotional problem solving can be seriously questioned for reasons based on what appears to be an inadequate operational definition of emotional problem solving—i.e., the MEPS story. First of all, if the MEPS measure of emotional problem solving were valid, and if the ability to cope effectively with one's negative emotions were, in fact, related significantly to IQ, then we would expect to find an inverse correlation between IQ and such emotional disorders as anxiety disorders, phobias, and depression. However, research in the field of psychopathology offers no evidence that such a correlation exists. Second, the MEPS definition seems to be based upon a questionable model of emotional problem solving which assumes that the major determinants of negative emotional states are mostly internal and inaccessible. The information provided in the stories is limited primarily to a description of a negative emotional state in the protagonist and the goal of reducing or getting rid of the unpleasant feelings. Minimal information is provided about possible situational or internal determinants of the emotional state, thus requiring the subject to focus directly on the emotional response itself. However, without any concrete problematic situation to deal with, the only "relevant" solutions available to a subject are likely to be abstract, subjective, or psychodynamically oriented solutions (for example, seeking insight through introspection, catharsis, accepting one's feelings, etc.). Such solutions would probably depend on a certain level of intellectual or educational sophistication, which might explain the correlation between IQ and the MEPS measure of emotional problem solving.

In contrast to the above model of emotional problem solving, D'Zurilla and Goldfried's (1971) approach is based more on a cognitive–behavioral model. According to this model, emotional responses are controlled and maintained by stimulus events in the person's environment and by certain types of accessible cognitive events (i.e., specific beliefs, expectations, and self-statements). D'Zurilla and Goldfried have pointed out that the same kinds of stimulus conditions that often make a situation "problematic" also tend to elicit negative emotional reactions (for example, threat, uncertainty, frustration, absence of reinforcement, conflicting stimulus demands). They have recommended that the problem solver focus his efforts not on the emotional response itself, but on the stimulus events producing it. The set is to use one's emotional response as a cue for seeking out and identifying the relevant stimulus determinants. When these determinants are found to include interpersonal factors, as they often do in real life, it becomes rather meaningless to distinguish between interpersonal and emotional problem solving. By solving the interpersonal problem, the emotional problem gets solved in the same process. Whether this process is referred to as interpersonal or emotional problem solving will depend simply on what outcome the problem solver chooses to emphasize. Therefore, when the studies on emotional vs interpersonal problem solving are considered from a behavioral viewpoint, it must be concluded that the emotionally oriented MEPS stories represent inadequately defined problems and misdirected problem solving, and that the distinction between interpersonal and emotional problem solving is mainly an artificial one.

There are some additional problems with the MEPS that raise further questions about its validity as a measure of SPS in the above studies.

One must use caution in interpreting MEPS performance as a measure of *general* SPS ability since it focuses on only one component of the SPS process—i.e., means–ends thinking. An adequate measure of SPS ability must assess the other important components as well, including the ability to adopt an appropriate problem-solving set, the ability to define and formulate problems adequately, decision-making ability, and the ability to monitor one's own behavior and evaluate the solution outcome.

Although MEPS stories are usually analyzed for several different elements (i.e., relevant means, enumerations, obstacles, time), most of the studies have focused on the number of relevant means and the relevancy ratio. The Hahnemann group has interpreted these scores as measures of the *spontaneous* capacity to generate a number of relevant means in a problem-solving situation, presumably because no prompting or probing is permitted during the administration of the MEPS, and concluded that this ability is an important factor in behavioral adjustment. While we do not question the assumption that the spontaneous tendency to generate means–ends thinking is an important element in SPS, there is some reason to question whether the above MEPS scores are valid measures of this ability. The instructions for the MEPS present the procedure as a test of imagination; there is no attempt to induce a problem-solving set. Generalization between a "test of imagination" and a real-life problem-solving situation cannot be assumed. Training programs in problem solving (especially *creative* problem solving) instruct individuals to use their imaginations in order to generate an abundance of new and original ideas (Osborn, 1963; Parnes, 1967). The set to use one's imagination on the MEPS might, similarly, *prompt* subjects to produce an abundance of means, which might not be their typical response when confronted with a situation which they define as a "problem-to-be-solved."

Although we may question whether MEPS scores such as the number of relevant means and the relevancy ratio are valid measures of the spontaneous generation of means in a problem-solving situation, these scores are more clearly an indication of the quantity and quality of a subject's social response repertoire for certain social situations. Interpreted only in this manner, the MEPS can be viewed as a behaviorally oriented test of *social competence* (i.e., effective social behavior), similar to the method proposed by Goldfried and D'Zurilla (1969). From this point of view, the results of the above studies would be interpreted as demonstrating a relationship between psychopathology and a general social-competence deficit, rather than a specific deficit in SPS.

In addition to the studies that focused on the MEPS, the Hahnemann group conducted two other studies related to the generation-of-alternatives process which focused on a measure of *alternative thinking*, or the ability to generate alternative solution possibilities in an interpersonal problem-solving situation. In this procedure, hypothetical interpersonal problems are presented to the subject along with instructions to provide possible solutions. For example: "Victor wants people to listen to him, but no one ever does. What can Victor do to get listened to?" Although the interpersonal problems are similar, the instructions for this measure differ from those used with the MEPS in two important ways. First, the task is presented to the subject as a problem-solving test, rather than as a test of imagination. Second, unlike the administration of the MEPS, "quantity instructions" and probing questions are used to encourage subjects to produce the maximum number of alternative solutions (for example, "Think of all the things he could do," "What else do you think he might do?" "Can you think of anything else?").

Using this alternative-thinking test, Platt et al. (1974) found that adolescent psychiatric patients generated significantly fewer alternative solutions and significantly more irrelevant solutions than did a normal control group. In addition, the alternative-thinking scores were found to be unrelated to IQ. In another study, Platt and Spivack (1973) found that adult psychiatric patients generated significantly fewer solution alternatives than did normal controls, but this difference disappeared when the influence of IQ was taken into account statistically. In this study, the alternative-thinking measure was found to be highly correlated with IQ.

At first glance, it would appear that the high correlation in the adult sample between IQ and the alternative-thinking measure is quite damaging to the Hahnemann group's interpersonal problem-solving model. If they concluded on the basis of a correlation between their measure of emotional problem solving and IQ that emotional problem solving is not an important factor in behavioral adjustment, then to be consistent they would now be forced to conclude that the generation-of-alternatives is not an important factor either. Before concluding this, however, we might consider the possibility that the problem is more methodological than conceptual. The critical element in the generation-of-alternatives ability is the *spontaneous tendency to think of alternative solution possibilities* when confronted with a problem, and not the absolute number of solution responses that a person is capable of producing (see D'Zurilla & Goldfried, 1971). By using prompting and probing procedures to elicit the maximum number of solution responses from a subject, the alternative-thinking test may be tapping verbal intelligence and/or the intellectual capacity for inventing a variety of novel and original solution ideas.

A more appropriate method for testing the generation-of-alternatives ability might be one which involves the presentation of problematic situations to subjects along with instructions requiring them to "solve the problem" and to "think aloud" while solving it (see Meichenbaum et al., 1979). The subjects' verbalizations could then be analyzed for alternative thinking as well as other cognitive problem-solving variables. While the use of quantity instructions and probing questions might not be an appropriate method for testing the generation-of-alternatives ability, it is likely to be quite useful for training in this ability, especially in the case of creative problem-solving training where novelty and originality are emphasized (see Osborn, 1963; Parnes, 1967).

Several studies have been done which are related to the decision-making component of SPS. In one study dealing with the evaluation of solution possibilities, Platt, Siegel, and Spivack (1975) presented adult psychiatric patients and normal controls with a list of the most commonly supplied relevant means for solving interpersonal problems from the MEPS and asked them to rank order the means in terms of effectiveness and social appropriateness. They found no significant differences between the two groups in their ability to recognize the relative effectiveness of the different solutions and concluded that this decision-making ability is not an important factor in adjustment. This conclusion may be premature. In the recent study by Appel and Kaestner (1979) comparing the MEPS performance of narcotic drug abusers in "good" and "poor" standing in a drug rehabilitation program, subjects were presented with a problematic situation from the MEPS along with a list of five relevant and five irrelevant means. Their task was to try to select the five relevant means. The results showed that the drug abusers in "good" standing recognized significantly more relevant means than did the drug abusers in "poor" standing.

The conflicting results in the above two studies might be due to the different testing methods used. Appel and Kaestner (1979) presented both relevant and irrelevant means to the subjects and had them choose the relevant ones. Platt et al. (1975), on the other hand, presented only relevant means, which the subjects were required to rank order according to degree of effectiveness and social appropriateness. The appel and Kaestner method seems to be more analogous to a real-life decision-making task, where an individual usually must choose from a variety of response alternatives varying in degree of relevancy and effectiveness. Perhaps an important decision-making factor in adjustment is the ability to discriminate between relevant and irrelevant responses in a problem-solving situation.

Although Platt *et al.* (1975) failed to find a difference between psychiatric patients and normals in their rank-ordering of problem solutions, they did find that the patients were significantly less able to provide a valid reason for choosing one alternative over another. This finding suggests that there may be a deficiency in the decision-making process among the patients which did not show up on the particular experimental task used in the study. The solutions presented to the subjects in this study are best described as *strategies* rather than specific means or tactics. As defined earlier, a strategy-level solution is a general course of action which describes *what* will be done without specifying exactly *how* it will be done. (For example, for a problem which involved the question of how to become a community leader, one of the solutions presented to the subjects in the study was "Offer plans on how to improve the community.") In D'Zurilla and Goldfried's (1971) SPS approach, the problem solver first considers different *strategies* for dealing with the problem, and then generates *specific tactics* or means for implementing the most relevant strategies (for example, "Write letters to the local newspapers asking for more recreational facilities for senior citizens," "Attend PTA meetings and argue for better personal counseling services in the schools"). The final decision as to the "best" solution is made at the specific level. While a knowledge of general social norms and standards may be adequate in many problem-solving situations for evaluating the relative effectiveness of different general strategies, effective decision making at the *specific* level may often require more complex decision-making abilities. In the D'Zurilla and Goldfried SPS model, for example, a utility-oriented decision-making method is recommended which is based upon the ability to predict and evaluate the likely consequences (personal, social, short-term, and long-term) of specific solution alternatives.

Two studies by the Hahnemann group are related to the D'Zurilla and Goldfried (1971) decision-making model. These studies have focused on a measure of *consequential thinking,* or the tendency to conceptualize consequences before taking action spontaneously. In one study, Platt and Spivack (1973) found that adult psychiatric patients were less likely to anticipate and evaluate consequences than were normal controls. Similar results were obtained by Spivack and Levine (1963) with impulsive adolescents. These findings strongly suggest that there is, indeed, a deficiency in the decison-making process, as it is defined by D'Zurilla and Goldfried (1971), in the maladjusted groups tested in these studies.

The Hahnemann group has also studied *causal thinking* (i.e., the tendency to think in terms of cause–effect relationships) and *perspective taking* (i.e., the ability to appreciate the point of view of others in a particular situation). These cognitive abilities are likely to be involved in all stages of the D'Zurilla and Goldfried (1971) model, but they are particularly important for the recognition and definition of problems. Platt and Spivack (1973) found that adult psychiatric patients were less likely than normal controls to think in terms of prior causes of events in a problem-solving situation. Deficits in the ability to see problematic situations from the perspectives of other involved persons have been found in both adolescent psychiatric patients (Platt et al., 1974) and adult psychiatric patients (Platt & Spivack, 1973).

Several of the studies referred to in the previous section support the hypothesis that deficits in the problem-orientation operation are associated with maladjustment. Results reported by Platt and Spivack (1974) showed that psychiatric patients are less likely than normals to include a "stop and think" element in their MEPS stories. Instead, they seemed to be more concerned with the taking of immediate action in a problem-solving situation. According to Meichenbaum et al. (1979), studies of the thought processes of individuals who tend to cope poorly with stress situations indicate that these individuals fail to adopt an appropriate problem-solving set. Instead of engaging in problem-solving-oriented thinking when confronted with stress situations, they tend to be preoccupied with "self-referent ideation" (i.e., thoughts focusing on one's personal deficiencies) that inhibits performance.

Two additional studies concerning the relationship between SPS skills and maladaptive behavior are worth noting. Perri, Richards, and Schulthesis (1977) conducted structured interviews with individuals who had a serious cigarette smoking problem and made a concerted effort to reduce or quit smoking on their own. Their objective was to determine which factors and methods, especially behaviorally self-control methods, are critical to successfully self-reduced smoking. They found that significantly more successful than unsuccessful individuals used problem-solving and self-reinforcement techniques. The operational definition of problem solving used in this study paralleled the five stages of D'Zurilla and Goldfried's (1971) SPS model.

In a similar study, Doerfler and Richards (1981) attempted to identify the factors and methods that are related to successful self-initiated attempts to cope with depression. They found that although both successful and unsuccessful individuals attempted to use problem-solving techniques, the successful individuals were more likely to define their life problems in effective, concrete terms while the unsuccessful individuals defined their problems in more vague and global terms.

A major problem in interpreting the results of all of these studies stems from the fact that they are correlational findings. As a result, no cause–effect relationship between any problem-solving variable and psychopathology or adjustment can be concluded from any of these studies. It is still possible that instead of the hypothesized cause–effect relationship between SPS and psychopathology, some factor associated with psychopathology might have produced the deficits in performance on the problem-solving measures (for example, distractibility, inability to concentrate, anxiety, psychiatric drugs, etc.).

For obvious reasons there are no experimental studies on the effects of problem-solving abilities on psychopathology. However, there are a number of laboratory analog studies which have provided some suggestive experimental evidence regarding the effects of one problem-orientation variable, namely, "perceived control." In these studies, the ability to solve an experimental problem or cope with an aversive situation is manipulated and the effects on responses analogous to abnormal behavior are observed. Basically, the experimental subjects are placed in an insoluable problematic situation where they lack control over aversive stimulation or some rewarding outcome. Using a variety of different behavioral measures, investigators have found that this type of experimental situation produces potentially maladaptive responses such as "learned helplessness" or depression (Hiroto & Seligman, 1975; see also Abramson, Seligman, & Teasdale, 1978), anxiety and stress (Geer, Davison, & Gatchel, 1970; Staub, Tursky, & Schwartz, 1971), obsessive–compulsive behavior (Marquart & Arnold, 1952; Jones, 1954; see also Mather, 1970), and even high blood pressure (Hokanson, DeGood, Forrest, & Brittain, 1971). Most importantly for this discussion, Geer et al. (1970) showed that it is not the actual uncontrollability that is critical in producing the effect, but instead the subject's *perception* of uncontrollability, even though it might not be accurate. Moreover, there is evidence which indicates that the resulting maladaptive responses tend to be most intense and debilitating when the individual attributes uncontrollability to some personal deficit or inadequacy (see Abramson et al., 1978; Bandura, 1977b). In terms of Bandura's self-efficacy theory, such an attribution would be expected to lower the individual's expectations of personal efficacy, resulting in negative emotional consequences and maladaptive behavior. These are the conditions that would tend to exist when an individual's SPS skills are poor and he or she recognizes the relationship between this skill deficit and his or her ineffective coping performance.

One must be very cautious in generalizing the above results to real-life problem-solving situations and the maladaptive behaviors involved in clinical disorders. It is possible that the differences may be too great to permit any meaningful conclusions. Another limitation of these studies as far as SPS research is concerned is that they focus on only one component of the problem-solving process—i.e., problem orientation or set. No information is provided on the effects of other SPS abilities. Studies that have provided more convincing experimental evidence on the effects of SPS on psychopathology and adjustment are those in which disturbed, maladjusted, or ineffective individuals are trained in SPS skills and the effects on behavioral competence and psychopathology are observed. We will review these outcome studies later in this article.

IV. ASSESSMENT OF SOCIAL PROBLEM SOLVING

In previous sections we have alluded to some of the problems involved in attempting to assess SPS. It has been suggested that some assessment problems can be avoided by distinguishing clearly between the concepts of problem solving (i.e., the process of discovery), solution implementation (i.e., the performance of the solution response), and behavioral competence (i.e., effective coping behavior and social skills). To clarify the concept of SPS even further, a distinction should also be made between SPS ability and SPS performance which parallels the distinction often made between academic ability and academic performance or achievement. SPS ability is assessed by focusing on the problem-solving process (i.e., the discovery process) and measuring the extent of an individual's knowledge or possession of the important component skills or specific abilities which are involved in this process. This can be done directly through the use of self-report questionnaires and inventories, or by analyzing an individual's verbal or written responses to specific test problems and identifying relevant problem-solving variables. Scores can then be assigned for specific component abilities (for example, problem-definition ability, decision-making ability, etc.) and/or a total score can be calculated for overall problem-solving ability.

While SPS ability refers to the possession of component SPS skills, SPS performance refers to the *implementation* of these skills and is assessed by evaluating the problem-solving *product* (i.e., the reported solution). This can be done by judging an individual's verbally reported solution to test problems or by observing and judging actual solution-implementation behavior in simulated or real-life problematic situations. In addition to assessing overall problem-solving performance by evaluating the chosen solution, it is possible for an investigator to assess performance with respect to more specific problem-solving skills by using measures designed to evaluate the effectiveness of these skills (for example, skill in defining problems, generation-of-alternatives performance, decision-making effectiveness). A measure of problem-solving performance can also be viewed as an *indirect* measure or sign of problem-solving ability, however, it must be recognized that factors other than problem-solving ability are likely to influence problem-solving performance, especially behavioral performance in the real-life setting (for example, specific skill deficits, emotional inhibitions, etc.).

According to the above distinction, a measure of SPS ability would tell us whether or not an individual has the necessary skills or potential to be a good problem solver, while a measure of SPS performance would tell us whether or not he is capable of applying these skills adequately so as to solve problems effectively. Which measure to use in a particular study would depend on the specific research question being asked. Whenever possible, however, it would seem desirable to include both measures in a study so that the relationships among SPS ability, SPS performance, behavioral competence, and psychopathology could be evaluated.

Two general approaches to the assessment of SPS can be identified: self-report or verbal assessment and observational assessment of overt behavior *in vivo* or in simulated problem-solving situations. Since SPS is primarily a *cognitive* process, the most direct approach is verbal assessment. The verbal assessment of SPS employs methods such as questionnaires, pencil-and-paper scales and inventories, interviews, and verbal problem-solving tests. A particularly useful method for studying problem-solving cognition is the "think aloud" or "think-and-write" procedure (see Henshaw, 1979). In this procedure, the subject is presented with a test problem which he is asked to solve. While solving the problem, the subject is instructed to verbalize or write down all the thoughts that come to mind. These verbal or written problem-solving responses are then coded and analyzed for various problem-solving skills and outcomes. This method can be used in the experimental setting with either hypothetical problems or the subjects' real problems. It can also be given as a "homework" assignment connected with the solving of real problems in the subjects' lives.

The verbal assessment of SPS ability and performance is subject to the same reliability and validity problems which are found when this method is used to assess any other behavior. The most serious problem is that the individual's verbal responses in the testing situation may not always be a valid report of real-life problem-solving behavior. Verbal reports may be influenced more by the individual's perception of the assessment situation and by anticipated consequences in that situation. This tendency would result not only in problems with validity but in unreliability as well, with responses varying from one testing situation to another depending on the particular demand characteristics of the situation. For example, an individual may report "rational" problem-solving thoughts and "good" solutions mainly because approval for these responses is anticipated from the investigator or therapist, and not because these are typical problem-solving behaviors in the real-life setting. On the other hand, an individual may report less effective problem-solving behavior than is likely to be performed in vivo if certain desired consequences are anticipated, such as sympathy and support from others, or the continuation of government disability payments.

Certain habitual response styles or "sets" can also influence the validity of verbal assessment. For example, an individual may tend to agree or disagree on questionnaire items, use the extremes on pencil-and-paper scales, exaggerate or minimize certain cognitive experiences, or report only socially desirable responses. If the individual tends to perceive a testing situation as a threat, anxiety and avoidance responses may disrupt or change performance. In interviews and during individual test administration, the expectations and bias of the interviewer or test administrator may also influence the subject's verbal responses in a subtle way. For example, if the test administrator expects improved problem-solving behavior after training, he may reinforce the more relevant and better quality responses by giving them more attention. In addition, if test instructions and questions do not introduce the appropriate "set" or clearly specify what kind of information is wanted, then the verbal responses obtained may be based on incorrect perceptions and idiosyncratic interpretations of the test stimuli and, as a result, reflect the wrong experiences. For example, because the instructions for the MEPS present the procedure as a "test of imagination" instead of introducing a problem-solving set, subjects may respond by trying to be as creative and imaginative as possible,

which might not be their characteristic way of responding in a problem-solving situation.

Despite the problems with self-report or verbal assessment, it is an
efficient assessment approach and the only means of obtaining direct
information about the cognitive skills involved in SPS. Procedures
designed to avoid these problems and maximize the reliability and
validity of verbal-assessment methods in general have been discussed
by Bellack and Hersen (1977). With specific reference to the assessment
of SPS, we offer the following recommendations:

1. Problem-solving tests which require the individual to perform on
a problem-solving task are probably less likely to be influenced by
extraneous factors in the assessment situation and by habitual response
styles than are questionnaires and inventories which merely require
the recognition of "correct" responses. This method, used with the
"think aloud" or "think-and-write" procedure, might be the most useful and valid self-report method for assessing SPS.

2. Instructions for problem-solving tests should clearly introduce a
problem-solving set, specify the kind of information that is sought
(i.e., the exact step-by-step thoughts or self-statements used to solve
the problem and the subject's final, "best" solution response), and
request that the subjects view the situation from their own personal
perspectives. The latter is designed to focus the subject's attention on
his own internal problem-solving tendencies instead of on external
influences.

3. Test problems should be used which approximate the subject's
real-life problems as closely as possible. If hypothetical problems are
used, they should be based on as much information as possible about
the current living environment of the subjects (for example, common
problems arising during the course of college life and work for college-
student subjects) (see Goldfried & D'Zurilla, 1969). When possible, the
subjects' *real* problems should be used. However, the use of different
problems for different subjects could result in methodological problems if the subjects are not adequately matched on the difficulty level
of their problems.

4. Procedures should be used to ensure that the test problems are,
in fact, "problematic." If the subject is already familiar with the situation from past experience, then his response may be based more on
prior learning, which may not have involved problem solving, than
on current problem-solving ability. Even if the subject is unfamiliar
with a particular "problem," it still may not be problematic enough
to discriminate between "good" and "poor" problem solvers if the

difficulty level is so low that an effective solution is obvious after a brief look. To avoid these difficulties, subjects can be asked to rate possible test problems for degree of familiarity and difficulty. For a particular subject, only the less familiar and more difficult problems would be used. Another possibility is to ask subjects to look at a problem briefly and then report the first solution that comes to mind. Only those problems for which no immediate effective solution is given would then be used with a particular subject. Once again, however, if different problems are used with different subjects, the possibility of confounding test variables with treatment conditions will have to be dealt with.

The second general approach to the assessment of SPS is the observational assessment of overt behavior either *in vivo* or in simulated problematic situations under experimental conditions. A major problem with this general approach for assessing SPS *ability*, or the process of problem solving, is that overt activities play a relatively minor role in the process as compared to cognitive activities. Overt problem-solving behavior is limited to activities such as information and advice seeking, "testing" or rehearsing different solution alternatives (when this is possible—i.e., when the consequences of testing an ineffective alternative are not likely to be serious), and monitoring or recording solution behavior and its effects.

The observational approach is likely to be more useful for assessing overt SPS *performance*. Because of the problems involved in the verbal assessment of SPS, investigators such as Krasnor and Rubin (1981) and Butler and Meichenbaum (1981) have argued that SPS assessment should focus on overt SPS performance in the natural environment (see also Kendall *et al.*, 1981). The major problem with this method is that it focuses on the assessment of coping behaviors and other goal-directed actions which are not always the product of problem solving. In some cases the situations focused on may not be problematic at all for the subject, who may simply be displaying previously learned habits. When the relevant situations are, in fact, problematic, the observed behavior may still represent the effects of other social-learning processes, such as modeling, direct verbal instruction, and instrumental learning. Even if it were possible to establish that the behavior being assessed is solution-implementation behavior, there are likely to be other non-problem-solving factors influencing the effectiveness of performance, such as specific skill deficits, emotional inhibitions, and motivational deficits. While the observational approach *in vivo* has serious problems as a method for assessing SPS, it is likely to be more useful for the behavioral assessment of *social competence*—a concept which takes in all forms of coping and goal-directed social behavior (see Goldfried & D'Zurilla, 1969). A behavioral measure of social competence in the real-life setting would be very useful in SPS research as an important criterion for determining the predictive validity of SPS measures as well as evaluating the effectiveness of SPS training programs.

Some of the above problems with the observational assessment of SPS can be avoided by using simulated problem-solving situations (i.e., "role-playing") and/or a combination of verbal and observational assessment. These procedures would permit more control over testing conditions to ensure that the behavior being observed is, in fact, problem-solving behavior, and minimize the effects of non-problem-solving factors on performance. For example, when using the simulated problem-solving method, procedures such as those recommended earlier can be used to identify test situations that are, indeed, "problematic" for the subject. Experimental instructions can also be used that specifically request subjects to apply their problem-solving skills in the test situation in order to ensure further that the observed performance will be mediated by problem-solving cognition. Verbal methods such as the "think aloud" or "think-and-write" procedures can then be used to obtain specific information about these mediating cognitions. Experimental conditions also permit the use of controls to minimize the possible effects of extraneous social influences on problem-solving performance. In addition, verbal reports can be used to identify the subject's *verbal* solutions, so that they can be compared with their *overt* solutions in an attempt to identify possible discrepancies that might be due to extraneous factors. Such procedures might help to shed more light on the problems involved in the transfer of problem-solving performance from verbal solutions to overt solution implementation (see Butler & Meichenbaum, 1981).

A very useful combination of observational and verbal methods for the study of couples' or group problem solving is the problem-solving discussion method. In this method, two or more individuals are asked to solve either hypothetical or real problems through group discussion. These verbal discussions are directly observed or tape-recorded and then later coded and analyzed for specific problem-solving skills and solutions. With this method, the problem-solving *process* can be directly observed in a controlled test situation which closely approximates the subjects' real-life problem solving.

A potentially useful method for individual problem solving is one that combines the verbal-assessment method with self-observation *in* vivo. In this method, subjects are asked to keep careful records of real-life problem-solving attempts as a "homework" assignment after being trained in the use of appropriate self-monitoring and self-report procedures. One possible format for this self-assessment method might be described as the A–B–C–D–E format. Under "A," the subject describes the problematic situation as it presents itself. The "B" is a "think-and-write" component. Here the subject describes in concrete terms all of his thoughts and self-statements which occur in response to the problematic situation. During or following SPS training, the subject would describe the step-by-step cognitive operations that he has learned to use in order to solve problems more effectively. Under "C," the subject describes and rates the intensity of his emotional responses to the problematic situation as well as those that are associated with his cognitive responses. "D" refers to the subject's overt behavior in response to A, B, and C. The subject would describe here his solution-implementation behavior. Finally, the "E" refers to the outcome of his coping behavior (achievements, personal consequences, social consequences, etc.). These self-assessment "homework" assignments could provide data on the subjects' problem-solving behavior before, during, and after training, including a follow-up evaluation.

In summary, two general approaches to the assessment of SPS are self-report or verbal assessment and observational assessment, each of which has its own problems which tend to reduce reliability and validity. Verbal assessment is preferred since it is the only means of obtaining direct information about the cognitive operations in SPS. Several recommendations are offered which may help to maximize the reliability and validity of these methods. The observational approach is more useful for assessing SPS *performance* than it is for assessing the SPS *process*. Observational assessment *in vivo* appears to be a more promising approach for the behavioral assessment of *social competence* than for the assessment of SPS. Observational assessment of SPS using simulated problem-solving situations under controlled experimental conditions has promise, especially when combined with self-report methods. A very promising method for assessing couples' or group problem solving is the problem-solving discussion method, which combines verbal and observational procedures. Similarly, the combination of self-report methods and self-observation *in vivo* also seems to be a promising approach.[3]

---

[3] For a description and critique of specific tests which have been developed to assess SPS, see Butler and Meichenbaum (1981), Kendall *et al.* (1981), and Krasnor and Rubin (1981).

V. OUTCOME OF SOCIAL PROBLEM-SOLVING TRAINING

SPS training may be used in several different ways. It may be used as a sole therapy approach, a treatment maintenance strategy, or a competence-enhancement program for individuals and groups which has implications for prevention and community psychology. A major criterion in the evaluation of studies on SPS training is the adequacy and appropriateness of the outcome measures used. Three measures are important for the assessment of SPS training effects: problem solving, behavioral competence, and psychopathology.

Measures of problem-solving ability and performance are necessary to evaluate whether training achieved its major objective of improving SPS skills and enhancing SPS effectiveness. A *specific* measure of behavioral competence would be important when the focus of treatment is on some specific type of coping behavior. A measure of *general* behavioral competence or positive adjustment is important for investigating the effects of training on the generalization of effective behavior, and to test the hypothesis that SPS operates to reduce psychopathology by facilitating general social or behavioral competence. *Specific* measures of psychopathology would be needed when the focus of treatment is on specific maladaptive behaviors, while a more *general* measure would be important for evaluating SPS training as a prevention approach. The following review of studies on SPS training is grouped into sections based on the type of subject population or target behavior focused on.

A. Hospitalized Psychiatric Patients

Siegel and Spivak (1976a,b) developed a problem-solving therapy program for chronic psychiatric patients in an attempt to improve their general social competence. The program focuses on four SPS skills: (a) ability to recognize interpersonal problems, (b) ability to define problems, (c) ability to think of alternative solutions, and (d) ability to decide which solution is best. Training consists of a series of 14 "gamelike" exercises involving the use of didactic presentations, slides, and cassette tapes. For example, one of the exercises for problem definition is called "Thirty Questions." Designed to train patients to seek relevant information, this exercise requires the patient to ask a maximum of 30 questions in order to obtain information about a problem from the therapist. An exercise for decision-making training is called "Impulsivity-Reflection Slides." This exercise involves the use of slides showing a model coping with various problematic situations, first in an impulsive, ineffectual manner, and then in a more reflective and successful way.

Two pilot studies were conducted to determine the feasibility and applicability of the training program. In the first study, seven patients volunteered to undergo the training. It was reported that four of these seven patients responded favorably to the program, accepting it as a "legitimate new therapeutic approach." No systematic attempt was made to assess the efficacy of treatment in this study.

The goal of the second pilot study was to evaluate the effects of SPS training on patients' problem-solving cognitions. Twelve patients who were involved in a partial hospitalization program were randomly assigned to either a problem-solving training group or a no-treatment control group. The training program was conducted on an individual basis. Both groups were pre- and posttested on six different SPS measures. Unfortunately, due to the small N and a problem with subject attrition, the investigators decided that any statistical analysis would be inconclusive; therefore, no systematic data were reported.

While the above pilot studies demonstrate only the feasibility of SPS training with hospitalized psychiatric patients, two studies by Coché and his associates (Coché & Flick, 1975; Coché & Douglass, 1977) have provided some objective data on its efficacy. Coché and Flick (1975) compared problem-solving training, an attention-placebo group, called "Play Reading," and a no-treatment control group. Problem-solving training was conducted in a group setting and covered four steps: bringing up a problem, clarifying the problem, generating alternatives, and discussing the feasibility or consequences of various solutions. Unlike Siegel and Spivack's (1976a,b) program, training did not involve specific exercises, but was conducted in a more general group-discussion fashion. In the play-reading group, subjects met to read and discuss various plays, with different subjects being assigned different roles from the play. Both the problem-solving and play-reading groups met for eight 1-hour sessions over a period of 2 weeks. The major dependent measures were three scores derived from the MEPS: number of relevant means, number of irrelevant means, and the relevancy ratio. The results showed that the patients who received the problem-solving training improved significantly more on all three MEPS measures than the attention-placebo and no-treatment control groups. No differences were found between the attention-placebo and no-treatment control groups on any measure.

While the investigators are to be commended for including both an attention-placebo group and a no-treatment group in their study, closer inspection of the placebo condition raises questions concerning its value as a control for nonspecific factors such as "faith" in the treatment and expectation of benefit. The major task of the subjects in this condition was to "read plays and find enjoyment and companionship in doing so" (p. 23). It is doubtful that this social activity would be capable of generating expectations of benefit equal to those of subjects in the problem-solving training condition. Equalizing the credibility of treatments is recognized as an important factor in controlling for nonspecific effects in therapy outcome studies (Jacobson & Baucom, 1977). It would be desirable to include measures such as ratings of expectations of benefit to confirm the comparability of groups on this important variable.

Another problem with the Coché and Flick study is that the MEPS was the only outcome measure used. Questions have been raised about the validity of the MEPS as a measure of SPS (see Butler & Meichenbaum, 1981). No measures of behavioral competence or psychopathology were included to help evaluate the clinical significance of the improved MEPS performance. Finally, there was no follow-up assessment, thus leaving unanswered the question of maintenance of treatment effects.

In an attempt to evaluate the effects of SPS training on outcome measures other than the MEPS, Coché and Douglass (1977) conducted a similar study with hospitalized psychiatric patients which included two self-report measures of personal adjustment in addition to the MEPS. Three groups similar to those in the Coché and Flick (1975) study were compared: problem-solving training, an attention-placebo group in which subjects read and discussed comedies, and a no-treatment control group.

Contrary to the findings of the previous study, no significant differences were found between the problem-solving group and the control groups on any of the MEPS measures. The authors explain the failure to replicate the MEPS results by pointing out that subject attrition resulted in a higher level of pretreatment SPS ability in the problem-solving group, leaving this group with less "room to grow" than the other two groups. Although the MEPS failed to provide support for SPS training in this study, the problem-solving group did show significantly greater improvement in several areas of personal adjustment, including better impulse control, more positive self-image, increased feelings of mastery and competence, and reduced depression.

The same criticism of the placebo condition in the Coché and Flick (1975) study applies to the placebo condition in the present study as well (i.e., reading and discussing comedies). Although the investigators suggest that follow-up assessments are important and should be conducted in the future, none was included in the present study. Finally, the subject attrition problem which resulted in a higher level of SPS ability in the problem-solving group indicates that much caution is needed in drawing any conclusions on the basis of these results.

Viewing SPS training as part of a deinstitutionalization program involving the teaching of practical skills to chronic psychiatric patients, Edelstein, Couture, Cray, Dickins, and Lusebrink (1980) conducted a problem-solving therapy program with 12 of these patients. Training involved a series of four modules which focused on five skills: problem identification and definition, generation of alternative solutions, selection of the best alternative, implementation of the solution response, and evaluation of resulting outcomes. Each training module was structured to begin with a didactic presentation of the underlying principle or principles, and then gradually increase patient participation while decreasing therapist involvement. Procedures were also employed to facilitate motivation and group participation. For example, during the generation-of-alternatives step, patients were separated into teams to foster competition.

The study used a multiple-baseline design with each subject serving as his own control. A verbal problem-solving test using an interview format was administered at pretreatment and after each of the four training modules. In this procedure, subjects were required to respond to hypothetical problems similar to those that might be encountered in the community after leaving the hospital (for example, problems preparing meals independently, conflicts with a landlord, problems budgeting money, etc.). Four problems were presented at each testing. Problem-solving performance was evaluated in four skill areas: correct identification of the "main problem," number of alternative solutions generated, adequacy and realism of stated consequences and solution choice, and adequacy of statements of solution implementation—i.e., how one would actually go about carrying out the solution. In addition to the verbal problem-solving measure, a combination behavioral-verbal problem-solving test was also administered at pre- and posttreatment to assess for generalization from verbal problem-solving to overt problem-solving performance. This test involved a simulated problematic situation in which a customer (the subject) is overcharged by the cashier in a grocery store. In addition to role-playing a response to the situation, the subject also responded verbally to questions regarding the same skills that were assessed on the verbal test.

The results for the verbal problem-solving measure showed significant increases in the four skill areas as a function of each respective training module. In addition, the data also suggested that training in

one SPS operation can affect the ability to perform other operations—
i.e., training in problem identification and definition seemed to facilitate the subjects' generation-of-alternatives performance, and training
in the generation of alternatives appeared to improve their ability to
evaluate alternative solutions. The former is consistent with results
reported recently by Nezu and D'Zurilla (1981b). Significant improvement in all four skill areas was also found in pre- and posttest comparisons. Analysis of the behavioral-verbal problem-solving data showed
significant pre-post increases in adequacy of solution choice and adequacy of solution implementation.

While these results for SPS performance are impressive, no measures
of psychopathology or general behavioral competence were included
in the study. Moreover, no follow-up assessment was included to
evaluate maintenance of treatment effects. Although the own control,
multiple-baseline design in this study reduces somewhat the likelihood of a confounding of SPS training with factors such as attention-
placebo and the mere passage of time, the possible confounding of
treatment effects with practice effects due to the repeated problem-
solving testing still cannot be ruled out. Finally, since a solution-
implementation component was included in the training program,
another possible confounding factor is performance-skill training. The
reasons for distinguishing between problem solving and solution implementation were discussed earlier.

Bedell, Archer, and Marlowe (1980) developed a comprehensive SPS
training program for severely disturbed patients which is based on the
first four stages of the D'Zurilla and Goldfried (1971) model (i.e., problem orientation, problem definition and formulation, generation-of-alternatives, and decision-making). In addition to didactic lectures and
exercises aimed at providing patients with an understanding of important problem-solving concepts, these investigators included a "skill
enhancement/generalization" training component designed to facilitate
behavioral problem-solving performance. This component of the program included the use of structured role-playing, journal writing, practice sessions, and "homework assignments."

Twenty hospitalized psychiatric patients, with varying diagnoses,
participated in a study designed to evaluate this problem-solving training program. In addition to their participation in the study, these
patients were also involved in a traditional residential treatment program involving both medical and psychiatric care. The patients were
divided into two groups: a problem-solving training group and a control group that engaged in a recreational program for an equal period
of time. Three self-report measures of problem solving were developed

for the study and administered before and after treatment: (a) the Problem Solving Knowledge and Information Test (PKIT), (b) the Problem Solving Self-Evaluation Test (PSET), and (c) the Problem Solving Performance Evaluation Test (PPET). The PKIT was a multiple-choice test designed to assess the subjects' knowledge about the SPS process. The PSET used a Likert-type scale to obtain self-ratings from the subjects of the frequency with which they actually performed various problem-solving behaviors. The PPET measured the subjects' verbal problem-solving performance in several specific areas: problem identification, listing the basic elements of the problem, generating possible solutions, rank ordering the solution alternatives with regard to feasibility, and providing reasons for selecting the different solutions.

The results showed that the problem-solving group improved significantly more than the control group on the PKIT and the PPET, but not on the PSET. No follow-up was reported and no measures of general behavioral competence or psychopathology were obtained. In addition, while the recreational control group was probably adequate as a control for time and attention, it does not appear to be an adequate control for placebo factors such as "faith" in the treatment and expectation of benefit.

To summarize, six studies which attempted to evaluate SPS training with hospitalized psychiatric patients were reviewed. Two were preliminary studies which reported no systematic, objective data. Four studies reported results supporting the efficacy of SPS training, but only one used a measure of personal adjustment or psychopathology and none included a follow-up assessment. Additionally, all of the studies have methodological problems which indicate that caution is needed in interpreting the results and drawing conclusions concerning the efficacy of SPS training with this population.

B. Substance Abuse and Addictions

SPS training has also been used with individuals who have problems involving drug addiction, alcoholism, and cigarette smoking. Copemann (1973) used a comprehensive behavioral approach to the treatment of heroin addicts which included problem-solving training based on the D'Zurilla and Goldfried (1971) model as a major component. In addition to SPS training, the treatment package included specific behavioral techniques such as aversive counter-conditioning and training in self-control principles. Analyzing the data for subjects who completed the treatment program, Copemann found that 86% were drug free at a 12-month follow-up evaluation. Fourteen percent of these subjects subsequently relapsed but were given booster sessions and found to be drug free after another 6-month follow-up period.

It is impossible to assess the specific effects of SPS training in this study because of the absence of control groups and the fact that problem-solving training was only one part of a comprehensive treatment package. Moreover, no measures of SPS or behavioral competence were included to determine whether or not SPS skills and competence were actually enhanced in the subjects who were drug free following the treatment program and might have contributed to this effect.

Intagliatia (1978) conducted a study to assess whether problem-solving training would improve on the results of a typical VA alcoholism treatment program involving 6 weeks of in-patient medical and psychiatric care. Sixty-three male alcoholic patients were randomly assigned to either an experimental group which received problem-solving training in addition to the VA alcoholism program or a control group that did not receive any problem-solving training. The problem-solving training group participated in 10 1-hour training sessions over a 4-week period which were designed to teach the problem-solving steps of problem recognition, problem definition, generation of alternatives, and selection of the best solution. The MEPS and a social competency scale were administered to both groups at pre- and post-treatment assessments. Additionally, shortly prior to discharge from the alcoholism program, all subjects participated in a structured interview to discuss "discharge planning," covering areas such as employment, living arrangements, and the use of leisure time. The subjects' interview responses were scored for (a) number of discrete instrumental acts described as plans for coping with problems, (b) number of obstacles recognized, (c) number of solution alternatives that were considered but not yet decided upon, and (d) number of discrete acts that the person planned to implement.

The results showed that the problem-solving training group improved significantly more than the control group on one MEPS score—i.e., the number of relevant means. Trends were observed in favor of the problem-solving group on the other MEPS scores but none of the differences was significant. With regard to the interview data, however, the problem-solving group performed significantly better than the control group in all four response categories, indicating better planning and preparation for coping with problems in living after returning to the community. No significant findings were reported for the social competency scale. A 1-month follow-up evaluation included only the problem-solving group to determine how well they remembered the problem-solving principles and whether or not they were applying these principles in real life. Although 14 of the 22 subjects contacted reported having used the problem-solving principles in coping with real-life problems, most of them had forgotten significant portions of the training information.

Although a follow-up evaluation was included in this study, it left much to be desired since it did not include any formal measures of SPS, behavioral competence, or maladaptive behavior, and did not include the control group. It would have been particularly useful to repeat the social competency scale after a follow-up period instead of doing only a pre–post assessment since it was only after being discharged from the in-patient program that the subjects had the opportunity to demonstrate greater competence. Another difficulty with the study is that it did not include a control for attention-placebo factors. Although both groups participated in the VA alcoholism program, the problem-solving group might have had greater expectations of benefit because of their additional "new" treatment.

A similar study using the same type of population which included an attention-placebo control was conducted by Chaney, O'Leary, and Marlatt (1978). The 40 male patients who participated as subjects in this study were also involved in an in-patient VA alcoholism treatment program. These subjects were randomly assigned to either a skills training, placebo control, or no-treatment control group. The skills-training program involved training in the five stages of the D'Zurilla and Goldfried (1971) SPS model, whereas the placebo-control group only met to discuss their feelings and reactions to various problematic situations involving alcohol. Both groups met for eight 90-minute sessions over a 4-week period. The no-treatment control group received only the regular VA alcoholism program.

The major outcome measure in this study was the Situational Competency Test (SCT), which involved the presentation of tape-recorded problematic situations involving alcohol which the patients might encounter in the real-life social setting. The subjects' task was to imagine being in the situation and then verbally respond to the question: "What would you do or say?" Verbal responses were scored for latency of response, duration of response (i.e., number of words), compliance (i.e., whether or not the subject "gave in" to the situation), and specification of new alternative behaviors. A second outcome measure was a "drinking profile," which involved the use of a structured interview to obtain information about the subjects' drinking behavior. The SCT was administered at pretreatment, at termination of training, and at a 3-month follow-up. The drinking profile was taken at pretreatment and after follow-up periods of 1, 3, 6, and 12 months.

The results for the SCT showed that the skills-training (problem-solving) group performed significantly better than both control groups on scores for duration of response and specification of new alternative behaviors; however, these differences diminished at the 3-month follow-up assessment. Since no significant differences were found between the two control groups on the measures of drinking behavior from the drinking profile, these data were pooled and then compared to the data from the skills-training group. For the 1-year period following treatment, the skills-training group was found to be significantly more improved on the following measures: number of days drunk, total number of drinks, and mean length of a drinking period. No significant differences were found in the actual number of relapses between the groups; however, one can conclude from the other drinking measures that the duration and severity of relapses were reduced as a function of the problem-solving training.

This study represents a significant improvement over the previous studies methodologically, since it included both an attention-placebo control and adequate follow-up assessments. It demonstrates solid, if not overwhelming, support for the efficacy of problem-solving training with a patient population that has difficulty handling problematic situations involving alcohol. However, the study is lacking in a measure of SPS to determine the actual degree of improvement in SPS skills. In addition, although the study includes specific measures of competency and drinking behavior, it would have been desirable to include more general measures of behavioral competence and psychopathology to assess the degree of generalization.

Karol and Richards (1978) investigated the use of problem-solving training as a maintenance strategy for cigarette-smoking reduction. Thirty-eight habitual smokers were randomly assigned to either behavioral treatment, behavioral treatment and maintenance strategy, or waiting-list control. The behavioral treatment involved five sessions over a 3-week period, consisting of self-monitoring, stimulus control, and alternative behavior planning. The goal of the program was to reduce smoking gradually and then quit completely by a predetermined target date. The maintenance strategy consisted of problem-solving training based on the D'Zurilla and Goldfried (1971) model and the use of a "buddy system" involving scheduled telephone contacts between pairs of subjects following the behavioral treatment program.

The results at treatment termination indicated a significant reduction in smoking frequency in both treatment groups, but not in the waiting list-control group. Follow-up assessments via telephone interviews were conducted after 2-, 4-, and 8-month periods. The group that received the maintenance strategy showed very little relapse on follow-up, whereas the relapse rate for the other two groups was substantial. For example, at the 8-month follow-up evaluation, the average number of cigarettes smoked above the posttreatment-assessment level was 1.1 for the maintenance-strategy group, whereas the number for the other two groups was 14.8.

While the above results for the efficacy of the maintenance strategy are impressive, it is not possible to determine the specific effects of problem-solving training in this study since the maintenance strategy also included the "buddy system." No measures of SPS or competence in handling specific problematic situations independently were included to help evaluate the possible role of problem-solving training in contributing to behavioral change. Finally, it is possible that the addition of the maintenance procedures to the behavioral treatment might have increased the effects of attention and expectations of benefit in this group. No procedures were included to control for this possibility.

To summarize, studies have reported positive behavioral changes in drug addicts, alcoholics, and cigarette smokers following treatment programs involving problem-solving training. In the one study with drug addicts, the effects of problem-solving training cannot be isolated because of several methodological problems. Two studies with alcoholics provided more convincing results. In one well-controlled study, significant changes were reported on measures of both drinking behavior and effectiveness in coping with problematic situations involving alcohol. One study with cigarette smokers reported results which suggest that problem-solving training might, indeed, be effective as a treatment maintenance strategy; however, methodological problems preclude any firm conclusions. A weakness in all of these studies is the failure to include more general measures of social or behavioral competence and psychopathology to assess the generality of problem-solving training effects.

C. Depressed Geriatric Patients

On the basis of the studies supporting the "learned helplessness" view of depression (see Abramson et al., 1978), and the study by Gotlib and Asarnow (1979) which found highly significant differences on several MEPS measures between depressed and nondepressed subjects, it would appear that problem-solving training might be a very appropriate treatment for depression. One study has been reported which

compared the use of problem-solving training with a social-reinforcement program for the treatment of depression in a group of geriatric
patients living in a nursing home (Hussian & Lawrence, 1981). Thirty-
six patients who scored in the severly depressed range on the Beck
Depression Inventory (Beck, 1967) were randomly divided into three
groups: problem solving (PS), social reinforcement (SR), and waiting-
list control (WLC). Both treatment groups met for five 30-minute training sessions during a 1-week period of time. Problem-solving training
was based on the D'Zurilla and Goldfried (1971) model. Training was
carried out on an individual basis and involved discussion of each of
the five stages of the model as well as practice solving real-life problems generated by the subjects in a previous pilot study. The major
objective of the social-reinforcement program was to increase the rate
of reinforcement the subjects were receiving in their daily lives. Subjects were prompted to engage in various activities such as arts and
crafts and given social reinforcement for attendance, participation in
a specific activity, perseverance, and interaction with other patients.

After the first week of treatment, each of the three groups was randomly divided in half to produce six subgroups. One PS subgroup
received a second week of problem-solving training (PS–PS) while the
second PS subgroup participated in the social-reinforcement program
(PS–SR). One SR subgroup received a second week of social reinforcement (SR–SR) while the second SR subgroup received the problem-solving training (SR–PS). Finally, one WLC subgroup remained
on the waiting list for the second week (WLC–WLC) while the second
WLC subgroup was changed to an informational control group (WLC–IC).
This subgroup met to discuss the various life changes that accompany
aging.

The major outcome measures were the Beck Depression Inventory
(BDI) and self-ratings of depression. Other outcome measures included
the Hospital Adjustment Scale (HAS), which measures the general
level of daily functioning and adjustment in the institutional environment, and a written problem-solving test using hypothetical problems. The BDI, HAS, and self-ratings were administered at pretreatment, at the end of the first treatment week, at the end of the second
treatment week, and after follow-up periods of 2 weeks and 3 months.
The problem-solving test was administered at pretreatment and at the
end of the first treatment week.

After the first week of treatment, both the PS and SR groups showed
significantly less depression on both measures than did the WLC group.
As expected, the PS group showed significantly better performance on

the problem-solving test than did the SR group. An analysis of differences between pretreatment assessment and the posttreatment assessment at the end of the second week provided for a comparison between the combined treatments. The results showed a significant reduction in depression on the BDI only for groups that received problem-solving training. The PS–PS group was significantly less depressed than both the WLC–IC and WLC–WLC groups, and the SR–PS group was significantly less depressed than the WLC–IC group. The differences between the SR–SR group and the control groups were not significant.

Differences on self-ratings of depression and on the HAS emerged in the analysis of differences between the end of the first treatment week and the end of the second treatment week. The groups that received problem-solving training during the second week reported less depression than the groups that received social reinforcement during that week. On the HAS, the group that received problem-solving training for both weeks showed significantly more improvement than the 2-week social reinforcement group and the 2-week waiting-list control group.

The superiority of problem-solving training was maintained at the 2-week follow-up. Two problem-solving training groups (PS–PS and PS–SR) were found to be significantly less depressed on the BDI than the 2-week waiting-list control group. On self-ratings of depression, the 2-week problem-solving training group was significantly less depressed than the 2-week social reinforcement group and the 2-week waiting-list control group. Although the differences were no longer significant at the 3-month follow-up assessment, the trends in the data were similar to the findings at the 2-week follow-up.

The Hussian and Lawrence study provides strong support for the efficacy of problem-solving training for reducing depression and improving adjustment, at least in the particular patient population focused on in this study. Problem-solving training was not only the most effective procedure at the end of the 2-week treatment period, but this superiority was maintained over a 2-week follow-up as well. Although the significant differences disappeared after the 3-month follow-up, the trends were the same and it is possible that a more extensive treatment program lasting for more than just 2 weeks might have produced more durable effects. It should be pointed out that a similar argument can also be made for the social-reinforcement approach to the treatment of depression. A more extensive program involving not only the prompting and reinforcement of activities, but also skills training and communication training as well (designed to increase positive social interaction and social reinforcement) might have produced better results.

D. Stress and Anxiety

Experimental studies have found that a perceived lack of control in stressful problematic situations can increase anxiety and other related maladaptive responses, such as high blood pressure and compulsive behavior. In addition, studies of individuals who tend to cope poorly with stress have found deficits in problem-solving behavior in these individuals, especially in the problem-orientation category (see Meichenbaum et al., 1979). Therefore, it might be expected that SPS training would be an appropriate and useful treatment for stress and its resulting anxiety.

Mendonca and Siess (1976) conducted a study to evaluate the relative effectiveness of anxiety-management training and problem-solving training for reducing anxiety resulting from vocational indecision in college students. Thirty-two undergraduate college students with this anxiety problem were divided into five groups: anxiety management, problem solving, anxiety management and problem solving combined, discussion placebo, and no-treatment control.

Anxiety-management training involved relaxation training, group systematic desensitization, and the use of self-coping imagery. Problem-solving training used a group-discussion format and was based on the D'Zurilla and Goldfried (1971) model. The combined condition included the essential features of both treatments with an equal emphasis on the two methods. The subjects in the placebo condition met to discuss their career indecision and to attempt to gain insight into the causes of their anxiety. Outcome measures included measures of the frequency and variety of vocational search behavior (for example, visiting a job site, discussing career plans with a professor), state and trait anxiety, and problem solving. The problem-solving measure was a timed written test involving imaginary role playing in response to tape-recorded vignettes of common problematic situations in a college setting. Three subtests produced scores for the following problem-solving behavior: concrete information gathering, generation of alternatives, and choice behavior.

Results for vocational search behavior showed that the combined-treatment and the anxiety-management group improved significantly more than the problem-solving and no-treatment control groups. There was no significant difference between the combined treatment and anxiety-management. No significant differences were found in anxiety reduction on either anxiety measure. On the information-gathering subtest of the problem-solving measure, the problem-solving group performed significantly better than anxiety-management and both control groups; the combined-treatment group performed significantly better than both control groups; and anxiety-management was significantly better than the no-treatment control. On the generation-of-alternatives subtest, the combined-treatment was significantly better than both control groups, and the problem-solving group performed significantly better than the placebo-control group. No significant results were found on the measure of choice behavior.

Although the findings for the problem-solving test supported the efficacy of problem-solving training in this study, the results regarding the measures of anxiety reduction and vocational search behavior did not. However, since none of the treatments produced significant anxiety reduction, it is possible that the vocational problems of the students were not sufficiently resolved by the end of the study for them to show a significant relief from the anxiety of their vocational indecision. A follow-up assessment would have been desirable to assess for possible later anxiety-reducing effects. With regard to vocational search behavior, it is likely that the college students in this study were already quite aware of the importance of exploratory behavior in making vocational decisions; thus, the problem-solving training would not be expected to add any new information or skills in this regard. The self-coping imagery and covert rehearsal involved in the anxiety-management condition might have been more useful in actually *facilitating* the students' search behavior. Finally, the failure to obtain significant results on the choice-behavior subtest might have been due to the unreliability of this measure. Parallel-form reliability was only .34 and an estimate of internal consistency was only .57. With such low reliability, the validity of this measure can be seriously questioned.

Another good example of the use of problem solving to cope with stress and anxiety can be found in the stress-inoculation training program developed by Meichenbaum (see Meichenbaum & Navaco, 1977; Meichenbaum & Jaremko, 1982). This training program is a multicomponent treatment method which includes problem-solving training, self-instructional training (for example, task-oriented self-statements, positive self-evaluations) (Meichenbaum, 1977), and training in specific coping skills such as relaxation and assertion. The problem-solving component emphasizes the adoption of a problem-solving set, problem definition, generation of alternative "solutions" or coping responses, anticipation of consequences, and evaluation of feedback. The program trains individuals to perceive a stress situation as a challenge or "problem-to-be-solved" instead of as a threat. They are taught (through verbal instruction, modeling, rehearsal, and feedback) to monitor their thoughts, images and behaviors in stress situations and to make problem-solving-oriented, facilitative self-statements instead of negative, inhibitive, or anxiety-provoking statements. In addition to training in problem solving and other cognitive coping skills, the program also provides training in direct action coping skills to facilitate effective performance in the real-life setting and strengthen self-efficacy expectations.

The stress-inoculation approach has been evaluated with a variety of different stress-related problems, including test anxiety (Holyroyd, 1976), speech anxiety (Meichenbaum et al., 1971), extreme anger Novaco, 1975), invasive medical procedures (Kendall et al., 1979), and interpersonal confrontation (Glass, Gottman, & Shmurack, 1976). Although these studies have provided support for the efficacy of the stress-inoculation package, the specific contribution of the problem-solving training component has not yet been determined. Thus, these studies offer only suggestive evidence regarding the effectiveness of SPS training for reducing stress and anxiety.

A study that provides more convincing evidence for the efficacy of a problem-solving approach to anxiety reduction has been reported by Jannoun, Munby, Catalan, and Gelder (1980). These investigators set out to replicate under more controlled conditions the findings of a previous study in which 12 agoraphobic patients were successfully treated with a home-based programmed-practice approach. This approach involves graded in vivo exposure to feared situations with assistance and social reinforcement provided by the patient's spouse (or some other significant person). As a comparison treatment, the investigators decided to use an approach that would enable them to establish whether exposure to the feared situations is an essential component of the treatment of agoraphobia. The treatment which they employed for this purpose was a problem-solving approach involving the identification of relevant life problems and stresses and the discovery of ways of solving or reducing them.

Twenty-eight agoraphobic patients were randomly assigned to the two treatment conditions and to one of two therapists. Each therapist treated seven patients in each treatment condition. Treatment was carried out in the home for a 3-week period. In both treatments, the patient's partner was actively involved in planning treatment targets and reinforcing progress. In the programmed-practice condition, patients were instructed in the use of the graded-exposure method and asked to practice going out for at least an hour each day. In the problem-solving condition, patients were instructed to keep a daily record of life problems and stresses and taught how to set problem-solving targets and deal with them. The patients and their partners were instructed to discuss relevant problems and stresses for at least an hour each day. The partners were instructed in how to assist the patients in solving these problems and reinforcing their attempts at doing so.

Dependent measures included ratings of phobic severity and anxiety by an independent assessor and by the patients themselves, and diary measures of time away from home and number of journeys made. Assessments were made before and after treatment and at 3- and 6-month follow-ups. On the measure of phobic severity, both the assessor's ratings and the patient's ratings showed significant decreases after treatment for both treatment conditions, with improvement continuing in both conditions during the follow-up period. Although improvement was significantly greater for the programmed-practice treatment at the 3-month follow-up, there was no longer a significant difference at the 6-month follow-up, indicating that the problem-solving group continued to improve at a faster rate. On both the assessor's and the patient's ratings of anxiety, both treatment conditions showed a significant decrease at the end of treatment, which continued during the follow-up period so that at the 6-month assessment both groups showed only mild anxiety. There were no significant differences between treatment conditions.

On the measure of average time away from home each week, the programmed-practice group reported a greater number of hours per week at the end of treatment than the problem-solving group, but the difference was not significant (it should be noted that the programmed-practice subjects were asked to go out daily as part of their treatment, whereas the problem-solving subjects were not). However, an unexpected finding was that the scores of the programmed-practice group decreased slightly between the 3- and 6-month follow-ups, while the problem-solving group reported an increase in time away from home during this period. The same pattern of results was found on the measure of average number of journeys per week.

The above results show that on follow-up evaluation, problem solving and programmed practice were equally effective in the treatment of agoraphobia. Moreover, there was some tendency for problem solving to be more effective than programmed practice in facilitating going out away from home during the 6-month follow-up period. According to the investigators, these findings challenge the hypothesis that systematic exposure to the feared situations is a necessary part of the treatment of agoraphobia. Instead, they show that a treatment aimed at anxiety reduction by solving life problems can also be effective, and might even result in better long-term maintenance effects. These results are particularly impressive in view of the fact that the investigators were clearly biased in favor of the programmed-practice treatment. Furthermore, the results for problem solving might have been even greater had it not been for the fact that one therapist was less effective than the other in conducting the problem-solving training whereas the two therapists were equally effective with the programmed-practice treatment. The more effective therapist obtained results with the problem-solving treatment that were comparable at all assessments to those that both therapists obtained with programmed practice.

E. Academic Underachievement

Richards and Perri (1978) evaluated the relative effectiveness of problem-solving training and faded counselor contact as maintenance strategies used in conjunction with a behavioral-counseling program for poor study habits and academic underachievement in college students. Sixty-nine introductory psychology students who volunteered for the study were randomly assigned to six groups: (1) study-skills advice, (2) self-control training, (3) self-control training with problem-solving training, (4) self-control training with faded counselor contact, (5) self-control training with problem-solving training and faded counselor contact, and (6) no-treatment control. In addition, a no-contact, nonvolunteer control group of 11 students was included in the study.

The study-skills advice group participated in a training program that offered direct information regarding textbook reading, study scheduling, note-taking, exam-taking, and writing. Self-control training provided instruction in the use of behavioral self-control procedures such as self-monitoring, stimulus control, and self-reinforcement in addition to the study-skills advice. Problem-solving training followed the five stages of the D'Zurilla and Goldfried (1971) model. The five treatment groups met for four sessions over a 3-week period. The two groups which included faded counselor contact met with 2-, 5-, and 14-day intervals between sessions. The other three treatment groups met with 1-week regular intervals between sessions. The outcome measures included exam grades from the introductory psychology course and semester grade point averages (GPA). Course grades were available during the week following counseling and at 6 and 12 weeks after counseling. GPAs from before counseling and 12 weeks and 1 year following counseling were analyzed. A written test designed to assess knowledge of the problem-solving skills was also administered at posttreatment and at a 12-week follow-up.

Results for the course exams showed that the groups receiving problem-solving training were significantly superior to all other groups at the 6- and 12-week posttreatment assessments. Results for GPAs also showed the problem-solving groups to be significantly superior to all other groups at the 12-week and 1-year posttreatment evaluations. The faded counselor contact procedure was not effective as a maintenance strategy. Results from the problem-solving test indicated that the problem-solving training groups did, in fact, learn the requisite skills and maintained this knowledge at the 12-week follow-up assessment.

The one possible control problem in this study is that the extra time and attention devoted to the problem-solving training might have contributed to the superior performance of these groups. However, it is not likely that this factor would be powerful enough to affect academic performance, especially after a 1-year follow-up. Therefore, the results of this study can be considered strong support for the efficacy of problem-solving training as a treatment maintenance strategy. They also support the view that the significant maintenance effect in the Karol and Richards (1978) study on cigarette smoking was primarily a result of the problem-solving training rather than the "buddy system."

F. Marital Problems

According to the behavioral view of marital problems, deficits in problem-solving skills play a major role in marital distress (Jacobson, 1981; O'Leary & Turkewitz, 1978). Following from this viewpoint, problem-solving training has always been considered an important part of marital behavior therapy (Weiss, Hops, & Patterson, 1973; Jacobson, 1981; O'Leary & Turkewitz, 1978). However, in most marital behavior therapy programs, problem solving refers to the *general* therapy process by which couples learn to resolve their marital conflicts, rather than to *specific* training in SPS skills. This process usually consists of communication training and contingency contracting. Although there is some overlap between communication training and SPS training, especially in the area of problem definition and formulation, most of the SPS skills described here are not emphasized.

One notable exception to the above is the marital behavior therapy program developed by Jacobson (1977a), which involves specific training in several of the SPS operations described by D'Zurilla and Gold-fried (1971), with particular emphasis on training in defining and formulating problems, generating alternative solutions, and evaluating solutions. In addition to problem-solving training directed specifically at improving couples' performance in discussing and resolving relationship conflicts, Jacobson's program also includes contingency contracting, which involves the negotiation of specific behavior-change agreements.

Jacobson (1977b) evaluated his marital behavior therapy program in an outcome study involving 10 couples. These couples were randomly assigned to either a treatment group, involving 10 sessions of therapy, or a waiting-list control group. The early therapy sessions focused on problem-solving training with contingency contracting beginning in the fourth session. In the remaining sessions, the couples applied all of their skills to the discussion of specific problems in their relationship. Outcome measures included a problem-solving performance test, in which couples were observed interacting in a problem-solving discussion situation, and a self-report scale of marital adjustment. Scores were obtained for problem-solving performance by coding the couples' verbal behavior into positive, negative, and neutral categories. Both measures were administered at pre- and posttreatment. The marital adjustment scale was also administered after a 1-year follow-up. In addition, throughout treatment couples were asked to monitor and record behaviors in the home which were defined as problematic during pretreatment assessment. This resulted in a multiple-baseline type of design, allowing for an assessment of the specific effects of the treatment intervention on particular problematic behaviors.

The results showed that the couples receiving marital behavior therapy improved significantly more than the waiting-list control group on both the measures of problem-solving behavior and marital adjustment. At the 1-year follow-up, the treatment gains on the marital adjustment scale were maintained. On the measure of frequency of problematic behaviors in the home, the treated couples showed significant improvement which could be attributed to the specific treatment procedures.

Jacobson (1978) conducted a second study designed to replicate the above findings with the addition of a nonspecific therapy group to control for nonspecific factors such as attention and expectation of benefit. The nonspecific group included all of the characteristics of the behavioral treatment group except for the problem-solving training and contingency-contracting procedures. The credibility of the non-specific therapy was checked by having the couples rate the therapists and the two treatment conditions on factors related to credibility, and by having an independent sample of subjects rate written descriptions of both treatment conditions. No significant differences in credibility were found between the two treatment conditions.

The results replicated the findings of the first study regarding the comparison of behavioral treatment with the waiting-list control. In addition, the results also showed that the behavioral treatment produced significantly more improvement than the nonspecific treatment on both the measures of problem-solving behavior and marital adjustment. The gains on the marital adjustment scale were maintained at a 6-month follow-up assessment.

Since both of the above studies focused on a university-based population (relatively young, moderately distressed, relatively high intelligence), Jacobson (1977c) conducted another outcome study with a more severely distressed population in an urban psychiatric hospital setting. These subjects were not only experiencing serious relationship problems, but many also had serious individual psychological problems as well. Six couples participated in the study, each of which was studied separately using a single-subject, multiple-baseline design, focusing on problematic behaviors recorded by the couples in the home. An important aspect of this study for SPS is that the behavioral treatment involved only problem-solving training; no contingency contracting was included.

Problem-solving training with each couple was compared to a baseline involving 3 to 4 weeks of an instructional procedure in which the couple was simply asked to increase positive behavior. After these 3 or 4 weeks, individual problem areas were treated with the problem-solving approach. The behavioral data recorded in the home showed significant improvement in five of the six couples from baseline to posttreatment. In the sixth couple, although positive changes were reported on a self-report measure, these changes were not substantiated by the home behavioral data. Of the five improved couples, four maintained their gains at a 6-month follow-up, as measured by the marital-adjustment scale. With four of the five improved couples, the problem-solving training appeared to be effective and sufficient for producing significant therapeutic change. However, the fifth improved couple needed further direct instruction aimed at increasing positive behavior before significant change could be produced.

Together, Jacobson's first two studies provide strong support for the efficacy of his marital therapy package. However, because this package

includes contingency contracting in addition to problem-solving training, no conclusions can be drawn concerning the specific contribution
of the problem-solving training to the overall outcome. Although the
single-subject methodology in the third study does not control adequately for attention-placebo effects and the effects of intercurrent life
experiences, this study is important for the fact that significant improvement was obtained with several severely distressed couples when
treated with a form of marital therapy based primarily on problem-
solving training. These findings strongly suggest that problem-solving
training might, indeed, be the most powerful ingredient in Jacobson's
marital therapy package.[4]

G. Facilitation of General Competence in "Normal" Individuals

Since the goal of SPS is to facilitate *general* social competence, it
is not surprising that there has been considerable interest in the use
of SPS training for *competence enhancement* in a variety of different
educational settings, including academic courses, workshops, seminars, conferences, institutes, and adult education programs. If these
programs prove to be effective, they could be very useful in clinical
psychology for *prevention* purposes with such "vulnerable" or "at
risk" populations as retired senior citizens, the recently divorced, single parents, the unemployed, and various other groups who are having
difficulty coping with changing circumstances or an increasing number
of problems in living and may be turning to maladaptive coping behaviors such as excessive drinking, overeating, and drug abuse.

Long before investigators in clinical psychology became interested
in the applications of problem-solving theory and research, Sidney
Parnes (1962) developed a very successful course in "creative problem
solving" at the University of Buffalo which is basically a training
program in SPS skills. A manual has been published for this program
(Parnes, 1967), which has been used to teach problem-solving skills
to college students and adults in all professions throughout the United
States.

Parnes' (1967) creative problem-solving course is structured as a 16-
session training program covering the same general SPS skills as de-

---

[4] Training programs similar to Jacobson's have also been used in family therapy,
where problem-solving training is one component of a larger treatment package which
also includes training in more general communication skills and contingency contracting
(Blechman, Olson, & Hellman, 1976; Robin, Kent, O'Leary, Foster, & Prinz, 1977). These
studies have been reviewed by Urbain and Kendall (1980).

scribed by D'Zurilla and Goldfried (1971) and Spivack et al. (1976). For example, the topics include "sensing problems and challenges," "fact-finding," "recognizing the real problem," "idea-finding," "evaluating ideas," and "preparing to put ideas to use." There is a special emphasis in the program on the creative process involved in "idea-finding" (i.e., the generation of alternatives), which is based primarily on Osborn's (1963) principles of "deferent of judgment" and "quantity-breeds-quality." Exercises and homework assignments are included to give students practice in applying the total problem-solving process to a variety of practical problems including impersonal creative tasks (for example, "How can you make a better mousetrap?"), individual and interpersonal problems in living (for example, "How can you get to your destination on time when your car won't start?" "How can you get your children to reduce their consumption of soft drinks and sweets?"), and broader community issues (for example, "How can merchants in town prevent further thefts from their stores?").

Parnes and Meadow conducted two studies designed to evaluate the creative problem-solving course at the University of Buffalo (Meadow & Parnes, 1959; Parnes & Meadow, 1960). In the first study, students from three problem-solving courses were compared to a matched control group of students from other courses on several measures of creative problem solving and three personality scales from the California Psychological Inventory (CPI) (i.e., "dominance," "self-control," and "need to achieve"). The problem-solving measures were based on responses to hypothetical problems and included two measures of quantity of ideas and five measures of quality of ideas. These measures were administered before and after the course. The results showed that the creative problem-solving group improved significantly more than the control group on both measures of quantity of ideas and on three of the five measures of quality of ideas. In addition, the problem-solving group increased significantly more on the dominance scale of the CPI, which reportedly measures characteristics such as confidence, self-reliance, persuasiveness, initiative, and leadership potential.

The second study was designed to assess the *maintenance* of improvement in creative problem solving following the completion of the course. Subjects who completed the creative problem-solving course an average of 18 months before the study were compared to two separate control groups of subjects who had registered for the course but did not actually take it, on the six creative problem-solving measures which produced significant or near significant results in the first study. None of the subjects had ever taken the problem-solving tests before. The results showed that the problem-solving group was significantly superior to one control group on all six creative problem-solving measures and significantly superior to the second control group on four of the six measures.

The results for the first study indicate that the major aim of Parnes' creative problem-solving course was achieved—i.e., an improvement in creative problem-solving thinking. The significant results for the dominance scale of the CPI also suggests that the course had a positive effect on personality. It is possible, however, that a "Hawthorne Effect" might have contributed to this outcome. That is, one cannot rule out the possibility that the students who took the course performed better on the problem-solving and personality measures primarily because they had been given attention and the expectation of improvement. In order to control for this effect, a nonspecific training program would be needed which provided attention and generated the same expectation in the students for improved performance but did not include any specific training in creative problem-solving skills. The results of the second study must also be interpreted with caution since no measures were obtained before the course to rule out the possibility that initial differences in creative problem-solving ability between the experimental and control groups might have contributed to the significant differences at follow-up. Another inadequacy is that no measures of personality adjustment or social competence were included in this follow-up study.

Dixon, Heppner, Petersen, and Ronning (1979) assessed the effects of an intensive problem-solving workshop with normal college student volunteers. SPS was conceptualized by these investigators as a lattice of five sequential phases: problem definition, goal selection, strategy selection, strategy implementation, and evaluation. Brainstorming and decision making were conceived of as generic skills applicable across the first three phases. Fifty undergraduates were randomly assigned to three groups: a treatment group (problem-solving training), a pretest–posttest control group, and a posttest-only control group. Problem-solving training was conducted in five, 1.5-hour group sessions consisting of didactic presentations, group discussions, and directed practice. Homework assignments were also given, which were designed to facilitate generalization and transfer of skills beyond the workshop setting.

The major dependent measure was the problem-solving test used in the Mendonca and Siess (1976) study on vocational indecision, which consisted of a generation-of-alternatives subtest and a choice-behavior subtest. As reported earlier, the validity of the latter subtest can be seriously questioned because of low reliability. Another measure was a self-report problem-solving inventory which assessed the subject's perceptions of their problem-solving skills.

The results for the generation-of-alternatives subtest showed that the problem-solving group and the pretest–posttest control group increased equally in the *quantity* of solution alternatives produced, but that the problem-solving group improved significantly more on scores related to the *quality* of alternatives. The brief opportunity to practice generating alternatives on the pretest seemed to be sufficient to produce a significant increase in the number of alternatives generated in the pretest–posttest group; however, the more intensive problem-solving training was required to produce a significant improvement in the quality of solution ideas. No significant results were found for the choice-behavior subtest, which might have been due to the low reliability and questionable validity of this measure. The results for the self-report problem-solving inventory showed that the problem-solving group performed significantly better than the combined control groups, with the difference resulting primarily from the subjects' report of less impulsivity in problem-solving situations. The study did not include a follow-up nor did it include an assessment of general behavior competence or adjustment.

Toseland (1977) developed a group problem-solving workshop for senior citizens in an attempt to improve their social effectiveness. The workshop provided training in the following skills: (a) problem definition, (b) evaluation of thoughts and feelings concerning the particular problematic situation, (c) explication of the desired emotion, behavior, and consequences for the problematic situation, (d) generation-of-alternative solutions, (e) decision making, and (f) practice in solution implementation. Although the workshop stressed the application of general problem-solving skills, the content of the group meetings focused on problematic situations requiring assertive behavior, such as confrontation, turning down unreasonable requests, and giving negative feedback.

Six volunteers from a senior citizen center participated in the six-session workshop. Dependent measures included a self-report assertiveness scale and a problem-solving performance test involving the role playing of responses to assertion situations. These measures were administered 1 week before and after training. The results showed a significant pretest–posttest improvement on both measures. Although these results indicate that improvement did occur, no conclusions can be made concerning the efficacy of the problem-solving training in this study because of the absence of control procedures and the small number of subjects.

To summarize, four studies were reviewed which evaluated competence-enhancement programs based on SPS training with normal individuals. Although all of these studies have produced promising results, methodological problems indicate that caution is needed in interpreting the results as support for the efficacy of problem-solving training. In addition to the methodological problems, only two of the studies included a measure of general competence or adjustment. Only one study included a follow-up assessment, and this study was inconclusive because the subjects were not tested on the dependent measures at the time of the problem-solving course. Only one of the studies included a "vulnerable" population which would be an appropriate target population for a prevention program. Therefore, although SPS training programs show promise for prevention, there is still no solid evidence available concerning their efficacy for this purpose.

H. Community Problems

All of the studies reviewed thus far have focused on the problem solving of individuals or, in one case, couples. SPS training may also have a useful application in community psychology to increase the effectiveness of special groups or committees in solving problems confronting entire communities (for example, crime, air pollution, inadequate services, unemployment, racial conflict, etc). The members of such groups might include volunteers from the community, elected officials, supervisors, employees, and management or administrative personnel. Problem-solving groups interested in SPS skills might also include committees from various professional and special interest organizations (for example, lawyers, doctors, psychologists, trade unions) who are charged with the responsibility of attempting to find solutions to problems facing the organization.

One study which evaluated SPS training for a community-based problem-solving group was conducted by Briscoe, Hoffman, and Bailey (1975). The study focused on a policy-making board from a university-sponsored rural community project. The nine board members were elected representatives from the community. The responsibilities of the board included the identification and resolution of community problems and the administration of a $20,000 budget for community projects.

Earlier assessment of the board's activities found that its problem-solving attempts were unsystematic and relatively unsuccessful. To remedy this, three problem-solving steps were identified for training: (a) problem identification and isolation, (b) generation and evaluation of alternative solutions, and (c) selection of a solution with concomitant plans for its implementation. A multiple-baseline design across subjects and skills was used. Seven of the nine board members received individual training in the problem-solving skills while the remaining two served as control subjects and received no training. Training methods included prompting, modeling, fading, role playing, and social reinforcement. The major outcome measure was verbal problem-solving behavior based on an analysis of videotapes of board meetings. The verbal statements of board members were judged by two university professors who taught problem-solving courses and by two active community leaders.

The results for both group and individual data generally showed increases in the use of key problem-solving statements following training in the relevant skill. Follow-up assessments of 1 week to 2 months following training in each skill indicated that although the positive changes were not always maintained at a high level, they consistently remained higher than baseline. The two control subjects did not show any changes in the quality of their problem-solving statements.

Although the possibility of a "Hawthorne Effect" cannot be ruled out in this study, the results demonstrate the feasibility of SPS training for community problem-solving groups and offer at least suggestive evidence for its efficacy. Future studies should explore the possible advantages of training the members in a group, instead of individually, and include measures of solution implementation and its effects in the community.

VI. CONCLUSIONS AND RECOMMENDATIONS

SPS has been conceptualized as a social-learning process and general coping strategy whose goal includes the discovery of effective behavior and the facilitation and maintenance of general social competence. As in any other research area in psychology, some terminological and conceptual confusion is apparent in the literature. Much of this confusion can be avoided by distinguishing clearly between (a) *problem solving* as a process of discovery, (b) *solution implementation* as the product of problem solving and a measure of problem-solving performance, and (c) *behavioral competence* as general coping behavior.

Most of the research on SPS with adults has been based on a model of the SPS process which includes the following five general skills or operations: (a) problem orientation or "problem-solving set," (b) problem definition and formulation, (c) generation of alternatives, including both strategy-level solution alternatives and specific step-by-step means,

(d) decision making, and (e) solution implementation and verification. These skills should *not* be viewed as five independent sets of specific cognitive abilities. Instead, each operation should be conceptualized as a different stage in the SPS process which has its own special purpose or function in facilitating problem-solving effectiveness and social competence. Empirical support for the important role of each of these operations comes from a number of SPS process studies as well as studies on the efficacy of specific cognitive–behavioral modification procedures. In fact, many of the elements in these stages are already well-established behavior-change procedures from other behavior therapy approaches.

Many studies have reported results supporting a relationship between SPS skills and psychopathology. The patient populations focused on in these studies have included psychiatric patients, "acting out" or impulsive adolescents, drug abusers, depressed counseling center clients, and depressed college students. There are several problems with these studies which limit the conclusions that can be drawn concerning SPS. First, most of the studies have focused on only one component of the SPS process—i.e., means–ends thinking as measured by the MEPS. Of the several possible elements of means–ends thinking that can be scored using the MEPS, most of the significant findings are based on only one element—i.e., relevant means. Second, the validity of the MEPS as a measure of SPS ability has been questioned (see also Butler & Meichenbaum, 1981). Third, most of the studies have focused on a severely disturbed hospitalized population; it should not be assumed that these findings can be generalized to other populations of less disturbed individuals, although the one study that involved depressed counseling center clients and introductory psychology students produced strong supporting results. Finally, the data are correlational; therefore, no conclusions are possible concerning a cause–effect relationship between SPS skills and psychopathology. Thus, while these findings are consistent with and supportive of the social-learning or social competence view of psychopathology, they cannot be considered as firm evidence for this conceptualization.

Several experimental analog studies have found that the perception of inability to solve specific experimental problems (i.e., the avoidance of aversive stimulation or the achievement of some desired outcome) can lead to "maladaptive" reactions such as anxiety, depression (i.e., "learned helplessness"), fixated or compulsive behavior, and increased blood pressure. Moreover, there is evidence that suggests that some of these reactions are likely to be most intense when the individual attributes his lack of control in the experimental situation to a deficit in *personal efficacy*. Although these findings help to strengthen the hypothesis that deficits in problem-solving skills might cause maladaptive emotional reactions and behavior, no conclusions can be drawn on the basis of these analog studies because of the possible limits on the generalizability of the findings to actual clinical disorders.

The two major approaches to the assessment of SPS are self-report or verbal assessment and observational (behavioral) assessment. Each approach has its own special problems which can reduce reliability and validity. Verbal assessment is necessary in SPS research because it is the only method that can directly assess cognitive problem-solving variables. Technical skills in developing self-report instruments can minimize potential problems and result in acceptable reliability and validity (see also Bellack & Hersen, 1977). The observational-assessment approach promises to increase validity by assessing problem-solving performance *in vivo* or in a simulated problem-solving situation which closely approximates real-life problem solving. However, the major problem with this approach to the study of SPS is that cognitive problem-solving variables cannot be directly assessed and it is not possible to distinguish adequately between problem-solving performance and other forms of behavioral competence. It is also difficult to assess and account for the possible effects on performance of variables such as performance-skill deficits, emotional factors, and motivational deficits. A promising alternative is an approach that combines verbal-assessment procedures with observational methods.

Outcome studies on SPS training have focused on the following patients and target behaviors: hospitalized psychiatric patients, substance abusers and addicts, depressed geriatric patients, stress and anxiety problems, academic underachievement, marital problems, general behavioral competence, and community problems. Taken together, these studies have produced very promising results supporting the efficacy of SPS training as a treatment approach, a treatment maintenance strategy, and a competence-enhancement program for individuals and groups which has implications for prevention. Although the overall results are encouraging, many of the studies have methodological problems which result in ambiguous findings and weak or limited conclusions, thus reducing their scientific value. The major problems are inadequate control groups or procedures, inadequate outcome measures, and failure to include follow-up evaluations.

The major control problem is the failure to account adequately for the possible effects of nonspecific factors associated with treatment. When a single treatment is being evaluated, it is necessary to include an attention-placebo group to control for these factors. Moreover, since nonspecific effects are often mediated by cognitive variables such as "faith" in the treatment or expectations of benefit, these expectations should also be assessed to ensure that they are equal in the treatment and attention-placebo groups (see Jacobson & Baucom, 1977). When the aim is to compare two or more specific treatments, it is not always necessary to include an attention-placebo group; however, it is still important to assess expectations of benefit to rule out the possibility that the superiority of one treatment over another might be due primarily to the fact that the treatment description and/or procedures generated greater expectations of benefit in the subjects.

With regard to inadequate outcome measures, some studies failed to include any measures of problem solving. Only a few studies included measures of both problem-solving ability *and* performance. Without these measures, it is not possible to determine whether or not the training program achieved its major purpose of improving problem-solving skills or problem-solving effectiveness. Some studies used problem-solving measures which focused on only one or two components of the problem-solving process (for example, generation-of-alternatives performance, decision-making effectiveness). In addition, most measures were developed for the particular study by the investigators without first evaluating their reliability and validity. Thus, there is a need for more comprehensive measures of problem solving which assess all the components of the process, and for more standardized measures for which data on reliability and validity are available.

A major weakness in some studies was a failure to include any measures of behavioral competence (i.e., coping behavior) or psychopathology. This inadequacy seriously limits the clinical significance of these studies. More studies are needed which obtain measures of behavioral competence and psychopathology *outside of the treatment setting* in order to evaluate the generalization of treatment effects to the real-life setting. There is also a need for more measures of *general* behavioral competence and *general* psychopathology to assess for possible *widespread* generalization effects, which would be important for prevention. A few studies included self-report measures of general social competence or personality adjustment, but no behavioral measures. A number of the studies failed to include follow-up evaluations; however, several of those which did found very promising results for the durability and maintenance of SPS training effects.

Although most of the studies are based upon D'Zurilla and Goldfried's (1971) SPS model, the studies are difficult to compare because different training methods have been used, different SPS skills have been emphasized, and some programs included certain components of the model while excluding others. In addition, some programs included training in solution-implementation skills in the program. This introduces a confounding in the study between the effects of SPS training and performance-skill training, which causes ambiguous results.

More studies are needed which focus on clinical problems such as stress and anxiety, depression, obsessive–compulsive disorders, and maladjustments involving personal–social inadequacy or incompetence. For example, Meichenbaum's stress-inoculation approach appears to be quite effective for the treatment of stress-related disorders (see Meichenbaum & Jaremko, 1982), but the problem-solving component has not yet been assessed for its specific contribution to the treatment outcome.

Finally, although the studies on competence-enhancement programs suggest that SPS training may play a useful role in prevention and community psychology, only one study to date has focused on a so-called "vulnerable" or "at-risk" population, and possible applications with community problem-solving groups are only beginning to be explored.

REFERENCES

Abramson, L. Y., Seligman, M. E. P., & Teasdale, J. D. Learned helplessness in humans: Critique and reformulation. *Journal of Abnormal Psychology*, 1978, **87**, 49–74.

Appel, P. W., & Kaestner, E. Interpersonal and emotional problem solving among narcotic drug abusers. *Journal of Consulting and Clinical Psychology*, 1979, **47**, 1125–1127.

Bandura, A. *Principles of behavior modification*. New York: Holt, 1969.

Bandura, A., Vicarious and self-reinforcement process. In R. Glasner (Ed.), *The nature of reinforcement*. New York: Academic Press, 1971.

Bandura, A. *Social learning theory*. New York: Prentice-Hall, 1977. (a)

Bandura, A. Self-efficacy: Toward a unifying theory of behavioral change. *Psychological Review*, 1977, **84**, 191–215. (b)

Beck, A. T. *Depression*. New York: Hoeber, 1967.

Beck, A. T. Cognitive therapy: Nature and relation to behavior therapy. *Behavior Therapy*, 1970, **1**, 184–200.

Bedell, J. R., Archer, R. P., & Marlowe, H. A., Jr. A description and evaluation of a problem solving skills training program. In D. Upper & S. M. Ross (Eds.), *Behavioral group therapy: An annual review*. Champaign, Illinois: Research Press, 1980.

Bellack, A. S., & Herson, M. Self-report inventories in behavioral assessment. In J. D. Cone & R. P. Hawkins (Eds.), *Behavioral assessment: New directions in clinical psychology*. New York: Brunner/Mazel, 1977.

Blechman, E. A., Olson, D. H. L., & Hellman, I. D. Stimulus control over family problem-solving behavior: The family contract game. *Behavior Therapy*, 1976, **7**, 686–692.

Bloom, B. S., & Broder, L. J. *Problem-solving processes of college students*. Chicago, Illinois: University of Chicago Press, 1950.

Briscoe, R. V., Hoffman, D. B., & Bailey, J. S. Behavioral community psychology: Training a community board to problem solve. *Journal of Applied Behavioral Analysis,* 1975, **8,** 157–168.

Butler, L., & Meichenbaum, D. The assessment of interpersonal problem-solving skills. In P. C. Kendall & S. D. Hollon (Eds.), *Assessment strategies for cognitive-behavioral interventions.* New York: Academic Press, 1981.

Chaney, E. F., O'Leary, M. R., & Marlatt, G. A. Skill training with alcoholics. *Journal of Consulting and Clinical Psychology,* 1978, **46,** 1092–1104.

Ciminero, A. R., Calhoun, K. S., & Adams, H. E. (Eds.), *Handbook of behavioral assessment.* New York: Wiley (Interscience), 1977.

Coché, E., & Douglass, A. A. Therapeutic effects of problems-solving training and play-reading groups. *Journal of Clinical Psychology,* 1977, **33,** 820–827.

Coché, E., & Flick, A. Problem solving training groups for hospitalized psychiatric patients. *Journal of Psychology,* 1975, **91,** 19–29.

Copemann, C. D. *Aversive counterconditioning and social training: A learning theory approach to drug rehabilitation.* Unpublished doctoral dissertation, State University of New York at Stony Brook, 1973.

Dixon, D. N., Heppner, P. P., Peterson, C. H., & Ronning, R. R. Problem-solving workshop training. *Journal of Counseling Psychology,* 1979, **26,** 133–139.

Doerfler, L. A., & Richards, C. S. Self-initiated attempts to cope with depression. *Cognitive Therapy and Research,* 1981, in press.

D'Zurilla, T. J., & Goldfried, M. R. Problem solving and behavior modification. *Journal of Abnormal Psychology,* 1971, **78,** 107–126.

D'Zurilla, T. J., & Nezu, A. A study of the generation-of-alternatives process in social problem solving. *Cognitive Therapy and Research,* 1980, **4,** 67–72.

Edelstein, B. A., Couture, E. T., Cray, M., Dickens, P., & Lusebrink, N. Group training of problem-solving with chronic psychiatric patients. In D. Upper & S. Ross (Eds.), *Behavioral group therapy: An annual review* (Vol. II). Champaign, Illinois: Research Press, 1980.

Ellis, A. *Reason and emotion in psychotherapy.* New York: Lyle Stuart, 1962.

Ellis, A. The basic clinic theory of rational-emotive therapy. In A. Ellis & R. Grieger (Eds.), *Handbook of rational-emotive therapy.* New York: Springer, 1977.

Ellis, A., & Grieger, R. (Eds.), *Handbook of rational-emotive therapy.* New York: Springer, 1977.

Gagné, R. M. Human problem solving: Internal and external events. In B. Kleinmuntz (Ed.), *Problem solving: Research, method and theory.* New York: Wiley, 1966.

Geer, J. H., Davison, G. C., & Gatchel, R. I. Reduction of stress in humans through nonveridical perceived control of aversive stimulation. *Journal of Personality and Social Psychology,* 1970, **30,** 30–43.

Glass, C., Gottman, J., & Shmurack, S. Response acquisition and cognitive self-statements modification approaches to dating skill training. *Journal of Counseling Psychology,* 1976, **23,** 520–526.

Goldfried, M. R. Psychotherapy as coping skills training. In M. J. Mahoney (Ed.), *Psychotherapy process: Current issues and future directions.* New York: Plenum, 1980.

Goldfried, M. R., & D'Zurilla, T. J. A behavior-analytic model for assessing competence. In C. D. Spielberger (Ed.), *Current topics in clinical and community psychology* (Vol. I). New York: Academic Press, 1969.

Gotlib, I. H., & Asarnow, R. F. Interpersonal and impersonal problem-solving skills in mildly and clinically depressed university students. *Journal of Consulting and Clinical Psychology,* 1979, **47,** 86–95.

Henshaw, D. A cognitive analysis of creative problem solving. Unpublished doctoral dissertation, University of Waterloo, 1978 (as described in Meichenbaum, Henshaw, & Himel, 1979).

Hiroto, D. S., & Seligman, M. E. P. Generality of learned helplessness in man. Journal of Personality and Social Psychology, 1975, 31, 311–327.

Hokanson, J. E., DeGood, D. E., Forrest, M. S., & Brittain, T. M. Availability of avoidance behaviors for modulating vascular-stress responses. Journal of Personality and Social Psychology, 1971, 19, 60–68.

Holroyd, K. A. Cognition and desensitization in the group treatment of test anxiety. Journal of Consulting and Clinical Psychology, 1976, 44, 991–1001.

Hussian, R. A., & Lawrence, P. S. Social reinforcement of activity and problem solving training in the treatment of depressed institutionalized elderly patients. Cognitive Therapy and Research, 1981, 5, 57–69.

Intagliatia, J. C. Increasing the interpersonal problem solving skills of an alcoholic population. Journal of Consulting and Clinical Psychology, 1978, 46, 489–498.

Jacobson, N. S. Training couples to solve their marital problems: A behavioral approach to relationship discord. Part I: Problem-solving skills. International Journal of Family Counseling, 1977, 5, 22–31. (a)

Jacobson, N. S. Problem solving and contingency contracting in the treatment of marital discord. Journal of Consulting and Clinical Psychology, 1977, 45, 92–100. (b)

Jacobson, N. S. The role of problem solving in behavioral marital therapy. Paper presented at the 11th Annual Association for Advancement of Behavior Therapy Convention, Atlanta, December 1977. (c)

Jacobson, N. S. Specific and nonspecific factors in the effectiveness of a behavioral approach to the treatment of marital discord. Journal of Consulting and Clinical Psychology, 1978, 46, 442–452.

Jacobson, N. S. Behavioral treatments for marital discord: A critical appraisal. In M. Hersen, R. M. Eisler, & P. M. Miller (Eds.), Progress in behavior modification. New York: Academic Press, 1981.

Jacobson, N. S., & Baucom, D. Design and assessment of nonspecific control groups in behavior modification research. Behavior Therapy, 1977, 8, 709–719.

Jannoun, L., Munby, M., Catalan, J., & Gelder, M. A home-based treatment program for agoraphobia: Replication and controlled evaluation. Behavior Therapy, 1980, 11, 294–305.

Jones, L. C. T. Frustration and stereotyped behavior in human subjects. Quarterly Journal of Experimental Psychology, 1954, 6, 12–20.

Kanfer, F. H. Self-regulation: Research, issues, and speculations. In C. Neuringer & J. L. Michael (Eds.), Behavior modification in clinical psychology. New York: Appleton, 1970.

Karol, R. L., & Richards, C. S. Making treatment effects last: An investigation of maintenance strategies for smoking reduction. Paper presented at the 12th Annual Association for Advancement of Behavior Therapy Convention, Chicago, November 1978.

Kendall, P. C., Pellegrini, D. S., & Urbain, E. S. Approaches to assessment for cognitive-behavioral interventions with children. In P. C. Kendall & S. D. Hollon (Eds.), Assessment strategies for cognitive-behavioral interventions. New York: Academic Press, 1981.

Kendall, P. C., Williams, L., Pechacek, T. F., Graham, L., Shisslak, C., & Herzoff, N. Cognitive-behavioral and patient education interventions in cardiac catheterization: The Palo Alto medical psychology project. Journal of Consulting and Clinical Psychology, 1979, 47, 49–58.

Krasnor, L. R., & Rubin, K. H. The assessment of social problem-solving skills in young children. In T. Merluzzi, C. Glass, & M. Genest (Eds.), *Cognitive assessment*. New York: Guilford, 1981.

Mahoney, M., & Avener, M. Psychology of the elite athlete: An exploratory study. *Cognitive Therapy and Research*, 1977, **1**, 135–142.

Marquart, D. I., & Arnold, L. P. A study in the frustration of human adults. *Journal of General Psychology*, 1952, **47**, 43–63.

Mather, M. D. Obsessions and compulsions. In C. G. Costello (Ed.), *Symptoms of psychopathology*. New York: Wiley, 1970.

Meadow, A., & Parnes, S. J. Evaluation of training in creative problem-solving. *Journal of Applied Psychology*, 1959, **43**, 189–194.

Meichenbaum, D. Enhancing creativity by modifying what subjects say to themselves. *American Educational Research Journal*, 1975, **12**, 129–145.

Meichenbaum, D. H. *Cognitive behavior modification: An integrative approach*. New York: Plenum, 1977.

Meichenbaum, D., & Cameron, R. Training schizophrenics to talk to themselves: A means of developing attentional controls. *Behavior Therapy*, 1973, **4**, 515–534.

Meichenbaum, D., & Jaremko, M. (Eds.). *Stress prevention and treatment*. New York, Plenum, 1982, in press.

Meichenbaum, D., Gilmore, J., & Fedoravicius, A. Group insight vs. group desensitization in treating speech anxiety. *Journal of Consulting and Clinical Psychology*, 1971, **36**, 410–421.

Meichenbaum, D., Henshaw, D., & Himel, N. Coping with stress as a problem-solving process. In W. Krohne & L. Laux (Eds.), *Achievement stress and anxiety*. Washington, D. C.: Hemisphere Pub., 1979.

Meichenbaum, D., & Novaco, R. Stress-inoculation: A preventative approach. In C. Spielberger & I. Sarason (Eds.), *Stress and anxiety* (Vol. 5). New York: Halstead, 1977.

Mendonca, J. D., & Siess, T. F. Counseling for indecisiveness: Problem solving and anxiety management training. *Journal of Counseling Psychology*, 1976, **23**, 339–347.

Nezu, A., & D'Zurilla, T. J. An experimental evaluation of the decision-making process in social problem solving. *Cognitive Therapy and Research*, 1979, **3**, 269–277.

Nezu, A., & D'Zurilla, T. J. Effects of problem definition and formulation on decision making in the social problem-solving process. *Behavior Therapy*, 1981, **12**, 100–106. (a)

Nezu, A., & D'Zurilla, T. J. Effects of problem definition and formulation on the generation of alternatives in the social problem-solving process. *Cognitive Therapy and Research*, 1981, **5**, 265–271. (b)

Novaco, R. *Anger control: The development and evaluation of an experimental treatment*. Lexington, Massachusetts: Health, 1975.

O'Leary, K. D., & Turkewitz, H. Marital therapy from a behavioral perspective. In T. J. Paolino & B. S. McCrady (Eds.), *Marriage and marital therapy: Psychoanalytic, behavioral, and systems theory perspectives*. New York: Brunner/Mazel, 1978.

O'Leary, K. D., & Wilson, G. T. *Principles of behavior therapy*. New York: Prentice-Hall, 1980.

Osborn, A. F. *Applied imagination: Principles and procedures of creative problem-solving* (3rd ed.). New York: Scribner, 1963.

Parnes, S. J. The creative problem solving course and institute at the University of Buffalo. In S. J. Parnes & H. F. Harding (Eds.), *A source book for creative thinking*. New York: Scribner, 1962.

Parnes, S. J. *Creative behavior guidebook.* New York: Scribner, 1967.

Parnes, S. J., & Meadow, A. Evaluation of persistence of effect produced by a creative problem-solving course. *Psychological Reports,* 1960, **7,** 357–361.

Perri, M. G., Richards, C. S., & Schulthesis, K. R. Behavioral self-control and smoking reduction: A study of self-initiated attempts to reduce smoking. *Behavior Therapy,* 1977, **8,** 360–365.

Phillips, E. L. *The social skills basis of psychopathology: Alternatives to abnormal psychology and psychiatry.* New York: Grune & Stratton, 1978.

Platt, J. J., Scura, W. C., & Hannon, J. R. Problem-solving thinking of youthful incarcerated heroin addicts. *Journal of Community Psychology,* 1973, **1,** 278–281.

Platt, J. J., & Siegel, J. M. MMPI characteristics of good and poor social problem solvers among psychiatric patients. *Journal of Community Psychology,* 1976, **94,** 245–251.

Platt, J. J., Siegel, J. M., & Spivack, G. Do psychiatric patients and normals see the same solutions as effective in solving interpersonal problems? *Journal of Consulting and Clinical Psychology,* 1975, **43,** 279.

Platt, J. J., & Spivack, G. Problem solving thinking of psychiatric patients. *Journal of Consulting and Clinical Psychology,* 1972, **39,** 148–151. (a)

Platt, J. J., & Spivack, G. Social competence and effective problem solving in psychiatric patients. *Journal of Clinical Psychology,* 1972, **28,** 3–5. (b)

Platt, J. J., & Spivack, G. Studies in problem-solving thinking of psychiatric patients: Patient-control differences and factorial structure of problem-solving thinking. In *Proceedings, 81st Annual Convention of the American Psychology Association,* 1973, **8,** 461–462.

Platt, J. J., & Spivack, G. Means of solving real-life problems: I. Psychiatric patients versus controls, and cross-cultural comparisons of normal females. *Journal of Community Psychology,* 1974, **2,** 45–48.

Platt, J. J., & Spivack, G. *Manual for the means-ends problem-solving procedure (MEPS): A measure of interpersonal cognitive problem-solving skills.* Hahnemann Community Mental Health/Mental Retardation Center, Philadelphia, January 1975.

Platt, J. J., Spivack, G., Altman, N., Altman, D., & Peizer, S. B. Adolescent problem solving thinking. *Journal of Consulting and Clinical Psychology,* 1974, **42,** 787–793.

Richards, C. S., & Perri, M. G. Do self-control treatments last? An evaluation of behavioral problem solving and faded counselor contact as treatment maintenance strategies. *Journal of Counseling Psychology,* 1978, **25,** 376–383.

Rimm, D. C., & Masters, J. C. *Behavior therapy: Techniques and empirical findings* (2nd ed.). New York: Academic Press, 1979.

Robin, A. L., Kent, R., O'Leary, K. D., Foster, S., & Prinz, R. An approach to teaching parents and adolescents problem-solving communication skills: A preliminary report. *Behavior Therapy,* 1977, **8,** 639–643.

Schwartz, R., & Gottman, J. Toward a task analysis of assertive behavior. *Journal of Consulting and Clinical Psychology,* 1976, **44,** 910–920.

Siegel, J. M., & Platt, J. J. Emotional and social real-life problem-solving thinking in adolescent and adult psychiatric patients. *Journal of Clinical Psychology,* 1976, **32,** 230–232.

Siegel, J. M., & Spivack, G. Problem-solving therapy: The description of a new program for chronic psychiatric patients. *Psychotherapy: Theory, Research and Practice,* 1976, **13,** 368–373. (a)

Siegel, J. M., & Spivack, G. A new therapy program for chronic patients. *Behavior Therapy,* 1976, **7,** 129–130. (b)

Siegel, J. M., Platt, J. J., & Spivack, G. Means of solving real-life problems: II. Do professionals and laymen see the same solutions as effective in solving problems? *Journal of Community Psychology*, 1974, **2**, 49–50.

Spivack, G., & Levine, M. *Self-regulation in acting-out and normal adolescents*. Research Report M-4531, National Institute of Health, Washington, D. C., 1963.

Spivack, G., & Shure, M. B. *Social adjustment of young children*. San Francisco, California, Jossey-Bass, 1974.

Spivack, G., Platt, J. J., & Shure, M. B. *The problem-solving approach to adjustment*. San Francisco, California: Jossey-Bass, 1976.

Staub, E., Tursky, B., & Schwartz, G. E. Self-control and predictability: Their effects on reactions to aversive stimulation. *Journal of Personality and Social Psychology*, 1971, **18**, 157–162.

Toseland, R. A problem-solving group workshop for older persons. *Social Work*, 1977, **22**, 325–326.

Urbain, E. S., & Kendall, P. C. Review of social-cognitive problem-solving interventions with children. *Psychological Bulletin*, 1980, **88**, 109–143.

Weiss, R. L., Hops, H., & Patterson, G. R. A framework for conceptualizing marital conflict. In L. S. Hamerlynck, L. C. Handy, & E. J. Mash (Eds.), *Behavior change: Methodology, concepts, and practice*. Champaign, Illinois: Research Press, 1973.

A Cognitive–Behavioral Approach to Recurrent Tension and Migraine Headache

KENNETH A. HOLROYD[1]

Stress and Coping Project,
University of California,
Berkeley, California

FRANK ANDRASIK

Department of Psychology,
State University of New York,
Albany, New York

[1] Present address: Department of Psychology, Ohio University, Athens, Ohio 45701.

ADVANCES IN COGNITIVE-BEHAVIORAL RESEARCH
AND THERAPY, VOLUME 1

I. INTRODUCTION

Headache may be the most common medical complaint. Survey data indicate 50 to 70% of all people experience headaches at some point (Andrasik, Holroyd, & Abell, 1979; Hurley, 1969; Kashiwagi, McClure, & Wetzel, 1972; Lance & Anthony, 1971; Waters & O'Connor, 1975) with 10 to 12% of these individuals seeking medical help for their headaches (Hurley, 1969). The overwhelming majority of headache complaints are diagnosed as either tension or migraine headache. Thus, a survey of 1152 patients attending a specialized headache clinic revealed that 94% of clinic patients were diagnosed as suffering from tension and/or migraine headache (Lance, Curran, & Anthony, 1965). In a less selected population tension and migraine headache probably account for an even larger proportion of headache complaints.

Considerable research effort has been devoted to headache because it is so pervasive. Until recently, however, investigations of headache were limited in number and focus and were conducted chiefly by members of the medical profession. In the early 1970s scattered reports of the successful application of biofeedback treatments for migraine and tension headache appeared in the literature, paving the way for a host of investigations of psychologically based treatments to follow and renewing interest in investigations of mechanisms of headache. Accumulated research findings now have considerably advanced our understanding of headache and have challenged a number of accepted notions about causes of headache and the procedures used in its treatment. The present article discusses these important findings from a cognitive–behavioral perspective.

II. DEMOGRAPHICS

Tension and migraine headaches are associated with similar demographic characteristics. Approximately 75% of adult tension and migraine headache sufferers are women (Friedman, Von Storch, & Merritt,

1954; Lance & Anthony, 1966; Olesen, 1978), although among children under the age of 10 years slightly more than half the headache sufferers are male (Prensky, 1976). Recurrent headache appears before the age of 40 in more than 90% of sufferers, and may appear prior to age 5 in as many as 25% of headache sufferers (Friedman et al., 1954; Selby & Lance, 1960). Tension and migraine headache do not appear to be related to social class, race, education, or intelligence (Friedman et al., 1954; Waters, 1971; Markush, Karp, Heyman, & O'Fallon, 1975).

III. SYMPTOMS

Descriptions of tension and migraine headache symptoms have been provided by the American Medical Association's Ad Hoc Committee on the Classification of Headache (1962) and the World Federation of Neurology's Research Group on Migraine and Headache (1969).

Tension headache is described by the Ad Hoc Committee (1962) as an "ache or sensation of tightness, pressure or constriction, widely varied in intensity, frequency and duration, sometimes long-lasting and commonly sub-occipital" (p. 128). A prototypic tension headache is characterized by persistent bilateral pain that is vise- or bandlike, dull and drawing, and slow in onset and resolution. These or similar symptoms will be diagnosed as tension headache when migrainous features (see below) are not reported, headaches are not associated with climate changes, allergies, or sinus problems, and there is no evidence of underlying organic involvement. The most reliable factor differentiating tension and migraine headache is said to be frequency of occurrence, with tension headache usually occurring more than twice a week and migraine usually occurring less frequently (e.g., Kudrow, 1978). However, because tension headaches tend to be less severe than migraine, this may be an artifact of severity; tension headache sufferers may simply not seek treatment unless headaches occur more than twice a week.

Migraine headache is characterized by the Ad Hoc Committee (1962) as "recurrent attacks of headache, widely varied in intensity, frequency and duration. The attacks are commonly unilateral in onset; are usually associated with anorexia and, sometimes, with nausea and vomiting; in some are preceded by, or associated with, conspicuous sensory, motor, and mood disturbances; and are often familial" (p. 127). When headache is accompanied by "sharply defined, transient visual, and other sensory or motor prodromes or both" it is termed classic migraine. Common migraine, which occurs more frequently, is "without striking prodromes and less often unilateral."

Migraine onset may be sudden or occur gradually over the course of an hour or two. Pain tends to be dull, deep, and steady when the headache is relatively mild, but becomes throbbing or pulsatile when the pain is severe. Anorexia and nausea are the most frequent symptoms accompanying migraine and are reported by as many as 90% of migraine sufferers, with vomiting, photophobia, and blurred vision also common (Lance & Anthony, 1966; Selby & Lance, 1960). Striking visual disturbances such as the appearance of moving shapes or colors or partial or total blindness are reported by about 40% of migraine sufferers (Hachinski, Porchawka, & Steele, 1973), and paresthesias such as prickling of the hands and feet or muscle weakness are reported by about 30% of migraine sufferers (Heyck, 1974).

Qualitative vs Quantitative Symptom Differences

The reports of the Ad Hoc Committee and World Federation of Neurology reflect the belief that tension and migraine headache are associated with qualitatively different symptoms. Recent research, however, has begun to question this widely accepted belief. For example, Thompson, Haber, Figueroa, and Adams (1980) found that if chronic headache sufferers were asked about all the headache symptoms they experienced, not just their typical headache symptoms, both tension and migraine headache sufferers reported the same vascular symptoms. However, individuals with less severe headache problems, who tended to be diagnosed as tension headache sufferers, reported experiencing vascular symptoms less frequently than individuals with more severe headache problems. These findings and results from other studies (e.g., Bakal & Kaganov, 1977, 1979; Phillips, 1977; Phillips & Hunter, 1980) suggest that vascular symptoms may be associated with increasingly severe headaches in both tension and migraine headache sufferers.

Not only are severe tension headaches likely to be accompanied by vascular symptoms but many vascular headaches appear to be symptomatically indistinguishable from tension headaches. For example, about 50% of migraine sufferers report, in addition to their clear-cut migraine headaches, headaches that are too diffuse to be characterized as migraine (Oleson, 1978). However, similar vascular processes probably underlie both types of headache since both are equally responsive to vasoactive migraine medication (Barrie, Fox, Weatherall, & Wilkinson, 1968). Many vascular headaches may thus have symptom features that are virtually indistinguishable from tension headaches.

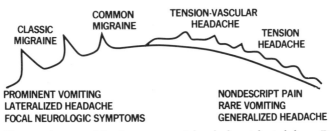

Fig. 1. The continuum of benign recurrent headache. Adapted from Raskin and Appenzeller (1980); reprinted with permission of W. B. Saunders, Philadelphia.

These findings suggest that differences between tension and migraine headache symptoms may be quantitative rather than qualitative (Bakal & Kaganov, 1977). According to this view tension and migraine headache are located at different points along a continuum of severity (see Fig. 1). The headaches of any given individual are likely to cluster around a particular point on the severity continuum resulting in a diagnosis of tension, migraine, or mixed headache. However, most individuals will also occasionally experience headaches at widely divergent points on the continuum.

IV. PATHOPHYSIOLOGY

The dominant model of the pathogenesis of *tension headache* attributes head pain to the "sustained contraction of skeletal muscles" usually occurring "as part of the individual's reaction during life stress" (Ad Hoc Committee on Classification of Headache, 1962, p. 128). Head pain is assumed to result from (a) the stimulation of pain receptors in the contracted muscles and (b) ischemia resulting from the compression of intramuscular arterioles (Haynes, 1980).

Migraine headache is thought to be primarily of vascular origin, with vasoconstriction in both the extra- and intracranial arteries occurring during the prodromal phase and vasodilation occurring during the pain associated with the migraine attack (Adams, Feuerstein, & Fowler, 1980). During vasoconstriction regional blood flow may be reduced by as much as 50% (Hachinski, Olesen, Morris, Larsen, Enevaldsen, & Lassen, 1977). The resulting focal cerebral ischemia is assumed to produce the altered sensory experiences or "aura" that frequently precede or accompany migraine. During vasodilation pain is positively correlated with pulse amplitude in extracranial arteries (Graham & Wolff, 1938; Sakai & Meyer, 1978) suggesting that vasodilation and head pain are intimately related. However, the fact that stimuli which induce vasodilation (e.g., hot bath, exercise) do not necessarily induce headache suggests that factors other than extra-cranial vasodilation are involved as well. It is likely that intracranial vasodilation is also involved in producing pain (Raskin & Appenzeller, 1980), although this has been difficult to document because intra-cranial vasodilation is also a response to pain (Ingvar, 1976).

A. Quantitative vs Qualitative Differences in Pathophysiology

There is little evidence to support the belief that tension headaches are of muscle-contraction origin and migraine headaches of vascular origin. Tension headache sufferers do not show higher resting levels of muscle activity or greater increases in muscle activity or response to stress than do migraine sufferers (Anderson & Franks, 1981; Bakal & Kaganov, 1977; Gannon, Haynes, Safranek, & Hamilton, 1981; Martin & Mathews, 1978; Philips, 1978; Philips & Hunter, 1980; Pozniak-Patewicz, 1976). In fact, the observation that muscle contraction is a common prodromal symptom of migraine (Pearce, 1977) raises the possibility that muscle contraction responses observed in both tension and migraine headache sufferers are secondary to vascular alterations and ischemia.

Moreover, because research on migraine seldom includes tension headache sufferers as a control group there is little evidence to indicate that the vascular and biochemical alterations associated with migraine do not also occur during tension headache. There is, however, some evidence to the contrary. Vasoconstriction, including constriction of the extracranial arteries, is associated with tension as well as migraine headache (Ostfeld, Reis, & Wolff, 1957; Tunis & Wolf, 1954). Other alterations in cerebral circulation observed during migraine can also be seen during some tension headaches (Sakai & Meyer, 1978), and at least some of the biochemical findings associated with migraine (e.g., low platelet serotonin levels) have been observed in tension headache sufferers as well (Rolf, Wiele, & Brune, 1977). Although it is commonly assumed that certain vasoactive drugs, such as ergot-amine preparations, are differentially effective with tension and mi-graine headache, there is no convincing evidence to support this belief (Barrie et al., 1968; Lance & Curran, 1964; Raskin & Appenzeller, 1980). These findings suggest that tension and migraine headache may be quantitatively different manifestations of the same underlying phys-iological mechanism. Furthermore, it appears likely that this under-lying mechanism involves vasomotor instability.

B. Mechanism of Vascular Instability

The physiological mechanism producing vascular instability associated with recurrent headache remains obscure. The release and subsequent depletion of vasoactive substances which produce a passive distension of the arterial wall and reduced pain threshold appear to play an important role (Fanchamps, 1974). Raskin and Appenzeller (1980) suggest that the modulation of serotonin at the central level (altered reactivity of brain stem serotonergic neurons) and at the peripheral level (regulation of the synaptic turnover of serotonin) is a crucial factor in pathogenesis of recurrent tension and migraine headaches. Serotonin is of particular interest because its actions on blood vessels (both vasoconstriction and vasodilation) parallel the vascular changes observed during migraine, and because serotonin has been implicated as an inhibitory transmitter in the brain stem pain-modulating system. The observation that drugs effective with migraine also act to depress the activity of brain stem serotonergic neurons is also consistent with this hypothesis.

V. HEADACHE PRECIPITANTS

A. Stress

Tension headache typically occurs in conjunction with life stress. For example, a recent multicenter study concluded that "emotional or situational" precipitants were of primary importance in 77% of 1420 carefully diagnosed tension headache sufferers (Friedman, 1979). There is no evidence, however, that tension headache sufferers are exposed to more severe stress than headache-free individuals. Thus, Andrasik, Blanchard, Arena, Teders, Teevan, and Rodichok (1981) found that tension headache sufferers and matched headache-free controls reported no differential exposure to stressful life events on the Social Readjustment Rating Scale (Holmes & Rahe, 1967). For the most part, tension headaches appear to be precipitated by everyday stresses that may be encountered by most people. For example, Howarth (1965) reported that, in 27.7% of his sample, headache appeared to be precipitated by domestic or social problems, and by problems at work in 19.4%.

It is less commonly known that stress is the most frequent precipitant of migraine (Henryk-Gutt & Rees, 1973; Selby & Lance, 1960). Yet, it is frequently observed that migraine tends to occur not at the peak of stress, but during a period of relaxation immediately following stress, for example, on April 16 for tax accountants and at the end of the school year for teachers. Data collected by Henryk-Gutt and Rees (1973) from a sample of migraine sufferers over a 2-month period revealed that over half of the reported headache attacks were associated with stressful events. Again, migraine sufferers do not report increased exposure to stressful life events when compared to headache-free controls (Andrasik et al., 1981). Exposure to laboratory stress has also been reported to precipitate migraine (Marcussen, 1950).

B. Other Precipitants

Migraine symptoms can also be precipitated by a wide range of stimuli that are not directly stress related (see Table I). The diversity of stimuli that can precipitate headache suggests that susceptible individuals may be characterized by a lowered biologic threshold to multiple external and internal stimuli (Raskin & Appenzeller, 1980). In spite of the diversity of stimuli that have been observed to precipitate headache only a small proportion of an individual's recurrent headaches are likely to be associated with the precipitants such as those in Table I (Gomersall & Stuart, 1973; Medina & Diamond, 1978).

Even when precipitants can be identified they tend to be variable in their effects, often provoking headaches following fewer than half the exposures. This suggests that precipitants must interact with other factors influencing vasomotor regulatory processes to produce headache.

VI. MAINTAINING VS PRECIPITATING FACTORS

Headaches that initially appear in clear association with life stresses may, as they become more severe, increasingly occur independently of observable precipitants. In an attempt to explain this observation Bakal and Kaganov (1979) have suggested that one consequence of recurrent headache is that physiological mechanisms underlying headache attacks may increasingly become autonomous of their original precipitants. Thus by the time headaches occur on a daily basis, fluctuations in vasomotor regulatory processes which largely occur independently of their previous precipitants may maintain headache symptoms.

Headache complaints can also be maintained by their environmental consequences (Fordyce, 1976). Headache symptoms may legitimize the avoidance of unpleasant activities or elicit sympathetic communications from the social environment. These reinforcements may maintain symptom reports or impede effective problem solving necessary to

TABLE I
Factors Precipitating Headache[a]

Common precipitants	Less common precipitants
Dietary tyramine, nitrite	Drugs (e.g., reserpine,
Glutamate, salt	histamine)
Oral contraceptives	Allergic reactions
Menstruation	Humidity
Hunger	Excessive vitamin A
Lack of sleep	Excessive sleep
Bright light, glare	Environmental chemicals
Alcohol	(e.g., ozone)
	Physical exhaustion

[a] Adapted from Raskin and Appenzeller (1980). Reprinted with permission of W. B. Saunders, Philadelphia.

control symptoms. Martin (1972) claimed to find evidence that such secondary gains were maintaining headache complaints in 56% of a sample of 100 headache sufferers. However, our experience as well as that of others (Haynes, 1980) has been that reinforcements for headache complaints are only likely to be of significance for a small minority of recurrent headache sufferers.

VII. VULNERABILITY FACTORS

A. Genetic Predisposition

The high incidence of recurrent headache in close blood relatives of both tension and migraine headache sufferers (often up to 70%) suggests that predisposition to headache may be transmitted genetically (Bakal & Kaganov, 1977; Dalsgaard-Nielsen, 1965; Friedman et al., 1954; Lance & Anthony, 1966; Ziegler, 1978). In their review Raskin and Appenzeller (1980) conclude that existing evidence is consistent with the hypothesis that a predisposition to vasomotor instability is transmitted via autosomal dominant heredity with incomplete penetrance. Unfortunately, at present there is no reliable method of assessing this predisposition.

B. Psychological Predisposition

Efforts to identify psychological characteristics that render individuals vulnerable to recurrent headache have focused on the assessment

of personality traits or unconscious conflicts, and have been guided
by the hypothesis that headache is an expression of intrapsychic conflict or a consequence of psychological disturbance (Friedman, 1979;
Martin, 1966; Philips, 1976; Wolff, 1963). However, because psychological variables typically have not been assessed prior to the onset
of headache symptoms, personality characteristics of headache sufferers may be consequences of living with recurrent pain, rather than
characteristics that predispose to headache. For example, in his review
Harrison (1975) concluded that chronic headache tended to be associated with high levels of neuroticism and elevated hypochondriasis,
hysteria, and depression scores on the MMPI. However, similar personality characteristics are associated with other chronic pain problems (Bond, 1976) and appear to be modifiable by medical interventions which successfully reduce or eliminate pain (Sternbach &
Timmermans, 1975). Thus these personality correlates may be consequences of chronic pain.

Depression and headache have a strong association. Not only are
recurrent headache sufferers frequently depressed, but headache is the
most frequent somatic symptom of depression occurring in over 50%
of depressed patients (Barolin, 1976; Cassidy, 1957; Dalessio, 1968;
Davis, Wetzel, Kashiwagi, & McClure, 1976; Kudrow, 1976; Ziegler,
Rhodes, & Hassanein, 1978). Obviously depression may be a consequence of recurrent headache in the same way that depression may
be a consequence of other chronic pain problems. It is also possible
that depression increases vulnerability to headache (Ziegler, 1978).
Although there is no hard evidence to support this contention, the
observation that depression may precede the onset of headache (Luborsky, Docherty, & Penick, 1973), and the fact that a significant number of individuals are troubled with headache symptoms only when
depressed, suggest that depression may increase vulnerability through
mechanisms that are not well understood at this time.

There has been virtually no research on the relationship between
efforts to manage or cope with stress in the naturalistic environment
and the frequency and patterning of headache symptoms. However,
a large body of research suggests that the way an individual copes
with stress can influence not only physiological stress responses but
also the onset and course of symptoms (Holroyd, 1979; Holroyd, Appel,
& Andrasik, 1982; Lazarus, 1966, 1982). Efforts to manage the stresses
that precipitate headache and to control the distress and pain of headache attacks may, therefore, influence the occurrence and patterning
of symptoms in important ways. Indirect support for this contention
is provided by evidence that therapeutic interventions designed to

alter the way headache sufferers cope with stress can successfully reduce headache symptoms (to be reviewed below). At this point we do not know if there are certain ways of coping with stress that render individuals vulnerable to headache attacks.

The major factors influencing headache are integrated in Fig. 2. Unlike medical accounts of headache, which often conceptually isolate physiological and psychological variables and assign physiological variables a preeminent causal role in headache, this model conceptualizes headache as what Bakal and Kaganov (1979) have termed a psychobiological phenomenon. Headache is seen as a function of reciprocally interacting psychological and physiological processes with neither psychological nor physiological variables assumed a priori to have preeminent causal status. This formulation suggests that therapeutic interventions which produce alterations in the psychological antecedents and correlates of headache will not only indirectly influence underlying physiological processes but also directly alter headache. In the sections to follow, we review the relevant treatment literature, bearing in mind these principal factors contributing to headache. Before doing this, however, it will be helpful to discuss headache assessment briefly.

VIII. ASSESSMENT OF THE HEADACHE CLIENT

The headache history is the primary basis for distinguishing migraine and tension headache from other types of headache. In this context, history taking serves two primary functions. The first is to begin to rule out headache as a consequence of trauma, significant psychopathology (such as depression, delusional, conversional, or hypochondriacal states), nasal vasomotor reactions, underlying disease processes, neurological or structural defects, or other organic involvement (such as circulatory insufficiency, hypoglycemia, or hypercapnia). The second focus of the history is to ascertain information for treatment planning and to quantify the patient's level of discomfort so that his/her treatment course can be meaningfully evaluated. Diamond and Dalessio (1978) and Lance (1978) provide comprehensive descriptions of the headache history, outlines or frameworks for organizing the information obtained, and illustrative examples.

In addition to the headache history, it is important to conduct a basic physical and neurologic examination, giving special attention to the head and nervous system, and to perform associated laboratory tests. Additional diagnostic procedures are reserved for difficult cases

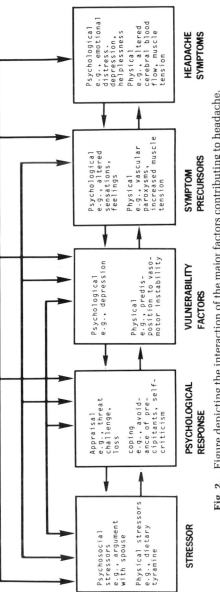

Fig. 2. Figure depicting the interaction of the major factors contributing to headache.

and are introduced in their order of invasiveness, beginning with procedures such as skull series, electroencephalogram, and computerized
axial tomography and continuing to the more invasive procedures,
such as ventriculography, angiography, and pneumoencephalography.
Lance (1978) reports that the more long standing the headache, the
less the need for additional evaluative procedures since, generally,
headaches with a duration of 5 or more years are most likely to be
migraine or tension and without underlying organic complications.

The headache history has been the primary method of collecting
information relevant to the differential diagnosis of tension and migraine headache. Although this differential diagnosis can be done reliably (Blanchard, O'Keefe, Neff, Jurish, & Andrasik, 1981), it does
not appear to correspond to headache syndromes with different pathophysiologies and symptom pictures as had previously been assumed.
Other evidence (to be reviewed below) further suggests that the global
categories of migraine and tension headache may be of little utility
in planning treatment. However, certain specific features of headache,
such as the intensity and temporal course of the pain (Bakal, Demjen,
& Kaganov, 1981; Blanchard, Andrasik, Neff, Teders, Pallmeyer, &
Rodichok, 1981b), do appear to have a bearing on treatment. We would
encourage clinicians and researchers to employ quantitative measures
of these specific features of headache in addition to or in place of the
more global classifications of tension and migraine headache.

IX. PHARMACOLOGICAL TREATMENT OF RECURRENT HEADACHE

Pharmacological agents, long utilized in the management of chronic
headache, are intended to serve (a) prophylactic functions (i.e., administered for the purpose of preventing the onset of a headache), (b)
abortive functions (i.e., administered for the purpose of interrupting
a headache cycle once it has begun), and (c) palliative functions (i.e.,
administered for the purpose of reducing the pain or discomfort experienced by the sufferer during a headache attack). A wide variety
of medications have been used with many of these agents serving
multiple functions. Pharmacological agents are selected specific to the
presumed physiologic etiology of migraine and tension headache.
Thus, medications administered to migraine sufferers are chiefly designed to counteract vasodilation of extracranial arteries and arterioles
during the headache phase and/or to block the action of humoral

mediators implicated in the migraine cycle, such as serotonin and histamine.

Prophylactic agents are reserved for those migraineurs troubled by frequent attacks (three or more per month) and consist of daily oral administrations of ergot alkaloids or derivatives, most commonly ergotamine tartrate (Gynergen) and methysergide maleate (Deseril, Sansert), which are reported to be effective with from 40 to 100% of patients (Barrie et al., 1968; Curran & Lance, 1964; Curran, Hinterberger, & Lance, 1967). Other prophylactic agents include antihistamines (Sandomigrain, Periactin), hypotensive agents (Catapress, Dixarit), β-adrenergic blockers (Inderol), antidepressants of the tricyclic type (Elavil, Endep) or the MAO inhibitor type (Nardil, Marplan), and anticonvulsants (Tegretol) (Anthony & Lance, 1969; Couch, Ziegler, & Hassanein, 1976; Diamond & Franklin, 1976; Forssman, Henriksson, Johannson, Lindvall, & Lundin, 1976; Stensrud & Sjaastad, 1976). Ergot derivatives and related formulations are most commonly utilized to abort the acute attack of migraine and may be taken by routes other than oral for those experiencing vomiting. Commonly utilized medications include ergotamine alone (Gynergen, Ergomar, Ergostat, Lingraine, Femergin) or ergotamine combined with caffeine, antispasmodics, antiemetics, and/or sedatives (Cafergot, Cafergot-PB, Wigraine, Migral, Ergodryl). All are administered at onset, may be repeated for a limited number of times at varying intervals, and are reportedly effective with a majority of patients, reducing durations of attack by as much as 80–90% (Saper, 1978; Selby & Lance, 1960). Individuals whose headaches are not successfully alleviated by the preceding medications are frequently treated symptomatically with analgesics (from aspirin to opiates), sedatives, and/or antiemetics. Intramuscular injections of steroids are sometimes successful for alleviating the sterile inflammation around the enlarged vessel which occurs during a migraine of long duration (Diamond & Dalessio, 1978).

Prophylactic treatments for tension headache are designed either to alleviate depression presumed to underlie the headache or to relax the affected musculature (Diamond & Dalessio, 1978; Lance, 1978; Martin, 1972). A variety of tricyclic and MAO-inhibiting antidepressants are used with tension headache sufferers. Tricyclics are thought to have an analgesic effect as well when used with headache sufferers (Diamond & Dalessio, 1978). Interestingly, antidepressants appear to produce similar outcomes whether or not the headache sufferer has any symptoms of depression (Lance & Curran, 1964). Thus, the benefits of antidepressant therapy may result from alterations in serotonergic activity and metabolism induced by these drugs and not from the alleviation of depressive symptoms. The more typical treatment involves palliative agents, ranging from self-prescribed over-the-counter drugs such as aspirin and acetaminophen to opiates and/or sedative–hypnotics (Diamond & Dalessio, 1978).

Reviews of the pharmacological treatment literature suggest that the aforementioned medications are effective with a majority of patients (e.g., Lance, 1978; Raskin & Appenzeller, 1980; Saper, 1978). Although often effective, pharmacologic treatments are not without costs (Diamond & Dalessio, 1978; Lance, 1978). For example, a host of side effects have been noted with ergot use: most common among these are nausea, epigastric distress, diarrhea, drowsiness, paresthesias, and cramping of the extremities; less common effects are insomnia, depression, sensations of swelling in the face, and weight gain. Many of these side effects pass with continued use. Chronic ergot use can, however, lead to ergot poisoning or ergotism, a condition resulting from damage to the endothelium of the capillaries and small blood vessels. In severe cases, gangrene may ensue (Diamond & Dalessio, 1978). The most serious side effects have been attributed to methysergide and concern the development of retroperitoneal, pleural, and cardiac valvular fibrosis, which are assumed to be due to this drug's serotonin-like effects (Graham, 1967). To prevent the deleterious effects of chronic methysergide use, practitioners regularly discontinue it for periods of several weeks occurring at intervals of 4 to 6 months. Other medications have their attendant side effects, as well as dietary restrictions in the case of MAO inhibitors.

Pharmacological vs Psychological Management

One research team has recently compared a pharmacological approach to a psychological approach in the treatment of severely distressed tension headache sufferers (Bruhn, Olesen, & Melgaard, 1979). Most of the patients included in this investigation had received previous physical therapy and paramedical treatments; all had received previous medical management. Of the 28 subjects entering the study, 5 dropped out for various reasons. Subjects were assigned to EMG biofeedback training or to the "most suitable alternative" medical/pharmacological treatment. Biofeedback participants received 16 treatment sessions designed to reduce forehead muscle tension levels (and tension levels in other muscle groups for a small number of individuals) plus 30 minutes of daily home relaxation practice. The alternative treatments were individualized and consisted of physical therapy, medication (analgesics, sedatives, antidepressants, or muscle relaxants), or combinations of both. Biofeedback participants alone displayed significant improvement on the various outcome measures (headache intensity, headache duration, headache index, and drug intake). Independent evaluations by referring neurologists, who were unaware of treatment assignment, were consistent with the above. Furthermore, improvements noted by biofeedback participants were maintained throughout the 3-month follow-up period.

An additional aspect of the preceding study requires mention. Bruhn et al. (1979) had subjects in the medical treatment group rate their headache pain on a daily basis, a procedure regularly used when psychological interventions are evaluated but one that departs from the periodic global retrospective approach typically used to assess outcome in pharmacologic investigations. When evaluated in this manner, Bruhn et al. found limited effectiveness for pharmacomedical treatment. Research indicates that the reports of pain obtained by these two assessment methods are discrepant and suggests that the global ratings of headache severity may overestimate improvement following treatment relative to daily headache recordings (Andrasik & Holroyd, 1980b; Blanchard, Andrasik, Neff, Jurish, & O'Keefe, 1981a). Estimates of the effectiveness of pharmacotherapy, therefore, may be inflated since evaluations of pharmacotherapy have used global ratings of improvement exclusively. The risks of permanent tissue damage and unpleasant side effects associated with medication usage, combined with the likelihood that medication effectiveness may be overestimated, support the pursuit of nonpharmacological alternatives to headache treatment.

X. RELAXATION AND BIOFEEDBACK TREATMENT OF RECURRENT HEADACHE

Relaxation training refers to a variety of procedures, which seek to dampen an individual's arousal to stressful stimuli. In the treatment of headache, relaxation has consisted of three basic types: (a) progressive deep muscle relaxation training as first described by Jacobsen (1938) and its subsequent variants (e.g., Warner & Lance, 1975), (b) passive relaxation or meditative procedures, such as transcendental meditation (Benson, Klemchuk, & Graham, 1974), and (c) components of autogenic training (Schultz & Luthe, 1969) which utilize self-instructions of feelings of warmth and heaviness to promote relaxation.

Biofeedback procedures have developed as another alternative for treating headache sufferers. Here, too, a variety of procedures have been utilized in an attempt to modify the physiological abnormalities underlying headache. In the biofeedback treatment of tension headache subjects are typically taught to reduce the tension levels of muscles in and around the forehead and neck (Budzynski, Stoyva, & Adler, 1970; Budzynski, Stoyva, Adler, & Mullaney, 1973). Daily home relaxation practice is usually added to the training procedure to augment training effects.

Biofeedback for migraine headache has consisted of two basic types: (a) thermal feedback from skin surface sites and (b) feedback of the vasomotor response of cranial arteries. Of the two procedures, temperature feedback has been most actively studied and is regarded by some as the nonpharmacological treatment of choice for migraine (Board of Directors, American Association for the Study of Headache, 1978). The basic treatment approach, developed at the Menninger Clinic (i.e., Sargent, Green, & Walters, 1972), combines temperature biofeedback with autogenic exercises resulting in what Sargent et al. term "autogenic feedback." In early applications skin temperature was monitored from two separate sites, hand and forehead, and subjects were instructed to warm their hands relative to their forehead in order to produce peripheral vasodilation and cephalic vasoconstriction. In more recent work monitoring has been accomplished from single sites, typically the hand or finger. Cephalic vasomotor conditioning is a more complicated biofeedback procedure and, as a consequence, has received only limited research attention at present. In this approach, pulse amplitude of the temporal artery is fed back to subjects to enable them reliably to produce vasoconstriction, which can be used as an abortive technique during headache (Bild & Adams, 1980; Friar & Beatty, 1976).

A. Treatment Effectiveness

At present a sufficient number of well-controlled investigations exist within the literature to permit evaluation of the outcomes of relaxation and EMG and thermal biofeedback treatments. Reviews of this literature indicate that relaxation and biofeedback treatments are efficacious and produce fairly equivalent results (Adams et al., 1980; Andrasik, Coleman, & Epstein, 1981; Beaty & Haynes, 1979; Blanchard, Ahles, & Shaw, 1979; Turk, Meichenbaum, & Bernstein, 1979; Williamson, 1981).

In a recent review, outcomes from available treatment studies were compared more directly by a statistical procedure known as meta-analysis (Blanchard, Andrasik, Ahles, Teders, & O'Keefe, 1980). To accomplish this, mean improvement scores for groups of subjects given a particular treatment in a particular study became the unit of analysis. Mean percentage improvement obtained by the treatment procedures as well as by varying control procedures (psychological placebo, medication placebo, and self-monitoring alone) is presented in Table II. Individual comparisons performed on both the migraine and tension headache investigations revealed all treatment procedures to be superior to placebo but not to be significantly different from each other. In the analysis of tension headache treatment the psychological and medication placebos were, additionally, superior to monitoring alone but not different from one another.

Review of the available research leads to the following conclusions. First, tension and migraine headache sufferers appear to be equally responsive to biofeedback and relaxation training. Relaxation illustrates this point most clearly as this procedure has been applied in a similar manner to headache sufferers of both types with nearly identical results.[2] A second major conclusion is that, even though relaxation and biofeedback treatments are efficacious, a sizable number of clients exhibit only minor improvement following treatment with these interventions. Our research yield would be enriched by closer scrutiny of these minimally responsive clients so that more efficacious treatments may be developed for them. Our knowledge of the characteristics of these minimally responsive individuals is meager. Preliminary data suggest that the following may be associated with a poor response to treatment: male sex (Diamond, Medina, Diamond-Falk, & DeVeno, 1979), advanced age (Diamond et al., 1979), high initial basal levels of forehead muscle tension and low initial basal hand temperatures (Bruhn et al., 1979; Diamond et al., 1979; Epstein & Abel, 1977; Hartje & Diver, 1978), depressive symptomatology (Blanchard et al., 1981a; Diamond & Franklin, 1976), anxiety (Blanchard et al., 1981a), and intense, unremitting pretreatment pain levels (Bakal et al., 1981; Blanchard et al., 1981a). Third, although treatment outcome studies abound, investigations of treatment processes are sparse. It is to this matter that we now turn.

B. Mechanisms of Change

In the treatment of tension headache, studies have shown relaxation and biofeedback to be superior to pseudotherapy control procedures,

[2] A recent study (Blanchard, Andrasik, Neff, Ahles, Arena, Jurish, Pallmeyer, Teders, & Rodichok, 1981) calls this conclusion into question by suggesting that relaxation training may be less effective with migraine than tension headache. If this proves true, it would have little implication for the two models of headache we are discussing because it is consistent with both.

TABLE II

Average Percentage Improvement in Migraine and Tension Headache Patients Treated by Relaxation, Biofeedback, or Placebo[a]

A. Migraine Treatment Studies

	Conditions			
	Thermal biofeedback with autogenic training	Thermal biofeedback	Relaxation training	Medication placebo
Average percentage improvement	65.1	51.8	52.7	16.5

B. Tension Treatment Studies

	Conditions					
	Frontal EMG biofeedback alone	Frontal EMG biofeedback and relaxation training	Relaxation training alone	Psychological placebo	Medication placebo	Headache monitoring only
Average percentage improvement at end of treatment	60.9	58.8	59.2	35.3	34.8	-4.5

[a]From Blanchard et al. (1980). Reprinted with permission of the Association for Advancement of Behavior Therapy, New York.

suggesting that outcomes with these treatments do not result merely from exposure to credible treatment procedures (e.g., Holroyd, Andrasik, & Noble, 1980). On the other hand, studies that have carefully examined the interrelationships between headache symptoms and treatment-induced alterations in physiological responding have found changes in these two variables to be markedly desynchronous. For example, Epstein and Abel (1977) found that after an extensive course of biofeedback, none of their tension headache clients was able to demonstrate significant abilities to lower frontal EMG. However, one-half of their subjects recorded marked headache improvement. Clearly these improvements were due to factors other than the learned control of EMG activity. Conversely, Holroyd, Andrasik, and Westbrook (1977) found that when EMG biofeedback was accompanied by counterdemand instructions (Steinmark & Borkovec, 1974) tension headache sufferers who demonstrated good control of frontal EMG activity did not necessarily show improvements in headache symptoms.

A most recent study was designed to examine explicitly the role that the learned control of EMG activity plays in headache improvement following biofeedback training. In this study (Andrasik & Holroyd, 1980a), tension headache sufferers were led to believe they were receiving feedback to reduce forehead muscle tension levels. Actually they were provided one of the following: feedback for decreasing muscle tension, the standard biofeedback treatment procedure (termed Decrease); feedback for increasing muscle tension (termed Increase); or feedback from an irrelevant muscle group, the forearm flexor, so that frontal muscle tension would remain constant (termed No Change). Since clients in all three groups received contingent "success" feedback, they were provided with the opportunity to attain a sense of mastery over the feedback task that noncontingent feedback control groups fail to provide. Although clients in the three conditions demonstrated self-control of muscle activity as intended (increased, decreased, or no change; see Fig. 3), clients in all groups showed similar reductions in headache activity relative to a control group (termed Recording) (see Fig. 4). Thus, symptom improvement was not mediated by learned reductions in forehead muscle tension.

Available evidence similarly suggests that improvements in migraine symptoms following thermal biofeedback may have little to do with the temperature changes that occur during treatment. For example, in a retrospective examination of migraineous treatment successes, Werback and Sandweiss (1978) found these treatment successes had not increased their hand temperatures to a statistically significant degree during treatment. Similarly, Turin and Johnson (1976) found their

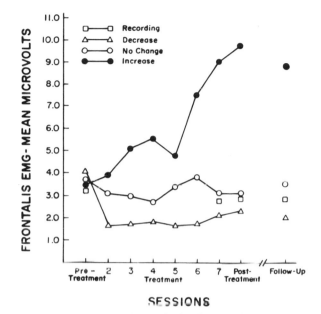

Fig. 3. Integrated EMG activity during biofeedback self-control periods. From Andrasik and Holroyd (1980a).

migraine clients displayed minimal temperature increases after extensive training, yet many of these individuals reported significant reductions in headache activity. The only study able to provide clear evidence of learned ability to increase hand surface temperature found this was inadequate to produce headache improvement (Elmore & Tursky, 1981).

Two studies have evaluated the role of temperature increases in mediating treatment outcome by comparing the symptom improvement of migraineurs taught to increase hand temperature to the improvement obtained by migraineurs taught to decrease hand temperature, while imparting similar positive expectancies to all participants. In both investigations (Kewman & Roberts, 1980; Largen, Mathew, Dobbins, & Claghorn, 1981) subjects in each condition displayed similar improvements, which argues convincingly that skin temperature alterations were not responsible for the symptom reductions reported by subjects. Mullinix, Norton, Hack, and Fishman (1978) employed a similar investigational strategy by comparing true thermal warming feedback to false feedback, while keeping demands for improvement equally high across all subjects. Again, both procedures produced similar patterns of improvement. Additionally, recent reviews of studies

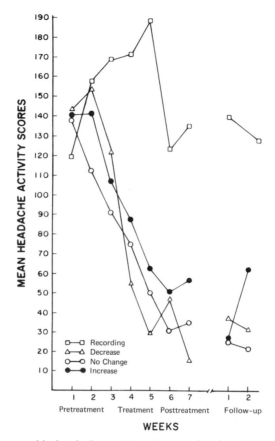

Fig. 4. Mean weekly headache activity. From Andrasik and Holroyd (1980a).

examining hand temperature self-regulation abilities have questioned whether subjects can exert any meaningful degree of control of hand temperature by biofeedback. Thus, for the most part, the evidence in support of physiologic mediation of relaxation and biofeedback is weak, suggesting that other change processes are operating in these procedures.

C. Coping and Headache Improvement

Change in cognitive processes has been hypothesized as a central mediator of the outcomes obtained with biofeedback therapy (Lazarus, 1975; Meichenbaum, 1976), but no direct tests of this hypothesis have appeared in the literature. Evidence from one of the studies discussed above is consistent with the notion of cognitive mediation of treatment outcome. In this study (Andrasik & Holroyd, 1980a), tension headache sufferers showed similar reductions in headache symptoms irrespective of whether their forehead muscle tension levels decreased, increased, or remained unchanged during biofeedback training, indicating that factors other than learned reductions played an important role in the therapeutic change process. Inquiries about the strategies clients used following treatment provide some insights into the factors possibly mediating change during biofeedback therapy.

Strategies used by the subjects in each of the three biofeedback treatment conditions are presented in Table III. Examination of these data indicates that (a) the three biofeedback groups were very similar in their reports of strategies used, (b) use of muscle relaxation strategies was infrequently reported for the two biofeedback control procedures (No Change and Increase), and (c) most of the strategies appear to be very similar to the coping strategies that are taught during cognitive–behavioral therapy, for example, cognitive reappraisal, attention deployment, and fantasy (Lazarus, Averill, & Opton, 1974). Thus, interview data indicated that clients in all three biofeedback groups made major changes in the ways they coped with headache-related

TABLE III

Strategies Utilized by Biofeedback Participants to Control Headache

Strategy	Group		
	Decrease	No change	Increase
Behavioral intervention	0	2	0
Controlled breathing	2	0	1
Focusing attention/ thinking of monotonous tasks	1	5	7
Focusing on body needs and sensations	3	0	0
Imagery or fantasy	16	15	10
Muscle relaxation	6	1	0
Nonfocusing of attention/ letting thoughts flow	2	3	3
Praying	1	0	0
Problem solving	2	0	0
Rational reevaluation	0	2	1
Self-instruction	0	1	0

stresses during treatment. One may speculate that the enhanced awareness of muscle tension resulting from biofeedback training sensitized
clients to tension preceding headache symptoms, and the contingent
success provided during training increased participants' confidence
in their ability to control their headaches. This sensitivity to cues
antecedent to the headache and enhanced self-efficacy may have then
led clients to attempt new ways of coping with headache-related
stresses. Thus, biofeedback and relaxation therapies may be effective
because they indirectly induce patients to alter their transactions with
the environment, not because they enable patients to directly control
problematic physiological responses.

XI. COGNITIVE–BEHAVIORAL TREATMENT OF RECURRENT HEADACHE

Cognitive–behavioral therapy treats recurrent headache by helping
the client to manage more effectively both headache-related stress and
the psychological component of headache rather than by teaching the
client to regulate stress-related physiological responses. This approach
to treatment has three potential advantages that biofeedback and relaxation training do not have. First, since stress responses are embed-
ded in the individual's transactions with the environment, attempts
to control specific physiological responses frequently fail because the
individual continues to cope with the stressful events in ways that
generate the very responses he/she is attempting to control (Holroyd,
1979). Cognitive–behavioral therapy, with its focus on altering the
way an individual copes with headache-related stresses, may enable
the individual to control stress responses in situations where biofeedback and relaxation are ineffective. Second, biofeedback and relaxation
training provide clients with only a single coping response (relaxation).
However, the complex demands of everyday life often require more
flexible coping skills, such as those included in cognitive–behavioral
therapy. Finally, cognitive–behavioral interventions appear better
suited to combat the depression that can be both a precipitant and a
consequence of headache, as well as the negative affect that arises
from unsuccessful attempts at managing headache (feelings of frustration, helplessness, and lack of control, for example).

The cognitive–behavioral approach to managing headache is governed by the same principles and general treatment strategies that
characterize cognitive–behavioral approaches to other disorders (cf.
Beck & Emery, 1979; Beck, Rush, Shaw, & Emery, 1979; Kendall &

Hollon, 1979; Meichenbaum, 1977). Specific interventions, however, will vary quite dramatically with different presenting problems. Even in the treatment of stress-related physical disorders very different kinds of interventions are likely to prove useful with different types of disorders (Holroyd *et al.*, 1982). In this section we will describe in as much detail as space allows an approach to the treatment of recurrent headache we have developed over the last 5 years. Within this general treatment framework other clinicians might, of course, use somewhat different interventions.

A. Treatment Techniques

Cognitive–behavioral treatment can be roughly divided into three phases: education, self-monitoring, and problem-solving or coping skills training. However, prior to initiating treatment, clients are taught to record the occurrence of headache and to rate the severity of head pain during each headache episode. Headache symptoms can be conveniently recorded on a pocket-sized card (see Fig. 5) with space for recording characteristics of headache symptoms (e.g., head pain location, presence of migraine-like symptoms), efforts to manage head

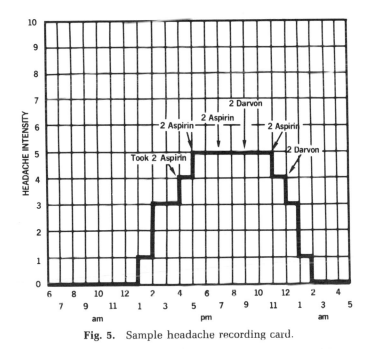

Fig. 5. Sample headache recording card.

pain (e.g., medication usage, psychological coping efforts), or precipitants and correlates of headache attacks (e.g., diet, sensations, thoughts
and feelings preceding and accompanying attacks) provided on the
back. Since global and retrospective questions about headache symptoms are only weakly correlated with these daily headache recordings
(Andrasik & Holroyd, 1980b) they cannot be assumed to provide equivalent information.

Occasionally someone will find headache recording upsetting. This
is most likely to occur with individuals who minimize the severity
of their headache problems and who cope with their symptoms by
ignoring their head pain. When headache recording disrupts these
familiar coping strategies, the individual may become anxious and
fearful about headache symptoms worsening. Usually in such cases
it is sufficient to reassure the client that their experience is not unusual,
and to emphasize that detailed headache recordings can help them
devise more effective ways of coping with their headaches than they
have been using.

> Ms. A described herself as "gritting my teeth and going about my business"
> during 20 years of migraine attacks that occurred approximately twice a month.
> When the attacks became more frequent and severe following separation from her
> husband and did not respond to medication she was referred for cognitive therapy.
> Following 2 weeks of headache recording she arrived at the second evaluation
> session looking obviously depressed. She reported that in the process of recording
> her headaches she had "discovered" that she regularly experienced headache of
> moderate severity, in addition to the more serious headaches she was seeking help
> with. She had been so successful at ignoring these headaches that she became
> depressed and discouraged upon realizing their actual frequency.

1. Educational Phase

The educational phase of treatment has four interrelated goals: (a)
to provide information about the pathophysiology and precipitants of
headache, (b) to combat the demoralization and depression frequently
associated with chronic headache, (c) to convey to clients that they
must take an active role in managing their headaches, and (d) to explain
what is involved in treatment. The coping efforts of the chronic headache sufferer are frequently undermined by the belief that headache
symptoms reflect global personal inadequacies or an inevitable response to overwhelming environmental pressures. A nontechnical
discussion of the pathophysiology and precipitants of headache which
emphasizes the determinants of headache as potentially under the
client's control can thus help combat feelings of helplessness and
encourage the client's active participation in treatment. Occasionally

the information will also provide symptom relief by disconfirming beliefs about headaches that are contributing to the client's problems.

> Prior to seeking help for her headaches Ms. B had received 3 years of psychoanalytic psychotherapy for other adjustment problems. For 12 years she had monthly migraine attacks that appeared to be associated with menstruation, as well as less regular attacks she said occurred when she was pressured or depressed. During the presentation of didactic information about headache she responded with obvious relief. When she was questioned about the response she reported she had regarded the continued occurrence of headache as a sign that she had failed to manage her life differently than her mother who also suffered from migraine. She experienced relief when she realized her susceptibility to migraine might be genetic and not an indication that she had failed in her efforts at personal growth. Following this interview she recorded no headaches for 6 months. At the 6-month follow-up she attributed the relief of her headache symptoms entirely to the increased sense of well being and confidence this information about headaches had provided.

In our didactic presentation we place particular emphasis on psychological stress as a headache precipitant and on cognitive processes as determinants of their responses. Written materials including the diagram in Fig ? and didactic examples from the therapist's personal experience are used to illustrate how psychological processes influence headache symptoms and to involve less psychologically minded clients in treatment.

2. Self-Monitoring

After the presentation of didactic information clients are taught self-monitoring skills so they will be able to identify the covert and overt events that precede, accompany, and follow stressful transactions. Clients record in a headache diary the sensations, feelings, thoughts, and behavior associated with stressful transactions and headache attacks. We also frequently have clients imagine themselves in stressful situations during the treatment session describing their experience aloud in a "stream of consciousness" fashion. Whatever the specific techniques that are used with a particular client the therapeutic task is to assist the client in becoming an observer of his or her thoughts, experiences, and behaviors. Our impression is that the most effective therapists are able to elicit finely detailed accounts of the client's response to stress rather than global reconstructions.

As the client becomes adept at this self-monitoring the therapist assists the client in identifying relationships between situational variables (e.g., criticism from spouse), thoughts (e.g., "I can't do anything right"), and emotional, behavioral, and symptomatic responses (e.g., depression, withdrawal, and headache). Table IV presents self-monitoring data which accompanied the headache recorded in Fig. 5. It can be seen that headache onset was preceded by resentment and anxiety over work demands and the apparent sexual overtures of a fellow employee, as well as by nausea and sensations of tingling and lightheadedness. The client appears unable to take actions that might resolve these conflicts or to manage the emotional distress and tension these situations arouse. We might also speculate that her inner dialogue of conflict undermines her efforts to cope with the situation.

Upon entering treatment, clients differ in their ability to identify headache antecedents and correlates. Some clients can describe the sensations, thoughts, and feelings that precede headache onset in considerable detail and can predict with considerable accuracy when and under what conditions headaches will occur. However, most headache sufferers experience at least some of their headaches as appearing without warning. Even following detailed self-monitoring training at least some headaches will occur without identifiable antecedents. These headaches are treated by modifying the psychological correlates of headache (e.g., feelings of helplessness, emotional distress) and altering factors in the client's life that may increase vulnerability to headache even when they do not occur in close proximity to the headache attacks themselves (e.g., depression, chronic daily stress).

3. Coping Skills Training

As the client becomes adept at self-monitoring, therapy begins to focus on altering the psychological antecedents and correlates of headache. This coping skills training may involve cognitive-restructuring, self-control relaxation training, behavioral rehearsal (Goldfried & Davidson, 1976), and, at times, marital or family therapy. Changes in environmental stimuli (e.g., elimination of possible chemical precipitants) or changes in diet also occasionally become the focus of treatment.

It is often useful to begin training with instruction in self-control relaxation (Goldfried & Trier, 1974) because, as noted earlier, some clients can abort, or at least reduce the severity of their headache symptoms, by relaxing prior to headache onset. Other clients, however, will receive little benefit from relaxation training, and occasionally relaxation training appears to aggravate headache symptoms. Therefore, the therapist should not place all his or her eggs in one basket and rely exclusively on the therapeutic benefits of this one intervention.

Bakal et al. (1981) have provided an interesting description of a woman whose headache attacks became more frequent when practicing relaxation training, but who could successfully abort her headaches

TABLE IV

Sample from Self-Monitoring Record of Events Associated with Onset of Headache

Time	Situation	Physical sensations	Thoughts	Feeling (0–100)	Behavior
8:00 AM	Breakfast, husband says I look "scattered"	—	Worry about getting to work on time (e.g., If I'm late Mr. _____ will notice)	Anxiety (25) Hurt (20)	Rush through breakfast, leave dishes in sink
10:00 AM	Given too many technical letters to type	Upset stomach from coffee, tense muscles	Everybody assumes I'm superwoman. No one takes account of other demands on my time	Anxiety (30) Annoyance (20)	Rushed typing, curt on telephone, take extra long break to calm down
12:00 noon	Jerry (fellow employee and supervisor) asks me to lunch. Talks suggestively about recent divorce	Lightheaded, tingling sensations in head and face, nausea	Jerry in on the make. I don't like fending him off—so why am I here. Am I seductive?	Anxiety (50) Awkwardness (40) Is that a feeling?	Try and offer sympathy but resent ulterior motive. Probably curt
2:00 PM	Spencer gives me long report with 5 tables to be done by 5:00	Headache—back of neck	F--- him—he didn't even ask what else I had to do. Fantasize Spencer stuck in elevator. No time to relax	Anger (60) Anxiety (60)	Typing report—distractedly
4:00 PM	Report completed	Headache worsening, nausea	If I could quit ruminating and was more organized I would get more work done	Anger (40) Anxiety (50)	Give report for correction. Complain to Susan. Type letters

by "becoming busy" when she sensed a headache attack was imminent. This woman's headache attacks were reliably preceded by scintillating scotomata (blind spot in the visual field surrounded by shiny, sparkling, prismatic figures) so she could use this symptom as a signal to become active, thereby preventing headache onset. Even when she had successfully aborted every headache for 6 months the scintillating scotomata continued to occur as frequently as before treatment.

Cognitive restructuring typically plays a central role in treatment because stress responses tend to be mediated by the individual's appraisal of the stresses they confront and of their ability to respond to the demands posed by the event. Often the role of cognitive processes in determining the client's stress responses is evident in the self-monitoring data the clients themselves have generated. The therapist can make sense of this information by suggesting that particular expectations or beliefs underlie stress responses in a variety of situations (e.g., "In each of these situations where you made a mistake, you criticized yourself harshly, became depressed and ended up with a headache. Are you expecting yourself to do everything perfectly?"). Clients are then pushed to examine the consequences of these hypothesized beliefs (e.g., "The requirement that you perform perfectly prevents you from attempting to learn new skills on the job, leads you to suffer unnecessarily over simple human errors, and contributes to your headaches and your having to leave work early to go home to bed."). It is the recognition of these consequences that often helps motivate the client to dispute thinking and change behavior interpreted as consistent with "irrational" beliefs.

The identification of specific beliefs that appear to underlie complex patterns of thinking, emotion, and behavior provides clients with a framework for organizing and understanding psychological responses to stressful events and thus for changing these responses. The actual change process, however, typically requires practice in the implementation of specific coping skills that enable the client to alter stressful transactions and to manage psychological stress responses. Coping strategies can be tailored to the specific stressful situations that confront the client and to the particular problems the client experiences with these situations, and can be practiced both imaginally and in role play enactments. Cognitive coping skills include (a) the use of self-instructions designed to maintain a coping orientation, to guide coping efforts, and to combat anxiety-arousing rumination, (b) the production of calming imagery, and (c) the application of rational problem-solving skills to practical problems (e.g., time management) confronting the client. Skills for self-assertion and for negotiating interpersonal conflicts also can be useful in managing particular stressful transactions.

Beck and Emery (1979) have provided a valuable description of cognitive therapy techniques and we draw heavily on their work. No collection of interventions can cover all situations that are likely to occur. Therefore, the therapist must be flexible in devising interventions that are capable of reaching particular clients.

> Ms. C's combined responsibilities at work and home kept her frantically pressed for time and overworked from 6:30 AM until 10:00 PM. Although the large quantity of nonprescription pain relievers she ingested had aggravated a stomach ulcer and she had been cautioned that she was becoming dependent on Darvon she could see no alternative to her demanding schedule and her methods of controlling her headaches. In the group of chronic headache clients she was assigned to she parried all suggestions with arguments that they were unworkable, financially burdensome, or dependent upon cooperation from others that could not be counted on. Ms. C appeared to take pleasure in articulately and convincingly demolishing the suggestions of group members, although she was arguing in essence that her situation was hopeless. Finally, the therapist led the group in constructing a table listing the emotional and health consequences of her lifestyle (which had been recorded in detail during self-monitoring) and all possible reasons Ms. C and the group could think of why change was impossible. She was instructed to study the table during the week and to try to devise counterarguments to each of the arguments in the table.

Where chronic stress in a marital relationship or in the larger family appears to be a major factor in the client's headache problems, or where family members undermine the autonomous coping efforts of the client, it can be helpful to include the client's partner or other family members in treatment (Coyne & Holroyd, 1982). The goals of these sessions are likely to be of two sorts. The therapist may simply give family members direct instructions to reinforce the client's autonomous efforts to manage headache symptoms and not to reinforce certain headache-related behaviors (e.g., overly dependent or helpless behavior). The therapist may also teach communication and conflict management skills to reduce family conflict and assist the client in verifying or disconfirming his or her expectancies and fears about other family members.

B. Treatment Effectiveness

In the first controlled evaluation of cognitive therapy for headache sufferers (Holroyd et al., 1977), 31 chronic tension-headache sufferers received eight sessions of cognitive therapy, eight sessions of frontal EMG biofeedback, or were assigned to a wait-list control group. Because this study was designed to determine if techniques specific to cognitive therapy would prove effective in reducing headache symptoms neither relaxation training nor marital and family interventions were included in the cognitive therapy treatment. In order to minimize the influence of implicit demands for improvement on headache-recording data clients were also told that improvement could not be expected until treatment had been completed (cf. counterdemand instruction, Steinmark & Borkovec, 1974). Otherwise cognitive therapy was conducted essentially as described earlier.

Cognitive therapy was found to be highly effective in reducing headache symptoms, with more than 80% of clients receiving the treatment showing at least a 50% reduction in headache symptoms (see Fig. 6). On the other hand, only about half the clients receiving biofeedback showed similar improvements in headache symptoms, in spite of the fact that all biofeedback clients successfully learned to control frontal EMG activity. The authors suggested that the relatively poor outcomes obtained with biofeedback may have resulted because "counterdemand instructions employed in the present study, but not in previous studies, counteracted strong implicit demands for improvement that are a necessary condition, at least for some clients, for the therapeutic effectiveness of biofeedback" (Holroyd et al., 1977, p. 131).

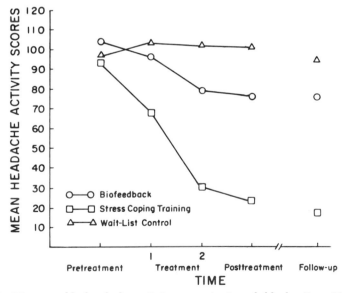

Fig. 6. Mean weekly headache activity scores in 2-week blocks. From Holroyd et al. (1977); reprinted with permission of Plenum, New York.

At a 2-year follow-up (Holroyd & Andrasik, 1980) clients who had been treated with cognitive therapy were still significantly improved with over 80% still showing substantial (greater than 45%) reductions in headache activity from pretreatment levels. Because only four bio-feedback clients contacted at follow-up had been improved following treatment, there were not sufficient numbers of subjects to compare directly the maintenance of gains produced with cognitive therapy and biofeedback. However, clients treated with cognitive therapy were somewhat more likely to maintain treatment gains than clients treated with biofeedback or relaxation training by other investigators (Budzynski et al., 1973; Reinking & Hutchings, 1981). These data suggest that cognitive therapy may be of particular value in facilitating the long-term maintenance of therapeutic gains.

At this follow-up evaluation clients also completed a Coping with Headache Questionnaire that inquired about the clients' use of nine commonly used methods of controlling headaches. Individual items asked about the use of prescription and nonprescription medication, the use of cognitive self-control strategies that had been taught during treatment, the use of relaxation, and the use of other commonly reported strategies for managing headache symptoms (e.g., exercise, sleep). On this questionnaire clients in both the cognitive therapy and biofeedback groups reported using multiple strategies for controlling their headaches. In fact, every client in both groups reported using at least half the strategies on the Coping with Headache Questionnaire. However, clients who had received cognitive therapy reported significantly more frequent use of the cognitive strategies they had been taught during treatment. This suggests that the use of these cognitive coping strategies may have facilitated the maintenance of therapeutic gains.

In a second study (Holroyd & Andrasik, 1978) cognitive–behavioral treatments with different coping skills training components were compared. Thirty-nine chronic headache sufferers were assigned to three treatments which differed only in the coping skills taught during treatment or to a wait-list control group. All three treatments included the headache recording, educational, and self-monitoring components described above. In addition, one group of clients was taught cognitive coping skills in the same manner as in the study of Holroyd et al. (1977). A second group was taught both cognitive coping skills and self-control relaxation. The third treatment group was taught no specific coping skills; clients in this group were told that their headaches would improve if they understood the "underlying cause" of their symptoms. Rather than teaching specific skills for managing headaches the therapist offered plausible interpretations of material generated during self-monitoring in terms of historical events in the patient's life. The therapist's interpretations were designed to provide an explanation for the client's distress and to increase the client's self-confidence and self-esteem.

Clients in each of the treatment groups showed substantial improvements in headache symptoms which were maintained at 1-month follow-up. Apparently, neither the elimination of cognitive coping skills training nor the addition of self-control relaxation altered the effectiveness of cognitive therapy. These results were further clarified by information collected during posttreatment interviews. Not unexpectedly, in the two groups taught cognitive coping or cognitive and relaxation coping skills clients reported during posttreatment interviews that they had used the skills they were taught during treatment to control their headaches. However, all but one of the participants in the group not taught specific coping skills reported they had devised and implemented specific techniques for controlling their headaches as well. Moreover, the one exception showed only minimal improvement in headache activity.

In some instances the methods clients devised to control their headaches were different from the methods that had been taught to clients in the other two treatment groups (e.g., imaginally reviewing karate exercises or praying when a headache was imminent); in other instances the methods were indistinguishable from those that had been taught in the other groups. This suggests that it is less crucial to provide clients with particular coping skills than to teach them to monitor the insidious onset of symptoms and to ensure that they are capable of interrupting the chain of overt and covert events that precipitate and aggravate symptoms. A comparison of these findings with those of the Andrasik and Holroyd (1980a) study further suggests that the psychological changes mediating the effectiveness of biofeedback and cognitive–behavioral therapy may be more similar than previously has been thought.

Figueroa (in press) also evaluated cognitive–behavioral therapy administered in a group format. Fifteen tension headache sufferers were randomly assigned to cognitive–behavioral therapy, an attention placebo discussion group, or a wait-list control group. Cognitive–behavioral therapy consisted primarily of the teaching of coping skills with modules on relaxation, the use of self-instruction and imagery to control pain and distress, and rational problem solving (cf. Goldfried & Davidson, 1976). In the discussion group psychological conflicts that might underlie headache symptoms were discussed. It appears, however, that these two treatments differed not only in the coping skills that were taught but in the opportunity they provided to learn self-monitoring skills. In the course of learning to use the coping skills, subjects in the cognitive–behavioral therapy group could be expected to learn to monitor psychological and environmental events associated with headache onset. However, subjects in the discussion group probably did not have an equal opportunity to learn self-monitoring skills.

Inspection of reported means indicates that subjects in the cognitive–behavioral therapy group showed more than a 50% reduction in headache symptoms, while subjects in the other two groups showed only minor improvements. However, because of the small number of subjects, differences between the cognitive–behavioral therapy group and the discussion group reached significance only on one of four headache measures following treatment and two of four measures at 1-month follow-up. Nevertheless, this study does provide some additional evidence that cognitive–behavioral therapy can yield substantial improvements in headache when administered in a group format.

The clients in the studies described above had been diagnosed primarily as tension headache sufferers. However, Mitchell and his colleagues (Mitchell & Mitchell, 1971; Mitchell & White, 1977) have used a similar treatment approach with migraine sufferers. Clients were taught to monitor cognitive and behavioral responses to stressful situations and to use specific strategies for coping with the stressful situations they identified (e.g., self-instruction, thought stopping, and assertion training). In the only controlled evaluation of the treatment, Mitchell and White (1977) assigned 12 migraine sufferers to either audio-cassette versions of this treatment or relaxation training or to one of two control groups. Both treatments produced significant improvements in migraine symptoms, with the coping skills treatment producing more improvement than relaxation training (73 versus 45% improvement). Subjects in the control groups showed no reduction in symptoms. These results are promising. However, conclusions about treatment effectiveness must be tempered because of the small numbers of subjects in this study.

Several investigators have treated chronic headache sufferers with a combination of biofeedback and cognitive–behavioral therapy. Bakal et al. (1981) report results from 45 chronic headache sufferers (17 tension headache, 15 migraine, and 13 mixed headache sufferers) treated with a combined treatment. Clients in this study recorded their headaches and monitored "the sensations, thoughts and feelings that preceded and accompanied their headache" for 3 weeks prior to treatment. During treatment clients were provided didactic information about their headaches, relaxation or EMG biofeedback during 7 of the 12 treatment sessions, and coping skills training during the remaining 5 sessions. Throughout treatment self-monitoring data were used to teach clients "to view previously undifferentiated attacks as consisting of a number of smaller and describable components."

Bakal et al. note that both relaxation and biofeedback training were used as part of self-monitoring to teach clients "to observe changes in bodily sensations, thoughts and feelings which accompanied any changes in EMG levels" and not to teach "direct muscle control." However, no data are provided to indicate that clients receiving this treatment failed to learn control of EMG activity. Coping skills training consisted of training in self-instruction, imagery production, and control of attention. Graduated homework assignments were designed to provide practice in the use of coping skills and to facilitate their generalization to the natural environment.

Clients receiving this treatment averaged approximately a 50% reduction in headache symptoms, and improvements were maintained at 6-month follow-up. Most patients showed clinically significant reductions in headache symptoms. Treatment outcomes were unrelated to the type of headache diagnoses clients received, head pain locations, or the presence or absence of migraineous symptoms. Clients with migraine symptoms were as responsive to treatment as clients with tension headache symptoms. However, a subgroup of clients who typically recorded 15 or more hours of head pain per day, or virtually continuous pain during waking hours, did significantly worse than the majority of patients with more episodic headache symptoms.

Steger and Harper (1980) treated 20 chronic tension headache sufferers with either relaxation training or what they termed a "comprehensive" biofeedback and cognitive therapy treatment. For 2 weeks prior to treatment all clients recorded headaches and "antecedent and consequent headache events" (p. 138) and had resting EMG levels recorded each week. Clients assigned to relaxation training were then provided with relaxation training tapes and instruction in the regular home practice of relaxation training. Clients in the combined biofeedback and cognitive therapy groups then received four sessions of EMG biofeedback and four sessions of combined biofeedback and cognitive therapy. These latter sessions consisted of 20 minutes of biofeedback training and 30 minutes of coping skills training that focused on the "identification of specific stressful situations and adaptive or maladaptive coping strategies" and training in the use of "general stress coping strategies (for example, thought stopping, assertiveness, marital disagreement reduction)."

Home relaxation training and the combined biofeedback and cognitive therapy treatment were equally effective in reducing resting EMG levels. Only the combined treatment, however, produced reductions in headache symptoms and psychological symptoms (as assessed by the Hopkins Symptom Checklist). Because clients receiving the combined treatment received 10 (2 assessment and 8 treatment) sessions of therapist contact while relaxation training subjects were seen for only 2 sessions, it is unclear whether these differing outcomes were a function of differences in therapist contact or the differing content of the treatments. Nonetheless the results of this study provide additional evidence that a combined biofeedback and cognitive therapy treatment can effectively reduce headache symptoms.

Lake, Rainey, and Papsdorf (1979) assigned 24 migraine headache sufferers to eight sessions of EMG biofeedback, temperature biofeedback, or a combined temperature biofeedback and rational–emotive therapy treatment, or to a wait-list control group. Unfortunately the rational emotive therapy treatment consisted of only three 30- to 40-minute sessions appended to the third, fifth, and seventh biofeedback sessions. The authors note that this brief intervention "did not constitute an adequate test of this treatment" (p. 138). Moreover, in most analyses no treatment effects were observed indicating that none of the interventions had a significant impact on headache symptoms. This study thus provides no clear information about the effectiveness of rational–emotive therapy in the treatment of chronic headache.

Although only a handful of studies evaluating cognitive–behavioral therapy have been published to date, findings from these studies are quite promising and amply justify continued evaluation of this treatment in the management of recurrent headache. We have suggested that because cognitive–behavioral therapy more comprehensively addresses the psychological antecedents and components of recurrent headache, it is reasonable to assume that for many individuals this treatment will prove more effective. However, when the recurrent headache sufferer presents for treatment, most therapists will probably begin therapy with relaxation training because of its efficacy, simplicity, and ease of administration. In this context it is important to determine if cognitive–behavioral interventions increase the effectiveness of relaxation training or benefit those patients who fail to respond to relaxation training. More information about treatment durability is also needed because our knowledge of the long-term effects of relaxation, biofeedback, and cognitive–behavioral therapy is meager. We have argued that cognitive–behavioral treatments, which teach clients general problem-solving strategies rather than a single skill such as relaxation, may more effectively prepare the individual for long-term management of headache than relaxation training or bio-feedback (Goldfried, 1980; Holroyd, 1979). Even if cognitive–behavioral interventions prove no more effective than relaxation in producing an immediate reduction of headache symptoms, they may prove helpful in promoting the long-term maintenance of treatment gains. One of the longest treatment follow-ups in the headache literature is encouraging in this regard (Holroyd & Andrasik, 1980).

XII. CONCLUSIONS

Several conclusions emerge from the present analysis of data pertinent to recurrent headache.

1. There is little evidence that tension and migraine headaches constitute different headache syndromes with distinctive symptoms and pathophysiologies. Thus (a) tension and migraine headache symptoms do not appear to cohere as qualitatively different syndromes but do seem to disperse along a headache severity continuum, (b) individuals diagnosed as tension and migraine headache sufferers display similar physiological responses both during and preceding headache as well as to stress, and (c) the effectiveness of both drug therapies and psychological interventions, such as relaxation training, biofeedback, and cognitive–behavioral therapy, appears to be unrelated to headache diagnosis.[2]

2. It was proposed that both tension and migraine headaches are manifestations of the same reciprocally interacting psychological and physiological processes. One important implication of this formulation is that alterations in the psychological antecedents and correlates of headache can be expected not only to influence indirectly underlying physiological processes but also to alter headache directly.

3. A sizable number of recurrent headache sufferers are not aided to a clinically meaningful degree by pharmacological agents, relaxation training, or biofeedback, and the gains of those initially helped may not be maintained for long periods. Thus, efforts to develop more

effective treatments and interventions capable of facilitating the maintenance of therapeutic gains seem warranted.

4. Minimal support was found for the hypothesis that headache improvement following biofeedback is mediated by the learned control of physiological activity. Evidence was reviewed suggesting that headache improvements are often mediated by cognitive and behavioral changes rather than by learned control of physiological activity.

5. It was argued that relaxation training and biofeedback ignore psychological variables that can be important in the genesis and maintenance of headache. A cognitive–behavioral treatment approach that more comprehensively addresses the psychological antecedents and components of headache was described. On theoretical grounds it was argued that this treatment may prove effective with some individuals who are not helped by relaxation training or biofeedback and may enable individuals who improve following relaxation training or biofeedback to maintain their improvement more effectively.

6. Results from small scale outcome studies provide empirical support for the effectiveness of cognitive–behavioral therapy in treating recurrent headache. However, comparisons of relaxation, biofeedback, and cognitive–behavioral therapy are needed to determine the comparative efficacy, utility, and costs of these interventions. The only direct comparison of these therapies to date found cognitive–behavioral therapy to be superior to EMG biofeedback in treating tension headache (Holroyd et al., 1977).

7. Salient characteristics of individuals who are unresponsive to relaxation training or biofeedback need to be identified so alternate methods of treating these individuals can be developed. In some instances there is reason to believe that cognitive–behavioral therapy will prove effective with headache sufferers who do not respond to relaxation or biofeedback. For example, when headaches are accompanied by depressive symptomatology there is a reduced responsiveness to relaxation training or biofeedback. Since cognitive–behavioral therapy effectively reduces both headaches and depression, it may prove to be the treatment of choice for these individuals.

8. Surprisingly, little is known about the long-term effects of any of the treatments for headache or about factors contributing to relapse. The limited available evidence suggests cognitive behavioral approaches may produce outcomes that are quite durable. Cognitive–behavioral therapy thus deserves the increased attention of investigators developing methods for facilitating the long-term maintenance of treatment gains.

REFERENCES

Adams, H. E., Feuerstein, M., & Fowler, J. L. Migraine headache: Review of parameters, etiology, and intervention. *Psychological Bulletin*, 1980, **87**, 217–237.

Ad Hoc Committee on Classification of Headache. Classification of headache. *Journal of the American Medical Association*, 1962, **179**, 717–718.

Anderson, C. D., & Franks, R. D. Migraine and tension headache: Is there a physiological difference? *Headache*, 1981, **21**, 63–71.

Andrasik, F., Blanchard, E. B., Arena, J. G., Teders, S. J., Teevan, R. C., & Rodichok, L. D. *Psychological functioning in headache sufferers*. Unpublished manuscript, 1981.

Andrasik, F., Coleman, D., & Epstein, L. H. Biofeedback: Clinical and research considerations. In D. M. Doleys, R. L. Meredith, & A. R. Ciminero (Eds.), *Behavioral psychology in medicine: Assessment and treatment strategies*. New York: Plenum, 1982.

Andrasik, F., & Holroyd, K. A. A test of specific and nonspecific effects in the biofeedback treatment of tension headache. *Journal of Consulting and Clinical Psychology*, 1980, **48**, 575–586. (a)

Andrasik, F., & Holroyd, K. A. Reliability and concurrent validity of headache questionnaire data. *Headache*, 1980, **20**, 44–46. (b)

Andrasik, F., Holroyd, K. A., & Abell, T. Prevalence of headache within a college student population: A preliminary analysis. *Headache*, 1979, **19**, 384–387.

Anthony, M., & Lance, J. W. Monoamine oxidase inhibition in the treatment of migraine. *Archives of Neurology*, 1969, **21**, 263.

Bakal, D. A., Demjen, S., & Kaganov, S. Cognitive behavioral treatment of chronic headache. *Headache*, 1981, **21**, 81–86.

Bakal, D. A., & Kaganov, J. A. Muscle contraction and migraine headache: Psychophysiological comparison. *Headache*, 1977, **17**, 208–215.

Bakal, D. A., & Kaganov, J. A. Symptom characteristics of chronic and nonchronic headache sufferers. *Headache*, 1979, **19**, 285–289.

Barolin, G. S. Brief report: Headache and depression. *Headache*, 1976, **16**, 252–253.

Barrie, M. A., Fox, W. R., Weatherall, M., & Wilkinson, M. S. P. Analysis of symptoms of patients with headaches and their response to treatment with ergot derivatives. *Quarterly Journal of Medicine*, 1968, **37**, 319–336.

Beaty, E. T., & Haynes, S. N. Behavioral intervention with muscle-contraction headache: A review. *Psychosomatic Medicine*, 1979, **41**, 165–180.

Beck, A. T., & Emery, G. *Cognitive therapy of anxiety and phobic disorders*. Philadelphia, Pennsylvania: Center for Cognitive Therapy, 1979.

Beck, A. T., Rush, A. J., Shaw, B. F., & Emery, G. *Cognitive therapy of depression*. New York: Guilford, 1979.

Benson, H. Klemchuk, H. P., & Graham, J. R. The usefuless of the relaxation response in the therapy of headache. *Headache*, 1974, **14**, 49–52.

Bild, R., & Adams, H. E. Modifications of migraine headaches by cephalic blood volume pulse and EMG biofeedback. *Journal of Consulting and Clinical Psychology*, 1980, **48**, 51–57.

Blanchard, E. B., Ahles, T. A., & Shaw, E. R. Behavioral treatment of headaches. In M. Hersen, R. M. Eisler, & P. M. Miller (Eds.), *Progress in behavior modification* (Vol. 8). New York: Academic Press, 1979.

Blanchard, E. B., Andrasik, F., Ahles, T. A., Teders, S. J., & O'Keefe, D. Migraine and tension headache: A meta-analytic review. *Behavior Therapy*, 1980, **11**, 613–631.

Blanchard, E. B., Andrasik, F., Neff, D. F., Ahles, T. A., Arena, J. G., Jurish, S. E., Pallmeyer, T. P., Teders, S. J., & Rodichok, L. D. *The short term effects of relaxation training and biofeedback on three kinds of headache.* Paper presented at the Association for Advancement of Behavior Therapy, Toronto, 1981.

Blanchard, E. B., Andrasik, F., Neff, D. F., Jurish, S. E., & O'Keefe, D. M. Social validation of the headache diary. *Behavior Therapy,* 1981. (a)

Blanchard, E. B., Andrasik, F., Neff, D. F., Teders, S. J., Pallmeyer, T. P., & Rodichok, L. D. *A sequential comparison of relaxation training and EMG biofeedback in the treatment of tension headache.* Unpublished manuscript, 1981. (b)

Blanchard, E. B., O'Keefe, D., Neff, D., Jurish, S., & Andrasik, F. Interdisciplinary agreement in the diagnosis of headache types. *Journal of Behavioral Assessment,* 1981, **3**, 5–9. (c)

Board of Directors, American Association for the Study of Headache: Biofeedback Therapy. *Headache,* 1978, **18**, 107.

Bond, M. R. The relation of pain to the Eysenck personality inventory, Cornell medical index, and Whiteley index of hypochondriasis. *British Journal of Psychiatry,* 1976, **128**, 280–289.

Bruhn, P., Olesen, J., & Melgaard, B. Controlled trial of EMG feedback in muscle contraction headache. *Annals of Neurology,* 1979, **6**, 34–36.

Budzynski, T., Stoyva, J., & Adler, C. Feedback-induced relaxation: Application to tension headache. *Journal of Behavior Therapy and Experimental Psychiatry,* 1970, **1**, 205–211.

Budzynski, T. H., Stoyva, J. M., Adler, C. S., & Mullaney, D. J. EMG biofeedback and tension headache: A controlled outcome study. *Psychosomatic Medicine,* 1973, **6**, 509–514.

Cassidy, W. L. Clinical observations in manic-depressive disease: A quantitative study of 100 manic-depressive patients and 50 medically sick controls. *Journal of the American Medical Association,* 1957, **164**, 1535–1546.

Couch, J. R., Ziegler, D. K., & Hassanein, R. Anitriptyline in the prophylaxis of migraine. Effectiveness and relationship of antimigraine and antidepressant drugs. *Neurology,* 1976, **26**, 121.

Coyne, J., & Holroyd, K. Stress coping and illness: A transactional perspective. In T. Millan, C. Green, & R. Meagher (Eds.), *Handbook of health care clinical psychology.* New York: Plenum, 1982.

Curran, D. A., Hinterberger, H., & Lance, J. W. Methysergide. *Research in Clinical Studies of Headache,* 1967, **1**, 74.

Curran, D. A., & Lance, J. W. Clinical trial of methysergide and other preparations in the management of migraine. *Journal of Neurology, Neurosurgery and Psychiatry,* 1964, **27**, 463.

Dalessio, D. J. Some reflections on the etiologic role of depression in head pain. *Headache,* 1968, **8**, 28–31.

Dalsgaard-Neilsen, T. Migraine and heredity. *Acta Neurologia Scandanavia,* 1965, **41**, 287–300.

Davis, R. A., Wetzel, R. D., Kashiwagi, M. D., & McClure, J. N. Personality, depression and headache. *Headache,* 1976, **16**, 246–251.

Diamond, S., & Dalessio, D. J. *The practicing physician's approach to headache* (2nd ed.). Baltimore, Maryland: Williams and Wilkins, 1978.

Diamond, S., & Franklin, M. *Indications and contraindications for the use of biofeedback therapy in headache patients.* Paper presented at the meeting of the Biofeedback Research Society, Colorado Springs, February, 1976.

Diamond, S., & Medina, J. L. Double-blind study of propranolol for migraine prophylaxis. *Headache*, 1976, **16**, 24.

Diamond, S., Medina, J., Diamond-Falk, J., & DeVeno, T. The value of biofeedback in the treatment of chronic headache: A five year retrospective study. *Headache*, 1979, **19**, 90–96.

Elmore, A. M., & Tursky, B. A comparison of two psychophysiological approaches to the treatment of migraine. *Headache*, 1981, **21**, 93–101.

Epstein, L. H., & Abel, G. C. An analysis of biofeedback training effects with tension headache patients. *Behavior Therapy*, 1977, **8**, 37–47.

Fanchamps, A. The role of humoral mediators in migraine headache. *Canadian Journal of Neurological Sciences*, 1974, **1**, 189–195.

Figueroa, J. L. Group treatment of chronic tension headaches: A comparative treatment study. *Behavior Modification*, in press.

Fordyce, W. E. *Behavioral methods for chronic pain and illness*. St. Louis, Missouri: Mosby, 1976.

Forssman, B., Henriksson, K.-G., Johannson, V., Lindvall, L., & Lundin, H. Propranolol for migraine prophylaxis. *Headache*, 1976, **16**, 238.

Friar, L. R., & Beatty, J. Migraine: Management by a trained control of vasoconstriction. *Journal of Consulting and Clinical Psychology*, 1976, **44**, 46–53.

Friedman, A. P. Characteristics of tension headache: A profile of 1,420 cases. *Psychotherapy and Psychosomatics*, 1979, **20**, 451–461.

Friedman, A. P., von Storch, T. J., & Merrit, R. H. Migraine and tension headaches: A clinical study of 2000 cases. *Neurology*, 1954, **4**, 773–788.

Gannon, L. R., Haynes, S. N., Safranek, R., & Hamilton, J. A psychophysiological investigation of muscle-contraction and migraine headache. *Journal of Psychosomatic Research*, in press.

Goldfried, M. R. Psychotherapy as coping skills training. In M. J. Mahoney (Ed.), *Psychotherapy process: Current issues and future directions*. New York: Plenum, 1980.

Goldfried, M. R., & Davidson, G. C. *Clinical behavior therapy*. New York: Holt, 1976.

Goldfried, M. R., & Trier, C. S. Effectiveness of relaxation as an active coping skill. *Journal of Abnormal Psychology*, 1974, **83**, 348–355.

Gomersall, J. D., & Stuart, A. Variations in migraine attacks with changes in weather conditions. *International Journal of Biometeorology*, 1973, **17**, 285–299.

Graham, J. R. Cardiac and pulmonary fibrosis during methysergide therapy for headache. *American Journal of Medical Science*, 1967, **254**, 23.

Graham, J. R., & Wolff, H. G. Mechanism of migraine headache and action of ergotamine tartrate. *Archives of Neurological Psychiatry*, 1938, **39**, 737–763.

Hachinski, V. C., Olesen, J., Morris, S. W., Larsen, B., Enevoldsen, F., & Lassen, N. A. Cerebral hemodynamics in migraine. *Canadian Journal of Neurological Sciences*, 1977, **4**, 245–249.

Hachinski, V. C., Porchawka, J., & Steele, J. C. Visual symptoms in the migraine syndrome. *Neurology*, 1973, **23**, 570–579.

Harper, R. G., & Steger, J. C. Psychological correlates of frontalis EMG and pain in tension headache. *Headache*, 1978, **18**, 215–218.

Harrison, R. H. Psychological testing in headache: A review. *Headache*, 1975, **13**, 177–185.

Hartje, J. C., & Diver, C. E. Variation in hand temperature as a correlate to migraine severity. *Proceedings of the Biofeedback Society of America's Ninth Annual Meeting*, 1978, 36–39.

Haynes, S. N. Muscle contraction headache: A psychophysiological perspective of etiology and treatment. In S. N. Haynes & L. R. Gannon (Eds.), *Psychosomatic disorders; A psychophysiological approach to etiology and treatment.* New York: Gardner, 1980.

Henryk-Gutt, R., & Rees, W. C. Psychological aspects of migraine. *Journal of Psychosomatic Research*, 1973, **17**, 141–153.

Heyck, J. R. S. Pathogenesis of migraine. *Research Clinical Studies in Headache.* 1974, **2**, 1–28.

Holmes, T. H., & Rahe, R. H. The Social Readjustment Rating Scale. *Journal of Psychosomatic Research*, 1967, **11**, 213–218.

Holroyd, K. Stress, coping, and the treatment of stress related illness. In J. R. McNamara (Ed.), *Behavioral approaches in medicine: Application and analysis.* New York: Plenum, 1979.

Holroyd, K. A., & Andrasik, F. Coping and the self-control of chronic tension tension headache. *Journal of Consulting and Clinical Psychology*, 1978, **46**, 1036–1045.

Holroyd, K. A., & Andrasik, F. *Do the effects of cognitive therapy endure? A two-year follow-up of tension headache sufferers treated with cognitive therapy or biofeedback.* Paper presented at the Association for Advancement of Behavior Therapy, New York, November, 1980.

Holroyd, K. A., Andrasik, F., & Noble, J. A comparison of EMG biofeedback and a credible pseudotherapy in treating tension headache. *Journal of Behavioral Medicine*, 1980, **3**, 29–39.

Holroyd, K. A., Andrasik, F., & Westbrook, T. Cognitive control of tension headache. *Cognitive Therapy and Research*, 1977, **1**, 121–133.

Holroyd, K. A., Appel, M. A., & Andrasik, F. A cognitive behavioral approach to the treatment of psychophysiological disorders. In D. Meichenbaum & M. Jaremko (Eds.), *Stress prevention and management: A cognitive behavioral approach.* New York: Plenum, 1982.

Howarth, E. Headache, personality, and stress. *British Journal of Psychiatry*, 1965, **111**, 1193–1197.

Hurley, F. E. *Practical management of headache in office practice.* Paper presented at the meeting of the Chicago Medical Society, Chicago, March, 1969.

Ingvar, D. H. Pain in the brain—and migraine. *Hemicrania*, 1976, **7**, 2–5.

Jacobsen, E. *Progressive Relaxation.* Chicago, Illinois: University of Chicago Press, 1938.

Kashiwagi, T., McClure, J. N., & Wetzel, R. D. Headache and psychiatric disorders. *Diseases of the Nervous System*, 1972, **33**, 659–663.

Kendall, P. C., & Hollon, S. D. (Eds.). *Cognitive-behavioral interventions: Theory, research and procedures.* New York: Academic Press, 1979.

Kewman, D. & Roberts, A. H. Skin temperature biofeedback and migraine headaches. *Biofeedback and Self-Regulation*, 1980, **5**, 327–345.

Kudrow, L. Tension headache. In O. Appenzeller (Ed.), *Pathogenesis and treatment of headache.* New York: Spectrum, 1976.

Kudrow, L. Managing migraine headache. *Psychotherapy and Psychosomatics*, 1978, **19**, 685–693.

Lake, A., Rainey, J., & Papsdorf, J. D. Biofeedback and rational emotive therapy in the management of migraine headache. *Journal of Applied Behavioral Analysis*, 1979, **12**, 127–140.

Lance, J. W. *Mechanism and management of headache* (3rd ed.). London: Butterworths, 1978.

Lance, J. W., & Anthony, M. Some clinical aspects of migraine. *Archives of Neurology*, 1966, **15**, 356.

Lance, J. W., & Anthony, M. Thermographic studies in vascular headache. *Medical Journal of Australia*, 1971, **1**, 240.

Lance, J. W., & Curran, D. A. Treatment of chronic tension headache. *Lancet*, 1964, **1**, 1236–1239.

Lance, J. W., Curran, D. A., & Anthony, M. Investigations into the mechanism and treatment of chronic headache. *Medical Journal of Australia*, 1965, **2**, 904–914.

Largen, J. W., Mathew, R. J., Dobbins, K., & Claghorn, J. L. Specific and nonspecific effects of skin temperature control in migraine management. *Headache*, 1981, **21**, 36–44.

Lazarus, R. S. *Psychological stress and the coping process.* New York: McGraw-Hill, 1966.

Lazarus, R. S. A cognitively oriented psychologist looks at biofeedback. *American Psychologist*, 1975, **30**, 553–560.

Lazarus, R. S. Coping and adaption. In W. D. Gentry (Ed.), *The handbook of behavioral medicine.* New York: Guilford, 1982.

Lazarus, R. S., Averill, J., & Opton, E. The psychology of coping: Issues of research and assessment. In G. Coehlo, D. Hamburg, & J. Adams (Eds.). *Coping and adaptation.* New York: Basic Books, 1974.

Luborsky, L., Docherty, J. P., & Penick, S. Onset conditions for psychosomatic symptoms: A comparative review of immediate observation with retrospective research. *Psychosomatic Medicine*, 1973, **35**, 187–204.

Marcussen, R. M. Vascular headache experimentally induced by presentation of pertinent life experiences: Modifications of the course of vascular headache by alterations of situations and reactions. *Research Publications of the Association of Nervous and Mental Disease*, 1950, **29**, 609–620.

Markush, R. E., Karp, H. R., Heyman, A., & O'Fallon, W. M. Epidemiologic study of migraine symptoms in young women. *Neurology*, 1975, **25**, 430–435.

Martin, M. J. Tension headache, a psychiatric study. *Headache*, 1966, **6**, 47–54.

Martin, M. J. Muscle-contraction headache. *Psychosomatics*, 1972, **13**, 16–19.

Martin, M. J., & Mathews, A. M. Tension headaches: Psychophysiological investigation and treatment. *Journal of Psychosomatic Research*, 1978, **22**, 389–399.

Medina, J. L., & Diamond, S. The role of diet in migraine. *Headache*, 1978, **18**, 31–34.

Meichenbaum, D. Cognitive factors in biofeedback therapy. *Biofeedback and Self-Regulation*, 1976, **1**, 201–216.

Meichenbaum, D. H. *Cognitive-behavior modification: An integrative approach.* New York: Plenum, 1977.

Mitchell, K. R., & Mitchell, D. M. An exploratory treatment application of programmed behavior therapy techniques. *Journal of Psychosomatic Research*, 1971, **15**, 137–157.

Mitchell, K., & White, R. Behavioral self management: An application to the problem of migraine headache. *Behavior Therapy*, 1977, **8**, 213–221.

Mullinix, J., Norton, B., Hack, S., & Fishman, M. Skin temperature biofeedback and migraine. *Headache*, 1978, **17**, 242–244.

Olesen, J. Some clinical features of the acute migraine attack: An analysis of 750 patients. *Headache*, 1978, **18**, 268–271.

Ostfeld, A. M., Reis, D. J., & Wolff, H. G. Studies in headache: Bulbar conjunctival ischemia and muscle contraction headache. *Archives of Neurological Psychiatry*, 1957, **77**, 113–119.

Pearce, J. Migraine: A psychosomatic disorder. *Headache*, 1977, **17**, 125–128.

Philips, C. Headache and personality. *Journal of Psychosomatic Research*, 1976, **20**, 535–542.

Philips, C. A psychological analysis of tension headache. In S. Rachman (Ed.), *Contributions to medical psychology*. Oxford: Pergamon, 1977.

Philips, C. Tension headache: Theoretical problems. *Behavior Research and Therapy*, 1978, **16**, 249–261.

Philips, H. C., & Hunter, M. *An alternative approach to tension headache: An investigation of the muscular, behavioral and subjective indices*. Paper presented at the Society for Psychophysiological Research, Vancouver, 1980.

Pozniak-Patewicz, E. "Cephalgic" spasm of head and neck muscles. *Headache*, 1976, **14**, 261–266.

Prensky, A. L. Migraine and migrainous variants in pediatric patients. *Pediatric Clinics of North America*, 1976, **23**, 461–471.

Raskin, N. H., & Appenzeller, O. *Headache*. Philadelphia: Saunders, 1980.

Reinking, R., & Hutchings, D. Follow-up to: "Tension headaches: What form of therapy is most effective?" *Biofeedback and Self-Regulation*, 1981, **6**, 57–62.

Rolf, L. H., Wiele, G., & Brune, G. G. Serotonin in platelets of patients with migraine and muscle-contraction headache. *Exerpta Medica*, 1977, **427**, 11–12.

Sakai, F., & Meyer, J. S. Regional cerebral hemodynamics during migraine and cluster headaches measured by the Xe^{133} inhalation method. *Headache*, 1978, **18**, 122–132.

Saper, J. R. Migraine II. Treatment. *Journal of the American Medical Association*, 1978, **239**, 2480–2484.

Sargent, J. D., Green, E. E., & Walters, E. D. The use of autogenic training in a pilot study of migraine and tension headaches. *Headache*, 1972, **12**, 120–124.

Schultz, J. H., & Luthe, W. *Autogenic training* (Vol. I). New York: Grune & Stratton, 1969.

Selby, G., & Lance, J. W. Observations on 500 cases of migraine and allied vascular headache. *Journal of Neurology, Neurosurgery and Psychiatry*, 1960, **23**, 23–32.

Steger, J. C., & Harper, R. G. Comprehensive biofeedback versus self-monitored relaxation in the treatment of tension headache. *Headache*, 1980, **20**, 137–142.

Steinmark, S., & Borkovec, T. Active and placebo treatment effects on moderate insomnia under counterdemand and positive demand instruction. *Journal of Abnormal Psychology*, 1974, **83**, 157–163.

Stensrud, P., & Sjaastad, O. Short-term clinical trial of propranolol in racemic form (Inderal), d-propranolol and placebo in migraine. *Acta Neurologica Scandinavica*, 1976, **53**, 229.

Sternbach, R. A., & Timmermans, G. Personality changes associated with reductions of pain. *Pain*, 1975, **1**, 177–181.

Thompson, J. K., Haber, J. D., Figueroa, J. L., & Adams, H. E. A replication and generalization of the "psychobiological" model of headache. *Headache*, 1980, **20**, 199–203.

Tunis, M. M., & Wolff, H. G. Studies in headache. Cranial artery vasoconstriction and muscle contraction headache. *Archives of Neurological Psychiatry*, 1954, **71**, 425–434.

Turin, A., & Johnson, W. G. Biofeedback therapy for migraine headaches. *Archives of General Psychiatry*, 1976, **33**, 517–519.

Turk, D. C., Meichenbaum, D. H., & Berman, W. H. Application of biofeedback for the regulation of pain: A critical review. *Psychological Bulletin*, 1979, **86**, 1322–1338.

Warner, G., & Lance, J. W. Relaxation therapy in migraine and chronic tension headache. *Medical Journal of Australia*, 1975, **1**, 298.

Waters, W. E. Epidemiological aspects of migraine. In J. N. Cumings (Ed.), *Background to migraine: Fourth migraine symposium*. Berlin and New York: Springer-Verlag, 1971.

Waters, W. E., & O'Connor, P. J. Prevalence of migraine. *Journal of Neurology, Neurosurgery and Psychiatry,* 1975 , **38,** 613–616.

Werback, M. R., & Sandweiss, J. H. Peripheral temperatures of migraineurs undergoing relaxation training. *Headache,* 1978, **18,** 211–214.

Williamson, D. A. Behavioral treatment of migraine and muscle-contraction headaches: Outcome and theoretical explanations. In M. Hersen, R. M. Eisler, & P. M. Miller (Eds.), *Progress in behavior modification* (Vol. 2). New York: Academic Press, 1981.

Wolff, H. G. *Headache and other head pain.* London and New York: Oxford University Press, 1963.

World Federation of Neurology's Research Group on Migraine and Headache. *Hemicrania,* 1969, **1,** 3–9.

Ziegler, D. K. The epidemiology and genetics of migraine. *Research Clinical Studies in Headache,* 1978, **5,** 21–33.

Ziegler, D. K., Rhodes, R. J., & Hassanein, R. S. Association of psychological measurements of anxiety and depression with headache history in a nonclinical population. *Research Clinical Studies in Headache.* Basel: Karger, 1978.

Index